D1607404

HUMAN SEXUAL ECOLOGY:

A Philosophy and Ethics of Man and Woman

Robert E. Joyce

University Press of America™

Library of Congress Catalog Card Number: 79-6727

Contents

iii

Chapter

Chapter

Chapter

vi

Chapter

Illustrations

Figure

Preface

Ever since the original Earth Day (April 1970) I have been heartened by the public growth in awareness of environmental problems and their solution. Of course, the problems remain critical, as intelligent proposals for solving them are so often begrudgingly entertained and reluctantly afforded a measure of implementation. But some rivers and lakes have been restored, some air has been rendered lung-worthy, some land has been released from the poisonous effects of pesticides, many people are beginning to turn from artificial (denatured) food to wholesome, field-fresh nourishment, and *ecology* has become a household word.

Before close attention to the care of the physical environment became a popular concern, pioneering biologists, chemists, and physicists were studying the problems, applying their scientific knowledge, and even issuing carefully-worded warnings. These well-founded efforts and responsibly articulated messages seemed to pass unnoticed by the public media until the strident, and partly irresponsible, rhetoric of *The Population Bomb* (1968) began to trigger the fear fantasies of millions. The revolution in physical ecology gained public momentum through the outspoken proclamations of a few exponents whose philosophical and moral values were not as acceptable as their scientific credentials. But, as a happy result, the environmental assessments and evaluations of saner scientific minds began reaching the people.

Human sexual ecology is an idea whose time is coming. The sexual energy crisis today is caused by the unbalanced regard for sexuality throughout human duration on the planet earth. The history of Western civilization provides ample evidence of one of the major symptoms of this crisis--the hypersacralization of sex as a subject too enigmatic to think about or to speak about openly. In our own century we have witnessed the ascendancy of its other major symptom--the trivialization of sex. Sex that was trivialized as a pleasurable means to get progeny in the puritan culture has yielded to sex that is trivi-

alized as a sophisticated means to get pleasure and ego-
satisfaction in the playboy culture.

Historically, human sexuality has been regarded
chiefly as a means to progeny and pleasure, rather than
as an essential good of personhood. Generally speaking,
it has never been viewed as, first of all, a good in itself, far more spiritual in its origin and meaning than
it is physical and emotional. Neither the Judeo-Christian
tradition, centered on the worship of God, nor the contemporary adventure into ego-fulfillment, centered on
on the worship of self, has seriously inquired about the
nature of man and woman as man and woman.

This book is an attempt to show the plausibility
of a deeper, more radical view of human sexuality. The
meaning and origin of human sexuality is seen as cosmic
and precosmic. The relationship of man and woman--an
ecosystem all its own--is portrayed as the heart of human
ecology.

Human Sexual Ecology is an attempt to span the vast
gulf between the old worldview of sexuality and a new,
integrated vision of man and woman. Its message regarding
the origin of sexuality and the meaning of sexual freedom
is distinctive and can only be appreciated through the
exercise of reflective consciousness. It may serve to
prepare the way for a more popular work that is being
planned to deal directly with the "copulation bomb" and
its disastrous effects on the ecosystem of human relations. The latter endeavor will be undertaken with the
hope that its rhetoric and moral conclusions are considerably more responsible than those of the "population
bomb" reactors.

I have tried to justify the imagery and ethical
judgments in the present work by sketching a sound philosophical framework that is sensitive to traditional philosophy as well as to certain phenomenological trends in
contemporary existentialism. However, it is only a framework. Certain other writings--noted in the text--must
be regarded as complementary to this one. An analysis
and direct refutation of opposing philosophical views
is planned for a later, more technical treatment of the
issues.

Fortunately, the practical base for a "Copernican
Revolution" in human sexuality is already building. Fertility awareness and natural family planning (not rhythm)
is growing throughout the world.

The casual observer may wonder at my optimism. The practitioners of natural methods of birth control are now only a small percentage of family planners. But one must take into account the underlying philosophy and genuine human good that springs from the educational efforts of those who competently and responsibly teach at the grass roots level. As one natural family planning (NFP) teacher recently commented in addressing an international gathering of teachers and researchers, "Who has not heard of Alcoholics Anonymous? Not too many years ago that movement was utterly unknown. Now we have it where I live in the Guatemalan countryside and it is well-known throughout the world. They had a good thing for people and it spread, person to person, and group to group. That is the way with NFP."

This book is an ethics for natural family planners and for all open-minded seekers of truth in sex. Many people become interested in the natural way of sexual living as soon as they are properly introduced to it-- free of the widespread ignorance and prejudice concerning its effectiveness and its family-enriching benefits.

The text is intended to be particularly helpful to college students and to educated adults who are sincerely trying to find deeper meaning in human sexuality. It can be used in college courses that introduce philosophy or that deal with ethical issues and perspectives. It can serve as a contemporary guide to sexual ethics in adult education courses that provide the rational basis for the traditional Judeo-Christian ethic. While being analytic along the way, I tried mainly to offer a panoramic perspective and a synthesis. The combined effect is both theoretical and, I hope, practical.

This book is written for both scholar and layperson. None of us are experts in the philosophy of human sexuality. It is one of those subjects in which the wise and perceptive layperson may have as much to contribute as the scholar.

I am grateful to many persons for a variety of contributions. The most important group of people are my students in courses on the philosophy of man and woman, which I have taught periodically during the past twelve years at St. John's University and the College of St. Benedict. Many individuals stand out in that group-- young people who asked important questions and who encouraged me to keep thinking and teaching in this subject area.

xiii

Among the individuals who were closely associated with the production of this volume I wish to acknowledge, first of all, Germain Grisez, distinguished professor of philosophy and ethics. His unique and creative interpretations of the moral theory of Thomas Aquinas served as both an inspiration and a norm in developing the general ethical framework for *Human Sexual Ecology*. His pointed comments on the work in progress, as well as his encouragement, were gratefully received.

William E. May, Associate Professor of Theology in the Graduate School at the Catholic University of America, also provided observations on the entire manuscript. Our discussions of it and his enthusiasm will long be remembered with gratitude.

Thanks are due to psychiatrist Conrad Baars of San Antonio for his careful checking of my treatment of affirmation in man-woman relations and for his encouraging comments on the project as a whole. The psychology of affirmation in this book appreciably accords with the theory of affirmation developed by Dr. Baars and by Dr. Anna Terruwe of the Netherlands, to whom I am also grateful.

Sociologist Paul Marx, founder and director of the Human Life Center--an organization of worldwide influence in educating professionals and laypersons on marriage, the family, and the crucial issues of human life--has provided a cornucopia of information on family planning, the sociological dimensions of sexuality, and the contemporary treatment of human life. The resources of the Human Life Center--physical and personal--were constantly available. For many years, Professor Marx has been an affluent source of education for me, as well as an inspiring colleague and friend.

Human Sexual Ecology is a project that received early encouragement from Professor Linden G. Leavitt, Academic Dean of International College, Los Angeles. Its viability as a publication was fostered by Dr. Paul O. Proehl, President of International College. I am grateful for their creative, humanistic support of the academic dimensions of this work.

A special thanks is due to Rev. Michael Blecker, O.S.B., President of St. John's University, Minnesota, and to Rev. Gunther Rolfson, O.S.B., Academic Vice President. They enabled me to take a sabbatical leave for research and writing in this special area of interest.

Kathi Hamlon made helpful comments on Chapter 13. Diane Craven did the same on Chapter 1. I am grateful to them, to Dr. R. Kenton Craven, Administrative Director, and to the entire staff of the Human Life Center for their practical support in the production of this work.

I will not begin to name the many couples who teach natural family planning in the United States and elsewhere in the world and whom I know personally. They know who they are, but they probably do not realize how thankful I am to them for their inspiration. I wrote this book as much for them as for anyone--that it might be a measure of rational support for them and for the growing numbers who teach and practice an ecological means of birth control.

The manuscript was typed by Marcy Lawrenz, whose excellence in typing is matched by her generosity and willingness to make many rough ways smooth. The illustrations were done by Bill Wander. Thanks also to Sheryl Guzek for helping to compile the Index.

Last, but most of all, I am grateful to Mary Rosera Joyce, my wife, whose philosophical and creative insights are esteemed and cherished. Her influence on this work is, in some way, present on every page. I dedicate the book to Mary, with joy in our love.

Robert E. Joyce, Ph.D.
St. John's University
Collegeville, Minnesota
October 15, 1979

Chapter 1

INTRODUCTION: PHILOSOPHY, ETHICS, AND SEXUAL ECOLOGY

In attempting to develop a personal philosophy and ethics of man-woman behavior, we are influencing ourselves for good or bad. Philosophies determine attitudes. Good philosophies determine good attitudes, and bad philosophies determine bad attitudes. These attitudes become the inner guides of every personal action.

Whenever we develop the underlying assumptions of our actions, we take a risk. Lack of insight and direction can lead to personal frustration and unhappiness. But if we either refuse or neglect to examine carefully the meaning of our life, the risk is greater. A healthy, well-developed philosophy of life is the anatomy of human happiness.

Philosophers can be said to be engaged in the science of integrative and ultimate meanings for reality--different kinds of reality and the whole of reality. But *anyone* who desires to develop a philosophy of life looks for meanings that are both ultimate and integrative. One wants to *bring all things together*. In our study of man and woman, I will try to sketch a philosophical picture of what we as sexual persons really are, and how our sexuality fits harmoniously with the other dimensions of ourselves.

We are interested not only in *what it is* to be sexual, but also in *how we should act* sexually. Ethics is the part of philosophy that studies the good and bad in human behavior. Our ethical concern is to develop sound criteria for determining whether a given personal action, freely chosen, is in accord with human nature or not. I will attempt to indicate general requirements for ethically good actions.

It is important to realize that ethics, as a branch of philosophy, does not deal with human behavior in every way. The special project is to examine actions, done by an individual or a group, precisely in so far as these actions are deliberately chosen. To the extent that our activity is merely habitual, unconscious, or done under constraint of one kind or another, it is not subject to ethical evaluation. So, if someone is walking along the street, the action is ethically relevant only to the degree that it is prompted by self-awareness, deliberation and freedom of will.[1]

Ethics can be general or particular. This book will offer some of the basic elements of both kinds of ethics.

In regard to general ethics, I will be expressing some of the ideas of Germain Grisez in his book, *Beyond the New Morality: The Responsibilities of Freedom*. This contemporary text provides background on the nature of ethics and a fuller understanding of basic principles.[2]

In regard to special ethics--the particular concern of the present work--I will be applying principles taken from general ethics (as well as from other areas of philosophy) to ethical problems in human sexual behavior. Many people are familiar with areas of special ethics concerning human behavior in fields such as law, medicine, politics, family relations, and others. But they do not necessarily know how sexual activity constitutes one of the most important areas for ethical development.

The special ethics of sexual love is the core of this book. What is authentic sexual love? How is it genuinely expressed? What is inauthentic sexual love? What are the ways in which it is expressed? These and similar questions will be our central concern. But, in order to attain a reasonably effective response to these questions, we must discover, to the best of our ability, the broadest and deepest meanings for being a person and for being sexual.

2

A person can swim freely and well only if the water is deep enough and plentiful. Similarly, a person can develop sound and effective ethical conclusions only if the meanings for the kind of human action at issue are deep enough and potentially integrative. We need in-depth, comprehensive meanings for terms such as man, woman, sexuality, love, friendship, if we are going to be able to see the true and the false prospects for human sexual behavior. These meanings come from the branches of philosophy known as philosophical anthropology and the philosophy of being. I will suggest some of them as we go along.[3]

Philosophy Is Personal

Everyone has a philosophy of life. Your particular philosophy of life is yours alone. Nobody can develop your philosophy for you. But it is personal, not private. Your philosophy is unavoidably public. It cannot be kept in the back room, because it determines everything you do. It affects your every action and thereby influences those people with whom you relate. Your philosophy of sexuality, for instance, consciously or unconsciously--for better or for worse--has a bearing on everything you do as a man or woman.

When you begin to make your implicit philosophy a matter for explicit attention, there are even less grounds for regarding it as somehow private. Philosophy is necessarily social and subject to critical examination by everyone else who philosophizes. There is no such thing as a private philosophy any more than there is a private chemistry or a private psychology.

If, for instance, you think that human beings have something about them that makes it possible for them to exist *personally* after death, you are right or wrong. Someone else who denies such a possibility is either right or wrong.[4] One of the necessary tasks in being philosophical is the attempt to examine the reasons or grounds for just such a philosophical claim and to test it in the laboratory of one's own consciousness. The laboratory of the philosopher is as real as that of the chemist or the biologist, even though the nature of the laboratory and the rules for evidence are quite different.[5]

Someone might be inclined to say, "Well, that's *your* philosophy of human sexuality, and this is *mine*." But that is very similar to saying, "Well, that's *your* anatomy of the human digestive tract, and this is *mine*." Philosophy, like biology, is *one science*. The difference is that philosophy analyzes people and things in their relationships at much greater depth than biology, and so it is more difficult to get agreement, even among the experts.

The aspects and relationships that philosophy studies are the ultimate and overarching ones, and they are naturally not visible to the eye in any way.[6] But they are visible to the non-manipulative, contemplative mind. The philosophical part of the mind by which we can see and grasp these relationships needs growth and strengthening. The exercise we get when thinking philosophically under sound guidance helps to strengthen the mind and enhance one's natural philosophical growth.

Why Human Sexual Ecology?

Human ecology is my expression for ethics or moral philosophy. In its attention to the necessary interrelationships of things, environmental biology, which gives us knowledge about the possibilities for sound management of our physical world, is similar to the structure of moral philosophy, which gives us knowledge about the possibilities for sound management of our totally human lives--including the ways we relate to the physical world. The particular branch of moral philosophy that deals with human *sexual* behavior can then be regarded as human sexual ecology.

Ordinarily, ecology is defined as the study of the relationships between organisms and their environments. The ecologist is concerned with the totality of interrelationships and interactions that influence or cause a given natural event. The ecologist is interested not simply in a given linear chain of cause and effect, but in the total effect of the environment with its super-multiplicity of elements, factors, forces and conditions.[7] So far in our contemporary understanding, the term ecology has been applied almost exclusively to the study of physical organisms and physical environment.

In this study of human sexuality, our use of the term *ecology* is applicable to the total human environment. Physical, psychic and spiritual environments are involved. None of these three general environments of the human person--which exist within the individual as well as between individuals--can be neglected when one is attempting to understand the meaning, value and function of human sexuality. The term *sexual ecology*, then, is used to suggest the supreme complexity, depth and pervasiveness of human sexuality in the lives and destiny of human beings.

One of the significant environments that will receive attention in this study has been largely neglected in the sexual ethics of the past: the intrapersonal area called attitudes. Attitudes are intimately influential in human sexual behavior. Human actions themselves are spawned, sustained, and nurtured by attitudes. Fresh and positive attitudes function ethically in a way not unlike clean, fresh air functions physically. Take-it-for-granted, negative attitudes function somewhat like stagnant, foul-smelling air.

One of the critical elements discussed in this book has been neglected in contemporary moral theory and practice: the inherent structure of every ethical action. Personal actions have characteristics that are independent of (though intimately related to) the intentions of the one performing them. Every human action has a body as well as a soul. Contemporary ethical theories that underscore the value of love as the motive for an action, without careful attention to the action itself, would seem to violate the ecology of the act (i.e., the coherence of essential parts of the act). Just as we must question industrial production and its environmental impact, we must always ask *what* an individual human action is doing; not just *why* it is done. Besides the motivation, there is a physical, psychic and spiritual structure to every human action. No one can kill an innocent person "out of love." To do so involves pollution of the motivation "love" and renders it non-love. Such an action violates the ecology of human behavior.

Human sexual ecology, then, means sexual ethics--an ethics of total relationships: within each person, between persons, between persons and the rest of the world. But, more importantly, it suggests man-woman friendship. A friend is a good environment. Friends are people who relate well with one another--directly and indirectly, verbally and non-verbally, in action and in attitude. Deep, rich friendships mean sound human ecology. Man-woman friendship is the key concept in human sexual ecology.

The Need for Man-Woman Friendship

Unfortunately, the friendship of man and woman never has been regarded as a broad cultural ideal. In both Oriental and Occidental cultures throughout the history of the world, man-woman friendship is the exception, not the rule. *As sexual*, men and women tend to be seen, almost inevitably, in a strictly functional way. They are rarely perceived in a celebrational way, too. Only here

5

and there do individuals arise, a man and a woman, who
are beloved friends without this beloved friendship apparently being a function of the married state, of a
genital liaison, or of their position in a family.

Nevertheless, the horizon is streaked with hope.
In her excellent book on women--written in the early fif-
ties--Anne Morrow Lindbergh quotes the poet Rilke:

Once the realization is accepted that, even between
the closest human beings, infinite distances continue to exist, a wonderful living side by side
can grow up, if they succeed in loving the distance
between them which makes it possible for each to
see the other whole and against a wide sky![8]

Lindbergh continues by saying:

This is a beautiful image, but who can achieve
it in actual life? . . . [T]heory precedes exploration; we must use any signposts that exist
to help us through the wilderness. For we are,
actually, pioneers trying to find a new path
through the maze of tradition, convention and
dogma.[9]

Rilke had spoken of a new man-and-woman love where "two
solitudes protect and touch and greet each other." Each
of these two solitudes is a profoundly rich environment
for the other person.

Human Sexual Ecology is written not only as an attempt to provide some of the theory which precedes exploration, but also to give expression to conviction already
attained through the experience of the kind of man-woman
friendship about which Rilke and Lindbergh speculate.
The ideas and perspectives of this book are shared with
Mary Rosera Joyce, my greatest friend, and wife. In our
twenty years of seemingly incomparable friendship--eigh-
teen of which have been blessed through marriage--we have
developed together the philosophy of man and woman outlined in these pages. It is not so much "our philosophy"
as it is our contribution to philosophy. With its
strengths and limitations it is presented to the reader
as an opportunity for learning what someone else has to
offer and as a help in making personal discoveries.

Philosophy: the Adult of the Personal Life

One further introductory perspective may help in
developing a philosophy of sexual love.

The central, ecological character of philosophical thought itself has been underplayed throughout the entire history of Western cultures.[10] Because of the specialization and fragmentation of intellectual endeavors that have occurred in recent decades, philosophy is often regarded as just another field of knowledge. This book, however, assumes a holistic, as well as personal, meaning for philosophy. It fosters a distinctive ecological perspective on what it means to develop a personal philosophy.

Philosophy, as the science of integrative and ultimate meanings for reality, has a crucial position in the maturation of human intelligence. In order to appreciate this central role of philosophy, we can relate the three areas of what might be called intellectual ecology to three readily identifiable areas of what might be called psychic ecology.

Specialists in transactional analysis regard three ego states as the natural parts of the human psyche. These ego states are called Parent, Adult and Child. In order to relate them to the three areas of intellectual ecology, it is first necessary to give them a philosophical interpretation. I will identify the root of each one of these psychic ego states and then indicate how a remarkably similar root is found in the life of the spiritual mind.[11]

The psychic Child can be understood as a person's inner capacity *to feel* from within and to respond instinctively to stimuli without inhibition and restraint. The baby tends to act almost entirely in accord with his or her feelings, sleeping when tired, crying when hungry or wet, and playing when contented.

The psychic Parent can be understood as a person's inner capacity *to be taught* and to receive direction for his or her life from others, especially parents. Those others include not only parents, but everyone else who exerts some influence on the person's behavior and in accord with whom the person is inclined to act. Brothers and sisters, playmates, and the television set are among the most influential *others* in the life of a child. Yet, later in life, teachers, friends, employers, and many different kinds of people, all constitute those others who have been definitely influential in the person's behavior. An individual must act not only as he or she feels, but also as *others feel*, if he or she is to survive and function maturely. But the key to doing so is an inherent disposition in the depths of the psyche that

7

naturally inclines the person to receive behavioral information from a world entirely beyond his or her own little
ego-world. This natural, inner capacity to be directed
by someone or something other-than-self is the root of
the psychic state called the Parent.

The Adult is the person's inner capacity *to interpret* and *to integrate* data from the Parent and the Child,
and *to respond* to the present situation thoughtfully and
wholly. The natural ability to use reason and to decide
what is the best course of action to follow at a given
time is the remarkably distinctive power of the human
being. This Adult ego state takes into account the instincts and demands of the Child and Parent within, but
acts independently. Like the others, it is present
from the beginning. But it is the last to become significantly activated, and it requires a certain amount
of development on the part of the Child and Parent capacities in order to operate effectively. The Adult also
depends on both the Child data and the Parent data for
effective functioning.

The counterpart of these three ego states is found
in the intellectual and spiritual life. Intellectually,
we all have a root Child. The Child is our natural capacity to know all created things and to respond naturally. We have a capacity and a natural desire to know,
ever more effectively and deeply, the things of the
world--inanimate, animate, and human. Our senses, memory,
imagination and intellect are knowing powers that put
us in touch with the created universe; and, if we are
healthy, the more we know, the more we want to know. All
of this knowledge comes from within our specifically human
inclination to know and lies within our natural capacity
to know. One can speak of the arts and sciences as the
specially developed ways of attaining the knowledge of
all the created universe that the liberated and growing
person desires to attain. The arts and sciences minister
to our intellective Child.

But there is another natural capacity to know. Everyone who has not had it squelched can recognize the
natural capacity to know uncreated reality or uncaused,
ultimate reality. Such knowledge cannot come from within
our finite capacity to know. It can only come (*through*
our natural desire to know) *from* the Creator, *the other*,
by way of some kind of special revelation. Such is the
kind of knowledge that the science of theology and religious studies purport to mediate and cultivate. This
natural capacity within us to know uncreated reality from
the Creator by way of special revelation is our intellec-

tive Parent. It is the natural capacity of the creature
to be taught from outside his or her own natural ability
to know created things, and to let his or her actions
be influenced by this uncreated Other.

The Adult in the intellectual life is that natural
capacity to interpret and to integrate data from both
nature (created beings) and supernature (uncreated being,
the Other), and to respond to the here-and-now situation,
meaningfully and wholesomely. Philosophy is the art and
science that cultivates this particular natural capacity
for interpreting and integrating *all* of one's knowledge
into a beingful whole.[12] *Philosophy* means "love of wisdom." And wisdom can be understood as a loving kind of
knowing and a knowing kind of love. A person might be
said to *be* Adult only to the extent that he or she is
well-integrated and wise.

In order to be wise, however, one need neither be
called a philosopher nor even have studied philosophy
in a formal manner. Surely, not everyone who is called
a philosopher or who has studied philosophy is wise.
Perhaps we can simply say that, other things being equal,
the individual has a better opportunity to grow in wisdom
if he or she studies philosophy under sound guidance than
if he or she does not. Becoming an intellectual Adult
requires careful guidance.

Pioneers in the Philosophy of Man and Woman

Even today any person who seriously reflects on the
ultimate meaning of sexuality can be regarded as a pioneer
in the philosophy of man and woman. In the Western world,
relatively little direct attention has been given to sexuality from a philosophical perspective. Baker and Elliston in their anthology, *Philosophy and Sex*, claim that
philosophers have all too readily abandoned sex to the
poets because they felt a conflict between the life of
reason and the inherent "unreasonableness" of sexual passion, and because they tended to regard the sensual world
as unworthy of philosophical reflection.[13] These generalizations seem to contain considerable truth.

But, more importantly, philosophy today is widely
conceived as having only incidental connection to theology
and religion. One of the major needs of our time is a
philosophy that incorporates theological data--as well
as natural, scientific and commonsense data--into its
organized reflections. Nowhere is this need more evident
than in the philosophy of man and woman.

Generally, philosophy in the Western world stops at the threshold of theology and religion, and refuses to incorporate data beyond the comprehension of the natural powers of the mind. While acknowledging that one of the major roles of philosophy is to help people examine things in accord with simple, unaided reason, I suggest that there is another and far more crucial role. The greatest task of philosophy is to help people experience wholeness in knowing, including what they acknowledge through faith. Theology deals directly with the contents of that faith; but it is not the integrative discipline as such. Philosophy, the traditional love of wisdom, needs expansion to include the highest Wisdom--without submerging either theology or itself.[14]

The reader is encouraged to develop a philosophy of man and woman as a kind of philosophy of life, including whatever he or she holds to be true in the area of religious belief. It is a mark of intellectual maturity to be able to respect differences in assumptions and presuppositions while examining the whole field of a person's organized reflection. In the dialogue proper to philosophy, often we can learn from others with whom we disagree on significant assumptions, if we bring these areas of difference into the light of consciousness, and if we treat the propositions of disagreement as hypothetical judgments. The differences are then recognized and respected. They can thus function as stimulants for thought and discussion rather than as unconscious sources of conflict.

Philosophies that always preclude or shy away from religious and theological knowledge tend to function like emotionally disturbed people who cannot relate well with their Parent ego state. Considering the history of human reflection, we might say that it is time to integrate. There is no more crucial area for this coming of age than in the endeavor of growing wise in the ways of being man and woman.[15]

Notes

1. The basic meaning of ethics is given by an authoritative historian of the subject in his comprehensive survey of the entire history of ethics in Western cultures: ". . . from the time of the first Greek philosophies, ethics has had but one meaning: it is the reflective study of what is good or bad in that part of human

10

conduct for which man has some personal responsibility." Vernon J. Bourke, *History of Ethics* (Garden City: Doubleday, 1968), p. 8.

2. Germain Grisez and Russell Shaw, *Beyond the New Morality: The Responsibilities of Freedom* (Notre Dame, Ind.: University of Notre Dame Press, 1974). Among other basic texts in moral philosophy, see Vincent Punzo, *Reflective Naturalism* (New York: Macmillan, 1969).

For background on the nature of Christian ethics, see, e.g., the helpful contemporary treatment given by William E. May in *Becoming Human: An Invitation to Christian Ethics* (Dayton, Ohio: Pflaum, 1975).

3. Since this book is mainly an ethics of sexuality, the meanings behind our basic terminology will not be discussed thoroughly. The origin, rational elaboration and justification for such terms will be, for the most part, presupposed. A development of the anthropological and metaphysical foundations is given by Mary Rosera Joyce and Robert E. Joyce, *New Dynamics in Sexual Love: A Revolutionary Approach to Marriage and Celibacy* (Collegeville, Minn.: St. John's University Press, 1970).

4. Not every philosophical question can be said to have a right or a wrong answer. This one is phrased so absolutely in order to point out the importance of striving for the truth, not just for further ideas. Most philosophical questions can be said to have relative responses, not absolute answers. Ideas are more or less adequate, valid or true. Some are more or less so than others. But in the midst of this relatively richer or poorer participation by the knower in the inexhaustible mystery of reality, there are some definitely attainable truths--at spiritual and psychic levels, as well as at the physically observable level. One can say "maybe" to the question of perceived immortality, but one cannot deny the implied truth or error that is the object of his or her doubt. Of course, among those who say it is a truth, there will be great diversity, and consequent relativity, in the *way* in which they characterize the nature of personal immortality.

5. By the philosopher's laboratory I mean the whole of one's personal consciousness and this consciousness taken precisely as a whole. When traveling, a philosopher takes his or her lab along. It is not localized in one place where instruments such as test tubes, Bunson burners, and hydrometers are kept. The practitioner directly observes real things in the lab (the whole of one's consciousness) just as they are experienced in everyday life. There is no attempt to manipulate the phenomena. One of the unique features of total consciousness is that it includes the spiritual power to be conscious of things without changing them by the very activity in which one knows them. In the philosopher's lab, experimentation is directly undertaken not upon the things known, but upon ideas that result from the knowing act itself.

The primary instrument of observation, employed by anyone doing philosophical reflection (experimentation), is what I call an intellectiscope. Basically, it consists of exercising one's conscious activity in a certain natural way, but with special focus. We let

11

ourselves become conscious of things precisely in and through our consciousness of them.

Instead of simply being conscious of things directly, as animals are, human beings are naturally conscious of things both directly and indirectly. Directly by simply seeing, hearing, touching, and the like. Indirectly, by being conscious of things in and through one's direct consciousness of them. Not only can I see (be conscious of) the paper which I am reading, but I can be conscious of my seeing (consciousness) of it. What I do when I think philosophically is to let my direct consciousness of something or someone serve as a magnifying instrument. Then I am conscious of things by using my indirect consciousness (reflective consciousness) to look *through* my direct consciousness of them, with the result that I see them as enlarged and as much more meaningful to me.

I am conscious of this piece of paper in and through my direct consciousness (seeing and touching) of it. The paper becomes meaningful to me, the more I see it *within* and *through* my direct experience (consciousness) of it. Just as the physical eye is clothed with a piece of curved glass (a microscope) in order to see physical dimensions hitherto unimagined, so too, our power to be reflectively conscious of things is clothed with our own direct acts of consciousness of things in order to see metaphysical (beingful) dimensions of those very same things, hitherto unsuspected. All true philosophical ideas can be, in principle, verified in the laboratory of one's personal consciousness in this real, but non-empirical, manner.

6. Good philosophers, of course, use all of their sense organs carefully and intelligently. Without physical sensation and its remarkable potential for intellective magnification, philosophy could hardly begin.

7. Barry Commoner, professor of biology at Washington University in St. Louis, offers perhaps the clearest treatment of the need for a non-linear, scientific approach to environmental biology in his book, *The Closing Circle* (New York: Knopf/Bantam, 1972).

8. Anne Morrow Lindbergh, *Gift from the Sea* (New York: Random House/Vintage, 1955), p. 98.

9. Ibid.

10. The common philosophical predicament of exaggerating one kind of being at the expense of the other kinds is discussed in my essay, "A Christian Will to Meaning in Everyday Life," *Cross Currents*, 17 (Winter 1967):25-38.

11. My brief characterizations which follow are made from a philosophical perspective. They do not necessarily coincide with the psychological descriptions of the ego states given by Eric Berne, original developer of transactional analysis, and by other TA specialists. For discussion of these three areas of the human psyche the reader is referred to the exceptionally helpful book by Muriel James and Elizabeth Jongeward, *Born to Win* (Reading, Mass.: Addison-Wesley, 1971).

12. As an art, philosophy works with a medium; namely, meanings. The more integrative and ultimate the meanings are, the more they are apt matter for the art of philosophizing. When a chemist asks,

"What is chemistry?" he or she is no longer in chemistry, but in philosophy. The meaning of chemistry—what it ultimately is and how it relates to all else—is a philosophical matter. When a theologian asks, "What is theology?" he or she is no longer in theology, but in philosophy. Yet, when a philosopher asks, "What is philosophy?" he or she remains right at home.

By saying that philosophy is an art I do not mean that one can make whatever one pleases. One is responsible to the truth of reality—the way things are essentially—for the shape of one's meanings. A person's philosophy is a unique artwork of integrative and ultimate meaning that distinctively reveals not so much one's ideas about reality, but the reality which one's ideas are about. A philosophy is only as beautiful as it uniquely *reveals* what is true and what is good.

13. Robert Baker and Frederick Elliston, eds., *Philosophy and Sex* (New York: Prometheus Books, 1975), Introduction. They also note candidly that articles on sex and sexuality have begun to appear in philosophical journals only since 1968.

14. The traditional notion of philosophy as handmaid of theology is not being dismissed. Theology as the Parent of intellectual discipline brings a *necessary* corrective to the instinctive direction of the egocentric, naturalistic propensity in human thought. What is being suggested is that theology not serve as a hyper-Parent—an intellective ego state that takes over the integrative functions of philosophy (the intellective Adult).

15. While the philosophy and ethics of human sexuality presented in this book is open to theological and religious truth, it is not a theological or religious ethics. One need not be committed to any religious doctrines in order to follow and appreciate many of its perspectives on the nature of human sexuality and behavior.

Part   I

SEXUALITY AND LIBERATION

Chapter 2

SEXUALITY MEANS SHARING

To be a man or a woman is to be sexual. Each person is a sexual being.

In considering our sexuality we are inclined, at first, to think that a person is sexual because of his or her distinctive physical organs of generation. But it is not really because we have different organs that we are male or female; it is because we are male or female that we have these distinctive organs.

Every cell in our bodies tells the story of our being man or woman. And yet it is not even because every cell in our bodies is sexual that we, as full persons, can be *called* sexual. Rather, it is because we are fully sexual in our being as persons that every cell in our bodies *is* sexual. Genital organs, cell structures, and hormonal systems, all reveal to us our inherently sexual being. But they do not *cause* us to *be* sexual. They cause us to *know* we are sexual.

If we are going to discover the true center and source of our sexuality, we will have to look deeper within ourselves. A person has emotions, an intellect, and a will that are just as integral and important as his or her body. It is often very difficult to say anything definite about the workings of these powers of the soul. It is much easier to know something definite about the body. Nevertheless, a person creates his or her life and destiny far more within the soul than within the body.

Sexuality so pervades the mind and heart--as well as the body--that it would be irrational to expect to find its center simply in the body. And yet most people tend to assume that sexuality is exclusively or primarily a bodily feature, because that is the first and most immediate way in which they come to know it. They confuse the way in which they come to know something with the thing itself that they come to know in that way. As a little child comes to know his body and bodily movements first (and in very definite ways) long before he or she ever suspects anything about an interior life that causes these movements, so we are naturally enamoured of the physical structure and function of human sexuality long before we begin to realize how deeply it is rooted in the spiritual depths of the person.

The immature inclination to restrict the consideration of sexuality and human sexual energy to the bodily or the physical part of human beings has been one of the most significant factors in perpetrating and perpetuating the crisis in human sexual ecology from which the world has suffered in many forms throughout the ages. We have not exercised our potential to be sexual ecologists, just as we have not exercised, until recently, our potential to be physical ecologists. We have considered only one set of relationships at a time, leaving out the practical realization that everything in the environment is related to everything else. So, we have concentrated almost exclusively on physical and genital sexual relationships without careful regard for the difficult-to-discern, but profoundly influential, spiritual relationships that are inextricably bound up with the psychic and physical.

Even the contemporary explorations of psychosexual relationships, such as those undertaken by Masters and Johnson, seem to have centered almost exclusively on the genital area of sexual dynamics. The brain is acknowledged as the main sexual organ in human beings. But it is regarded primarily as a service organ of the genitals, rather than of consciousness and of the spiritual in human sexuality. Because of the very pervasive tendency in science and in everyday life to narrow down one's field of investigation and to isolate a single chain of causes and effects, we have neglected the task of understanding the total complex of processes in both the environmental ecosphere and the sexual ecosphere.

18

Sexuality, Genitality, Coitality

At the outset of our study, therefore, I will attempt to provide a broad perspective for understanding man and woman. I will define sexuality, at least hypothetically, in such a way that it embraces all three basic ecosystems within the individual person and between individual persons.

The intention here is not to prove the adequacy of the definitions. The testing of these definitions can only be done in the laboratory of one's own individual consciousness, reflecting on experience and on the results of study in many areas of life. The consistent way in which these definitions will be used throughout this book may serve additionally as a suggestion of their adequacy. But the individual reader can try these definitions on for size by thinking over matters in man-woman relations to see whether, or to what extent, the definitions make sense.

Sexuality, then, can be defined as the personal power *to share* (physically, psychically, and spiritually) *the gift of self* with self and with others.[1] Sexuality is basically the power of sharing self. Sharing involves giving and receiving--not giving and getting. In Chapter 5, male and female sexuality will be defined in terms of these elements of sharing--giving and receiving. For now, I will simply suggest that every person may be regarded as *sexual* (male or female) in as much as he or she has the natural power to share self.

A mother and child are exercising this power, for instance, when the mother is teaching the child how to peel an orange. To some extent each of them is sharing *self* with the other. Of course, they may be regarded as sharing the orange and the knife. But the exercise of their sexuality does not consist in the sharing of things, but in the sharing of selves. It occurs naturally and fluently to the extent that they are sharing *themselves* with each other. If they are enjoying, not so much the instruction, but the *being together*, they can be said to be sharing themselves, and in that way they are fundamentally expressing their sexuality. Sexuality is the sharing dimension of personality.

If two people are members of the same sex they are sharing themselves with each other differently than if they were of the opposite sex. In any event, sexual activity is basically a sharing of self. It is not

19

necessarily genital activity--although genital activity is necessarily sexual activity.

Sexual activity is an interaction with people of either sex. But it is also an activity simply within the self. That is why care was taken to say that sexuality is the power to share the gift of self *with self*. Sexuality is, first of all, an interior condition and activity.

A person walking along the street enjoying the trees, the birds, the passing people and so on is sometimes said to be "enjoying himself." This is an instance of sexual activity. The person is sharing these enjoyable beings with self. So, the crucial test of sexual development often comes in the person's power to be alone creatively and joyfully. In those times of being alone, the degree of functional sexual power--sharing self with self--is necessarily revealed.

But sexuality is not genitality. We often fail to distinguish the two. Genitality is our personal and social power *to share the gift of life* in space and time with a new human being. Genitality is a special, dramatic physical power--the power of *sharing life*. It is a natural power to share our space-time life with another person of either sex, a child. In exercising one's genitality a person does *not specifically* share the gift of self. One shares specifically the gift of life. Naturally, the individual wants to share self, too, and does--in that action generally, but not specifically. Genitality is a power different from sexuality. Genitality is a power that has specific organs pertaining to it. Sexuality does not.

Moreover, genitality is *not specifically* a personal power. It is generally a personal power, but it is specifically a power of the human community as such. When a child is conceived, that child belongs to and is the responsibility of the community in a definitive way. For instance, both parents may die shortly after the birth of the child. Yet that child will be in the arms of the community until death; and, if the child becomes a parent later in life, many generations of people may be afforded nurture in the human community because of the one conception of two parents many years before. Our genital power is a personal power in that it is *ours*, and not that of another individual. But the child who may be conceived through that power is not simply the responsibility of the parent. That child is much more broadly

20

and definitively the responsibility of the whole human family.

Sexuality is not genitality. Nor is it coitality. Coitality is another power, different from both sexuality and genitality. It is the power that most people seem to confuse with sexuality. Coitality is the personal power *to share the gift of genital life* with a person of the other sex. It is the power to engage in coital union with someone of the other sex. Like genitality, it is a physical power. Coition, the actual activity of sharing one's genital life with a person of the other sex, is but one obvious form of expressing sexuality physically.[2] *Every* shared look, touch, conversation and the like involves some form of sharing oneself physically with another person.

Perhaps the prime ecological disaster in human sexuality has been the culturally reinforced tendency to assume that physical sexual fulfillment can *only* come through this one dramatic form of physical sexual activity: coital intercourse. When people hear of sex and sexuality, almost always they think of coital union which tends to culminate in orgasm for one or both partners. Because of the intensity of the satisfaction often accompanying this union, all other forms of less dramatic physical satisfaction such as touching, kissing, or delighting in the visual and auditory presence of one another have been--as *sexual* interactions--culturally neglected or repressed.

Coital union is but one form of one specific kind of physical sexual intercourse; namely, touching. Although the senses of hearing, seeing, smelling and perhaps even tasting are often involved, the activity itself is specifically one of touching. If it happens to come to fruition in the special touching of sperm-nucleus and ovum-nucleus, coital union results in the most dramatic kind of all physical sexual intercourse; namely, the causing of another human being in the world.

The child, however, is the *specific* result of the exercise of the *genital* powers, not of the coital powers. The coital powers are the natural *means* by which two people together share the gift of life with another person. But the coital union itself is specifically the sharing of one's own genital or generative life with a person of the other sex. This kind of distinction is important (along with others made later) if we would appreciate the beautiful complexity and unity of the human sexual ecosystem. Failure to make such distinctions, while regarding the remarkable interrelationships involved, muddies the waters of human sexual expression.

Coitality, genitality and sexuality are powers that are quite distinct within the human person. Each is associated integrally with the human body in a different way.

Coitality is specifically related to the organs of coition, primarily penis and vagina, as well as to the auxiliary organs such as the clitoris.

Strictly speaking, genitality is specifically related to the organs of generation, the testes and ovaries. Gestation, which naturally requires the womb; birth, which naturally requires the vaginal canal; and nursing, which naturally requires the breasts, are further physical sexual processes consequent upon coition and generation. They are modalities within the personal and social power of genitality.

Sexuality is not, as such, a specifically physical power. However, this personal power to share oneself with self and with others--for human beings in space and time--is always specifically related to the body. The whole body of the person is its "organ."[3]

Sexuality is the overarching and radically intimate source of vitality for the other powers. So, we can say that everything coital is sexual, although not every-thing sexual is coital--since *every* action of a human being has the power to share self within it.[4] We can likewise say that everything genital is sexual, although not everything sexual is genital--for the same reason. But it is also true to say that everything coital is genital, although not everything genital is coital--because, for instance, penis and vagina are always nec-essary for a natural act of generation, but the ovaries are not necessary for coition. In other words, every coital organ is a genital one but not every genital organ is a coital one.

Recognition of the unity and distinctness of these natural powers is crucial if we are going to develop a sexual ethics that is faithful to the integrity of the human being's radically natural structure and dynamics. Moreover, all of these powers and their activities or processes--sexuation, generation, coition, gestation, natalization, and lactation--are personal. They are powers and actions that can only be attributed to persons, not to animals.

Only Persons Are Sexual

If sexuality means sharing, then only persons can be said to be sexual in the fundamental sense. Animals and plants have sex and sex functions, but they are not, properly speaking, sexual. Sexuality is a component of personality, not of "doggality" or "rabbitality." In mating, animals do not *share* life with their offspring, because they are not capable of appreciating life *as a gift* and because they do not have the capacity to give *themselves* as a gift to another.

Animals beget or reproduce offspring. They function as sheer instruments in transmitting life. People have the power to transmit life as a gift. Animals mate or copulate. They function in this way unselfconsciously and by instinct. People have the power to *share* their very *selves* within an act of coital communion.

In the definitions, I have indicated that *sharing* is the key to all forms of authentic human sexual intercourse. People *sharing* their very selves in myriad ways of tender human intercourse: this is sexuality in action. People *sharing* the gift of life with another whole human being: this is genitality in action. People *sharing* the gift of their generative lives with each other in that most obvious of sexual acts (coital intercourse): this is coitality in action.

Sexuality Is Necessary for Love

All loving begins with sharing. For those of us who are Christian, Jesus came into the world first through the activity of God sharing Self with us. For those of us who are Jewish, Yahweh is a loving, ever-caring Lord leading his people. For those of us who believe in a less personal God, it still may seem that the Absolute Power or Self in reality shares itself with all creatures in varying ways and degrees.[5] We all seem to have a share in Divine energy. In any event, if we ourselves can be said to love, we will have to be able to relate to our beloved in a sharing way. We must be willing to *share* our very *self* with another in order to love that person. In doing so, we are acting sexually.

There are many kinds and forms of love, but there would seem to be one essential meaning. Love is *willing* the truest and the best for the one loved, and being willing to show we mean it. To the extent that we really do desire--not just "wish"--the truest and the best for someone in a given circumstance, despite what it may

23

cost us to help it come about, we can be said to love. Our giving and receiving capacities need to be in a condition of expansion if we are really to love. We love only by giving of our time, talent and efforts in such a way as to do all that we can to make the truest and the best come to the ones we love because they are so good and valuable in themselves.

In giving of ourselves for the good of the beloved we are likewise called to receive whatever comes to us. We may receive the bitter as well as the sweet. After all, our love may not be reciprocated. But if we love and are truly sharing, then we are receiving in a way that is as expansive as possible.

Love necessarily involves giving and receiving. Giving and receiving are the prime components of sharing. And sharing is at the heart of sexuality. The more we actually love, the more functionally sexual we become.

Persons Are Not Animals

Animals are not capable of love. Even their most humanlike actions which resemble love--such as when a faithful dog dies trying to save a drowning child--are the product of instinct. Love requires the capacity to know one's self as a self, and to be willing to share this self for the good of the beloved as a self. Animals know things, but do not know them *as* things or *as* selves. A dog knows his bone, but does not know it *as a bone* or in its boneness. The dog may be said to know himself, but he does not know himself *as a self* or in his selfhood.

This observation is not intended to disparage the remarkable and beautiful powers of dogs and many other animals. Perhaps, some people's difficulty in accepting the fact of an animal's inability to love comes from their own inability to experience or discern what real love is.

Love is not affection. Animals as well as people can be affectionate--they can "give affection." Yet many people seem to be, at times, functionally incapable of *giving themselves* (loving) while they are expressing affection. They can give affection, but they cannot give love. They can show how much they *like* someone, but they cannot intend genuine good for the other person, if that would mean they would have to suffer in some way. Such a condition in an animal is not a defect at all. In a human being it is a great paralysis--whether it is recognized or not.

24

Love transcends affection. Love is an activity that is just as appropriate to one's enemies as to one's friends. In an animal, the inability to love an enemy is a natural inability. In a human being, it is a functional inability. Persons are naturally capable of love for all beings, friend and adversary alike.

Unfortunately, in the history of the Western world-- most notably through the long, classical tradition of philosophical thought--"man" has been called a "rational animal." But it is difficult to see how man can be called an animal in any proper sense. We are animal*like* in many ways. Yet we are not basically animals.[6]

Human beings are not rational animals any more than animals are sentient plants. Animals, in turn, are not basically plants. They are a unique kind of living creature that has many properties similar to those of plants. But this unique kind of living creature is radically different from plants in the power to sense and to feel, as well as in the power of local motion. Similarly, human beings are like both plants and animals in many of their powers and activities, but they are radically other than plants and animals in their power to know the essences of things and to love.

Human Persons Defined

Human beings are a unique kind of creature. On the one hand, they are radically other than animals in being capable of self-reflection and love. On the other hand, they are radically other than angels or pure spirits in the power to eat, defecate, assimilate nutrients, be healed by natural self-repair, procreate, have sensations and emotions, make deliberations, and so forth. So, the human person may be defined as a unique being which is *naturally*--though not necessarily functionally at any given time with respect to all of these qualities-- capable of living through processes of nutrition, growth, self-repair, procreation, feeling, imagination, emotion, ideation, loving, willing, and relating to self and others in a self-reflective way.[7]

Perhaps, humans may be rightly regarded as the "lowest order" or the lowest type of persons. But humans ought not to be confused with the other lower kinds of creature any more than they are to be confused with "higher-order" creatures. We are spirit*like*, God-*like*, animal*like*, and plant*like* in many ways. We are even rock*like*. When dropped, we fall like a rock. But we

25

are in no proper sense--only figuratively, perhaps--
rocks, plants, spirits *or animals*.

In fact, if we are going to make an ecologically
philosophical breakthrough in our self-consciousness and
our understanding of the proper balance of interrelationships among planetary creatures, we may come to see
that we have held the likenesses in reverse. It is not
so much that humans are like animals, but that animals
are like humans. A dog with his tail between his legs
looks as though he is ashamed. But it is not shame. It
is a likeness to (human) shame, but the latter is the
primary reality. Just as human beings can bark like a
dog, but it is not really a bark; so dogs can cower like
humans, but it is not really shame.

Even in regard to more common activities we may have
our priorities of vision reversed. Probably, we should
not so much assume that people consume food like dogs
and cats, but that dogs and cats consume food like people.
Likewise, people do not grow and reproduce so much like
plants; it is rather that plants grow and reproduce in
likeness to the total growth (bodily, mental, spiritual)
and procreativeness of people. Failure to respect the
direction in which creaturely likeness flows inevitably
results in a poor interpretation of total ecology in
general and human ecology in particular. One can readily
acknowledge that plants and animals existed on the planet
before humans and yet realize that what is chronologi-
cally first may be ontologically (beingfully) last.

Person-Based Biology

Every action and function of a human being is primarily a person-action, not a biological one. Primarily,
the action of a person; secondarily, the action of an
organism. Even the flow of blood in the veins or the
flow of nerve energy or the fantastically complex enzy-
matic activity in the body is the activity of a person.
It is the activity of a person who *is* an organism; and
not the activity of an organism that happens to belong
to a person. We are person-al organisms, not animal
organisms.

A person is one whole being, in which all of the
powers are activated by a single principle of life and
action. That principle of life in a person has been
known as the rational soul. It is the intrinsic reason
why a person can both think and copulate, love and sleep,
and do all of the other multitudinous activities and
functions--conscious and unconscious. There is an

absolute unity to the human person, as well as to each animal and plant. The soul of the person is the all-pervasive source of every kind of structure in the individual. No power, organ, or function in the individual can be what it is or act as it does, except in virtue of the unique and singular character of the soul.

In the light of this unitary source of power and action, even the most biological and physical of functions must be regarded as primarily personal. We have a person-based biology, not a biology-based personhood. There is an enormous difference in the two ways of viewing humanity.[8]

The traditional way is to think of human beings as having a biology-based personhood, in contrast to spirits or higher-order creatures, who are thought to have a biology-less personhood. In this way of viewing it, the biological part of personhood is looked upon as a drag or a limitation--even, for many persons, an indecency or punishment.[9]

But this perspective comes about largely through an unreflective and almost literal acceptance of Aristotle's definition of man as a rational animal. Thus, man is thought to be basically an animal, a biological organism; but with a difference, rationality. Biology is then inevitably regarded as primary, and rationality as secondary. (Of course, much of this biologistic orientation is formed unconsciously.) Many otherwise sophisticated persons today accept this perspective rather uncritically. Not a few seem to regard the bodily and the biological reprehensively, as Plato seems to have done. The body is often subtly (or not so subtly) treated as a kind of animal to be trained and subjected to our will, as a pet to its master.[10]

However, in the history of Western philosophy there are periodic insights into the remarkable unity of body and soul. Some of these insights can convince the open-minded person that the body and biology, while an essential part of the person, are not the primary source of even the most elemental energy and activity. The primary source is his or her radically spiritual soul, which causes even the most basic biological processes. Ours is a person-based biology.

The implication here is the reverse of the traditional perspective. The rational soul is not seen as stuck within and confined by one's biology. Rather, the biology of the person is seen as both emanating from and being within a spiritual and incorruptible soul. The human person is not regarded as a high-class animal. Nor is the person considered to be a low-class spirit, contaminated by a body. The human person is valued as a being of a unique kind--both bodily and spiritual.[11]

The human soul is--unlike the souls of plants and animals--spiritual.[12] Thus, the spiritual is the source of life in every part of the person, and the body is one of those real parts. Through the power of his or her spiritual life the human person is able to share with self and with others in innumerable ways. This giving and receiving activity has different dimensions and many forms. But the personal power to engage in it can be called human sexuality.

NOTES

1. This definition and others in this book presuppose a sense of human beings as structured beings, having a stable, dynamic nature. The idea of human life and existence having a structure is not exclusively the province of traditional, Aristotelian-influenced philosophy. Contemporary phenomenologists are also inclined to this way of thinking and articulating. See, for instance, the work of existential psychologist Adrian van Kaam, *Sex and Existence* (Chicago: Franciscan Herald Press, n.d.).

The present volume is not necessarily concerned with what has been traditionally called the natural law. Nevertheless, the theory of sexual ecology is quite consonant with this perspective. Recognition is given to the natural structures of things--inanimate objects, plants, animals, persons--and to their role as built-in "rules" for human responsiveness. Traditionally, these "rules" have been called "laws of nature" as distinct from "natural law," which refers to the unique capacity of human beings to reflect upon and know themselves and determine *how* they are freely to act or not act.

2. Obviously, if coital union is done well, profound psychic and spiritual relationships are quickened or enriched. But the interaction itself is--unlike the interaction of sharing as such (the exercise of one's sexuality-power)--*specifically* a physical, interpersonal activity. Human coition is one particular kind of physically interpersonal behavior.

3. The implication here is that sexuality is a power common to humans and to non-bodily creatures. *Human* sexuality is essentially a *bodily* species of sexuality--not, however, specifically genital. But this personal power to share self with self and with others (sexuality) can reasonably be attributed (by those who believe in them) to purely spiritual creatures. Later, it will be claimed

28

that sexuality is an aspect of God's personality, from whom all sexuality takes its likeness. "God created man in the image of himself, in the image of God he created him, male and female he created them" (Gen. 1:27).

4. A human being has the *natural* power to intend or not to intend whatever is taking place in him or her—even something involuntary, such as breathing, dreaming, or conceiving a child (an act of generation). One can be willing or unwilling that these involuntary movements occur. They can be at least virtually voluntary. The quality of one's willing—especially including one's self-concept and motivation for sheer living—is decisive in determining the degree to which even involuntary acts or acts that are sometimes only partially voluntary (e.g., coital intercourse in a state of inebriation) are sharing (giving and receiving) rather than anti-sharing (putting out and getting).

5. Belief in the existence of God is not necessary for appreciating, to some extent, the nature of sharing and the general theory of sexuality and ethics in this book. But those who believe in God's existence and care for creatures will likely appreciate more readily the philosophy of human sexual ecology.

The existence of God and God's nature are subjects for the philosophy of being and cannot be discussed in this work. A brief outline of a guided reflection on the question of God's existence follows.

In the world of matter and motion, of space and time, everything that causes something to happen causes it *only in so far as* it is itself *being caused* by another cause or causes.

But whatever causes something only in so far as this cause itself is being caused by something else does not explain adequately *why* the caused event is happening; i.e., it contributes, in itself and in its causing action, *zero value* of explanation as to *why* the event is occurring *at all*. (A bat propelling a ball across a baseball diamond may partially explain why the ball travels in such a direction and at such a speed, but it explains *nothing* as to why the motion of the ball *exists at all*. And all the causes "behind" the motion of the bat, such as the batter's arm motion, his brain motions, his parent's act of generating him, and their parents' act of generating them, etc., only do their causing in so far as they themselves are caused by other causes.)

Now, an *infinite* series or an infinite number of such causes, which cause only in so far as they themselves are caused, would still not *explain adequately why* the event is *actually happening now*. Zero plus zero plus zero (explanation) equals zero explanation, whether the number of zeroes is finite or infinite.

But, here it is! The event *is* really *being*, really *occurring* (I *am* writing, you *are* reading, the clock *is* ticking, the world *is* spinning).

Therefore, there must be a cause of *this event* that is not causing it only in so far as it is caused by another, but is *causing* the event in and by itself—immediately! This cause of the real event—explaining its *be*-ing—most people call "God".

Each of the premises for this argument can be given extensive support, especially once the thinker gains an insight into the real difference between *what* something is and its being-at-all, and between the cause of something's *coming* to be (and to be *this* rather than *that*) and the cause of its *being*-at-all. God is the cause of the being-at-all of the simplest motion, thought, or act of love and is not to be confused with the cause of, say, the motion as this motion rather than that, as a *motion* rather than a thought, as coming into existence now rather than then, and so forth.

6. Human beings are, in some sense, rational organisms. By the term *animal* Aristotle meant a *living organism*, not simply a brute. But even with that point clearly understood, I find the definition less than desirable because it implies that the human being is fundamentally an organism without making it clear that this being is just as fundamentally a person.

7. The key distinction revolves around the radical difference between natural and functional capacity. A person is an individual (no matter how undeveloped or misdeveloped) that is naturally capable of these operations and activities. That which makes someone or something what it *is*, is its nature, not its function. Nature is the radical principle or source of all activities and functions of the individual. (See Aristotle's meaning in Phys., Bk. II, ch. 1, 192b, 21-23; cf. James Weisheipl, "The Concept of Nature," *The New Scholasticism*, 28 (1954):374-408).

Unless one is clear about the profound difference between natural capacity and functional capacity, all kinds of unethical behavior can result. The issue of abortion is a prime instance of the confusion that arises. Many people do not seem to be able to see that a human zygote has the *natural* capacity, though not the functional one, for reading, writing, speaking and loving in a self-reflective way; whereas a rabbit zygote, as well as the rabbit adult, has neither the natural nor the functional capacity for these activities. Judging who is a person can only be made rationally on the basis of natural capacity; never on the basis of functional capacity.

For an account of the ethical consequences of this distinction, see Robert E. Joyce, "Personhood and the Conception Event," *The New Scholasticism*, 52 (Winter, 1978):97-109.

8. This idea is treated by Mary R. Joyce, *How Can a Man and Woman Be Friends?* (Collegeville, Minn.: Liturgical Press, 1977), p. 17. Also, see her chapter on the unity of the person in *Love Responds to Life* (Kenosha, Wisc.: Prow, 1970), pp. 41-46.

On the remarkable unity of body and soul in the context of human sexuality, see Germain Grisez, "Natural Family Planning is not Contraception," *International Review of Natural Family Planning*, 1 (1977): 121-26.

9. The body as the locus of punishment and imprisonment seems to be the common view of the Platonic and neo-Platonic traditions. Christian pastoral practice in many ages, including our own, has not been immune to this unfortunate metaphysical rejection of bodies as essential to the human person.

10. This perennial view of the relationship of body and mind (consciousness, soul, personhood) has devastating consequences for human life. The major rationale for permissive abortion statutes today seems to derive largely from the assumption that the human body as such is not a person and that personhood is an achievement, not an endowment. This gradualist or developmental approach to the origin of human personhood was implicitly espoused by the majority view of the U. S. Supreme Court in its 1973 (Row v. Wade) opinion on legalized abortion. The rationale for this implicitly separational view of body and soul or body and personhood—in which the soul or the supposedly person-part of self is regarded as the owner and tamer of the body, even in adult life—is well formulated by Daniel Callahan, *Abortion: Law, Choice and Morality* (New York: Macmillan, 1970), especially pp. 384-401. The separational view of body and self is not always so grossly exposed as in the popular cry of body-ownership, "I have a right to control my own body." Callahan and others have concealed their view (perhaps from themselves) by misunderstanding the meaning of the term *potential* as applied to living beings. So, they regard the tiny human body, developing in the womb, as a "potential person" rather than an actual person with great potential. For a critique of the developmentalist notion, see R. Joyce, "Personhood and the Conception Event," especially pp. 105-106.

11. The philosophy of human nature and personhood behind these remarks is compatible with either an evolutionist or creationist interpretation of the origins of human beings. It does require a recognition of human nature as unique and singularly endowed among all presently-known physical creatures.

12. *Spiritual* is the positive term for the quality of the soul commonly known as *immateriality*. Discussion and demonstration of the immateriality and incorruptibility of the person (at least that decisive part of him or her called the soul) is an issue in philosophical anthropology. A guideline for awareness of the immateriality of the human soul is provided in the following outline of a traditional argument.

Think of a triangle. The triangle (not the *image* of it or the drawing of it, which merely signifies or symbolizes it) of which you are now thinking is not a material thing and thus is not subject to any change by motion or by concept in any way. Of course, it can be known more and more clearly, and certainly. But once triangularity is basically apprehended in its nature (e.g., stated as a 3-sided plane figure of straight lines), it is rightly understood as never changing. So too, in the case of non-mathematical realities such as truth, beauty, goodness, et al. We may apprehend or know them weakly or poorly, and we may misuse or misapply them much of the time, but they are themselves incorruptible and not subject to any change of matter and motion. (If anything, all matter and motion in the world are in some way governed by and subject to *them*. What is good is good, even if no one exists who exemplifies it. Thirty-sixness is thirty-sixness, independent of whether there are thirty six things existing to be counted and no matter *what* those things might be.

Now, my *knowledge* of the triangle may not be the same reality as the triangle itself. But my *knowledge* of it is essentially like it in being *unchangeable*. (Of course, I can change the degree and depth to which I understand the triangle and its "properties." But I cannot change *either* the triangle itself in its triangularity *or* my knowledge of it as far as its essence goes; i.e., as a 3-sided plane figure, etc.: or some such words which amount to the same thing.) If I could change essentially my knowledge of a triangle, it would not be a triangle that I was knowing in the first place. Therefore, my knowledge of a triangle, or of goodness itself--however weak this knowledge might be--is *essentially* unchangeable.

Furthermore, *I* am the *cause* of my thinking of and my knowledge of these "abstract" realities, such as triangularity, goodness, truth, and so forth.

But an effect cannot be greater than its cause. Thus the *knowledge* that I have (the effect) cannot be greater than *I* (its cause).

Therefore, I am, like triangularity, goodness, truth, and the like, immaterial and incorruptible or immortal--at least in the part of me by which I *cause* my knowledge of these things. (That part has been called traditionally the soul.)

Every aspect of this argument can be given extensive support, especially once the thinker realizes that abstractions are real-- just as real, though intangible, as concrete things (treeness is just as real as this oak tree in my backyard). Neither abstraction nor concrete thing are reducible to the other (treeness is radically other than this oak tree).

Chapter 3

SEXUAL ENERGY

In *any* living being of our experience, the soul may
be regarded as the unitary source of life and activity.
In the case of human beings, we can identify certain
activities that are intrinsically independent of matter
and motion. These activities, such as knowing things
in an immaterial way (knowing one's knowing of things,
knowing the essences of things, and doing abstract thinking), may not get their start without the experience of
sensations and images, but they are recognized--upon
serious reflection--to be themselves immaterial acts.[1]
Along with the person's activities of seeing, hearing,
feeling, imagining, and the like, these immaterial or
spiritual acts occur by virtue of the same mysterious,
unitary source within the individual person who engages
in them. This common intrinsic source within the human
person for *all* of his or her life, energy, and activity
can be called the spiritual soul.

This spiritual principle of the person pervades the
whole being, encompassing every part and making it to
be personal. A crucial aspect of being personal--a dimension of every part of the individual--is the power to
give and to receive self and others as unique, intimately
related beings. This power--physical and psychic, yet
specifically spiritual--is what I have defined as human
sexuality. It is the personal power to share the gift
of self with self and with others that leads to increasing
intimacy and co-creativity.

As one develops an ethics of man and woman, one
attempts to determine how a person should act *sexually*.
The whole human person is taken into account and the
essence of human sexuality is sought. Crucial questions
are asked. What are the deepest sources of sexuality?
What are the basic dynamics of human sexual energy? Adequate responses to these and other questions are necessary
in order to develop sound judgments concerning what is
ethically viable behavior. A decisive step in that direction can be taken by considering the meaning of sexual
energy.

Energy has been commonly defined as the capacity
to do work. Sexual energy may be understood as the capacity to share. Sharing is the particular kind of work
that is proper to sexual energy. An analysis of the two
intrinsic components of sharing (giving and receiving)
will help to enrich this concept of sexual energy, and
further reflections will develop our concept of human
sexual ecology.

Giving and Receiving

Giving is not simply handing over. Receiving is
not merely getting. Giving and receiving are very special
kinds of doing.

When a man gives a woman a diamond engagement ring,
what is he really doing? Is he just getting it to her?
Delivering it? And when the woman receives the ring, is
she simply taking it? Is she just getting it? We would
probably agree that giving and receiving involve much
more.

Giving is a human action that implies a certain
attitude. We use the word "giving" very loosely most
of the time. We often mean little more than "handing
over" something to someone. But genuine giving is handing
over something to someone while *presenting yourself*.
Genuine giving means that there is a gift and a giver.
The gift is given by the giver with an attitude that
says, "Here *I* am, too . . . open to your every good."

In giving, the giver delivers himself or herself
"within" the item given. This kind of giving tends to
unite the giver and the one who receives, because the
giver is present in the gift, the symbol of self. The
kind of giving that is merely a "handing over" tends to
disunite the giver and the recipient because the giver
is alienated from the "gift" through indifference or
even mental conflict.

Receiving is likewise a human action that implies
a certain attitude. We use the word "receiving" less
loosely than we do the word "giving." But we often seem
to use words such as "get" or "took" when we mean "receive." There is the common expression: "She got her
ring!" Or someone might say, "He took the gift and
thanked his friend." Not infrequently one hears the word
"receive" used to indicate something very passive. "He
received a terrible beating from the muggers." "She
was received coolly by the attendant." But genuine receiving is the condition of being dealt something or
handed something by someone while *presenting yourself*.
Genuine receiving means that something is recognized and
accepted as a gift, and someone as a giver. The gift
is received with an attitude that says, "I am grateful
for your presence in your gift."

In receiving, the receiver is open gratefully to
both the giver and the gift. This kind of communication
tends to unite more closely the receiver with the giver.

Giving and receiving, then, are different human
actions and attitudes. But they are intimately related.
We might say that they occur simultaneously in the same
person.

Giving, after all, is a receiving kind of delivering
or of "handing over." The giver does not impose the
"gift." The giver acts in a receiving kind of way. The
young man is *offering* the engagement ring to the young
woman. He is not forcing it upon her. He gives the
ring to her in such a way as to be open gratefully to
her for being there and for being a gift in his life.
As the giver, he is dominantly saying, "Here *I* am,
too . . . open to your every good." But he is also
saying, subdominantly, "I am grateful for your presence
and for the gift that *you* are."

Receiving is likewise a reciprocal kind of activity.
Genuine receiving is a giving kind of "being done to."
The receiver does not demand the "gift." The receiver
acts in a giving kind of way. The young woman receives
the ring with awe and gratitude. She does not take it
for granted. She receives the ring from her beloved in
such a way as to be open to his every good. As the receiver, she is dominantly saying, "I am grateful for
your presence and for the gift that *you* are." But she
is also saying, subdominantly, "I give you myself, open
to your every good."

Giving is a receiving kind of action. Receiving is a giving kind of action. When a person gives and receives he or she is sharing--even though the *other* person does not reciprocate. Sharing is the activity of giving in a receiving way and receiving in a giving way. *Sexual energy* is the capacity or power for this kind of giving and receiving.

As I have already indicated, sexuality itself can be defined as the personal power to share the gift of self with self and with others. The sexual energy involved in this power comes in degrees and is found diversely in human beings. Individuals vary tremendously with regard to their capacities for sharing, in attitude and in commonplace actions.

The Sources of Sexual Energy

What are the sources of this sexual energy? Where is the person's sexual energy located or centered? Where is it coming from? What is the root of this capacity to give in a receiving kind of way and to receive in a giving kind of way? Perhaps these questions can be answered, in part, by suggesting an analogy with physical energy sources.[2]

There are various sources of physical energy. We speak of petroleum energy, nuclear energy, geothermal energy, solar energy, and others. Each of these sources is a distinctive one. If we are to use the source, we must take special steps to attain, store, and distribute that particular kind of energy. But there is one, overriding fact; and, in an age of energy crisis, people become more aware of it. The one supreme source of all physical energy in our planetary system--a source of the sources-- is solar energy. All other energies seem to be forms of what is called solar energy.

Without the energy emitted from the sun, there would be no energy in the whole solar system. The sun is the supreme source of all energy, motion, heat, light, and so on. Without the sun, there would be utter death and desolation in the world. When science finds relatively inexpensive and effective ways to tap directly and to utilize efficiently the energy of the sun, technological civilization will take a gigantic leap in freedom and creativity.

When we regard sexual energy, the special *capacity* for doing the human work of sharing, the situation is somewhat similar. There are various sources or areas

36

in the human being where sexual energy resides. The most
obvious area is the genital area. Human genital energy
is a form of sexual energy and it is very strong in most
people, ready to be put into use at a moment's notice.
Coital energy is likewise obvious and is used extensively
by individuals throughout the world.

The sources of sexual energy are remarkably differentiated. In the body, every somatic cell represents a
source or center of sexual energy. Each cell is male or
female and might be said to "house" a bit of the person's
ability to share self as a man or woman. Deeper within
the person, the psychic areas of the personality are
other than somatic, yet inseparably united with the body.
Men and women store up sexual energy in their feelings
and emotions, in their imaginations and fantasies. Still
further, in the depths of the person's spiritual life,
there are concepts, ideas, and self-concepts as man or
woman. Wherever sexual conditions form or take shape,
sexual energy must be present.

So, we can see that the particular sources of sexual
energy in the human person are many and diverse. They
are found everywhere in his or her being. Each of these
sources is distinctive. If a person is to use one or
more of them, he or she must reflect, at least minimally,
and then take measures to express these energies. Sharing
is an activity that presupposes intention.[3]

The Primary Source: "Soular Energy"

Unfortunately, most people seem to exist in a kind
of sexual energy crisis. Many couples draw too heavily
upon genital and coital energy, and then they wonder why
their sexual life is not very satisfactory. Regular
depletion of one or two sources of sexual energy, or an
imbalanced use of many sources, inevitably leads to a
state of crisis.

The way out of this sexual energy crisis is available. There is a supreme source of sexual energy that
is comparable to the sun as the primary source of physical
energy. People need to become aware of, to learn about,
and to utilize the soul-energy within the inner "space"
of his or her being. The person's individual soul is
the ultimate source of all sexual energy. The ability
to do the work of sharing (sexual energy) comes ultimately
from the spiritual soul.

Contrary to a traditional notion that has culturally
inhibited inner-space sexual adventuring, there *is* sex

to a soul. The soul is the only ultimate source of all forms of sexual energy. Without a human soul, there is no sharing in the world--no giving and receiving of self with self and with others.

People have not yet made the connection. They are still confused by the age-old, popular notion that the soul is "free" of sex. The distinction between sexuality and genitality has not been discerned. It is true that there may not be any genitality to a soul; nor any coitality. But the soul is the only ultimate source of sexuality in the human being.

The human soul is also the *source* of genitality and of coitality, even though these human powers are specifically bodily powers. They are *human* bodily powers, and are thus caused from within by the soul.[4] All genital and coital sexual energy is, one might say, a derivative of human sexual energy. Genitality and coitality are particular forms of the capacity to share. They are particularly definitive expressions of the person's general and all-pervasive sexuality.

The sun can be regarded as the ultimate source or the master energy within the physical world. Similarly, the individual human soul can be regarded as the ultimate source or the master energy within the sexual world (which involves the physical, psychic, and spiritual areas of the person). Without the life and energy of the soul nothing would move. The body, mind, emotions, and spirit of the person would be dead. All sexual energy is fundamentally "soul-ar" energy.

The "Copernican Revolution" in Human Sexuality

In order to appreciate the sexual power that is available to everyone, the world needs a *real* sexual revolution. What has been called the sexual revolution in our time is not a significant revolution. It merely represents a transition from the "old" morality to the "new" morality which is really quite old.

Both the so-called new morality and the so-called old morality share the same basic premise: there is no sex to a soul. Sex is not soul-deep. It is only body-deep. The "old morality" tended to train and discipline the body and its coital-genital urges for the sake of the soul's mastery. The "new morality" tends to use and exploit the body and its coital-genital urges for the sake of the soul's pleasure.[5] According to both orientations, the soul can enjoy sex, but it is actually not itself sexual. Neither viewpoint seems to recognize that sex urge and sex pleasure are not only bodily but soular.

A genuine sexual revolution will be the effect of a radical shift in vision, not unlike that which occurred in the physical world of energy when Copernicus announced that the sun does not go around the earth, but the earth goes around. The aged Ptolemaic notion of the earth being the center of the system died hard. People merely had to open their eyes and see that the sun rises in the east and sets in the west. Copernicus was up against the obvious. Nevertheless, his view has prevailed.

As a result of this opposite view regarding the center of the physical world, space exploration has become possible. Orbiting space ships, satellite stations, and outer-space probes to Mars and beyond are taken in stride. If people had continued to live by the common-sense perspective of the past, outer-space travel would still be only a fantasy.

A similar revolution is imperative if the world is going to survive the present sexual energy crisis. Many millions of abortions, raw sewerage pornography, pandemic V.D., rapidly spreading use of contraceptives among teens and children, and many more evidences of sexual conges-tion around the world demand a new vision of the meaning and value of human sexuality. In the midst of the present breakdown there must be a breakthrough. The time has come for the people of the world to be alerted to the true center of the human sexual system.

The sexual morality of the past and present has been founded on the "obvious" fact that coital-genital sex is the center of human sexual energy. All one has had to do is *feel* one's genital drive to know this "truth." But sooner or later the reflective person is going to realize that the opposite is true. Human sexual behavior does not really revolve around genital inter-action and orgasm. Rather, genital and coital sexuality are satellites of the human sexual energy in the soul.

The crucial truth about human sexual energy is some-thing that no one ever dared to say about sex, but you somehow already knew. The crucial truth is a revolu-tionary one--contrary to an assumption shared by Augustine and Havelock Ellis, by Thomas Aquinas and David Reuben. The truth is that human sexual energy is not fulfilled or consummated in genital intercourse and orgasm. It only looks that way. Human sexual energy does not move around the human genitals, but the genital and coital expressions of sexual energy move around the true and ultimate source of sexual energy, the soul--the inner sun, radiating its supreme power and fullness within the inner space of each individual person. Genital sexuality is meaningless apart from the source of sexual energy in the person's brain and in the vast depths of the person's inmost self (the spirit).

Without a true revolution that amounts to an evolution regarding the dynamics of the human sexual ecosystem, we will not begin to explore our inner personal life where sexuality and sexual energy are really consummated as well as begun. Those who would start such a revolution, foster it, or even simply try to put it into practice in their own personal lives may have to be willing to take more flak than Kepler, Galileo, and others took from many Christian churchmen and people generally at the time.[6] But until we acknowledge (and desire to live by) deeper sources of sexual energy we cannot even begin to take human sexuality seriously. Most reflective persons somehow know intuitively that these deeper sources exist, but they do not take the time, or else they do not *care* to take the time, in order to locate and develop them.

The task of effecting within one's own individual life--not to mention society-at-large--a revolution in the flow and use of one's sexual energy requries attention to insights in the biological and social sciences, in art and psychology, in religion and philosophy. But the needed sexual revolution poses a special challenge to one's philosophy of life. Until the radical change of vision becomes rather commonplace in the culture, good will and uncommon philosophical reflection are required of those who would enjoy the expansive, practical benefits of this revolution within their own lifetime.

The "Copernican Revolution" in human sexuality means that human sexual energy is centered *and* articulated much more in human consciousness than in human genitals, and that human sexuality is consummated and fulfilled in attitudes rather than orgasms. Later, a few of the implications of these truths will be discussed in greater detail. For now it may be appropriate to emphasize that people generally know these things to be true. But they do not seem to *know* that they know it. These truths need to be raised to consciousness. With conscious reflection and discussion the person takes a first great stride toward living them.

Three Areas of Energy in the Person

In the science of physical ecology, the supreme role of the sun and its energy is well recognized and forms the major focus in determining the direction and amount of energy-flow within the various ecosystems. Once a science of sexual ecology is developed, there will be a similar attention to the soul as the source of all sharing (sexuality). The sexual energy of the soul will be studied and related to the sexual energy in the mind or psyche and in the body. In fact, we might see a kind of analogy between the three elementary areas to which ecologists refer in studying the flow of solar energy and the three elementary areas involved in the flow of sexual energy.

Scientists point to the earth itself (the planet and its surface) as one area for the reception of solar energy. Obviously, it is the area that receives the least amount of radiation. The atmosphere surrounding the earth is a second general area of concern and it receives far more penetration by solar radiation. The third area that may be distinguished is simply called universal space, the interplanetary "outer space," within which solar radiation is more simply operative.

In studying the source of *sexual* energy--soul-ar energy--we can likewise distinguish three areas. (See Fig. 1, p. 42)

First, the body. We notice not only that human genitals are structured distinctively because of some kind of bodily sexual energy, but also that each cell in the body has a sexual character (notably in chromosomal structure) and is, therefore, the inherent residence of some measure of this energy. Gonads and hormones reveal other ways in which the body absorbs and utilizes the sexual energy of the soul. The body is the "ground" of our personhood and our sexuality.

Second, the psyche. Just as the atmosphere mediates the earth's reception of solar energy, the human psyche--seat of emotions, fantasies, and incomparable depths of feeling--mediates the body's reception of sexual or sharing energy. Much more of the soular energy is absorbed by the psyche than by the body.

In our perennially backward view of the sexual flow we have credited the human psyche with merely reflected sexual energy. And, of course, there is a partial basis for this view. Just as the ground reflects both heat

41

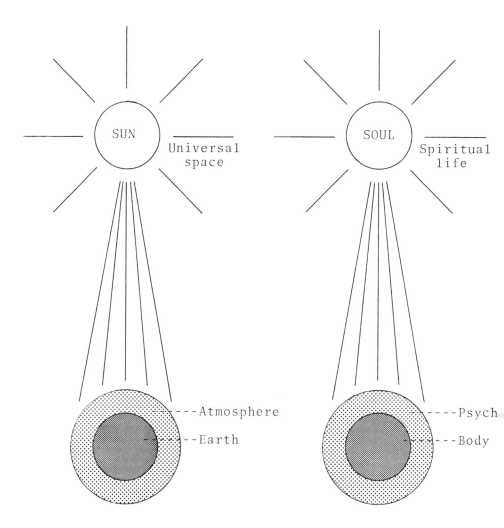

Fig. 1.   Energy Flow: Solar and Human

The individual human soul is compared in a figurative
parallel with the sun.   Both soul and sun are regarded
as the absolute sources of energy in their respective
systems.

and light from the sun back into the atmosphere, so both the "heat" of coital-genital passion and the "light" of erotic bodily form are "reflected" into the psyche, eventuating in emotional attachments, and in endless images and fantasies.

However, while we are quite willing to credit the mind and emotions with this *reflected* sexual energy, we seem to be almost totally unaware that the major thrust of sexual energy, like that of solar energy, must pass straight through the psyche "on its way" to the body. The human psyche, like the earth's atmosphere, must *absorb directly* much more energy than is reflected to it "from below."[7]

Third, the spirit. The person's spirit or spiritual life is a kind of interior universal space. The soul radiates, as it were, most simply and freely within the spiritual life of the person. A person is vastly more sexual and capable of sharing in his or her spiritual life than in psychic or physical life.

Through this likeness of spirit and space, psyche and atmosphere, body and earth, a very important philosophical truth can be appreciated. A double revolution in perspective is possible: one, on the part of the relation between bodily life and psychic life; and the other, on the part of the relation between the psychic life and the spiritual life.

We now know, from a panoramic perspective, that the earth stands (or revolves) *within* its surrounding atmosphere and that it is not so much a case of the atmosphere simply being "on" the earth. Similarly, we can realize, from a philosophical perspective, that the person's body is *within* his or her mind and psyche, and that it is not so much a case of the mind and psyche being somehow "in" the body.

We know, too, from a panoramic perspective, that the earth's atmosphere obviously stands (or moves) *within* universal space and that it is hardly a case of universal space being "in" the atmosphere. Similarly, we can acknowledge, from a philosophical point of view, that the psychic life of the person exists *within* his or her spiritual life and that it is not simply a case of the spiritual "touching upon" the mind and the psyche.[8]

This reversal of perspective can be viewed in another way. When a child first learns about the soul and the body, he or she is inclined to think, and may well be

43

taught, that "the soul is in the body." This perspective comes about because the child is taught to distinguish the soul as that which makes the body alive. The mountain is not alive because it does not have a soul in it. The tree is alive because it has a soul or principle of life. The human organism is a person and is capable of living after death, we are taught, because it has a special kind of soul in it--a spiritual soul. We are given the definite impression that the "soul is *in* the body."

As a person grows older, however, and engages in reflection and discussion, he or she may eventually do an "about face" in perspective. The realization may come that it is truer to say the body is in the soul than to say the soul is in the body. One can begin to see how people have, only through their spiritual souls, the *potential* to know all things--whatever is physically, mentally, or spiritually distant.[9] Our soul, then, must be somehow--even *before* we know something--in primitive contact with the reality that we come to know. So, the soul can be understood as a kind of magnetic field radiating well beyond the body. The body begins to appear as the center of this magnetic field, a place of concentration for the being, but in no way the exclusive "place of residence" for the person in his or her power and activity.[10]

The soul includes the body within its power and influence somewhat as the sun includes the earth within its power and radiation. Philosophically, then, as we stand here right now, knowing our personal self in body and soul, we are like a person standing on earth, *feeling* that he is in the center of everything, including the sun's "attention," but *knowing* that only a minute fraction of the sun's power and radiance is necessary for the support and maintenance of the earth. (According to scientific estimates, perhaps only one fifty-millionth of the sun's energy output reaches the earth's outer atmosphere.) Our ordinary, take-it-for-granted consciousness inevitably inclines us to feel that our bodies are somehow "where we are really at." But our self-reflective, critical consciousness can help us to see how our bodily life, as important as it is, probably is receiving a very small part of our soul's power and activity.

Eventually, the science of human sexual ecology will have to include attempts to assess the ratio of sexual energy actually available to the body, and it will suggest ways in which the body, like the earth, can more effectively utilize and transform the ample energy that it does receive. This latter kind of endeavor will probably entail a considerable analysis of how bodily actions and functions can become simultaneously more giving and receiving. Contemporary studies of body-relaxation techniques, as well as ancient practices such as yoga, already anticipate this kind of problem.

The Ecosystems Within

Just as there are many and varied ecosystems in physical ecology, so there are many and varied ecosystems in human sexual ecology.

A physical ecosystem is any basic functional unit for study. It includes all living and non-living elements that have a functional effect on one another. Some eco-systems are large, or vast, such as a lake or a continent. Others are small, such as a pond or a garbage can. The ecosystem is the basic nature of the place, with *all* of its elements adequately regarded.

Similarly, in human sexual ecology we can deal with large or small sexual ecosystems. They are innumerable. As long as we take into account *all* of the basic sexual (*sharing*) elements we are functioning properly. In the human being there can be no rightful attention to the bodily dimension without adequate regard for the psychic and the spiritual dimensions. And there can be no genuine attention to the spiritual or to the psychic, without the other two areas being given considerable regard.

If we examine a deliberate genital activity (for instance, masturbation or coital intercourse) we cannot simply regard its psychological causes and effects. We must examine all the relevant influences that inevitably flow into the ecosystem where this action occurs. These influences will require a consideration of all three areas of sexual energy: the physical and the spiritual, as well as the psychic.

Any human action involves a human ecosystem and will entail an elucidation of the basic elements from all three energy areas. Of course, in a given instance, it is not necessary to express all of the influences. (That would be impossible.) Nor is it always necessary to refer expressly to each of the other energy areas. Often, many factors can be left unexpressed. But in doing ethi-cal thinking about a human action one must, at least mentally, review the total ecosystem or environment in which the act is done and be willing to deal with its most significant features. This total ecosystem includes:

first, the environment *within* the doer himself or herself; and secondly, the environment involving human and
non-human others that are being affected or that are
having a distinctive influence.

Sexual energy, then, is the energy of sharing, of
giving and receiving. Its release and articulation in
the human being is incredibly complex. We do well to
stand starkly in awe, as primitives, before the unimaginably vast world of time and eternity, in which this
energy radiates.

NOTES

1. The relevant distinction is between intrinsic and extrinsic
dependence. When I know the essence of a tree, for instance, my
concept (treeness)--which is abstract, imageless, and has no material dimensions to it--exists both dependently and independently
with respect to my physical experiences of particular trees. This
timeless, motionless reality (my *concept* of treeness) is dependent
on the sensations of trees and treelike material beings that I have
experienced. It is dependent on these sensations in one way: for
its coming into existence. Unless I had sense experiences, this
concept would not have come into existence. But once it comes into
existence I can recognize that the concept itself is, in its *being*,
independent of the conditions of matter and sensation which insti-
gated it and which can continue to nourish many features of its
development. Thus, I can say that the concept is *extrinsically
dependent* on matter and motion inasmuch as it *comes to be* through
material agency (at least in part), but *intrinsically independent*
of matter and motion inasmuch as there are no characteristics of
matter and motion with respect to the concept itself. It is "sense-
less" and changeless in its essence. Treeness is treeness is
treeness, despite the wide variety of diverse physical things to
which it refers and even despite the total destruction of all of
them.
Perhaps this distinction between intrinsic and extrinsic depen-
dency can be better understood if it is applied to a more concrete
case. If I want to go from my home in St. Cloud, Minnesota, to
Minneapolis (about 70 miles away), I can take an auto, a bus, a
bicycle, an airplane, or even walk. I am dependent on one or other
of a variety of means in order to come to Minneapolis. But, once
I get there, I am no longer dependent on those means. My *coming
to be* in Minneapolis is quite different from my *being* there. Once
I am there, the bus could disintegrate or my legs could be ampu-
tated; but I would still be there. I could be said to be, then,
extrinsically dependent on the means by which I arrived, but intrinsically independent of those means.

46

There are many philosophy texts which deal with the close unity, yet difference, between sensation and intellection and with the implications for evaluating the paradoxical nature of the human person as *both* physical *and* spiritual. For instance, see James E. Royce, *Man and His Nature: A Philosophical Psychology* (New York: McGraw-Hill, 1961), pp. 88-149.

2. The following analogy is strictly illustrative and didactic.

3. The intention need not be explicit. Most of the time people are spontaneously, but implicitly, sharing things and themselves with other people.

4. The manner in which a soul causes the body and the specifically bodily powers, such as genitality and coitality, is through formal causality, not efficient (agent) causality. As a formal cause of the body and its parts, the soul constitutes the form or structure of the body. Simply by being itself--what it is--the soul makes the body to be what *it* is--this body. The soul is not a mini-agent inside a hunk of matter, fashioning it into a body by means of its acting upon it. The soul does *not act upon* the body in any way. It *is*, rather, the intrinsic *act* by which the whole being--body and all--is *what* it is, and by which it can do what it can do. Cf. Royce, *Man and His Nature*, pp. 289-303.

This theory of body-soul relationship is called hylomorphism. Originated by Aristotle, it has been developed and refined by Thomas Aquinas and by many subsequent philosophers. See, e.g., Thomas Aquinas, *The Soul*, trans. John P. Rowan (St. Louis: Herder, 1949).

5. Rollo May, for instance, has written incisively on this condition. See his *Love and Will* (New York: W. W. Norton, 1969), especially Chapter 2 on "The Paradoxes of Sex and Love," pp. 37-63.

The "new morality" takes many forms--even that of dissociating sex completely from morality. Contemporary sexual revolutions that purport to get to the *roots* of human nature, such as that advocated by Wilhelm Reich, tend to suffer from unawareness of the ground in which the roots are planted. The transcendent, spiritual sources are denied or overlooked in an effort to explicate many other important areas, such as the economic, emotional, and physiological. Human beings are inevitably conceived as no more than high-class animals. See, e.g., Wilhelm Reich, *The Sexual Revolution: Toward a Self-Governing Character Structure*, trans. Theodore P. Wolfe (New York: Farrar, Straus and Giroux, 1969). Although this major exponent of the popular "sexual revolution" makes an attempt to expunge from himself and his readers the moralism of the past--which is admirable enough--he falls headlong into psychologism, the backside of moralism. Psychologism is the attempt to reduce all explanations of human behavior to psychological ones. It is an amoral approach to human emotions--especially sexual emotions--and involves all sorts of backhanded moral injunctions, such as "never impede the drive to orgasm."

6. It has been reported that Kepler and Galileo once had a good laugh at the Churchmen who refused to look through a telescope to see the evidence of a Copernican worldview. But today one could be inclined to laugh at many scientists and the deeply entrenched

positivistic philosophers in our culture who refuse to acknowledge even the existence of what might be called an intellectiscope-- the intellectual power to see the super-empirical structures of things and of human nature itself--much less to use that native, intuitive power to make a behavioral breakthrough. Because the inner sources of sexuality--in psyche and spirit--are not empirically verifiable and cannot be intellectually possessed or manipulated, our positivistically utilitarian culture is disinclined to take them seriously. One can hardly be blamed for recalling analogously one wag's comment on the reticence of our industrial society to invest in solar energy research and implementation: "After all, General Motors doesn't own a piece of the sun."

7. One might readily engage in protracted speculation on this point. How, for instance, do we explain not only the stability of archetypes that Jungian analysts and others acknowledge in the depths of the psyche, but also their universality and depth of meaning. Unless we admit a direct and intimate relationship of these psychic sources with the spiritual destiny of the person, we have little ground for anything more than the glib dismissal of all psychic reality as epiphenomenal--which is so characteristic of rationalistic reductionisms since the time of Descartes.

The immediacy, but non-identity, of the psyche with the spiritual soul is portrayed in this chapter as figuratively akin to the relationship of the earth's atmosphere with the sun.

8. Another aspect of this tripartite analogy is that the earth represents the visible and tangible part of the person, the body. The earth's atmosphere represents the rather intangible and open, but still restrictive area of the person, the psyche, which envelops the body and protects it from the extreme power of the soul and potentially destructive bombardments of certain forces in the spiritual world. Universal space represents the utterly intangible and endlessly expansive character of the spiritual life, which nonetheless can be said to encompass the psyche and body, to put them in touch with all other beings (other "galaxies"), and to be the ultimate "medium" of the soul's existence and its influence on the individual mind and body, as well as on other beings ("galaxies").

9. Cf. Josef Pieper, *Leisure, the Basis of Culture*, trans. Alexander Dru, with an Introduction by T. S. Eliot (New York: New American Library/Mentor-Omega, 1963), pp. 83-96.

10. Cf. William Barrett's characterization of Heidegger's *Dasein* as a magnetic field or region of Being. *Irrational Man: A Study in Existential Philosophy* (New York: Doubleday/Anchor, 1962), especially p. 218.

Chapter 4

TOWARD SEXUAL LIBERATION

A revolution in *thinking about* human sexuality is not enough. We are challenged to live these new ideas and new perspectives. Contemplating the nature of human sexual energy, its flow patterns, and authentic ways to participate in them may reveal the need to sacrifice some very deeply engrained attitudes, feelings, and ways of behavior. A "Copernican" sexual revolution invites us to undergo a liberation that affects every area of human life.

The whole human being ought to be released from enslavement to meaningless, sterile attitudes and from unproductive ways of behavior. To the extent that this liberation is accomplished the person's authentic sexual structure--which exists at the heart of personality-- becomes accessible. The individual becomes capable of in-depth sharing.

The ecosystem of sexual freedom is part of the larger ecosystem of personal freedom. Perhaps we can appreciate the magnitude of the task of becoming sexually liberated by contemplating the challenge to faith, courage, patience, persistence, intuition, and reasoning that is involved in specifically human liberation.

In *The Republic*, the early Greek philosopher Plato, who lived near the headwaters of all philosophical thought in the Western world, provides a striking image of human liberation that can assist in evaluating prospects for

a genuine evolution and growth in our personal lives.[1]
Accompanied by appropriate commentary, Plato's allegory
of the Cave can serve as a power-picture motivating us
to persist through the difficult stages of sexual liberation.

In this chapter, first, I will review Plato's archetypal story of liberation by offering an updated and
accommodated version. Instead of a cave, a motion picture theatre will provide the setting. Then, in the
light of our needs for sexual liberation, I will examine
three stages of human liberation.

The Movie Theatre

Imagine yourself as always having lived in a movie
theatre, tied to a front-row seat in such a way that
you cannot turn around. You can only view what you see
ahead of you on the big screen. Other people are similarly affixed to chairs in the front row, none of them
being able to see anything but the moving pictures on
the screen. You and they can know one another only by
hearing voices and speaking obliquely to your fellow
prisoners. There is no way of knowing that you are imprisoned there. You naturally assume that the colorful
figures on the screen, including the sounds, are the
only things about which to think and talk.

You and the others occupy yourselves the whole
day with viewing, hearing, thinking about, and talking
over the continuous moving pictures before you. You
start to name the figures and to associate the sounds
with them, thinking that the sounds naturally come from
the figures on the screen. You are thoroughly absorbed
by the reality of the moving pictures.

Now, suppose that one day someone releases your
bonds to the chair and begins to induce you to turn
around. You are extremely reluctant and do not want to
bother. It hurts your neck to turn around. Suppose
further that someone, gently but persistently, points
your head in the direction of the projector in the back
of the dark theatre. You see only a small source of
light and little else. You wish to get back to the real
thing, the movies.

But suppose that your guide pulls you along to the
back of the theatre and leads you to the projection
booth. There in the dull light of the little room you
are shown the film with the figures on each little frame
and it is explained to you, painstakingly and with much-

...eeded repetition, that what you have always thought
as real is but a projection of the tiny images on the
film--an *image* of an *image*. You are told how the light
in the projector shines through the film and causes the
images to be projected on the big screen.

At first, you cannot believe it, and do not want
to believe it. You try to return to the comfort of your
seat and to the ease of seeing the bright and colorful
images you have always known as the really real world--
the nitty gritty, no-nonsense, down-to-earth life. But
your guide constrains you. He says you are now seeing
things a little more as they really are, and that to go
back would be great foolishness--more foolish than before,
when you had no idea there was anything more to life.

You struggle, but you are somehow jostled down to
the lobby of the theatre. There you can see vaguely
the daylight coming from the street outside. Your eyes
are not at all adapted to daylight and you are afraid
of it, yet somehow intrigued. Your guide pulls and tugs
and talks in encouraging tones until he finally gets
you to the doorway. In one great effort he pushes you
out onto the sidewalk in the full light of midday.

You are stunned. You cannot look up. You keep
your eyes downcast and, at first, are quite satisfied
to see only the shadows of the people passing by.

Suppose that, as you get enough courage to raise
your eyes, you happen to look at the theatre wall and,
by chance, catch sight of the *reflections* of the people
passing by and of the building across the street in the
plate glass of the theatre's "Now Showing" case. You
stare in amazement at this moving scene, knowing that
the real cause of what you see is right behind you.
Eventually, you make bold to see directly the things
themselves: the people, the automobiles, and the buildings.

In time, you view the sky with the moon and stars
by night and the sun by day. The sun is the most difficult to view. But you finally begin to appreciate
how all the light and color you have ever seen ultimately
comes from this radiant source and you bask gratefully
and joyfully in its warm and brilliant presence.

Suppose that you are eventually reminded of the
place from which you came and the "wisdom" of the people
there. Would you not give praise to God for being free
and able to enjoy the whole world directly? Would you

51

not feel sorry for those who remain bound to a hapless life of knowing only the images of the images of things? And if you happened to recall how the theatre prisoners would praise each other and give honors to the ones who could name the movie figures best and who could most accurately predict which ones would come next and how they would act, do you think you would envy them and desire ever again to be an expert among them?

But, then, imagine yourself going back into the theatre and returning to your old seat. If you began talking again to those around you, trying to tell them that what they were seeing was a very insignificant part of reality and life--even though it did reveal a little bit--do you think they would believe you? Would you not be treated by many of them as a mad person who had come to disrupt the obviously good order of life?

Many of them would probably laugh at you and accuse you of being idealistic, unrealistic, and impractical. If you tried to release one of them in order to help the individual come to a new and fuller realization of what life really means, would there not be some who would like to get rid of you entirely?

If you were a person of good will, you would probably desire to live life in the outer world and not return permanently to your old position. But you would want to make strenuous efforts to help those of the imprisoned who would be willing to learn a better life.

You would never give up the perspective of the world of sunshine, people, and real things. You could not. Once you had experienced the most fundamentally real dimension of life, everything would necessarily be seen in that context. You would be endowed with an ever-expandable, ecological sense of life.

Three Phases of Liberation

In this modernized parable there would seem to be three basic human conditions and three phases of libera- tion. The three basic human conditions are enslavement, becoming liberated, and freedom. Descriptively they might be termed image-watching, light-awareness, and sun-basking.

The three phases of liberation might be conceived as a beginning, middle, and end to the liberation process itself. The first phase of liberation is breaking the chains and looking around. The second phase could be

52

egarded as struggling with the light, since it consists
n coming to awareness of the causal nature of reality
nd in becoming somewhat familiar with the artifactual
ight (of the film-projector), which symbolizes and
artially reveals the ultimate source of all light and
isual structure in life (the sun). The third phase
ight be known as adapting to the sun. This is the final
tage of the liberation process. The person gradually
ecomes accustomed to being a child of the sun. In
rief, the three stages of the *human* liberation process
re breaking, struggling, and adapting. I will now apply
his perspective to the personal process of *sexual* libera-
ion.

Stage One: Breaking the Chains and Looking Around

We all suffer from a general human ignorance con-
erning who we are. Consequently, when we come to know
urselves as sexual beings we are inevitably overimpressed
ith genital drives and orgasms. Cultural conditioning
ends to reinforce and sophisticate these primitive im-
ressions. We readily become fixated in our perspec-
ives. Our sexual awareness amounts to a fascination
ith the obvious and dramatic aspects of human sexuality
evolving around genital intercourse. The meaning of
exuality takes shape in our souls, first of all, as
 superattachment to the power and action of genital
rgans. We all seem to begin as "movie-watchers," and
he importance of genital orgasm is an ever-recurrent
heme.

We may have been educated in the puritan culture
f the past or in the playboy culture of the present.
et, an overwhelming fixation on coital-genital rela-
ions as the goal of sex is the common ground. The
uritan consciousness tries to get us to repress or
gnore the movie-picture notion of sexuality, and the
layboy consciousness teaches us to ogle it and exploit
t. But both are very sure they know "where sex is
eally at."

Occasionally, perhaps, there is an attempt to turn
he's head and to see something more causal and vital
n human sexual dynamics. The puritan consciousness
ight be briefly perturbed when it hears the passage
rom Genesis about God making man in his image and like-
ess, male and female. Or a contemporary sexologist
ich as David Reuben might insist that the brain is the
ain sexual organ. But the puritan can rationalize the
enesis message as an unfathomable mystery. And the
exologist simply means that the brain is the main

53

service-organ of the penis and vagina, and not the other way around. His basic principle is maximum copulation frequency. Both are opposite angles on the same idea. Sexual action *is* genital action.

Obviously, the playboy is a winner in predicting accurately the next "figures" on the sex scene. He has his eyes wide open. During such segments of life's movie, the puritan's eyes are closed--or they are suppose to be. And the female members follow the "lead" of the males. When it comes to sex, Madam Puritan and Bunny Playmate have eyes only for what their mates desire.

The whole spectrum of puritan to playboy sex-wisdom constitutes a front-row seat in the spectator meaning for human sexuality. Everyone seems to be born and raised at some point between these poles of "consumer sexuality." Most people seem to die there, too.

Nevertheless, at times, individuals and groups have broken the cultural chains on the meaning of human sexuality. They have strongly suspected that sex was more than body-deep. They surmised that it came from a source that was beyond their bodily control. At least, the chains were broken and they turned around.

They have been able to do better than the puritan who, as it were, simply closes his eyes during most of life's sex scenes in his own experience. They have been able to break through the playboy fixation on gourmet sex. These chain-breakers have developed the strength to suppress coital-genital sex in their lives.

Suppression is not the same as repression. Repression is an unconscious action; one does not know one is doing it. Suppression is a conscious, mental put-away, usually done for a particular reason or to attain a special goal. It may be the result of a temporary or permanent commitment. Its motivation may be good or bad.

The most notable examples of this pulling away from a front-and-center view of sex might be the countless persons who, throughout the ages, have chosen to remain single and to abstain from coital-genital activity out of religious motivation. Their works of mercy and praye did not fit with child-begetting, which they rightly saw is entailed in the exercise of genital sex. Historically, almost all of these celibate people did not think enough about sexuality to do more than make a break from the usual social perspective. They did not explore the causes or the deeper meaning of human

54

sexuality.[2] They were being sexual without knowing and appreciating it.

This kind of liberation is a first stage in the process toward true sexual freedom. Today many people seem to be aware of its possibilities.[3] In fact, many seem to be moving into a second phase of the liberation process.

Stage Two: Struggling With the Light

One of the most significant groups of people today who seem to be struggling in the second stage of sexual liberation are women who identify with the feminist cause. These women want to be free of stereotyped sex-roles, into which they and all humankind seem to be born. They examine themselves as persons who are also women, rather than as women who happen to be persons. They know that personhood is the source of both womanhood and manhood. They want to act as persons first, no less so than men, and not as pelvic appendages of the male. These women are not the strident, man-castigating feminists who would obliterate all roles and overlook all sex differences other than the begrudgingly-endured, anatomical ones. They *like* men, as well as themselves. They somehow know that it is crucial to their being and their personhood that they *be* women, and act as women. But they do not know with great certainty just what their ways of behaving should be.

These women are sure of one thing. The puritan and playboy ways of relating to sex are puerile, immature, and stifling. There must be something better.

The widespread questioning and discussion about the meaning of being a man and woman in the contemporary world includes many people who seem to have entered a phase of liberation we might regard as struggling-with-the-light. The explaining and counter-explaining, the confusion and anxiety, resulting from all the views to which they are constantly exposed is represented in the parable by the turmoil and ambivalence of the released prisoner who is being shown the projector-light at the back of the theatre and is then brought into the projection booth for an explanation.

"The guide" in the story can represent different things for different people. Some may wish to regard the guide as one's conscience. Others may think of him as "the Lord" or the grace of God. Still others may regard the guide as a good friend or a specially good

book that they have read and followed. The point is
that someone or something is pushing the individual along.
That individual's inevitable resistance comes from famil-
iarity with the old and fear of the new. If one were
not confused, it would probably mean that one was fooling
oneself and was still back at the start, fantasizing a
liberation experience rather than living it.

Considerable reading, discussion, and personal
reflection, as well as prayer, can bring the person to
a very great sureness. One can become certain that the
definitive source of sexuality is to be found neither
in the psychological dimensions of the person nor in the
sociocultural, role-conditioning areas of human living.
And yet, like the released theatre-prisoner who has heard
the explanations and seen things for himself in the
limited light of the projection booth, the person struggling for sexual liberation will inevitably hesitate,
and even resist, when confronted by the possibility of
actually acknowledging the ultimate source of enlightenment on the subject. Someone or something very forceful
may have to push or draw the individual into the realization that sex comes from the spiritual life of a person--
a woman is a woman from her ova to the depths of her
being; a man is a man from his sperm to his spirit.
Authentic sexual life starts with, and remains within,
the "inner space" of one's personal and profound spiritual
being.

Stage Three: Adapting to the Sun

Once sufficient evidence and good will force the
person to acknowledge that, by far, most sexual energy
is spiritual energy, he or she can adapt gradually to
this new realization. Many things begin to come into
focus.

The person starts to evaluate the sexual ecosphere
in a revolutionary way. Just as the moving pictures on
the big screen *do* represent a kind of reality and are
derived from the world of pre-manipulative nature, so
genital drives and coital activity are really sexual,
but derivatively so. Consciousness of coital-genital
sex is an important feature of sexuality. But sexuality
can get along well without immediate attention to coital-
genital concerns. The world of total, human sexuality
does exist and function--with or without the release of
a person's consciousness from the chains of a genital
fixation.

56

If love is necessary for genuine sharing and if
sexuality is the sharing of self with self and others,
a liberated person is going to spend much of his effort
to become sexually integrated by learning the difficult
art of loving. Adapting to the sun means living in the
light of one's own deepest nature and loving it.

Love makes demands. The sexually liberated person
will not be satisfied to enjoy his or her new-found freedom unless it is shared with those who seem to be fet-
tered and with those who continue to falter in the struggle with the light. The beautiful unity between coital-
genital sex and sexuality motivates such a person to
return to the theatre and to help others who are willing
to develop.

An Integrative Interpretation

It is critically important that this modernized
parable be given an integrative interpretation. There
are many other facets of the story that are applicable
to sexual liberation. But one facet ought to be stressed
above all. Moving pictures are *good* for people. It
is likewise good to examine *all* the bodily aspects of
human sexuality. What is not good is to "sit fixed in
the front row" as though there is no other way to see
and experience the beauty of human sexuality.

Unfortunately, traditional interpretations of Plato's
original story of the cave tend to disparage the reality
of the shadows that the prisoners are viewing on the cave
wall. Shadows are real. They are not "imaginary" in
the sense that they do not exist. It is true that a
shadow on a wall or a picture on a screen cannot be
"touched" by the hand and handled. But it can be
"touched" by the eye. And it is not an hallucination.
The shadow is a genuine beginning or clue to a wider
world. As a participation in that world, it should
never be disparaged.

Plato's application of his own parable seems to
have been gravely misleading in regard to the relation
of the body to the soul--of the world of the cave to the
world of sunlight. Plato held that our bodies are necessary evils and that they are really prisons in which
we are somehow enslaved. All education, he thought,
involved a liberation of the person from concern with,
and control by, the body and its passion. The implication was that sex is a necessary evil. And, of course,
for Plato and the Greeks, as well as for philosophers
ever since, there was no sex to a soul. Sex was generally

57

regarded as a passion of the body that severely hampered the soul-concerns of the intellectual and spiritual life.

Despite this common interpretation of severely disparaging the body and physical sexual passion, Plato's image itself is extremely fruitful. One remarkable feature implied in the image is that the prisoners are *always in* the outer world, even though they do not know it. They are being influenced by the wider world, without knowing it. If the sun failed to function in that wider world, their image-watching and their very lives would cease.

In Plato's original story the enlightened, liberated prisoner would come back and make efforts to free the other prisoners. He would exhibit an admirable concern for his enslaved fellows. He would attempt to rescue them, even risking death at the hands of some of them. Of course, this is what Plato's hero, Socrates, actually did. And he was executed for his efforts.

If one develops the basic analogy somewhat further, in accord with the accommodated version of the story, there is another prospect for the enlightened prisoner. Not only should he want to return in order to help liberate his fellows. He should want to return at times just to enjoy theatre life itself. He might like to see what they are showing "these days." He might like to enjoy a particular film-showing. Or he might like to go to learn more about the movie-projection operation and the motion-picture business. Psychologists, social scientists, and natural scientists can be regarded as persons who are largely concerned with *how* the existentially human and physical world behaves or operates. They might be represented in the allegory by persons who spend a great deal of time in the theatre learning about the way the movies are projected, how they are made, and how the process can be altered in order to effect a better picture.

Most of these scientists might be represented as never having stepped outside the theatre. They know there must be an outside. That is, they know or suspect there is a region in an individual's life deeper than the body and mind. But they are generally so taken with the practical and useful things that can be done within the theatre, that they do not spend much time exploring the most expansive world.

Nevertheless, all theatre residents and practitioners exist *thoroughly within* the world of the sun. All individuals have a spiritual life. This spiritual life is not so much something within them as something they are within. The movie viewer is within the control of the projectionist, somewhat as the body is within the control of the mind or psyche. But both the viewer and the projectionist are themselves within the control of the "outer world." Theatre space is a microscopic part of universal space, somewhat as a human being's body and psyche are a microscopic--but crucial--part of his or her spiritual life.

Paradoxically, this microscopic part of our spiritual life--our bodily and worldly concerns--is the place where we first come into consciousness of ourselves. We are fully bodily beings. The body is the part of ourselves which we most readily begin to know. Knowledge of the spiritual--and with it a truer perspective on our bodies and minds--comes only with inner-space adventure.

No one can come into a measure of genuine sexual freedom without study, reflection, discussion, and prayer. There is no chance of taking a shortcut from the front row of the theatre to the sidewalk outside. Our initial bodily condition of rigid attention to the immediate world of color and sound prohibits even thinking of making such a move.

The microscopic part of the person's being--called the body--should never be disparaged, even after we are able to know and experience the rest of our being. The body is like the theatre. It is *part* of the world of personal being.

The theatre belongs to the world. It is good. It deserves physical and cultural support at all times. Even though it should go into the business of pornography, thus directly polluting the minds of the captive (or not-so-captive) viewers, the rational remedy is to change its programming by social pressure and persuasion, not to burn it down.

Similarly, the body belongs to the spiritual being. It is good and always deserves moral and physical support. Even when the body becomes ill or paralyzed, it should be cared for as worthy of existence. Healing remedies must be tried. One can undertake a change of diet and sleeping habits. One can submit to medication or surgery. The remedy is not to kill the body.

Unfortunately, many people through the ages, following the lead of Plato, their philosophical patriarch,
have attempted to kill the body mentally. They have
tried, as it were, to burn down the theatre once they
have become "enlightened." The various forms of repressive asceticism and exploitative rationalism in cultural
history may represent the actions of spiritual arsonists
who suffer from lack of adaptation to the sun.

Body-negative philosophers may be like a released
prisoner from the theatre who does not allow himself
sufficient time for gaining perspective in the outer
world. So many things that are natural to this outer
world enthrall and occupy him that he forgets about being
a creature needing shelter. So, why not burn down all
buildings so there will be no temptation to go back and
be trapped? Spiritual insecurity can be the stimulus
for devastating effects on the body and the mind, even
in otherwise enlightened and good-willed philosophers.[4]

Who Is Liberated?

Many facets of the sexually liberated personality
might be exemplified in order to give some clue to the
meaning of sexual liberation. Some of these will be
indicated throughout the remainder of this book. At
this point, a major attitudinal difference between authen
tic and inauthentic sexual liberation can be illustrated
by the story of two individuals whose lives are very
similar, yet whose sexual attitudes are quite diverse.
One of them is obviously struggling with the light and
ready to burn down the theatre. The other is basking
in the sun and experiencing the joy of soular sexual
energy.

Tanzan and Ekkido were two zen monks who were walkin
down a muddy road.[5] A heavy rain was falling. They
came round a bend in the road and there they saw a lovely
young woman in a silk kimono and sash, who had paused
before a large stretch of water, unable to get across.
Perceiving her predicament, Tanzan said, "Come on, girl."
He picked her up and carried her. Slushing through the
water, he gently put her down on the other side.

The monks went their way. Neither of them spoke
until that night when they reached a lodging temple.
Then Ekkido could no longer restrain himself. He said,
"Why, why did you do that? We monks don't go near females." Especially not young and lovely ones!"

Tanzan, surprised, looked at him and said, "I left
the girl there. Are you still carrying her?"

NOTES

1. Plato, *The Republic*, VII.
2. This observation is not made in order to suggest that religious
celibates generally have been rather unsharing, uncaring people
who were at best only partly liberated as human beings. Quite
the contrary, in many cases, and with respect to the ideal of religious celibacy itself. The suggestion here is simply that they
did not think *through* sex and sexuality to any great degree. They
thought *around* it.
3. The recent phenomenon that is called "asexualism" is an
example. Certain prominent people have revealed that they are not
having genital intercourse over extended periods of time. The
public response has been surprisingly positive. However, the term
asexualism is but another example of the misplaced identity of
genitality and sexuality. Such people are not being asexual, but
"acoital."
4. Many philosophers in the Western world, particularly since
the time of Descartes and the rationalist tradition, seem to suffer
from what I regard as this unconscious intellectual debility. An
illuminating characterization of this condition is given by William
Barret under the chapter title "Flight from Laputa," in *Irrational
Man*, pp. 120-146.
5. A slight modification of a Zen anecdote in *Zen Flesh, Zen
Bones*, a collection of Zen and pre-Zen writings compiled by Paul
Reps (Garden City: Doubleday, 1961), p. 18.

61

Chapter   5

THE MEANING OF MAN AND WOMAN

Sexuality means sharing the gift of self. Human sexual energy is the ability to do this great human work of sharing by mutually giving and receiving everything in life.

In Chapter 4, I indicated how sexual liberation--the process of growing toward a condition of sexual freedom--is necessary for opening up new levels of sexual energy. Through the process of genuine sexual liberation we are led into the depths of our own spiritual life where we can attain a much more integrative view of our whole being. The present chapter assumes this broader, integrative view of the total sexual ecosphere and takes a closer look at our sexual self. After considering the meaning of man and woman we will be better able to discuss, in Chapter 6, the nature of sexual freedom.

What does it really mean to *be* a man? What does it really mean to *be* a woman?

We need to seek a sexual identity that is deeper and far more pervasive than sociocultural identity. Roles that different societies expect of men and women, such as hunting and fishing for the men and child-care for the women, do serve to give us some clues regarding the ultimate nature of men and women as sexual beings. But such roles are not wholly decisive. Sometimes they are found to be opposite or exchanged in different societies. Socionatural roles are much more revealing. They are

stable across cultural and historical lines because they
stem from, and are formed around, the basic structure
of men as men and women as women. Only men are fathers.
Only women are mothers. Only a man can produce human
sperm. Only a woman can produce human ova. Only a
woman can gestate a child within her body for nine months
and then give birth.

Socionatural roles, such as fatherhood and motherhood, are roles that relate more to the person's *being*
than to his or her *doing*. They are the kind of roles
that people can *do* very well or very badly, but they
cannot really undertake the opposite role at all. Someone might say that a woman can play the role of father
or a man can play the role of mother. But it can only
be role-*playing*. A woman cannot *be* a father. A man
cannot *be* a mother. They can simply act like father or
mother in many ways. When a man diapers a baby, he is
fathering, not mothering. When a woman teaches her son
how to conduct his newspaper business, she is mothering,
not fathering. A father always fathers, never mothers.
His hands, eyes, and heart are strictly male hands, eyes
and heart. And a mother is a woman through her whole
being. A mother always mothers, never fathers.

As individuals, men and women can often *do* a better
job at the sociocultural aspects of fatherhood or motherhood than a person of the sex to whom this role naturally
(essentially) applies. But there remains a radical difference in the *being* of what they are doing.

Biology-Based Sexuality or Sexuality-Based Biology?

Most people are inclined to think that these natural
roles of man and woman are stable and irreversible simply
because they are based on anatomy. The old adage "anatomy
is destiny" seems to be applicable. But this inclination
to see the potential for fatherhood or motherhood as
based in biology amounts to a short-sighted, "Ptolemaic"
view of human sexuality. It arises from our position as
front-row theatre patrons (image-watchers) in the philosophy of life. Physical anatomy must be caused by something deeper within one's being.

The "Copernican" view of human sexuality allows
us to assert that "destiny is anatomy." Destiny reveals
itself in anatomy--but also in psyche and spirit. The
structure of a person's whole being is harmonious. We
are destined to be a man or woman throughout our whole
being. We are not man or woman simply because we happen
to be anatomically such. Our sexuality is not biology-

based. Our biology is sexuality-based. Our genitality (fatherhood-power or motherhood-power) is a special kind of capacity for sharing the gift of self (sexuality). An integral understanding of human nature demands that we realize how man and woman are soul-deep and that their individual souls are the ultimate causes within them for everything that they *do* and *are*.

In order to appreciate the soul-pervasive character of human maleness and femaleness we will need to examine some of the evidence existing at all three levels of sexual energy: the physical, the psychic, and the spiritual. But before doing so, we may be aided if I suggest general definitions of what a man is and of what a woman is.[1] I will give definitions that are very general and applicable to the basic energy-structure on all three levels. As a prelude, it will be helpful to reflect on the fruitful concept of androgyny.

Everyone Is Male and Female

Androgyny literally means man-woman or male-female. Every person is both male and female. Members of both sexes have male and female hormones within their bodily systems. In early embryogenesis the incipient genital organs appear to be identical or very similar. Both men and women are recognized as having something of the mental and emotional characteristics of the other sex as well as their own. The traditional qualities of male and female in the mind or psyche have been called, by Carl Jung, Animus and Anima (male and female forms of the Latin word for *soul*).

The contemporary women's movement has been responsible for considerable spread of this concept. However, for many feminists it seems that men and women are thereby thought to be sexless within, rather than sexful. They do not seem to be able to assert that there is anything distinctive about man and woman beyond physical anatomy. They seem to assume that there is no distinctive psychic anatomy to a man or a woman. And they entirely neglect the possibility that there are distinctive structures to men and women in their spiritual lives.[2]

What seems to be working in many minds is this notion: "If we cannot see any difference empirically between men and women at these deeper levels, then there is none." This idea exemplifies one of the most characteristic philosophical fallacies of our century: the positivist fallacy. The mistaken assumption is that *only* something which can be proven true or false, either

65

by means of the senses or by sheer logic, is really meaningful. According to this view, the statement that the moon is made of green cheese is a meaningful statement because it can be proven true or false by means of the empirical methods of science. "Go up there and see for yourself." Likewise, according to this view, the statement that God exists is a meaningless statement because there is no way to prove it true or false either by empirical means or by pure logic.

One of the big problems with this view is that it is self-refuting. The statement that only empirically grounded fact and logical truths are meaningful is itself neither empirically grounded nor logically true. We can never prove this statement to be true or false by empirical methods. We can never finally see, hear, touch, taste, or smell the evidence of it. Nor can we see its truth by merely logical analysis.

What contemporary feminists and others should be saying is that we find it most difficult to define what is male and female beyond the physical and empirical areas of the person, but there *must be* such a difference because the body is a self-revelation--an outward sign and expression--of the mind and spirit.

Something as dynamically different as the bodily sexuality of man and woman must represent a difference that is likely to be even more dynamic in the psyche, and most dynamic in the spiritual depths of the person. If we can assume that there is such a difference to be discovered and appreciated, there is hope for a genuine evolution in man-woman behavior and a better day possible in sexual relations.

If we assume that there is no such difference, then we will continue to spin our technological wheels, looking for the physical techniques that will make things right. This approach has been tried, for instance, in the use of contraceptives. Women were told that with the contraceptive pill they were now the equal of men in their sexuality. But that was only the conscious-level message. Subconsciously, women were being told that their genital systems were naturally defective and had to have a technological adjustment in order to bring them up to the status of the natural male. Such an approach is based upon a weak and negative concept of a woman. It bespeaks a philosophy of inequality between men and women, while using the rhetoric of equality. The promised freedom for the woman has not been forthcoming. With readily

66

available contraceptives women find it more often necessary, and no less difficult, to say no.

Androgyny, the male-femaleness of every person, need not imply that men and women are really the same down deep, but that the definition of man and woman is complex and requires philosophical insight, as well as liberation from the condition of prostitution to empirical evidence. We ought to start with our best intuition of what it means to be a man or a woman. Then we can proceed to determine the extent to which our intuitive definition fits the known physical, psychic, and spiritual features of the human person, and can modify it accordingly.

Defining Man and Woman

Man and woman are the two ways of *being* sexual. A person is either a man or a woman. In a rare instance, it may be difficult to tell whether the person is a man or a woman since both kinds of genitals are present (hermaphroditism). But it is reasonable to think that such a person is either one or the other and that the condition of double genitals represents a defect in nature somewhere below the surface. Even in the case of someone who is genitally and genetically one sex in physical structure but the other sex in feeling and emotion (transsexualism), we can reasonably say that such a person is either man or woman in the depths of his or her being. The gravely unfortunate distortions and conflicts of body-mind functioning need not blur our judgment on the ultimate exclusivity of each person's sexual being. People can look, feel and act *like* the members of the other sex, but they can only *be* a member of one sex.

If sexuality is the personal power to share the gift of self on all levels of one's being, then being a man must be a very distinctive *way* of doing this sharing. The way a man shares himself (physically, psychically, and spiritually) must be different from the way a woman shares herself. In articulating this difference, I will be defining man and woman correlatively. They cannot be defined except in terms of each other.

There are two complementary, component dimensions to any activity of sharing: giving and receiving. Thus, I would define a man as a human being who both gives in a receiving way and receives in a giving way, but is so structured in his being that he is emphatically inclined toward giving in a receiving way. The nature of being a man is an emphasis on giving in a receiving way.

67

A woman is a human being who both gives in a receiving way and receives in a giving way, but is so structured in her being that she is emphatically inclined toward receiving in a giving way. The nature of being a woman is an emphasis on receiving in a giving way. (Later, I shall criticize the widespread bias in the Western world by which receiving is regarded as inferior to giving). The sexuality of man and woman (their personal power to share the gift of self) is orientated in opposite but very complementary ways.

This way of defining man and woman takes into account that every person is male and female within. Every person has a human nature, which includes the ability and tendency to share the gift of self. Both a man and a woman are structured in a way that naturally enables them to give in a receiving sort of way and to receive in a giving sort of way. When a man exercises his sexuality well, he gives to himself and to others in a receiving sort of way (whenever he gives something). And he receives in a giving sort of way (whenever he receives something from someone). A woman exercises her sexuality in a similar way. But the nature of man is a dynamic orientation to emphasize, at all levels of his being, the receiving kind of giving; while the nature of a woman is a dynamic orientation to emphasize, at all levels of her being, the giving kind of receiving.

Men and women are not static structures. They are stable structures--dynamic, stable tendencies toward sharing in the world. Men are called, from within their being, both to give and to receive, but dynamically and emphatically to give. Women are called from within their being, both to give and to receive, but dynamically and emphatically to receive.

There is no single, empirically-observable kind of action that demonstrates the truth of these definitions. But there are many empirical clues, some of which we shall consider. First, I want to propose another set of *philosophically* testable definitions--based on certain absolute (metaphysical) attributes of every being.

What Is a Man, What Is a Woman?

The definitions of man and woman in terms of giving and receiving distinguish man and woman (the two mutually exclusive ways of being sexual) on the basis of how differently they are disposed to *act*. An even more substantial form of definition can be offered--based on how differently they are created to *be*. This alternative kind of definition, which I am going to offer after developing the ground-work for it, is indicative of the essence of man and woman. It portrays the in-depth significance of man and woman as complementary symbols of the most radical features of all being.

The *beingful* dimension of man and woman (or of anything whatsoever) is the least obvious immediately, the most difficult to discern clearly, but the most important. A person who is being authentically sexual--sharing more and more richly with self and others--grows deeper and deeper roots in this dimension. In order to appreciate the meaning of man and woman from this beingful (ontological) perspective, we must consider a few basic truths.

Every being that we can ever know--including ourselves, this-worldly creatures, other-worldly creatures, and God--is utterly unique. No being is the same as anything other than itself. No two blades of grass, no two hydrogen atoms, no two moments are the very *same*. If they were, they would not be two. This is the first basic truth that we need to contemplate. Every being is unique and *other than* all else.

But besides being unique and wholly itself, every being that we can ever know--no matter what *kind* of being it is--is superrelated to other beings. *Each* unique being is related, in unique ways, to *every* other being that exists. No being is unrelated to any other being. All beings affect one another, even though we cannot begin to say *how* in most cases. The slightest molecular movement in one part of the universe affects all others. Our sciences only scratch the surface of the unfathomably myriad ways in which individual beings and kinds of being interrelate with one another.

So, one can confidently assert two basic things about any and every being. Everything that exists or can exist has these characteristics. It is *unique* and really other than every other being. And at the same time it is *superrelated* because it has a unique relationship to each and every other being that is.

Additionally, we should note that the kind of relationship to which we refer is not a relationship that we make with our minds. It is the relationship that each has with each, independent of our minds and their knowing process. Every being, from within its own depths and not just through some kind of spatial or surface contact, affects every other being. As a being, a

69

particular tree in New York is related to a particular
tree in San Francisco--from within. The one tree is
within the influence of the other, and vice versa. This
interior kind of relating or being-within is a fundamental
characteristic of every being. Every being is *within*
every other being--not spatially or temporally, but by
virtue of their existing or *being* together. Every being
affects every other being in countless, subtle ways,
right within their community as beings.[3]

   Man and woman together, by their distinctive powers
to share, participate in these primary qualities of each
and every being. A man, then, can be defined as a unique
human being who is called, from his very depths, to instantiate (to be a concrete instance of), in his attitudes and actions, both the uniqueness and the superrelatedness of all beings, but especially the uniqueness.
A woman can be defined as a unique human being who is
called, from her very depths, to instantiate in her attitudes and actions both the uniqueness and the superrelatedness of all beings, but especially the superrelatedness
or withinness. Man is an emphasis on symbolizing and
celebrating uniqueness or otherness. Woman is an emphasis
on symbolizing and celebrating superrelatedness or withinness.

   These definitions can be tested philosophically by
taking the designatable attributes (giving and receiving;
otherness and withinness) and applying them to the powers
and activities of man and woman, deciding whether it is
fitting to say that men symbolize one combination and
women the other--at least in general, with respect to
most physical and mental features. The term *emphasis*
in the definitions allows for the vast relativity which
is naturally found in the actions of men and women as
individuals.

   While one cannot cite direct examples of these definitions, one can discover indirect examples by examining
at least some of the evidence from each of the sexual
energy levels of the human person.[4]

Physical Sexual Identity

   In an act of coital intercourse, the man gives his
penis to the body of the woman. But, if he is acting
in accord with his genuine power to share, he acts in
a receiving sort of way; not simply for his own satisfaction, but for hers, and in a manner that is open to
the potential for new life. The woman receives the man's
penis. But, if she is acting in accord with her power

70

to share, she acts in a giving sort of way; with vaginal
secretion and sensitivity, and in a manner that gives
an opportunity for full coital play and total generative
contact. The man does not force himself upon the woman,
but gives himself in a receiving manner. The woman does
not simply submit herself to the man, but receives him
in a giving manner. Coital union is a remarkable structural evidence for the meaning of man and woman.

In normal coital intercourse, gametes (genital
cells) go forth from the body of the man and are received
within the body of the woman. The woman's gametes do
not go out into the man's body. They remain within her.
She emphasizes in this way the receiving power of her
being and the *withinness* of every being in the universe.
The man emphasizes, in his way, the giving power of his
being and the *otherness* of every being in the universe.
Coitality, the personal power to share one's genital life
with someone of the other sex, is a definite sphere of
revelation concerning the being of man and woman.

Genitality, the personal power to share the gift
of life with another person (a child), also clearly mani-
fests the fundamental characteristics of being man and
woman. The man's body generates many millions of sperm
for every ovum maturated in a woman. This dramatic fact
ought to tell us something about the mutual emphases in
being that man and woman really are. The man naturally
emphasizes (with his sperm-production) manyness, differentiation, and plurality. These characteristics are
based on uniqueness and otherness, rather than oneness
and sameness. The woman naturally emphasizes (with her
ova-production) oneness and sameness. These characteristics are based on withinness or superrelatedness. To
the perennial philosophical question, how can reality
be both one and many, man and woman constitute a remarkable response.

Relative to a woman, a man's gamete production is
an emphasis on manyness, differentiation, and just plain
otherness. In his nature he is saying, "Let's have another and another and another!" Correlatively, a woman's
gamete production is an emphasis on oneness, centeredness
and just plain *superrelatedness*. Her one ovum relates
to super-many sperm--all potential impregnators. In
her nature she is saying, "Let's be one and intensify
our oneness and receptivity!" When a man gives sperm
he emphasizes "gives." When a woman gives (releases)
ova she emphasizes receiving.

71

At the critical point of the generative action, the moment of conception (fertilization), there is further evidence of the mutual definition of man and woman for those who choose to acknowledge it. The dynamic interaction of conception occurs outside the body of the man and inside the body of the woman. Man's symbolization of otherness and woman's symbolization of withinness continue. The single, penetrating sperm of the man is received by the single, penetrated ovum of the woman. Another important testimony to the nature of these two co-sharers is given by this kind of interaction. The sperm's thrusting, penetrating characteristic is an emphasis on giving and on otherness--on being beyond or being elsewhere than its point of origin. The ovum's characteristic of stability and its selective manner of being penetrated is an emphasis on withinness, continuity and centeredness. (Note: only an *emphasis*; not an exclusiveness.)

Other aspects of physical sexual being could be cited and interpreted to show that man and woman do have discernible clues to their own identity within the sphere of their natural physical behavior. One might note, for instance, that the male gamete is the one that determines the sex of the offspring. The XY chromosomal characteristic emphasizes *differentiation* on the part of the male in contrast to the homologous XX chromosomal structure of the female, which emphasizes sameness or *oneness*. The global character of a woman's erogenous zones in contrast to the man's more localized zone is another difference that is common among all women and men, independent of cultural attitudes and roles.[5] The reader can probably think of other male-female structures by which the definitions of man and woman can be tested further. In making one's interpretation and evaluation, care must be taken with our ideological and cultural biases. The meaning of *receiving* is a case in point.

Receiving Is as Important as Giving

Before continuing this evaluation and analysis at deeper levels, we need to acknowledge the equality of giving and receiving. Most people seem to have a bias toward giving as the paramount kind of action. There is a prejudice against receiving. Receiving is commonly regarded as an inferior behavior, fraught with passivity and acquiescence. The degree of cultural bias against receiving is so strong in the Western world that further elucidation seems necessary.

The perennial prejudice against women may be linked to an inadequate appreciation of *how active* an act of receiving really must be. Authentic receiving is just as active as giving. Receiving is a *letting* something be in distinction to giving, which is a *making* something be. In the Western world we are so product-oriented that we unconsciously accord priority to giving. But *letting* is just as much a *doing* as making. In some respects, it takes more doing to *let* something be than to do something to it. All true discipline and self-control are based more on *letting be* than on *doing about*; on receiving, more than on giving. The importance of meditation in Hindu and Buddhist cultures is a dramatic witness to the power of receiving or letting be--through the *action* of stillness or through "taking no action."

The ordinary concept of God in the Judeo-Christian tradition is a major stumbling block for appreciating the value of receiving. God is known as Father, but unrecognized as Mother. God is the father, provider, the one who calls and who heals, the one who rewards and punishes. God is little known as mother, nurturer, comforter. For the most part, women in Western societies have been bereft of an anchor in the Divine Nature for their self-concept as women.

God as Creator is thought to be the absolute one who gives being to his creatures, but not the absolute receiver of their being as well. Before being understood as giving being to others, God needs to be understood as eternally receiving Being (as well as giving Being) right within the Godhead. Christian theology has celebrated God as three Persons sharing Divine Nature with one another in an eternal, interflowing activity. With this understanding of God, there is much room for an interpretation that would bring out the infinitely *receiving* power of the Divine Persons within their own Nature.[6]

The ancient Chinese tradition, Taoism, teaches that the Absolute, called the Tao or the Way, is female and maternal. This tradition leaves open the possibility for identification with the Absolute in an opposite kind of exaggeration to that of the Judeo-Christian West. The intellectual history of man has not been noted for its balance when characterizing the Divine in sexual terms.

A more open and insightful understanding of the root meanings of giving and receiving would help to establish some kind of improvement in our appreciation of

Divine Nature, as well as our own sexual nature.   I
would like to suggest a further line of thought.

While it is true that in giving we receive, it is
likewise true that in receiving we are able to give.
Both are important to each other. Giving and receiving
are the essential poles of sharing. A person who gives
a gift to someone, but has the gift rejected and returned,
has still really given. He or she has given only because
there was a radical receiving in the action. Not, in
this case, a receiving on the part of the other person.
But a receiving within the giver himself or herself.
The giver gave the gift in a receiving sort of way. Receiving is as essential as giving in the life of any per-
son--human or Divine.

Man and woman, as the concelebrants of the uniqueness and withinness of all reality through their giving
and receiving, are equal in personhood and sexuality.
The perennial indignity of woman in relation to man
derives largely from our inability to see and respect
the excellence of a receiving emphasis in all authentic
being and behavior. The injustice will never be remedied
by rejecting a woman's natural orientation toward an
emphasis on the receiving side of human nature.

Psychic Sexual Identity

Once we leave the physical area of sexual energy
it becomes more difficult, but not impossible, to con-
ceptualize one's identity. We can no longer point to
physical structures such as penis and vagina, testicle
and ovary, sperm and ovum. But we can point to general
psychic tendencies in men and women throughout most
cultures and times. Even though these general characteristics do not seem to apply to every instance of man
or woman, they signify *that* man and woman are fundamentally different in the psyche as well as in the body.[7]

Every culture has had different roles for men and
women. This fact is much more important in determining
whether man and woman are diverse psychically than is
the fact that in some cultures these roles are the reverse
of what they are in most cultures. By assigning different roles or role-tendencies to men and women, every
culture exhibits an unconscious recognition *that* men and
women are different beyond physiological functioning.
If someone were to identify a living culture where all
the roles of men and women are identical, then we might
begin to wonder whether there is a definite difference

between men and women in their emotional lives and psychological roots.

Carl Jung was the most prominent analytic theorist of the twentieth century who acknowledged the male and female differences in the human psyche. Every man, he said, has within his psychic depths--well beyond his conscious control--an Anima. This Anima is something that he needs to integrate into his masculine personality if he is to be healthy. A woman, he said, has within her psychic depths the male counterpart, the Animus, which she is naturally called upon to integrate into her whole personality.

Many phrases have been used to articulate distinctively male and female personality traits. But the issue is not one of personality. It goes deeper. Animus and Anima are primary *roots* of the personality, not really manifest parts. Carl Jung called them archetypes, which meant that they are, so to speak, psychic genes transmitted to the individual unconscious from ancestors and from the basic psychic structure common to human beings at all times and in all places. Jung discovered what he called the collective unconscious, a universal seat of meaning and empowerment for individual and communal human personalities.[8]

Whatever one might think of the collective unconscious or of archetypes, it would seem very rash to deny that the psyche--so intimately related to bodily health and activity--possesses sexual depths. These depth-principles within the human soul, Animus and Anima, are structures of every person. They might be regarded as the Giving and Receiving roots of emotional life.

Perhaps these primary sexual sources of emotion in man and woman can be illustrated by considering a typical young man and woman who are "in love." When Jack sees or thinks of Laura he tends to want genital union with her. He is strongly pulled in that direction. Laura, on the other hand, tends to want affection, attention and devotion. She is not nearly so pulled in the direction of satisfying a genital urge. Jack's genital urge is very strong. Laura's affection-and-tenderness urge is very strong.

If these relatively raw urges are going to be gratified at this juncture, Jack will probably give Laura tenderness and affection in order to get sex and Laura will probably give Jack sex in order to get tenderness and affection. Before attaining sexual maturity, young men are inclined to make love in order to "have sex" and young women are inclined to have sex in order to "be loved."9

Before Animus and Anima are integrated in the young person, he or she is beset by these exaggerated emotional tendencies. The young man is inclined toward a rather raw form of giving. Genital interaction makes something happen and projects the participants outside themselves. Jack is emphasizing otherness in what he wants. Laura, however, as a young and undeveloped woman is inclined toward a rather raw form of receiving. Affection, tenderness, and devotion to her are actions of receptivity. It is something she loves to let happen--although, in this crude form, it is not so much a letting as a getting. Jack in his mind would like to say, "Come on, Baby, let's give!" Laura in her mind would like to say, "Oh, Jack, let's receive each other as a special kind of unity or oneness, a twosome taken up within each other's hearts."

While the young man is psychically wired for lots of "giving forth" activity, the young woman is psychically wired for lots of receiving (for superrelating and withinness kinds of activity). Later, as each becomes a mature individual, the various emotions become integrated not only among themselves but also with the body and with the spiritual life. In the universal space of the individual's spiritual life, a wider world of meaning is designed to *lead* feelings, not to follow them.

In the relatively mature couple we are likely to find two complementary psychic states of emotion that continue to reveal the universal nature and definition of man and woman. In any man-woman relationship--especially a romantic one--there is a natural inclination in the couple to hold and to be held. They want to embrace physically, mentally, emotionally, and spiritually. This embracing is a holding and being held. But the emphasis in the man is on holding and the emphasis in the woman is on being held. A man's body being generally larger than a woman's complements the male tendency to hold somewhat more than to be held, and a woman's tendency to be held somewhat more than to hold. Even holding hands can reveal this natural quality in man and woman. Body complements mind.

A woman loves to be held by a man. This being-held feeling is an emotional or psychic indication of the woman's basic nature as emphatically a giving sort of receiver. She emphasizes receiving in the embrace. The

76

man emphasizes giving. Being held is also a kind of being within and being the center of a field of multidirectional relations. A woman emphasizes, right within her emotional life, the withinness and superrelatedness of all things. The man, by being the "other" in a woman's life, reciprocally emphasizes the otherness of all things.[10]

Many other facets of psychic life reveal the fundamental nature of man and woman. But there is no doubt that proper applications of the definitions are more difficult in the psychic area of sexual energy because this dimension of human nature is so deep and complex. The unconscious life of the mind and its basic structures are even more mystery-filled than are the microscopic structures of human bio-chemistry.

Nevertheless, one should hardly abandon the search for the general structure of human nature and of human sexuality in the world of the psyche simply because the particular structures of *individual* lives and activities are bewildering in their complexity and often unattainable. Search into psychic identity is at least as exciting as probing the physical universe.

Spiritual Sexual Identity

The range of religious and theological literature is very broad and the content extremely rich for speculating on the spiritual dimensions of sexual identity. The many purposes of the present study permit time for centering only on the major example.

In Genesis the story of Adam and Eve is almost always regarded as the story of a first, unfortunate couple, who deliberately estrange themselves from God and from each other and who start, thereby, all the woe that humans experience in being born into the world of space and time on the planet earth. This story, however, may also be considered for its potential to reveal the spiritual structure of our sexual lives.

Adam may represent the Giving power within each person. Eve may represent the Receiving power. The story portrays Eve as being fashioned out of Adam's rib.[11] This manner of speaking could easily be interpreted as describing the Receiving power of the person being structured right within the Giving power. It is not good for Adam *within*--our power to give in a receiving kind of way--to be alone. Adam needs Eve *within*--our power to receive in a giving kind of way.

Every person is created by God to be fully and harmoniously Adam and Eve within and to share self with all
being--without disunity and conflict, trouble and pain.
But, in those human creatures who exist on the planet
earth, there is an original alienation of Adam and Eve,
their Giving and Receiving powers.[12] Somehow, at the
moment of being created, they must have said no or hesi-
tated, so to speak, in the reception of their own being.
(Christians regard Jesus as an exception.) In effect,
by their Receiving power they reached for the being of
the Giver, not the gift. They wanted to *be* God, and
not to be the unique creature of God that God was giving
and receiving them to be. The Eve in them turned away
from the Adam and tried to receive the being and power
of God. The Adam in them (their Giving power) going
unreceived, followed the lead of their Eve by attempting
to *be* something other than the Creator desired. The
first sin might be regarded as a sin of sexuality--a
sin of attempting a gravely unnatural kind of "sharing."

In any event, the story of Adam and Eve can be
reasonably held (by those who believe it is important)
to be the story of our creation as male and female within
the depths of each person, in the likeness of God. It
can be the story of a great spiritual disobedience which
has radically affected our sexuality, genitality, coitality, and every other dimension of our lives. Life in
space and time can then be regarded as an opportunity
for healing this fracture of Adam and Eve. (Christians
believe that Jesus is the saving presence that comes
to heal the whole person, including his or her gravely
weakened and damaged powers to Give and Receive.)

Concelebrants or Co-Functionaries?

Are men and women, then, related to each other as
two broken halves that need each other to make a whole?[13]
If the definitions set forth in this chapter are generally
accurate, men and women are each whole human beings--each
with maleness and femaleness in their physical, psychic,
and spiritual spheres of relationship. Every person is
sexually complete in himself or herself. (Those who
believe in original sin acknowledge that each man and
woman needs others of both sexes to help in healing
the wounded whole that each one is.)

Although men and women are co-functionaries--designed
to accomplish things together in uniquely effective ways--
they are, even more radically, concelebrants of the goodness and beauty of all being. By virtue of the particular
kind of creature each of them is, they are called to

celebrate the otherness and relatedness of all things, and to do so in ways that are unique to each of them.

When a person celebrates something, such as a birthday, he or she does things simply out of joy over the event. A celebration is a joyful and symbolic way to participate in an important event or significant attribute. It says, "We are so glad this being (person, event, thing) *is*." By their very nature, man and woman are called to participate joyfully and symbolically in the goodness and beauty of *every* being's uniqueness and superrelatedness.

Because, in their own being's structure, there is a reciprocal emphasis on reality's most fundamental attributes (uniqueness and superrelatedness), man and woman can celebrate together (concelebrate) the goodness and beauty of being, and can do so in a superabundantly rich and dynamic way. Even their simplest tasks together can be done in a celebrational, as well as a functional, way. The fact that their celebrational potential is, so often, only weakly realized makes it nonetheless real. It simply underscores the profound challenge to consciousness-raising--a challenge built into their everyday relationships.

As celebrants of being, man and woman do not *absolutely* need each other. Each one is androgynous, symbolizing the radically reciprocal characteristics of reality. A man or woman is a whole sexual person in himself or herself. At all times, a person can celebrate within self, and share in, the goodness of being. While concelebration may be a superabundant sharing, single sharing is itself abundant.

Of course, a man's way of sharing himself within himself, with other men and with women, is different from a woman's way of sharing herself within herself, with other women and with men. Both man and woman celebrate the otherness (uniqueness) and the withinness (superrelatedness) of every being with respect to every other. But they do this celebration and sharing with opposite (not opposed) orientations.

Man and woman do not need each other to *become* a whole. They need each other to help in becoming healed and *healthfully* whole persons. Men need women in order that women can help them recognize and develop their power to receive in a giving sort of way as well as to give in a receiving sort of way. Women need the opposite kind of help from men. Quite obviously, men and women need one another in actions as well as in attitudes. Their mutual need is manifest in the bearing and educating of children as well as in everyday accomplishments and the attainment of sexual identity.

Men and women are like two hands of the same person. The person needs a right hand and a left hand. Two right hands or two left hands will not do. Yet these hands are equal in size and quality. Each has five fingers, a palm, and other common features. The main difference is that they face in opposite directions. They *face each other*.

Only a man and a woman can *face* each other fully, being to being. Just as the fingers on a hand can relate by touching each other side to side, front to back or back to front; so, people of the same sex can relate to each other supportively in various ways. But, like fingers of the same hand, they cannot relate face to face. Any finger, however, can relate to the thumb not only by touching side to side and front to back or back to front; it can also relate face to face. Man and woman are structured similarly. When any man and woman relate to each other--no matter what their ages or style of life--there is the relatability of face-to-face interaction.

The best way a man and woman can relate is face to face, even as it is the best functional way for finger and thumb to relate. Coital intercourse is the most evident way in which we see that *sexually* only a man and woman can relate face to face. In that *particular* form of face-to-face interaction they have, additionally, the potential of co-functioning in the parenting of a child.

Most "face-to-face" interaction of man and woman is not readily definable and is unknown to them at the time they are engaged in it. But that is also true of the "side-to-side" action of any individuals, whatever their sex.[14]

Man-woman identity operates, consciously or unconsciously, at every level within each person. A healthy sexual self-concept--so crucial to sound sexual behavior-- will be guided by these general, but definite meanings for being man and woman. Some of the countless implications and applications of the definitions which are offered in this chapter will be indicated throughout the remainder of the book.

The Value of These Definitions

These definitions of man and woman (in terms of giving in a receiving way and receiving in a giving way; and in terms of otherness/withinness or uniqueness/ superrelatedness) are attempts at stating the most radical "roles" of all. They respond to the question, What is the role of a man or a woman as a *being*? They reach within and beyond sociocultural roles and socionatural roles. They suggest basic guidance for anyone who would inquire, "What am I called to *be* as a man or as a woman?"

One might naturally wonder how these radical "roles" are practiced concretely. So, it is important to realize that there are many and various ways in which an individual can and does fulfill these "roles."

Within the faithful response to the ways of moral responsibility, which will be discussed in later chapters, the individual man or woman is free to practice the creative art of living sexually. For instance, it is strictly impossible to indicate, in any direct way, *how* a man *shares* (expresses his sexuality) interiorly in a manner that is different from a woman. Even the most effeminately acting man is sharing in a distinctively male sort of way, despite the fact that we cannot *see* it or put our finger on it. He may be doing the sharing poorly. Chances are good that if we culturally regard a certain way of acting as effeminate for men we are recognizing an exaggeration or distortion in natural male behavior. But cultural evaluations are relative in this regard, and could be false, especially in reference to a particular individual.

The question then arises whether there is any practical value in defining man and woman in a non-empirical way, since we cannot apply these definitions to behavior in a direct way. My response is, in part, that these definitions can be applied very effectively in an *indirect* manner. They are provided for men and for women so that the individual can meditate on their meaning and then, unconsciously and spontaneously, begin to realize them in everyday action.

One of the immediate benefits of taking these definitions seriously and letting them sink into the depths of the mind is that the person can substantially increase his or her sense of sexual identity. Lack of any sense of sexual identity beyond bodily anatomy is one of the prime reasons for anxiety and meaninglessness in many different kinds of sexual relations. We need to know

81

something of our anatomy and physiological functioning
in order to know how and why to feed ourselves certain
kinds of food and to avoid other kinds. Similarly, we
need to know something of the anatomy and functioning of
our psychic and spiritual lives--including the sexual
dimensions--in order to know how and why to guide our
own lives as a whole.

The definition of sexuality given earlier has now
been extended to man and woman specifically. Man and
woman are the two correlative ways of sharing the gift
of self. The intent of these definitions is to offer
something to ponder in one's heart in order to become
surer *that* sex is soul-deep and to grow in the knowledge
of *what* it basically involves. The deeper our root
meanings for man and woman, the better the opportunity
to grow rich as sexual persons. *How* we can really express the depths of sex through the concrete actions of
everyday life is another distinctive question. But
this challenge of becoming effective in expressing the
unique person each of us was created to be is profoundly
conditioned by our ultimate meaning for being a man or
a woman.

Notes

1. In any science, definition is crucial to progress. Definitions serve as general maps of the territory we are attempting
to explore in our knowledge endeavors, as best we can sketch out
this territory on the basis of preceding adventures into it. Obviously, we desire to modify our definition-maps as we discover,
through subsequent exploration, inaccuracies in the previous for-
mulations. When the knowledge of a field progresses, definitions
can become more refined and precise, just as maps can. Also,
at times, and for certain practical purposes, we do not use our
most refined definitions because they can, like superdetailed maps,
make use more difficult.
2. Many contemporary feminists seem to be trying to solve the
sexual energy crisis through the idea that men and women are really
the same or should be treated the same--even, if possible, with
respect to exercising their physical powers of generation. Women
have been and continue to be--in many ways--oppressed. But that
is only one side of the symptoms of the sexual energy crisis. The
neuter concept of androgyny, which so many feminists regard as crucial to freedom, is itself devastating.
3. To affect something, however, is not necessarily to exert
a causal influence, if a cause is regarded in the traditional,
Western way as that upon which something *depends* for its existence

or coming into existence. At least certain kinds of beings--
most notably God--can be affected by others without thereby being
or becoming dependent upon them.

4. For an integrative approach to data from biology, psychology,
and medicine concerning fundamental differences (not inferiorities)
between the sexes, see Judith M. Bardwick, *Psychology of Women: A
Study of Bio-Cultural Conflicts* (New York: Harper and Row, 1971).

5. This observation has been made by Margaret Mead and others.
An excellent anthropological source for the empirical *clues* on
male-female difference is Margaret Mead, *Male and Female: A
Study of the Sexes in a Changing World* (New York: New American
Library/Mentor, 1955). The philosophical concepts in this Chapter
regarding man-woman difference are thoroughly consonant with Meade's
observations and with most of her generalizations.

For philosophical-phenomenological approaches to the differences of the sexes, cf. F. J. J. Buytendijk, *Woman: A Contemporary
View*, trans. Denis J. Barrett (New York: Newman Press and Association Press, 1968); and Abel Jeanniere, *The Anthropology of Sex*,
trans. Julie Kernan (New York: Harper and Row, 1967), especially
pp. 77-85, 97-125.

6. The receiving power of God can be seen through the Christian
concept of the Pleroma--the idea of a super-fullness at the end of
the world in which Christ gathers all into himself so that God
may be all in all. Even in his "empirical" life Jesus seemed to
be in touch with his Anima, as when he said he would like to
gather the people of Jerusalem under his wings as a hen gathers
her chicks. In the Christian worldview, Creation seems to emphasize
the male side of being--giving being and performing. But Redemption seems to emphasize the female. Jesus as the Word of God empties
himself in the redemptive action. He undergoes willingly and unconditionally the plight of those needing redemption. (Mother-
love is an unconditional kind of love according to Eric Fromm and
others.) After he empirically leaves the world, Jesus still continues to knit the family together by a dynamic, but unobservable
presence and by nurturing, through the sacraments, the premortal
children who are willing to partake. The Alpha may be masculine,
but the Omega seems to be feminine. The redeemed universe which
was created in, through, and with the Word is, in the end, restored
by God, the Mother, to God, the Father. (This nucleus of a theology
of God's femaleness has been stimulated by and shared with Mary
R. Joyce and Germain Grisez.)

7. The psychologically reflective basis for these philosophical
claims about the definitions of man and woman is indicated by
Erik Erickson, *Identity: Youth and Crisis*, especially Chapter 7,
"Womanhood and the Inner Space." (New York: W. W. Norton, 1968).

8. E. g., Carl G. Jung, et al., *Man and His Symbols*, eds. Carl
G. Jung, M.-L. von Franz, and John Freeman (Garden City: Doubleday,
1964). In this volume, see Jung's section on the analysis of
dreams, pp. 55-66, and especially his section on the archetype
in dream symbolism, pp. 67-82. Interesting background on the
theory of the collective unconscious is given by Jung in Chapter

7, "Archaic Man," *Modern Man in Search of a Soul*, trans. W. S. Dell and Cary F. Baynes (New York: Harcourt, Brace and World/ Harvest, 1933). A developed treatment occurs in *The Collected Works of Carl G. Jung*, eds. Sir Herbert Read, Michael Fordham and Gerhard Adler, trans. R. F. C. Hull, 19 vols. (London: Routledge and Kegan Paul). See especially "The Concept of the Collective Unconscious," in Volume 9, Part I. Also found in *The Portable Jung*, ed. Joseph Campbell, trans. R. F. C. Hull (New York: Penguin Books, 1971), pp. 59-69.

Human Sexual Ecology would seem to be supported by the thinking of Carl Jung more than by any other major psychological theorist. The philosophical and psychological approaches are necessarily different, and some of the philosophy of sexuality is even conceived in a somewhat divergent way--notably the Animus and Anima. But the inspiration for much of my philosophical conception of psychic life--especially in regard to the Animus and Anima--is provided by the brilliant, scholarly, and clinical synthesis of Carl Jung.

On the Jungian interpretation of Animus and Anima as major archetypes (contents of the collective unconscious) see Emma Jung, *Animus and Anima*, trans. Cary F. Baynes and Hildegard Nagel (New York/Zurich: Spring Publications, 1972). This publication is available from the Analytical Psychology Club of New York, Inc., 28 East 39th St., N.Y.C. 10016.

9. For a synopsis of how sexual maturity can be attained in man-woman relationships, see Mary Joyce's *How Can a Man and Woman Be Friends?*

10. Obviously, the question of holding and being held is very complex. There are different kinds of holding and being held, and different kinds of male holding and being held as well as of female holding and being held. Here we attempt to discern the most general, yet viable, notion of holding and being held in relationships that are man-woman.

11. See M. and R. Joyce, *New Dynamics*, p. 53.

In regard to the spiritual dimension of male and female one can consult commentators on Biblical sources. E.g., W. Cole, *Sex and Love in the Bible* (London: n.p., 1960) or T. C. De Kruijf, *The Bible on Sexuality*, trans. F. Vander Heijden (De Pere, Wisc.: St. Norbert Abbey Press, 1966).

12. This idea is treated at greater length by Mary R. Joyce in *The Meaning of Contraception* (Collegeville, Minn.: Liturgical Press, 1970), pp. 89-93.

13. This idea originates in Plato's *Symposium*. According to June Singer, that work makes the first mention of the figure of the Androgyne in Greek philosophy. See her chapter entitled "Plato's Androgyne: Origins of Heterosexuality and Homosexuality," in *Androgyny: Toward a New Theory of Sexuality* (Garden City: Doubleday, 1976).

Perhaps this common notion of another person as "the other half" ("the better half" yet?) is a case of misplaced identity. Animus and Anima are sufficient within a single person to constitute a sexual whole. What is needed by the person is not a half to be wholed, but a whole to be healed.

14. The phenomenon of sexual interaction is fantastically complex. In accord with the general definitions, however, we can begin to indicate the basic pattern of sexual interaction by theorizing that the giving power of one person relates with the receiving power of the other (of the same, as well as opposite, sex). When two people of the same sex relate ("side to side") the emphasis on giving or on receiving is the same or is going in the same direction. But when people of different sex relate the mutual emphases balance each other ("face to face") structurally, if not concretely. Not only do a man's and a woman's various dimensions of giving relate naturally with corresponding dimensions of receiving, but their *emphases* (giving in a receiving way and receiving in a giving way) *also* reciprocally relate--which cannot be the case with people of the same sex. Man-woman interrelationship is always a mutuality of emphasis at the basic structural level, along with the general background network of mutual giving and receiving potencies that are normally interacting in any human interaction.

Part   II

FREEDOM AND FRIENDSHIP

Chapter 6

SEXUAL FREEDOM

Sexual freedom is popular. Many talk about it. Books and magazine articles are written about it. Films are made. People explore and experiment. But an underlying question remains. How many people have found genuine freedom in their sexual behavior?

For many individuals freedom seems to be, for the most part, the release of inhibitions, the coddling of instincts, and the release of tension. Do they experience great joy in their many pleasurable activities? Why is there so much sadness and social disorder in the lives of those for whom freedom means nothing more than choosing a goal and going after it? Perhaps the lack of joy and the scarcity of genuine freedom comes partly from most people taking it for granted that they know what freedom is.

Like sexuality and love, freedom involves in-depth experience. Freedom comes from the attitudinal heart of the person. It does not come from an individual's instinctive behavior, nor from the opportunity for options, nor from the mere desire to be free. Human freedom is ecological: deep and complex, involving several major dimensions and interrelated levels. If an individual is going to experience genuine and lasting freedom, all levels of the person need to be working in harmony with one another.

Sexual freedom is essentially human freedom within the powers of sexuality, including the genital and coital powers. Therefore, defining basic *human* freedom, in a reasonably adequate way, is important for anyone who would actually succeed in making the difficult, but incomparably rewarding, journey into the area of genuine sexual freedom.

In Chapter 4, I discussed the liberation process and, by means of the story about two Zen monks, briefly suggested the *attitude* of freedom. In Chapter 5, we considered the nature of sexuality and sexual identity. Now we are in a position to examine the basic conditions of freedom. Once these conditions are established, one can root his or her sexual attitudes and behavior in such a way that they have the best chance to grow vigorously.

Human freedom can be understood as having three basic levels. Besides the three levels, one can speak of a fourth kind of freedom that is found in the mature person. By this latter, full-bodied freedom all three levels of freedom are included and integrated. The three levels can be called freedom of movement, freedom for goals, and freedom for goods (values). The integrative kind is called freedom of self-perfection.[1]

Sexual freedom will be defined in the light of these fundamental dimensions of freedom.

Freedom of Movement--Level One

The first level of freedom is essentially a freedom of movement. It is shared by all things in the material world. It is freedom from restraints. Leaves blowing in the wind, a rock falling from a cliff, a deer racing in a meadow, a baby kicking in his crib. These instances of freedom essentially involve going from one point to another without a choice. The mere absence of physical restraint makes this freedom possible.

Humans share this kind of freedom with all other space-time creatures. All of our bodily functions--such as the flowing of blood, cell metabolism, and fluctuation of temperature--are instances of first-level freedom. But this freedom is also found in the human psyche as well. All of our instincts, feelings, and emotions are essentially a going from one condition to another without choice entering into the action itself. All the movements of our unconscious drives and feelings are included in first-level freedom.

Even the spiritual powers of the human person are involved in this level of freedom. All acts of thinking, knowing, willing, desiring, and the like--inasmuch as they are radically natural acts, not under our specific direction--are first-level actions and are instances of spiritual freedom, independent of our personal control. We cannot help but think, know, will, desire, and so on. These actions flow from us as naturally as breathing, hungering, or feeling. They are instances of freedom of movement or act.[2]

First-level freedom is the ability to go or to pass from one condition to another, gradually or immediately. It is a non-choice or a pre-choice freedom.

Freedom for Goals--Level Two

The second level of freedom is not specifically a freedom of movement, but it is natural. Human beings are a particular kind of natural being in which a unique type of freedom-potential resides. The human person has the freedom-power to choose. This freedom to choose is natural only to human beings. It is crucial to the activity of both second and third levels of freedom.[3]

The person has a power to choose a particular goal, and then to set about achieving it. This freedom to choose an objective, and to find an appropriate means of attaining it, is second-level freedom--the freedom for goal-directed behavior. A goal is a particular set of circumstances or conditions that is not now present, but which the person desires to put into effect. The person *freely* decides to pursue this objective and freely acts toward its accomplishment.

If someone is *forced* to strive toward a particular objective, he or she is not enjoying freedom for goals. If either the goal or the means to the goal are not freely chosen by the individual, the action is *not* a second-level freedom. Animals, therefore, do not enjoy this level of freedom, even though they sometimes engage in choice*like* behavior.[4]

This level is a means-end freedom. The free action does not include within itself the reality toward which it is leading. The goal is a condition not yet present in the action. Driving home from one's job can be an action of second-level freedom inasmuch as the person really chooses to get home (the goal) and is using an appropriate means (automobile, motorcycle) of his or her choice. Many people live much of their lives at this

91

level of freedom. Their *every* action is a means to an end. Few of their actions are ends in themselves to any great extent.

Freedom for Goods (Values)--Level Three

Third-level freedom involves a different kind of choice. At the second level a person exercises a freedom to get something not yet possessed. In order to do so, one *chooses to be determined* by a goal outside self and outside one's present conditions. But, in so far as a choice is being made at the third level, the person is *choosing to determine himself or herself*. Third-level freedom is freedom of *self*-determination.

With the freedom of self-determination, the person chooses to participate in some human good that is part of his or her very nature--such as knowing for the sake of knowing, telling the truth, or worshipping God. The chosen good is not outside the action by which the person participates in it. In this sense, there is a world of difference between a goal and a good.[5] A goal is some-thing one chooses to get. A good is something one chooses to let--to let be or let happen. It is a choice to let oneself be determined in one's action, not by something other than self but by a human good that is an essential part of oneself.

If a man chooses to marry in order to get something for himself from his partner, he is acting largely on second level. But if he chooses marriage to this woman as a great opportunity to participate in the fundamental goods of human life, such as friendship and life itself, then he is acting on the third level. People generally make choices on both levels at once.

Since the freedom of self-determination is the free-dom to participate in fundamental human goods that flow from the depths of the soul, it is a freedom that is never exhausted. We can never participate too deeply in friend-ship or in life itself. They are not goals or limited objectives. They are goods or ends in themselves.

When a person acts at this third level, he or she experiences the chosen good all during the action. The good that is experienced is like a sunbeam that comes from the depths of one's inexhaustibly good self, and it lights up the action by which the person is enjoying it. One can think of someone standing in a dark cave looking at the light coming from the entrance. He can see the light by the light itself. And it is this light

92

which is present all along the route as he makes his
way toward it and toward fuller participation in it.

Only this third level of freedom affords the person
the possibility of becoming an abundantly human individual. A human being has the natural power to choose to
participate--or to refuse to participate--in the basic
structural values that help to constitute his or her
very being as a human person.[6] He or she can choose to
participate very deeply or very weakly. The ability to
participate in third-level freedom admits of incalculable
degrees. It is the freedom to be a deeper and deeper
person. It is the freedom to be more and more richly
who you already are.

In order to increase one's participation in the
goods of human life one needs second-level activity, too.
For instance, in making a commitment to marry, two people
are determining themselves and their lives to a considerable extent. But they cannot practically carry it out
unless they engage in countless acts of goal-directed
behavior. Deciding on and doing the multitudinous tasks
of preparation for the wedding is largely action at the
second level--not to mention the numerous practical decisions and goal-attainment activities through the marriage itself. These actions receive their character as
truly human actions in so far as they embody the choice
made at another level, in which the partners more or
less deeply determine themselves to participate in fundamental human goods, such as integrity, friendship, and
life itself.

Moral Action

We are studying human sexuality so that we can learn
to determine what are morally good and bad ways of man-
woman behavior. Therefore, we should note carefully
that an action is moral only to the extent that it is
a third-level action. A moral action is one that involves
freedom of self-determination. This third-level action
requires and embraces considerable second-level action.
But the core of human freedom and moral action is action
by which the person himself or herself determines, to
one degree or another, who he or she shall be.

By moral action I do not necessarily mean morally
good action. Moral action is simply action that effectively makes oneself good *or* bad, *so* good or *not so* good.
An action is morally good to the extent that it involves
a deliberately intended, genuine participation in one
or more human goods. It is morally bad to the extent

93

that it involves a deliberately intended failure to participate adequately in one or more human goods. The person, through knowledge and will, creates his or her moral life out of the relatively inexhaustible "material" afforded by the basic goods structured within human nature.

Later, we shall have occasion to study the most fundamental goods and inherent values of human life. For now, it is important to realize that any human freedom, including sexual freedom, involves the way in which a person participates--or fails to participate--in the structure of himself or herself as a human being.

Every person engages in action that is moral--action that is morally good or bad, depending on the *way* in which the self-determination is effected. We are created to be free. We cannot not be free. Even if we choose not to choose, we have chosen.[7] This choice affects the whole character of our life. The choice not to choose--not to engage in much action at the third level, for instance--inevitably and incalculably pollutes our entire moral life.

But choosing to choose is only a step in the right direction. We can readily choose to participate in the human goods of life through ways and means that act against the very good we intend to enjoy. Learning to act morally well (like learning to walk) involves falls, bumps, and bruises, so to speak. Beginning with childhood, we gradually grow into the use of our knowledge and free will concerning our own actions. If we are sincere, we *can* gradually add dimension to our freedom. We can move from an emphasis on first-level freedom as a baby, to an emphasis on second-level freedom as a child and adolescent, to an emphasis on third-level freedom as an adult--from impulsive freedom to goal-centered freedom to value-centered freedom.

These three necessary levels of freedom correspond with the three basic ego states of the human psyche as delineated by transactional analysis.

Freedom of movement (impulse) is the raw, untutored freedom that comes from within our nature and lies beyond the determination of self or others. It might be regarded as Child freedom. It is necessarily involved in any thoroughly human action.

Freedom for goals is a freedom to be directed by something outside oneself. This kind of orientation is

found deep in the human psyche. It is the natural power
to be determined in our behavior by others. This inner
Parent keeps saying to us, "Do this, don't do that.
Choose this goal, don't choose that. This is the way
(means) to do it, not that." The psychic Parent itself
is *not* a level of freedom, but it does provide the main
psychic orientation for goal-directed freedom.

Freedom for goods is a freedom to determine one's
personal destiny. This freedom of self-determination is
the ultimate source of specifically moral action, whether
good or bad. In its activity it requires the integration
of first-level and second-level free actions. Similarly,
the psychic Adult is that ego state in which our rational
judgments take place and we decide our courses of action.
It integrates into its operation the other two ego states
and their contributions. The Adult ego state is the
psychic counterpart of the main freedom-area of the per-
son--which is a spiritual area. In some respects, we
can say that third-level freedom is Adult freedom.

Freedom of Self-Perfection

Within the third level of freedom there is the possibility for exercising the kind of freedom that everyone
seems to be talking about, but few seem to attain. Everyone wants freedom to mean self-perfection. We are created
to enjoy the perfection of our God-given beings. We
deeply long for a freedom to be perfectly who we are.[8]

But freedom of self-perfection is the result of the
right exercise of this third-level freedom--the freedom
of self-determination. If our self-determination is
poor, we will be failing in self-perfection and will be
developing self-defection. We will be growing further
and further away from our true selves. This misuse of
the freedom of self-determination leads inevitably into
a wild and chaotic kind of growth--a morally cancerous
condition. (In traditional terminology, such a condition
is called *sin*.)

We are all susceptible to the inauthentic freedom
of self-defection because we tend to confuse second-
level and third-level freedom. We think that freedom
of choice necessarily means freedom of alternatives and
options. We become fixed on a kind of supermarket concept of freedom. As a result, we are inclined to demand
as many alternative ways of acting in a given area of
human behavior, such as sexuality, as our feelings or
our friends will permit. The attitude that it is OK as
long as you do not hurt anyone seems to stem from this

misconception of human freedom. The result is that the person tends to grow horizontally, but not vertically. He or she becomes fat with options, but thin with meaning. The metabolism of everyday moral decisions tends to be seriously upset.

People are inclined to think that human actions are good if one is sincere and open-minded. But, despite their importance, it is not sincerity and open-mindedness that makes one free. Only the truth will make us free, as Jesus once said. Only true alternatives and true goods--honestly and sincerely enjoyed--will create the kind of freedom in a person for which he or she was made.

Freedom of self-perfection is the kind of freedom that results from the true exercise of one's power for self-determination. When the fundamental human goods and values of life are participated in, such that they flow freely from the person and are not being exploited, freedom of self-perfection is growing. The more it grows, the greater the person becomes. Good actions produce healthy persons somewhat as nourishing food causes health in the body. The human being is a moral autotroph, a self-feeder, a self-determined entity.

Growth in self-perfection requires growth in self-knowledge. A very important part of self-knowledge is learning what truly human freedom is and entails. Human freedom is an essential structure of the person. It requires a knowledge that is deep. Its aspects are many and complex.[9] The present sketch of freedom is intended to give some general direction in our ongoing discovery of the freedom into which we are called by our God-like natures.

In light of this general orientation on freedom, I will define sexual freedom itself and show how it relates to the three levels of freedom.

Sexual Freedom

Sexual freedom is a form of the freedom of self-perfection. It has nothing specifically to do with having and choosing alternatives.[10] It is a participation in the fundamental human goods of personhood.

Sexual freedom is a *sharing* freedom: the freedom to share self with self and with others. Sharing self is a necessary feature of perfecting oneself. Giving and receiving within self and with others is the first fruit of love and of self-perfection. If sexuality is the *power*

96

to share the gift of self, sexual freedom is the *functional ability* to exercise this power.

Sexual freedom is not basically an instinctual freedom. It is not a species of first-level freedom. Removing inhibitions and social restraints concerning genital and coitional behavior does nothing necessarily to foster sexual freedom, and may even hinder it. Some inhibitions and social restraints represent an important human regard for the specific nature of genital and coital sexuality. Others may be hang-ups or hindrances. It all depends on *which* restraints. The widespread notion that sex is a bio-psychic necessity--an essential, physical need of the human person; a kind of high-class rutting behavior--suffers from the misconception that sexual freedom is simply a freedom of movement.[11]

Sexual freedom is not basically a second-level freedom of behavioral options. It is third-level. For sexual freedom to be present only one "option" is needed-- the option of saying yes or no to the opportunity to do one's action in a sharing manner.

Sexual freedom includes second-level action as well as first level action. Some measure of second-level freedom to "do as you choose" as well as of first-level freedom to "do as you feel" is always involved. But sexual freedom does not essentially mean the pursuit of limited sexual objectives.

The common cultural playboy-freedom, to create your own recreational sexual pleasures and then pursue them, is a form of sexual enslavement because it perverts the structure of freedom written into the person's being. Play and recreation are great human goods in sexuality as well as in other aspects of life. But they are not designed to be treated as limited personal objectives. Play is a fundamental and inexhaustible human good that is not itself created by the human creature and deserves the person's utter respect and reverence as he or she participates in it. This personal regard for the inexhaustible good of play requires careful attention to the nature of the play in which one appears to be engaged at the time.[12]

Sexual freedom is basically a freedom of self-determination. Sharing the gift of self is the very touchstone of participating in fundamental human goods. The inner sexual life of giving and receiving one's self within oneself--the interaction and communion of Animus and Anima, of Adam and Eve--is the prime activity of any

self-perfecting instance of third-level action. To be
human is to share; not simply to act or interact. The
only genuine way to participate in a fundamental human
good is to *share* in it, not simply to *react* to it or
use it.

Reacting to or interacting with a basic good of
human life is not enough. A person can be "enjoying" a
fundamental good such as human companionship by torturing
someone. He or she can participate in this good of companionship by getting sexual or genital kicks out of
torturing someone. The torturer reacts to or interacts
with the human good of companionship. Such action is a
third-level act of freedom. But it is a kind of action
that is opposed to sharing. Sharing means non-abuse of
the gift of self and of the other. Sadism is an instance
of the freedom of self-determination which abuses that
freedom itself by abusing one's own self and others as
well.

Self-perfecting sexual freedom means enjoying the
good of human sexuality at all levels in the God-given,
nature-structured ways appropriate to this good. The
truth about human sexuality and its distinctive structures
is what makes a person free, because it is the truth that
the person lets penetrate himself or herself more and
more deeply. Letting the truth of an action and of oneself penetrate from within the action itself and flow
freely to all around is an act of sharing--rather than
an instance of simply reacting to--the dynamic structure
of oneself. Ecologically sound self-determination--
letting nature have its rights--develops a freedom of
self-perfection. The more that self-perfection grows,
the easier true self-determination becomes, and the fuller
and richer the person becomes.[13] Sexual freedom is an
intimate part of this development.

Genital and Coital Freedom

Everyone has the *natural* ability to share the gift
of self. But sexual freedom--the *functional* ability to
share the gift of self--comes in degrees. Some rare
people are willing to share themselves thoroughly, even
to the point of giving their lives for fellow human beings
in need. Others seem very little able to share even
crumbs from their table. They are almost completely
dysfunctional sexually.

However, the question may arise concerning whether
one can be almost sexually dysfunctional, yet genitally

or coitally very active. This question prompts a consideration of the nature of genital and coital freedom.[14]

We commonly hear much talk about the sexual activity of teenagers; how it is on the increase, and how it can best be dealt with. Such discussion almost inevitably labors under the "Ptolemaic" notion of human sexuality that genital or coital performance *is* sexual activity. Of course, a person who performs an act of coition *can* be said to be genitally and coitally active. But, since sexuality means sharing, there is a question about how much sharing--and hence, sexual activity--has taken place. In immature teens there can be little question about any high degree of *sexual* activity. Moreover, when these young people continue their behavior through the use of contraceptives, they only serve to fixate their *sexual* development at a very low level of activity.

Genital sexuality is the power to *share* the gift of life with someone else (a child). When genital intercourse is not much more than a self-centered reaction to feelings of passion and romance, little sharing has been done with the child that might be conceived.[15] Should a child happen to be conceived, then one can say that by the action of coitally genital intercourse the participant has *caused* a child to come into the world, but has done little to share life as a gift. Yet there must be a minimal degree of sharing activity taking place if the child is to be conceived at all. The sharing, however, is so minimal and distorted that in this kind of generative behavior the participant can be said to be largely dysfunctional as a *sexual* person.

Coital sexuality is the power to *share*, with a person of the other sex, one's power to give life. When a man and a woman mutually engage their coital sexuality, motivated by the pleasure one or both gets from the action, but without having regard for the operation of the genital powers that they share, they contaminate their own moral lives. In disregarding the rights of nature that pertain to their own genital powers, they cause pollution of the coital (sharing) act itself. Such activity is self-negating to an appreciable degree, and, to that degree, their sexual freedom (the functional ability to share self) is diminished. In this kind of coital action the partners are "giving without receiving" and "receiving without giving." They are not genuinely *sharing* their powers and organs of generation. Yet their actions themselves are naturally designed to be sharing ones--actions in which coital-genital powers are not simply exchanged or used, but shared.

Actually, there has to be a slight amount of receivingly giving and givingly receiving, otherwise the penis would not even penetrate the vagina. But no matter how vigorous, exciting, and pleasurable the interaction may be from a performance standpoint, it puts out of play the very special powers it is structured to share. The *feeling* of these powers may be quite real. But their *meaning* has been put out of commission right within their very action.[16]

Genital and coital freedom, then, can only occur to the degree that there is genital and coital meaning in the action. Human freedom requires a special level of meaning. The meaning of the action must be third-level. It must come from participating in a human good already present and continuing throughout the duration of the action itself.[17] Human freedom is a freedom to let, rather than to get. It is a freedom to let the good of nature permeate the whole ecological system of the participant. Humans are always right in letting nature be in basic control.[18] Only in that paradoxical way can a human being become positively (rather than negatively) self-determining, and hence self-perfecting.

Genital and coital freedom is no exception. The exercise of genital and coital powers is free only to the extent that, in the very activity itself, they can be self-perfecting rather than self-defecting. When a person engages his or her genital and coital powers, the action is as free as the person is truly open to all of nature's inherent purposes in the actions themselves-- including their unique and remarkable manner of expressing and celebrating the gift of self to another self, which is authentic sexual freedom.

Genital and coital union should be a matter of personal choice.[19] The generation of offspring, one of the naturally inherent goods of coital union, is a *fundamental* good of the human community. Since this kind of union is not a *necessary* good for the perfection of the individual human person, genital and coital powers need never be deliberately exercised by a given individual. Individuals need to be functionally free as persons in order to choose wisely whether or how they will participate in this kind of community-building.

The ecosystem of freedom in the human person is ultimately governed by the freedom of self-perfection. Sexual freedom comes from the heart of the self-perfecting activity of sharing self. For this reason we can say that sexual freedom is the functional ability to *be* love and to *make* love, without *necessarily* making love in any one particular way.

Persons who *must* make love in a coital-genital way--at any time in their lives--cannot be regarded as sexually free to that extent. On the other hand, persons who regard this kind of love-making as basically inferior to other ways of human love-making are likewise unfree. *Coital-genital* freedom is primarily a freedom of *choice*--freedom to choose or not to choose coïtion, depending on one's life-commitments, life-style, and particular circumstances as they accord with God-given nature. *Sexual* freedom is primarily a freedom of *being*, the freedom to be a sharer of self, ever more deeply, richly, and continuously throughout life, at all times and in all circumstances.[20]

NOTES

1. On the whole range of meanings of freedom, see Mortimer Adler, *The Idea of Freedom*, 2 vols. (Garden City, N.Y.: Doubleday, 1960-61).

2. This first-level freedom, as found in human beings, largely corresponds to what traditional ethicists have called "an act of man," in contrast to "human act." Actions that flow from a person, inasmuch as they are not deliberately chosen, are called "acts of man"--which I will refer to later as non-personal acts (Chapter 9). "Human act" is the term reserved for any act of a person in so far as it is caused by that person's freedom of choice. Yet, the next level of freedom--freedom for goals--does not, of itself, enter the heart of specifically human action in the moral sense. Goals are not values, and hence cannot as such help to constitute a person's act as either morally good or bad. Action that qualifies as morally significant--for good or bad--must involve, as part of its very content, human values. But it can be said that whenever a person engages in second-level freedom (freedom for goals) he or she is always simultaneously acting--minimally, at least--at third-level (values-freedom). Specifically human values are always implied in any person's free exercise of the power to choose a goal, to choose the appropriate means to the goal, and to choose to move toward it. Thus, materially, if not formally, the distinction between acts of man and human acts is paralleled by distinguishing first-level freedom from second and third level, taken together.

3. On the existence and nature of freedom of choice see Joseph M. Boyle, Germain Grisez, and Olaf Tollefsen, *Free Choice: A Self-Referential Argument* (Notre Dame, Ind.: University of Notre Dame Press, 1976).

101

4. Sometimes people will ask whether second-level freedom is proper to animals as well as people. They point to the fact that animals naturally exhibit goal-directed behavior and select appropriate means to attain their goals. Domestic pets often display appropriate behavior, such as assuming a begging position or purring softly, in order to get what they want. But it must be observed that these pets do not know their goal *as* a *goal*, nor do they know the means *as* a *means*.

5. The psychological counterpart of this philosophical distinction between second and third levels of freedom and action is remarkably developed by Abraham Maslow, who envisions the unity and diversity of the states of Becoming and Being. In his book, *Toward a Psychology of Being* (New York: Van Nostrand, 1968), one can find considerable psychological perspective and analysis that complements and supports the philosophical theories of *Human Sexual Ecology*. See especially pp. 149-214.

6. Throughout this work the terms *value* and *good* are used interchangeably. They do not necessarily serve as synonyms. The term *value* is a relatively new term in the history of philosophy and has a more subjective connotation, being used most readily in the field of economic and political thought. *Good* emphasizes the objective pole in the commonality of meaning shared by these two terms. The "basic structural values" or goods to which I refer here are regarded as part of the individual's nature as a person. They are *given* (not acquired) ingredients of being-a-person, just as common to all individual persons as eyes, ears, lungs, etc. They also transcend the confines of the individual. Later, I will call them fundamental human Goods or Values and delineate their meanings. (Chapter 10).

7. The nature of freedom is regarded as an authentic participation in one's own God-given, natural self. We are created to be free--created to become (if we so choose) more and more richly and fully the being we were given to be. This kind of freedom is quite opposite to that of Jean-Paul Sartre and the whole ethos of the "do your own thing" culture. The basic attitudes are different. Sartre says we are *condemned* to be free. He finds--at least implicitly--our *givenness* as undesirable and regards it as a condemnation. Despite its brilliant psychology of radical personal responsibility for our actions, Sartrean existentialism amounts to a dreary ontology of creation as condemnation. Both worldviews on freedom, however, clearly espouse the idea that we cannot not be free. We *must* choose, for better or worse.

8. Freedom of self-perfection is not at all the same as freedom of self-actualization or self-realization. The latter terms would suggest attainment of possibilities strictly in accord with what one desires, not necessarily in accord with a transcendent source of one's being. A person can be actualizing his or her possibilities for self-deception and self-satisfied exploitation of others. Self-actualization theories like that of Maslow or the transactional analysis of Berne are very helpful to the moralist and to ethical pursuits. But they are not enough. Ethics must be specifically

102

the result of development in philosophical theories of self-identification (*Who* am I given to be?) and transcendental analysis (*What* are the absolute relationships in my life?).

9. Essentially, human freedom has little to do with the number, variety, and refinements of one's options. If a person is chained to a wall and is being beaten to death by a mob, he or she has, at best, only two options as such, but inexhaustible opportunity to exercise personal freedom. The victim may either bless or curse his or her persecutors. But the quality of benediction or malediction interiorly, if not exteriorly, expressed can be ever increased. Great love for one's enemies is a supreme act of freedom—a freedom of values and self-determination (third level) that constitutes self-perfection as a person and as a unique individual.

10. The essence of sexual freedom is not in the numbers of coital sex partners one can have, but in the depth to which one can functionally share self with whomever is, or morally could be, that partner. Sexual freedom does include choosing alternatives. Under certain conditions, it is better to have many more alternatives than two. A young woman, for instance, who goes steady with the same fellow from junior high school through college is probably not as free functionally to share with him or with anyone else as she would be had she dated many different fellows along the way.

11. Concerning the biomorphic conception of sex underlying this idea of biopsychic necessity a thorough characterization is given by Peter Bertocci, *Sex, Love, and the Person* (New York: Sheed & Ward, 1967), pp. 73-83.

12. Andrew Greeley treats extensively the idea that authentic sex play is founded only on a permanent relationship. He indicates the impact of the Judeo-Christian worldview and liturgical symbols on the meaning and value of sex play. He also provides a kind of internal critique of the playboy philosophy. *Love and Play* (New York: Seabury, 1977).

13. There is a misunderstanding on the part of many moralists that an action must be difficult in order for it to be good or to involve appreciable moral values. My theory, however, follows the ideas of classical moralists who place moral value in the total quality of the individual act as well as in the total virtue of the person. The significance is that the exceptionally moral person finds the virtuous life and morally good acts increasingly fluent, if not always easy.

The basis for the relative ease with which the virtuous person acts can be found in the delight in goodness which motivates and causes his or her acts. The virtuous person knows how to act by a kind of connatural knowledge that represents an immediate delight in the good. See, e.g., Thomas Aquinas, *Summa Theologica*, I-II, 23, 4.

For an excellent exposition of the pre-puritanical ethics of delight in doing good, see Albert Plé, *Chastity and the Affective Life*, trans. Marie-Claude Thompson (New York: Herder and Herder, 1966), especially sections on pleasure as the test of virtue and on the morality of pleasure, pp. 92-97. In this book, Plé clearly explains the tradition of sexual morality developed by Thomas Aquinas and others. He shows how this morality has been grossly misunderstood and prejudged by so many thinkers, particularly by two groups: psychiatrists and Christian educators. The nature of a moral act and the meaning of the virtue of chastity are the two major areas of attention.

In my opinion, ethical thinking during the modern and contemporary periods of philosophy has suffered greatly from an antithetic dualism fostered especially in Kantian and neo-Kantian spheres of influence. Goodness has been identified almost entirely with rationality and evil has been identified largely with the sensual and the emotional. As a result, moral virtue amounts to a kind of self-mutilation, rather than a gradual growth in perfective integration of the person as a person. Many psychiatrists and psychotherapists, as well as many Christian educators, have reacted negatively to that approach--and rightly so. But generally they are ignorant of the earlier integrative approach that has been muffled and distorted. There is a critical need for creative integration of will and intellect, the spiritual and the sensual, the beingful and the bodily, into sexual ethics of the future.

14. Cf. Mary R. Joyce, "What is Sexual Freedom?" in the *International Review of Natural Family Planning*, 1 (Fall 1977):271-75.

15. This is true whether the genital intercourse was coital or non-coital. Functionally speaking, of course, only coital intercourse between two positively fertile people has a chance of conceiving a child. But from a nature-sensitive, philosophical perspective all genital intercourse is in itself structured to celebrate, if not functionally effect, the coming into existence of persons other than the couple. Genital intercourse cannot be properly a *sharing* activity if the natural possibility of a child is precluded.

Coital intercourse is the essence of the genital interaction of man and woman. Non-coital, genital intercourse between people of the same or of different sex is essentially an act against itself.

The bonding between parents and child, as well as parent-child interactions (prenatally and postnatally), might also be called genital intercourse (non-coital)--in a positive sense.

16. For a basic treatment of the relationship of feelings and meaning in the exercise of coital-genital powers, see Mary R. Joyce, "The Sexual Revolution Is Yet to Begin," in *Abortion and Social Justice*, ed. Thomas W. Hilgers, M. D., and Dennis J. Horan (New York: Sheed & Ward, 1972), pp. 221-229.

17. Also, the action must not directly violate any of the other fundamental goods of life. This requirement will be discussed in Chapter 11, Evaluation of a Moral Act.

18. Cf. analogously Barry Commoner's Third Law of Ecology: "Nature knows best." *The Closing Circle*, pp. 37-41.

19. See, for example, M. Joyce, *Love Responds to Life*, Chapter 8. Also, *How Can a Man and Woman Be Friends?*, Chapter 4.

20. On sexual freedom in its ontological dimension, see M. and R. Joyce, *New Dynamics*, Chapters 3 and 10.

Chapter   7

THE EVOLUTION OF RELATIONSHIPS

One of the most poignant questions that can be asked
about human sexuality is whether a man and a woman can
ever be friends.

Friendship would seem to be one of the first fruits
of true freedom. If a man and a woman have attained in
their individual lives an appreciable degree of the freedom of self-perfection, deep friendship can develop quite
naturally and joyfully.

Unfortunately, there is a long-standing assumption
in our culture that a deep and lasting relationship between a man and a woman who are sexually attracted to
each other, is impossible apart from marriage and coital
relations. As a result, such a relationship is almost
a rare phenomenon. In Euro-American societies of the
past, when a man and woman were attracted to each other
and had values in common which they desired to share
deeply, but were unfree to marry, they were often enjoined
to keep the relationship "Platonic." Loving, physical
expression of their growing friendship was regarded as
exceedingly suspect, if not downright pernicious.

Today, particularly in some new-mode women's maga-
zines, there is serious thought about the possibilities
of man-woman friendship. Most people who would advocate
such a relationship include coital relations as a possibility or as a foregone conclusion. They continue
to labor under the "Ptolemaic" worldview of human sexu-

ality. Coital union is considered to be the ultimate
act of a man-woman relationship. All other expressions
of affection and approval are regarded basically as possible steps to coital orgasm. Almost everyone still
subscribes to a falling-domino theory of man-woman affection: one thing rather inevitably leading to another;
holding hands leading to kissing, kissing to bodily embracing, bodily embracing to genital petting, and petting
to orgasm.

     But there are men and women--especially women--in
the contemporary world who are seriously questioning
whether there is a natural necessity to this sequence.
They are beginning to suspect that the problem is an
attitudinal one. They may have experienced a sexual
energy crisis in their own lives. Or they readily recognize it in those around them. They also believe in a
truer and better destiny for humankind. And so, they
are ready for the "Copernican" sexual revolution.

     Many people are inclined now to believe in the idea
that was announced by William James, when he said that
the greatest discovery of his generation was that human
beings, by changing the inner attitudes of their minds,
can change the outer aspects of their lives. This manifesto of human potential can readily be applied to human
sexuality. Just as the original Copernican revolution
changed humankind from an earthbound creature to an outer
space explorer, so a Copernican-like sexual revolution
can change people from genitocentric sexual relations
to unimaginable depths in the inner space of man-woman
friendship.

     Only a genuine revolution in our thinking about
ourselves as sexual beings will make it possible for
loving friendships to develop between men and women.
But what would such relationships really entail? What
are the essential ingredients in a man-woman relationship
that is not necessarily a marital one and that is not
a repressive "Platonic" affair? And how can such relationships be developed, granted the bias toward genitocen
trism? These are the questions addressed in this chapter

     The response to these questions is meant to apply,
in many respects, to relationships between persons of
the same sex. These latter relationships are very important. People of the same sex are attracted to each
other in ways that invite acts of sharing themselves as
gifts. *How* man-man and woman-woman special relationships
can grow well is very similar to, yet different from,
the way in which man-woman relationships grow. A devel-

oped philosophy of interpersonal relationships--neces-
sarily sexual in their structure--is outside the scope
of this book. Therefore, the focus of this chapter and
of Chapter 18 is on the most crucial kind of relationship in human sexual ecology: man and woman.

The Four Qualities of Friendship

Whether a man and a woman are married to each other
or not, there are four qualities which seem to be essential to a mature relationship. These qualities will be
found in any true friendship--of the same or different
sex.[1] But they have special potential for richness and
depth when found in the relationship of a man and woman
who are particularly attractive to each other. (I have
noted in Chapter 5 how man and woman are so structured
that only they--unlike people of the same sex--can relate
to each other "face to face" on all three levels of their
being.)

The first quality of friendship might be regarded
as the foundation quality. *Equality* is a bedrock necessity if the relationship is going to grow into genuine
friendship. Because of ignorance and cultural prejudices,
men and women often have difficulty seeing themselves
as basically equal. Besides, men tend to be superior
in certain traits, such as the physical ability to protect self and others. Women tend to be superior in other
traits, such as the ability to nurture.[2] But whatever
superiority or inferiority may be attributed to an individual or to a sex in regard to particular qualities
of body, mind, and spirit, all of these qualities are
rooted within a person and a sexual being who is endowed
with human nature--common to all. No matter how superior
a person may be in many ways, he or she can still regard
the other as basically equal, by reason of personhood
and sex. If either the man or woman is posturing as a
master or a servant, friendship is impeded. Even Jesus,
who proclaimed himself God's equal, once said to his fol-
lowers, "I no longer call you servants . . . but friends"
(John 15:15).

Besides equality, *esteem* is essential to friendship.
The man and woman must value highly the person and sex
of the other. Friends are precious in each other's sight.
A man, for instance, who values the complex life of a
woman--the particular mystery of her being--reveals his
considerable potential for friendship with her. A woman,
for instance, who intuits in a man a potential greatness
that he himself cannot see, and treats him accordingly
(despite his errant behavior), is doing him the service

107

of a friend. Men as men are mysteries, too; and women as women sometimes need men to help them see their potential greatness.

A third necessary ingredient in friendship is *affection*. All friends experience feelings of liking each other. They want to express their feelings in word and touch. The kinds of things they say will vary greatly with the particular relationship. So, too, their ways of physically expressing affection will have a pattern of their own. Friends need not violate their friendship or their commitments when they kiss or embrace, as long as it is not done in order to stimulate generative powers or to alienate the affection they have for other people.

Loving, physical embraces can be positive signs of friendship, which include in their meaning all other existing friendships. Any loving relationship--including a marital one--is, by its very nature, open to all relationships that the partners have with other people. Exclusivist friendship is a contradiction in terms. Many relationships once regarded as friendships show themselves to be much less than that as jealousy overcomes them. Friendship is a relationship that is open and honest, and so is any of its delightful signs of affection in word, gesture, or touch.

Value sharing, the fourth quality of friendship, is the depth-dimension. Values, especially the more important goods of human life, are the content of any friendship. Sharing interests in sports, politics, religion, health-care, and in many other areas of life, is the occupation of friends. If friends have little in common, their friendship is correspondingly weak. If they have much in common, they can become intimate friends, on condition that they also develop the other qualities of friendship: a sense of equality, esteem, and affection.

But value sharing does not simply consist in having common interests and pursuing them. *What* are the *particular* values shared within the areas of sports, politics, religion, and the others? People will not be friends to the extent that they hold incompatible commitments with respect to these goods. Friendships that are broad and deep allow for contrary values in many areas of life. But as one attends to values that represent the deeper levels of life, the room for being contrary (yet maintaining genuine friendship) becomes smaller and smaller.

108

A theist and an atheist, for instance, can be good friends to some degree. But the *possibility* for deep, rich friendship among people who share the same religious and philosophical values in a heartfelt way--not just superficially--is incalculably greater than for those who do not similarly share in these areas. Two people can vigorously disagree on who was the greatest home-run hitter of all time, Babe Ruth or Hank Aaron, yet be fabulous friends because of the very many things they agree upon in sports, politics, religion, and so forth. But two people who vigorously disagree--meaning that their hearts are as involved as their heads--concerning whether Jesus is God may find a deep and lasting friend-ship next to impossible, even though their friendship may remain quite viable on lesser grounds.[3]

Value sharing is the very activity and practice of friendship. Sharing values is what friends as friends really *do*. Inasmuch as the sharing activity involves the *self* of the participants, sexuality is involved. Friendship between people of the same or of different sex requires *sexual* activity. Just as any two persons *as persons* will share differently because of their unique-ness of personhood, so people of the same sex will share differently from people of different sex. But the dis-tinctive kind of giving-receiving orientation proper to the persons' sexes will be uniquely activated in their value sharing.[4] Friendship is naturally sexual.

Friendship Defined

Christians, and others, believe that people are called to love their enemies, not only their friends (Luke 6:27-35). We are not called to like our enemies, but to love them. We are not called to try to treat our enemies as friends. (That would be a deception, a lie.) But we do need to love them, which means that we intend to do what is the truest and best for them, despite the cost. (When he saw it was the proper time, Jesus *died* for his enemies--all of us, who have sinned.) Jesus loved both friends and enemies alike.

Friendship is the enrichment of love. It adds to love the reality of positively liking someone. Enemies are not liked--at least to the extent that they are ene-mies or in the way that they are enemies. They are not liked--they are not attractive to us--because we do not share certain important values with them. In fact, we hold contrary values. So, people can be enemies to one another in some respects and friends in others. Few of us are totally friends.

109

Friendship that is true and lasting *is* a love relationship. But it is more. Friendship is love that is
enriched by equality, esteem, affection and, above all,
value sharing. Friendship is true love, genuinely shared.
It means willing the truest and best for someone, despite
the cost to self, and *liking* it. The degree of friend-
ship--its relative authenticity--depends on both the
intensity of love and the depth of *mutual sharing*. Lovers
are not necessarily friends, but true friends are necessarily lovers (in the truest sense of the word).[5]

Stages of a Relationship

Authentic man-woman friendship is possible only
when the two people are relatively mature sexually. Most
people are not mature enough to sustain a heterosexual
relationship of growing involvement and intense attractiveness, when this relationship is not supported in its
ups and downs by the commitment of marriage or the prospect of it. People who would "blast off" into the inner
space of such a relationship are very likely to drift
apart or to crash land--in bed.

How a person can prepare for special man-woman relationships through growth into a relatively mature sexual
life will be discussed in the next chapter. First, it
may be helpful to consider the main evolutionary stages
that erotically stimulating relationships normally entail
for persons who would progress from sexual immaturity
to maturity.

When a sexually immature person meets someone of
the other sex who is very attractive, he or she needs
to be prepared for the natural evolution of their relationship. Such a person can anticipate three levels of
growth in the impending relationship. There are many
different forms or kinds of development within these
three phases, depending upon whether the two persons are
not married but are looking for a marriage partner, or
are not married and not looking, or are married to two
others (or one of them is married)--not to mention the
many different facets of interaction flowing from their
individual personalities. I would suggest, however, that
three phases or stages--overlapping and interpenetrating
one other--describe the basic contours of evolution in
any emotionally involving relationship. The awareness
of these essential horizons provides support, especially
for those who enter such relationships as man and woman,
independent of considerations about marriage.[6]

110

The Romantic Stage

The first stage in the relationship might be called the romantic stage. Very often it happens that two people are suddenly taken up with each other. They alone really exist. The whole world seems to drop out of sight and the newly-found beloved is everywhere. For days or even weeks, the spell may remain. The two people may look into each other's eyes and feel each other's hearts beating with a single pulse. There seems to be only one practical purpose in living: to work themselves free from the many encumbrances of existence so that this new heaven can be experienced as totally and exclusively as possible. A new and exquisitely beautiful friendship may be dawning. Theirs is a sunrise freedom and friendship.

Almost all "special" love-relationships begin this way. Some are less dramatic. But, generally, a person meets someone and is rather readily enamoured of certain features of his or her personality, bearing, and being. The new friend probably strikes a deep chord in the unconscious life of this person. While the relationship need not be with a person of the other sex, the romantic overtures are usually more compelling between a man and a woman.

Young people are especially susceptible to intense relationships in this first phase. Almost inevitably these relationships fade and pass away, but not before the person has been exercised impellingly in his or her emotional life. Unfortunately, if the person is old enough to marry at the time when a relationship of this kind develops, there is a strong inclination to regard the object of one's fluently ravished desires as "the only one for me." "My beloved, my darling, my beautiful one has captivated me and I deeply desire to be wafted away into a life of never-ending marital bliss." This potentially ruinous attitude can be mitigated only by previous exposure to sound education in human sexuality.

At the risk of oversimplifying the process, one can reasonably suspect the silent workings of an untutored drive arising from the person's unconscious life. The romantic love that leads directly into marriage-- especially into teen-age marriages--is often the result of a psychic projection.

Every person has, dwelling in the depths of the psyche, certain erotic ideals or images of the perfect mate. For a man, the ideal might be blue-eyed, blonde-haired, curvaceous and might look remarkably like a well-known movie actress. Perhaps he has an alternate erotic ideal that highly resembles a popular rock and roll singer. For a woman, the erotic ideal might be medium-build, blond, curly haired and very romantic. Or tall, dark, handsome, and very gentle. Films, television, and novels are standard sources for the largely unconscious, but not infrequently articulated, psychic ideal in sexual otherness. The possibilities are limited only by one's most creative imagination.

When a person of the other sex comes into one's life and that new person tends to approximate the characteristics of one's erotic ideal, a deep psychic need is awakened. The erotic image in the unconscious mind largely represents a longing for integration of one's own personal life--an integration of one's psychic sexual other, one's Animus or Anima. The young or immature person is in critical need of this fulfillment. He or she needs the marriage of Animus and Anima within; and, in place of that marriage occurring, the psychic life provides erotically ideal images. But the immature person may not realize what is happening or even that he or she has a need for interior sexual fulfillment prior to a balance and healthy relationship with an attractive person of the other sex.

So, the sexually unintegrated person will not only feel the orchestration of romantic emotions within--which is normal and natural for anyone--but will feel a necessity to satisfy his or her needs for integration by mating with the newly discovered person, who is an unconscious substitute for the unintegrated Animus or Anima. If marriage is undertaken in this condition, the couple is headed for a very rude awakening. Someday they will be jarred into the realization that "this isn't the person I married or that I fell in love with!"

Unfortunately, it *is* that person, but he or she did not know the person as a person to any great extent. He or she was knowing and reacting to the erotic ideal, deeply rooted in the psyche, representing his or her own lack of sexual integration and development. The beloved one was used unconsciously as a means to compensate for a great gap in sexual development.[7] When reality finally strikes, the person is faced with the challenge of letting his or her marriage commitment be the opportunity to grow through the second stage of evolution and into the third without the benefit of a relatively healthy romantic stage to begin with.

112

The Realistic Stage

Any relationship (marital or not) will fail to mature unless it involves a realistic process which purifies. Eventually two romantically involved people are forced, by the weight of practicality and sheer existence, to look around and work out a place for themselves in relationship to other people and to life's total circumstances. They begin to see the other's limitations and faults. They become painfully aware of their own naive projections of erotic or romantic imagery by which they had, as it were, coated the being of their beloved. After an initially intense, mutual liking for each other--sanctified by that very telling phrase, *falling* in love--they begin to sustain a counterforce of disappointments and even dislikes.

The disillusionment is rarely total and the original beauty of the beloved may often be glimpsed. But it is impossible ever to return fully to the simple and unadulterated romance they once knew. Despite the waning brilliance of their mutual presence to each other, many people continue to love and to will good for each other. Nevertheless, their relationship has become a kind of sunset freedom and friendship. For many--perhaps, for most, if they are not committed in marriage--the ensuing night is too long or too cold, and the relationship dissolves.

The realistic stage is a time for growth and for opening out to the world. As Antoine de Saint-Exupéry has said, "Life has taught us that love does not consist in gazing at each other but in looking outward together in the same direction."[8] If the seed of love (hypermagnified in the original romantic stage) is allowed to grow, the two people have the opportunity to know and understand each other more deeply. Disillusionment is but a purifying of the unique and irreplicable relationship that any two people can mutually develop, if they have the willingness for it.

The Sharing Stage

A new day can dawn within each person. Through the ministry of this relationship and of other friendships, each one can gradually realize that we are our own best friends--or worst enemies. *I* am the one who brings freedom and friendship to any relationship.[9] Within myself, I can open up to the inner sun--the free source of sexual energy--by which I share myself with self and with all being. I can let this ultimate source of sexual energy

shine on my beloved, my friend. Then, I no longer suffer
from sunrise-sunset freedom and friendship.

The sharing phase of a relationship reveals and
makes possible a joy over the great good in myself, in
my friend, and in reality itself. I begin to live the
truth that *every* creature is essentially a unique mystery
and an immense good. I also sorrow over the evil in
myself, in my friend, and in the world because of wrong-
doing. Deep sharing in friendship brings one largely
beyond the egocentric sphere of happiness and sadness--
the sphere of reacting moodily to the inevitable highs
and lows of life.

As genuine love for my friend (and thus for all
other persons and things) grows by gradually increasing
the depth of sharing self with self and with others, I
am capable of consciously experiencing more reality. I
lessen my inclination to escape the realities of pain,
sickness, and suffering that abound in the world. I am
capable of greater sorrow over them. Sorrow and joy grow
together as the whole fruit of a mature person. Sorrow,
not depression. Joy, not elation or getting high.

The third stage of relationship--authentic friend-
ship--is attained to the extent that my beloved and I
are free and friends in the mutually "sun-drenched space"
of *being* our love, where we are not just trying to feel
it or to "make it." In order to come into this level
of mature relationship, we need a new vision of self as
a sexual being and the patience to wait for our emotions
to catch up with the vision.

Meaning Matures Emotions

Through the three stages of relationship one is
taken from a condition of feelings leading meanings to
the ecologically balanced state of meanings leading and
supporting feelings.

In the romantic stage, feelings rise to such a high
pitch that the real persons are obscured. The participants are emotion-centered, rather than meaning-centered.
The relationship may be described as very "meaningful."
But the meaning lies more in "how great we *feel*" than
in "how great we *are*."

In the realistic stage, the persons are required
to receive meaning and motivation from their surroundings,
circumstances, and past history because the disillusionment is so great. They are not capable of receiving most

114

of their meaning for the relationship from their *being*.
In order to sustain themselves, they must reach for principles and commitments such as marriage and family responsibilities. The second stage is very functional. The
relationship perdures *in spite of* how they sometimes *feel*.

The breakthrough into an emphatically sharing phase
of relationship--never an absolutely realized phase--
requires a living beyond the egocentric desires of romantic attraction while incorporating them within the whole
of one's life. The breakthrough likewise involves a
living from within oneself as an autonomous and co-
creative person. Principles and commitments of life are
highly regarded and lived, but not mainly because they
function well and serve to give us needed guidance. They
are lived because they are the deeply human ways of *being*
our union with people and with things in the difficult
art of loving. In the sharing phase each person is no
longer chiefly a function of his or her friend and of
society itself. Each one has evolved into a great solitude who shares deeply and richly from within the total
self. As Rilke says, "Two solitudes protect and touch
and greet each other."[10]

Child, Parent, and Adult Relationship

The romantic phase is a relationship dominated by
the inner Child. The relationship is feelings-centered,
and takes its simplicity from the healthy, but quite
limited, experience of fusing one's feelings with some
one person we desire.

The realistic phase is a relationship dominated
by the inner Parent. A relationship cannot be sustained
and grow if it is ruled by how the parties *feel*. In
order to come to their senses, people have to receive
direction from others: from counselling, from reliance
on past experiences in which they survived crises, and
from the basic circumstances and commitments of life that
are *other than* the particular friendship itself. They
must learn how to act toward each other *in spite of* how
they feel at times. This second stage of relationship
is goal-centered, and takes its complexity from the
healthy, but still limited, experience of fusing one's
projects and plans not only with those of the beloved,
but with those of many significant others whom we desire
to please.

The sharing phase is a relationship flowing from
the inner Adult. The participants have become autonomous
and integrative persons. They are able to discern what

115

is good and healthy in their present and future romantic
inclinations. They are careful to preserve the inner
power that protects and nurtures their cherished relation-
ship--a power which they have drawn from the second stage.
They learn how to act toward each other *together with*
their feelings, their projects, and their meanings. They
integrate the strengths of the two earlier phases and
share freely from within.

In mature friendship, a man and woman protect (Parent) and touch (Child) and greet (Adult) each other.

NOTES

1. These are the qualities of friendship delineated by Mary
Joyce in her book, *How Can a Man and Woman Be Friends?* pp. 10-11.
2. For a thorough discussion of the relative superiorities
of man and woman, see Lucius Cervantes, *And God Made Man and Woman:
A Factual Discussion of Sex Differences* (Chicago: Regnery, n.d.).
Also, Theo Lang, *The Difference Between a Man and a Woman* (New
York: John Day/Bantam, 1971).
Margaret Mead (*Male and Female*) and other anthropologists have
likewise delineated relative superiorities in the sexes.
3. I do not mean that two people who sincerely, yet firmly,
disagree with each other on the divinity of Christ cannot have a
rich and relatively rewarding friendship. If they are open-minded
and each can discern good will in the other, their friendship can
grow in many satisfying ways. I simply wish to point out that if
one of the parties believes in Jesus as God incarnate and the other
does not, the nature of the issue at stake is very profound. Their
opposite stands--if held out of deep convictions--place them on
opposite sides of the "sharing world," so to speak. The deeper
the conviction, the less common ground they have for enjoying other
things together. In cases where the question of Christ's actual
nature or role in the world is not a great issue, one way or the
other, there is less of an obstacle to mutual depth in the friendship, but--since the truth or falseness of the claim of believers
is something everyone should reckon with--the lack of shared commitment on this crucial issue impedes growth, whether the partners
realize it or not.
4. On the basic PAC structure of the giving-receiving orientation
in man and woman, see Chapter 18.
5. Not necessarily lovers in the usual erotic sense, but in the
fundamental, erotic sense of making love by coming into union with
another. Eros is a primal energy and desire for union with everything that is true, good, and beautiful.
For an excellent exposition of the nature of lovers see William
McNamara, *Mystical Passion: Spirituality for a Bored Society* (New

York: Paulist, 1977), especially Chapter 6, "From Romance to Mysticism."

6. The following three stages in relationship generally correspond to those of which Anne M. Lindbergh writes so beautifully: the double sunrise, the oyster bed, and the argonauta--three stages symbolized by three kinds of sea shell. See *Gift from the Sea*, Chapters 4, 5, and 6.

7. Lack of integration in one's relationship to the sexual other--Anima, in the case of men--has far more consequences than a difficult marital relationship. According to psychiatrist-philosopher Karl Stern, it constitutes a predominant flaw in the intellectual history of the West. Taking care to recognize the pitfalls of psychologism--the reduction of human behavior to a solely psychological explanation--he analyzes the inner relevance of the lives of several great thinkers of the modern era to see how they related to their own Anima and what philosophical consequences seemed to ensue: Descartes, Schopenhauer, Tolstoy, Kierkegaard, Goethe, and Sartre. Karl Stern, *The Flight from Woman* (New York: Farrar, Straus and Giroux, 1965), Chapters 5, 6, 7, 9, 10, and 11.

8. Antoine de Saint-Exupéry, *Wind, Sand and Stars* (New York: Time Reading Program, 1965) pp. 209-10.

9. See Mildred Newman and Bernard Berkowitz with Jean Owen, *How to Be Your Own Best Friend* (New York: Ballantine, 1971).

10. Quoted in Lindbergh, *Gift from the Sea*, p. 94.

117

Chapter 8

THE DYNAMICS OF GROWING IN FREEDOM AND FRIENDSHIP

Nearly everyone wants to be free and to enjoy friend-ship. But many are apparently not willing to make the determined effort that moral growth requires. Others may fail because they do not know how to proceed effec-tively. Courses and programs in personality development, group encounter, problem-solving, and the like, can be helpful in the outward workings of self-development. But they give little guidance to the person's effort to explore, and to be at home with, the soul-radiated regions of inner space.

Love and good will are crucial, but not enough. Basic knowledge is needed. In preceding chapters, I have outlined *where* growth in freedom and friendship leads. This chapter offers a few basic ideas on *how* to attain sexual freedom and friendship. Attention will be given to the importance of self-concept, the need for natural sexbirth, what to do about one's sex drive, the development of *intra*personal dialogue, and the art of centering.

Self-Concept and Sex-Concept

The crucial importance of sclf-concept in determining any personal behavior is a dogma of contemporary psycho-logy. A good self-concept bears good fruit and a bad self-concept bears bad fruit. People need strong, whole-some, positive and, above all, truthful self-concepts in guiding their behavior constructively and creatively.

Sexual behavior is no exception. A person's self-concept, for better or for worse, directs his or her sexual energy. This direction is done largely at a preconscious or unconscious level. Sexual energy can be increased or dissipated depending upon the creative or uncreative, positive or negative, character of the person's self-concept. Some psychologists claim that a person burns three times more energy when thinking negatively than when thinking positively.

This ecological phenomenon is surely at work in our sex-concepts--our self-concepts as sexual persons. There will be a vast difference in the person's behavior if he or she sees self sexually as a Playboy/Playmate; or as a blind instrument of nature's impersonal forces; or as a concelebrant of the primary goodness and most profound features of all being.[1]

Men, in our society, have special problems because of unbalanced self-concepts. They have been conditioned excessively toward the idea of *doing* things, performing, making, accomplishing, getting things done. They need to learn how to *let* things *be*, how to receive things without doing anything about them.

Unfortunately, deep within the space of a man's spiritual life, Adam has turned away from Eve. The Anima in a man--that beautiful capacity to receive in an unqualified way--is neglected or even avoided. Eve is alienated from the heart of a man. He finds it strange and difficult when he thinks of relating to his own inner power to receive. Therefore, he is automatically inclined to *take* rather than to receive--to take from his environment, to take from himself, to take from God, and, above all, to take from a woman--the person in his life who symbolizes outwardly his very own power to *receive* being in a pure and uncontaminated way.

Of course, a woman has a reciprocal problem. She is likely to be lacking in assertiveness. She is taught to give in, be passive, and often to engage in mock receptivity. She may "play it passive" in the presence of a man in her life who unconsciously symbolizes to her the assertiveness that she refuses to receive and integrate within herself. She may withdraw or "clam up" as a mechanism of escape. Or she may become an aggressive competitor with him, and, in that way, try unconsciously to compensate for a lack of integrating her Animus.

120

Both men and women tend to neglect or avoid the
deepest area of the self, because there is literally
nothing that one can *say*. We cannot *"make* something
of it" in words. This ineffable quality of the self is
a kind of unconscious scandal and stumbling block to
every red-blooded American pragmatist. Our avoidance
and ignorance of this preconscious self--which we can only
receive and cannot literally or practically express--is
Adam, turning away from Eve. It is existence breaking
away from essence. It causes the driving power of Animus
to go off on a mad, wild, self-indulgent spree in the
spirit and in the psyche of everyman. The not-OK Child
in us is having a quiet, all-pervasive temper tantrum
in the depths of our being. This avoidance and ignorance
of our in-depth self could be regarded as a major symptom
of original sin.

How, then, can a man or woman positively strengthen
his or her sexual self-concept? How can a cure be found
for the common refusal to accept the radical female (or
male) within personal nature?

On the one hand, we can probably do no better than
to point to the practical necessity of faith. The ineffable depths of our being can be infused with the redemptive power of God. On the other hand, we can open ourselves to the natural depths of our ineffable selves.
We can come to know the sexual life of Adam and Eve within
each of us. As men and women living together and educating one another, we need to make deliberate efforts to
encourage the growth of the marriage of Animus and Anima,
Adam and Eve, Giving Self and Receiving Self, within ourselves and our friends. A big step is taken when a person finally acknowledges this inner sexual life and permits the gradual formation of an in-depth sex-concept.

Natural Sexbirth

Today we are witnessing the exciting social movements of prepared (natural) childbirth, breast-feeding,
and natural family planning. Such developments are heart-
ening signs that sexual ecology is more than just a
dream. Nevertheless, the movements toward prepared childbirth and breast-feeding minister to the rediscovery
and support of emphatically female concerns in sexual
behavior. Men are very important in these endeavors, but
only a woman can give birth to, and nurse, a child.

People who are concerned with the natural flow of
human sexual energy are inclined to give first attention
to the highly complex and immediate needs of female

sexuality. A woman's sexuality is immediately more global·that a man's. Her whole body is an erogenous zone. Her sexuality is more *obviously* an all-pervasive condition.

But male sexuality may be just as all-pervasive as female sexuality, and just as influential in the health of the family. Through the development of human sexual ecology, we may come to see that the male potential for a rather global sexual experience is, at first, a latent one. It needs awakening. Women themselves may be particularly endowed with the power to bring out this male potential. But women first have to realize the male potential itself and their natural gift for cultivating it in a man.

The situation may be like the way in which genital energy is exercised differently in men and women. A young man is immediately and obviously attuned to the expression of coital-genital energy. Erections are common and the coital-genital urge is strong and insistent. A young woman's coital-genital drive is initially latent. Later in life, particularly through exercise, it can become as strong or stronger than that of a man. Men are immediately genitocentric in their drive; women are not, but eventually can become so. Similarly, a woman is immediately more global in her physical sex life; men are not, but eventually can become so, if they are willing to be helped by a woman. A man can learn gradually to identify with psychic and physical receiving powers--so immediate in a woman's sexual nature--without loss or threat to his maleness.

On the horizon of human sexual ecology we can look for a natural sexbirth movement, especially for men. Sex (sexuality) is like a child to be born within each person in the course of sexual maturation. Male sex, is, for the most part, unborn--at least, in our society. But a man can be taught to become aware of his Anima, his radical receiving power. He can be given instruction in how to think about himself as androgynous and as fully sexual within himself. He can be taught to let the Eve within proceed from the rib of his Adam. Anima can be regarded as an intimate friend. The Book of Genesis can serve as one of his sources of sex education.[2] The outward-directed and performance-oriented tensions and drives can be moderated within him by his learning to think differently, and by his letting them *be*.

Natural sexbirth requires intelligent motivation. The young man can appreciate how he is exercising his

Anima by letting his tensions and drives *be*, rather than by having to do something about them. He can come to realize that he is really *doing* something *by letting* them be. He is *performing* a profound activity of *receiving* himself.[3] His characteristically male other-directedness is given an interior depth by emphatically and intimately directing himself to the "other" that he is to himself. He is on the way to becoming his own best friend. Through the overflow of this interior friendship with himself he can become a more authentic friend to other people, male and female alike.

A natural sexbirth movement would mean the development of natural methods of sex control. Natural birth control methods, such as the temperature-rise and mucus-observation methods, depend upon natural sex control.[4] A man needs to realize that natural sex control is something that he can--paradoxically--*do* for himself, as a man, and as an autonomous sexual being. Natural child-birth is something that only a woman can do. Natural conception regulation is something it takes both of them to do. But natural sex control is something that only he can do for himself. It has enormous benefits for his wife and family. Yet the crucial benefit is found in his positive self-concept and heightened self-esteem.

A man's self-concept rightly requires something he can *do*. His self-concept should include a sex-concept that goes far beyond an ability for copulatory orgasm. Much more challenging and deeply natural is a man's ability and responsibility to *perform* acts of *receiving* his sexual tensions and drives without "doing anything about it"; without masturbating or without seeking a sex partner. He can be taught that this *receiving* that he *does* is *sexual activity*. It is a kind of natural sexbirth that only he can *do*. It is a kind of know-your-body-and-your-being form of sex control. It may not be the sympto-thermal method of conception control based on awareness of temperature rise and various other symptoms. It may not be the ovulation method of conception control based on mucus-consistency awareness.[5] But the practice of natural sexbirth is the receiving method of sex control based on friendship-motivation awareness.

Natural sexbirth is crucial to the friendship of man and woman, in marriage or not. It is more challenging and rewarding than natural childbirth or natural family planning.

Sex Drive Internally Expressed

Both men and women need to learn natural sexbirth. But the urgency is greater for men.[6] The man is the one who initiates copulatory union resulting in the unwanted pregnancies and the spread of V.D. that directly contribute to the sexual energy crisis. (Contraceptive intercourse, especially among the unmarried, merely hides the real problems and delays serious attempts to alleviate them. It tends to fixate people at the genitocentric level of sexual behavior and increases the social, if not individual, desire for abortion as a "back-up measure" of birth control.)[7] Only a man can be the main initiator of copulation, because he has the power to control himself in the presence of the erection that is necessary for vaginal penetration. A woman cannot rape a man because she cannot force an erection upon him, as he can force penetration upon her. Even the most loving and cooperative activity of coital union requires a special initiative from the man in permitting and sustaining an erection.

Nevertheless, both men and women need natural sex control. They need to learn how to receive their genital urges and drives, without necessarily "doing anything" about them.[8] The human genital drive and its tension is good for people. It reminds them of their great power and dignity in being able to share the gift of life. Whether it is ever activated or not, a coitional urge is, in itself, a thoroughly natural and human expression of one's selfhood. The coital-genital drive is not simply an instrument to be *used* when life is to be physically shared. It is likewise a natural physical means whereby we are constantly made aware of our responsibility to protect and nurture all helpless human beings, whether they happen to have been physically generated by us or not.

Our social responsibility is structured into the drive itself. Young people can be taught to realize the inherently social meaning of their sex drives. Once a person acknowledges that coital-genital urges are specifically social in their nature, he or she is very readily disposed to develop the ability for natural sexbirth.

The coital-genital drive, which can be so imperious in an individual, is basically a *physical*, *social* good. It is structured and directed *specifically* toward the generation of other persons, and *not specifically* toward the fulfillment of individual needs. When the coital-genital power is activated deliberately in the natural

124

way (through copulatory intercourse), it essentially disposes the couple to become parents physically.[9] But the child that could naturally result from this action is *ultimately* the responsibility of the community rather than the couple. As I mentioned earlier, both parents can die shortly after childbirth, leaving the child in the care of the community.

The coital-genital drive is a physical drive *within* the individual, but not specifically *of* the individual. Genital organs are *social* organs. They are unlike any other organs in the individual's body. The eye, for instance, is an organ *of* the individual *as well as within* the individual. When the eye is engaged in seeing and its ultimate objective is attained--the apprehension of color--it is the individual alone who receives the benefit. The community does not actually receive the color that is apprehended. Only *this* individual. And when he or she dies, the color-seeing stops. But this is not the case with the receiving of the ultimate good in the use of one's genital organs. The child--unlike the color or the sound or the flavor that are received by organs which are specifically *of* the individual--continues to be received by the community.

Natural sexbirth, which is a giving birth to nature's procreative power within, is a serious social responsibility on the part of the individual. He or she is naturally created to hold carefully within himself or herself the human community's generative trust. *Having* the drive is not necessarily the same as *receiving* it. Only when the drive and the tension accompanying it are consciously received just as they are, without manipulation, is the individual able to act responsibly with this community trust.

Sex drives and sex emotions, like inner movements such as anger and fear, need to be acknowledged and expressed. Every emotion needs expression--at least internally to oneself.[10] Not to express an emotion is to repress it, to deny it a place in consciousness where it naturally tends to go. Repression is the unconscious, but very effective way, of refusing to admit or to receive the existence of a drive or an emotion.

But expression does not mean exploitation. We need to learn where the impulse itself desires to go. Human impulses and drives are naturally designed such that they do not need to be given overt expression. Overt expression, such as shouting loudly in anger at someone who has been mean and hurtful, is something for a person to decide to do or not to do in accord with reason and will. What the anger impulse demands is not overt expression but conscious acknowledgment--at least to oneself--that one is angry.

Similarly, with respect to impulses and drives of our genital and erotic orientations, we need to acknowledge consciously their presence and express how we feel-- always to ourselves, if not always to others. On the one hand, we should not repress or deny their existence. On the other hand, we should not necessarily give them overt expression in word or deed. We should always try to let our emotions be internally expressed in our consciousness. For instance, a man might say inwardly to himself, "Oh, is she gorgeous, and would I ever like to hold her in my arms!" A woman might think, "Hmm, what a man for me!"

Internally expressing one's drive is not the same as an *intention* to express it outwardly when an opportunity arises. For instance, one could say to oneself something like this: "I would *like to* fantasize erotically and get rid of this physical tension by masturbating." One does not intend to act, but simply *admits* the desire. That would be giving internal expression to one's strong genital and erotic impulses, and would give them credit for being what they are without intending to actuate them. But to say to oneself, in effect, "If I get a chance today, I'm going to get rid of this tension by masturbating," is to intend something well beyond the nature of the drive itself. The *intention* here is not simply to permit an internal acknowledgement of the drive but to perform an external expression of it in an exploitative manner. The external expression of a genital drive has complex ecological requirements that go well beyond the relatively simple receiving of it within conscious life. (Of course, one may also abuse one's sexual [sharing] nature internally, such as by artificially stimulating erotic fantasies with the use of pornographic material, without ever intending to perform any overt action.)

The reception of one's genital drives and erotic feelings may seem to be simple. But many people have great difficulty in receiving them. Repression on the one hand and exploitation on the other seem to be much easier than simple receptivity. One cannot deny that lack of good will and an inclination to short-cut nature is very influential. Yet, the problem is much more complex and profound. People lack the knowledge of what is going on. They do not know the meaning of genital or erotic feelings. These factors also contribute to the difficulty of attaining freedom and confidence as a sexual person.

Boys and girls need to know their spiritual, mental, and psychic sexual selves far more than they need to know their physical sexual selves. The practice of natural sex control, based on healthy, in-depth self-concepts concerning one's sexual being, is difficult and, at times, especially for young men, next to heroic. But men, today as never before, need heroes and a challenge to greatness--in sexuality and spirituality.

Our technocratic conquest of outer space continues. It is obviously a predominantly male accomplishment. But there is an air of futility surrounding these extra-terrestrial endeavors when one adverts to the massive needs for inner-space exploration. A breakthrough is necessary in solving the problems of human life. The challenge to life on this planet is immense and most urgent. Outer-space endeavor will continue; but it may do so as a symbol of the inner-space demands of the spiritual, intellectual, and psychic development of human sexuality, even more than as a physical accomplishment.

In the coming age of human sexual ecology, every young man can be encouraged to begin this inner-space adventure by becoming truly a receiver of his sexual energy and coital-genital drives. Space heroes will have to make room for many soular-energy heroes. Men, young and old, need to be liberated from the Masculine Mystique, in which a whole culture is devoted to phallic "freedom" at the expense of the most cherished values of human life and love. Every child can learn how to become his own best friend, his own deepest receiver and lover of the unique self that he is. Young men and women can be taught how to listen to themselves as to their own best friend, how to love themselves, and how to go into solitude with themselves in order to grow in self-knowledge at deeper levels of sexuality.

A Date with Oneself

In order to prepare oneself for genuine man-woman friendship, nothing is more important than to love oneself and to develop a friendship with oneself. Solitude ministers to friendship. Only through solitude can a reconciliation take place in the originally disrupted marriage of Adam and Eve within. Only through periodic solitude can this inner intimacy grow.

A young person can develop the practice of having
a date with self now and then. Even "going steady" with
oneself is not a bad idea for anyone, as long as it does
not mean cutting out other meaningful relationships.
Any two people in love desire to be by themselves often
so that they may enjoy, share, and grow together. Many
couples particularly enjoy something like a quiet, candle-
light dinner, alone together. These special dates nourish
love, young and old. It is even more important that, with
some frequency, *individuals* go apart and be alone for
awhile. Not in order to feed narcissistic tendencies,
but in order to develop the inner communion of self with
self. In that inner union with self, the person can commune more authentically with God and with all his or her
other friends.[11]

A young man, especially, should be encouraged to
meet and get to know his inner female self. The avoidance
or escape from women as persons, so common among older
men, begins in the home of oneself. Freedom with women
can only begin in the hearth of a self-esteem that listens
with simple receptivity and desire to the speech of his
God-given self.

Centering

The attainment of sexual freedom and friendship is
an art, as well as a gift. It can be taught to some
extent. Some people will be more ready to learn and more
talented. But everyone needs to be taught the practice
of centering one's genital and erotic drives. Centering
is crucial for sexual integration. Learning to center
is an indispensable topic for sex education in the future.

The centering process in the art of pottery-making
can serve to suggest what is to be done. Centering is
the key to success in pottery-making. Nothing can be effectively done about shaping a piece of clay into a vessel
that is both useful and beautiful until centering is attained. Once it occurs the artist can then open the clay
with certain hand movements and can move the clay upward
upon the revolving wheel, into the desired shape.

The beginner at pottery is inclined, however, to
start by taking a hunk of clay, throwing it on the wheel,
and then trying to get the clay centered or balanced internally by ever so slightly pushing and pulling it with
the hands. This performance is useless. The potter must
learn how to center the clay. Eventually, through a series
of frustrating attempts, he or she does learn. Often
months go by before a consistent centering is accomplished.

The potter learns to take the clay in hand and hold it
firmly, but non-manipulatively, on the wheel as it turns.
The potter must be patient and not try to "do" the centering. He or she does not "perform" the centering action, but learns how to let the clay find its own center.
In the presence and the embrace of the potter and through
the natural turning of the wheel, the clay centers itself.
Then the artisan can go ahead and shape it.

A young man or young woman is almost inevitably like
the beginning potter. The youth thinks his sexuality,
the stuff of which his life is made, can be centered by
manipulation and direct attention. A young man has special problems because his genital drive is so strong and
immediate. He is very inclined to do something with it--
manipulate it. He, especially, is prone to overt action.
He instinctively desires to make something of this drive
and to release the tension. But deliberate masturbation
or experimentation with genital intercourse is as futile
as trying to shape up the clay with no centering having
occurred. Such attempts always make the needed centering
process all the more difficult because they work against
the sharing nature of the genital drive itself.

The person must let his or her genital and erotic
drives be, and be themselves. These drives and urges
must be allowed to find their own center within his or
her total sexuality. One's sexuality must be allowed to
find its own center before it is shaped into a lifestyle.
Somewhat like the potter who patiently and feelingly com-
munes with the spinning clay, a young man learns to take
hold of himself and to persist patiently in dialogue
with his deeper, total self.

Somewhat like the potter in the act of holding the
clay firmly and patiently while it finds its own center,
the person can prayerfully receive--with his whole mind
and heart, and even in a sense with his body--all his
physical urges, emotional reactions, fantasies, ideas,
and even the buzzing confusion of contradictory inner
messages. He can receive them all as good in themselves,
just as they are. Our sexual nature with its beautiful
and mysterious depths, as well as its powerful physical
urgencies, must be allowed to find its own center. We
cannot adequately become centered simply by means of
direct, rational control.

Natural sex control, far more than natural birth
control, is an in-depth art. It involves working with
a mysterious centering activity. There are bound to be
failures on the way to the attainment of practical success

in the art of sexual expression. Yet, the heart of the
method of natural sexbirth is itself practically a non-
method. As the good potter can only receive the centering
of the clay from the spinning clay itself, so the authentic practitioner of natural sexbirth can only receive
the centering of his or her sexuality from deep within
the self--well beyond the relatively superficial area of
strict rational control.

But once centering occurs--and to the extent that
it occurs--self-control in relating as a totally sexual
person to members of the other sex can take place with
remarkable freedom. When the clay is centered, the potter can bring it up into any one of many forms and shapes.
Similarly, when a person is really centered sexually, he
or she can freely choose to live a life of many different
friendships with others of the same and the other sex,
consonant with his or her vocational choices and commitments. (The key to personal freedom and integration is
the capacity to use one's powers in the service of commitment. It includes the conscious ability to activate
or not to activate these powers.)

The power of centering is crucial in disposing a
person to love sexually every person he or she meets.
Being personally centered is a necessary condition for
another kind of centering--centering with others. The
person who really loves is one who can readily let the
other become a center of radical concern--whether in a
conversation or in the total network of an ongoing relationship. For a sexually mature person everyone, including himself or herself, is a unique center for worldwide
concern. The freedom to let other people be individually
and communally true centers of the whole world within
one's consciousness and devotion is the mark of sexual
maturity.[12]

The contemporary sexual energy crisis has developed
because people have never really learned to attain the
mutual centering at the heart of their own sexuality,
to which they were called by receiving the gift of being.
Every person, therefore, who lets his or her sexuality
do its own centering might be said to take a giant step
for mankind in solving the sexual energy crisis.

NOTES

1. These general characterizations of sexual-concept represent the three basic kinds of such concept that tend to fall under the Child-Parent-Adult classifications. Playboy/Playmate is a self-concept that tends to exaggerate immediate gratification or else tolerates the postponement of gratification for the sake of a limited, though intense, kind of pleasure: genital orgasm ("the only true payoff"). It is a Child sex-concept. The idea that one is sexually the tool of nature's blind forces beyond one's significant control tends to exaggerate the dictates of the non-self (the other-than-self) in the regulation of one's sexual activity. It is a Parent sex-concept. By recognizing, and growing in conscious participation in, the ontological foundations for being sexual, a man and woman celebrate together the goodness of each and every being and tend to transcend the biases toward self and others, indigenous to the other sex-concepts, while integrating what is good and true about each of them. They develop an Adult sex-concept, which includes and moderates the other two.

2. Scriptural sources for sex education abound. But they cannot be regarded as *the* source of sex education, and they must be meditated on, and integrated with, secular sources and philosophical reflection. Fundamentalist usage of biblical texts would seem to be one of the critical ways in which we can constrict our notions of sexual maturity. Such rigid and unthinking application has often done considerable damage to the natural process of sexual self-knowledge. However, today we have a widespread attempt to repair the damage by a rigid and unthinking application of the theories and ideologies of sexologists and researchers whose world-view of human nature often seems to be even more decidedly canalized than their perspective on human sexuality itself.

3. A discussion on how this liberating process can occur is given by M. Joyce in *How Can a Man and Woman Be Friends?* Chapters 3, 4, and 5.

4. In these methods—commonly known as the basal body temperature method and the ovulation method—periodic abstinence from coital intercourse is only the ostensible side of the sex control. The underlying features of sex control include the couple's positive attempts to communicate effectively on all levels of personhood and on the total spectrum of common concerns with respect to each one's sexual behavior. The most important basis for the sex control is found on the level of communion that the couple can grow into as two sexual persons sharing their whole being, independent of coital-genital functioning. This communion is experienced in simple and meaningful touches, loving and tender embraces, and meaningful conversations, with or without attempts at genital gratification. Further discussion of these methods is given in Chapter 13.

5. In these natural methods of conception control the husband can participate by helping his wife record her signs and by thus observing the couple's fertility. NFP instructors like to convey the idea that fertility is a conjoint reality (hers + his = theirs).

Nonetheless, the primary agent of these methods is the woman. In natural sexbirth, the individual (man or woman) is the primary agent of awareness.

6. In my opinion, men are generally much less free about sex than women. Men are much more likely to take their erotic-genital urges too seriously and to fall for the latest form of rationalizing them. Regarding the male plight in the spurious sexual revolution of our time, Merle Shain has many incisive comments. For instance, on the "sexual revolution" she remarks: "Once we couldn't speak of sex and now we can't speak of love, and strangers go to bed together instead of shaking hands." *Some Men Are More Perfect Than Others* (New York: Charterhouse Books, 1973), p. 28.

7. On the relationship between the widespread dissemination and use of contraceptives and the legalization of abortion as a method of birth control sociologist Paul Marx makes a strong case for an existential connection. See his "Contraception: The Gateway," *International Review of NFP*, 1 (fall 1977):276-78. Leaders in the movement to spread contraceptive intercourse recognize very well that the demand for abortion follows the widespread practice of contraception. (Each contraceptive method has a significant failure rate.) Guttmacher, Tietze, Potts, Bungaartz, Schearer, and others have pointed out the connection. Of course, many individual couples do resist the cultural drift in this direction, because they allow themselves to see the difference between preventing a life and killing a life.

8. On the internal expression of the sex drive, see M. Joyce, *How Can a Man and Woman Be Friends?* pp. 24-47.

9. The implication here is that any *deliberate* exercise of one's genital powers that does not include the possibility of attaining, through the action itself, the specific purpose for which it obviously exists is an anti-natural activity. One is acting against the natural fertility of the act. And to act against the natural (even though not exclusive) purpose of an act is to act against the Composer (the One who created it) as well as against the person whose act it is. I do not intend to imply that involuntary genital activity (conscious but accidental, or unconscious as in nocturnal emissions) is in any way unnatural. That is why deliberation is emphasized. Voluntariness is essential for morally significant behavior.

10. The philosophical foundation for this claim is the innate goodness of all emotions. No emotion as such is bad. All emotions and psychic movements are good, just as all bodily and spiritual instincts and processes are good. There are no evil processes to the body, to the mind, or to the spirit. It is people who make "dirty parts" or "dirty thoughts" by regarding something good and natural as bad or by treating it badly through irresponsible behavior (commission or omission of certain ways of behaving).

This philosophical conviction concerning the goodness of all emotions was expressed 700 years ago by Thomas Aquinas. An integration of the rational psychology of Aquinas with contemporary psychotherapeutic practice, in which the inviolable goodness

of all human emotions is affirmed both theoretically and practically,
has been done by Anna Terruwe and Conrad Baars in *Loving and Curing
the Neurotic: A New Look at Emotional Illness* (New Rochelle, N.Y.:
Arlington House, 1972); *Healing the Unaffirmed: Recognizing Deprivation* (New York: Alba House, 1976); and Baars, *Feeling and Healing Your
Emotions* (Plainfield, N.J.: Logos International, 1979).

11. The special efficacy of solitude is its power to dispose the
person for communion as distinct from communication. Communion is
an abiding, continuous spiritual unity with someone. Communication
is a special, discrete interaction with someone. Communication can
be only as effective as it flows from an implicit communion in
which it is grounded. On the difference between communion and communication in human sexuality, see M. and R. Joyce, *New Dynamics
in Sexual Love*, pp. 28-30, and 58-61. On the essential meaning of
solitude for contemporary activists, cf. William McNamara, *The Human
Adventure: Contemplation for Everyman* (Garden City: Doubleday,
1974).

On listening to God with one's whole being--emphatically a power
of our Anima--John Powell offers a personal testimony in *He Touched
Me* (Niles, Ill.: Argus Communications, 1974), pp. 70-82. Catherine
de Hueck Dougherty offers a similar example of radical listening
in her book on the Russian tradition of contemplative solitude,
Poustinia (Notre Dame, Ind.: Ave Maria Press, 1975).

12. An excellent exposition of the power of sexual centering--
without using the term--is the discussion of John McGoey, *Through
Sex to Love* (Toronto: Gall, 1976), especially Chapters 5, 6, and
7 on "The Sexual Emotions," "Understanding Sex," and "The Power
to Love."

Part   III

LOVE AND MORALITY

Chapter 9

PERSONAL ACTS

Physical growth can occur only through individual acts of eating and drinking. Bodily health is maintained, enhanced, or weakened through individual acts of food consumption and exercise. Physical well-being can only be present by constant attention to particular actions of the individual. One cannot simply *will* physical health. A healthy attitude is not enough. The person must engage in specific behavior that will determine largely whether or not--and how well or poorly--the person will live as an organic reality.

Similarly, psychic and spiritual growth can occur only through individual acts of the person. Just as a small child needs to exercise his undeveloped power to walk by individual acts of walking, so this child needs to exercise his other undeveloped powers, such as the emotive and rational powers, by giving them individual acts of direction. Persons are self-directing creatures at all levels of their being.

Traditionally, moralists have distinguished between human acts and acts of man. Human acts are those actions that proceed from both knowledge and free will. Acts of man are all other acts; those that do not proceed from knowledge and free will, such as breathing, sleeping, metabolizing, and even those acts which proceed from emotional and spiritual powers--such as impulses of anger, love, aversion, or any thoughts, imaginations and tendencies that arise before the person is aware of them.

Human acts can be called personal acts because they are acts that involve the presence of the person to himself or herself. They require conscious, self-reflective attention and some degree of freedom to let them be or to direct them. Acts of man can be called non-personal acts in that the person is not present to the acts, although he or she is the one from whom they are proceeding. The person does not consciously and freely advert to such acts. They are acts of the person (person-acts), but not personal acts.

If a person is going to grow in freedom and potential for friendship, he or she will do it only by engaging in countless personal acts, in which the spiritual powers of the human person (known as intellect and will) are deliberately exercised. It is not enough just to *be* a person. Intellect and will, as well as brain, heart, liver, and lungs, can be quite active without a high degree of self-conscious and self-directive action. Not only performing deliberate acts of doing what is against one's nature, but also failure to do much deliberate activity will impede, retard, or even kill one's growth in freedom and potential for friendship. The abiding attitude and habit of *sharing* things and one's very self with others can only be developed and maintained by constantly acting with the deliberate intention of being personally present in one's individual actions.

When we act with deliberate intention to do what we know we are doing--and thus are not being forced into an action--we are, to that extent, *personally present* in the action. The action is an expression of our freely-choosing, destiny-making self. It can be separated neither from the self who is doing it nor from the extent to which it brings this self in the direction of a particular moral (spiritual) destiny. When a person freely engages in shoplifting he or she not only "does shoplifting" but *is* a shoplifter to some real extent. The person *is* in his or her acts.

These morally significant acts (as well as all other acts of the person) do not "hang on" the person. They inseparably flow from and really help constitute the person as a self-determining being. Only a distinct act of sincere regret and intent to amend the effects of one's action can remove the person from *being* a shoplifter. That act of authentic repentance changes the person himself or herself from one condition of being to another. Like the earlier act of shoplifting, the act of sincere, purposeful regret affects the being of the person who is present in it by *being* it.

138

Just as the *movement* of one's fingers is not merely something the person does, but is a vital part of the person himself or herself--along with the fingers them- selves--so the deliberate act of any part of one's being, through the specific mediation of intellect and will, is a vital part of that person--along with all of the powers through which it occurred.

A *human* person is a very complex, as well as pro- found, creature. Such a person may be distinguished from any other kinds of created person--the non-complex, but profound beings that the Christian tradition has called angels--by noting the brain and the organismic powers of nutrition, growth, procreation, and self-repair. The sexual freedom of this person as well as the functional capacity to be a friend can develop only in and through individual acts of knowing, willing, desiring, and relat- ing to reality in a self-reflective and self-directive way. A human person--as distinct, perhaps, from some exclusively spiritual being--does not determine himself or herself as a whole and at once. Self-determination is normally accomplished only in and through particular acts. Even in the slightest of personal acts the person is self-determining to a certain degree.

The Person and His or Her Acts

Why are even the least of one's personal acts-- slightly conscious and deliberate--self-determining? Because they determine *who* the person will be, not just *what* he or she will be. *What* a person is, is not deter- mined by him or her, but by nature and the author of nature. Nature is continuously acting within the person making him or her to be *what* he or she is. The flow of blood in the veins, the flow of nerve energy, the spon- taneous activity of the emotions, indeliberate acts of knowing and willing--these and innumerable other non- personal acts--ceaselessly make the person to be *what* he or she is. But every conscious, deliberate act of the person--however weak or strong--has a proportionately determining influence on *who* the person *will* be. This kind of act determines what his or her *destiny* will be *as a person*, not simply as a being.

Who the person *will be*, of course, is *not* the same as who the person essentially *is*. The person is this particular human being and will always remain such. John is John is John. Nancy is Nancy is Nancy. But the ul- timate destiny of John *as a person*, as a being capable of self-determination, is necessarily in John's hands-- or, more accurately, in *how* John freely exercises his

139

personal powers of intellect and will. John does not determine John to be John, but he does determine John to be uniquely loving or unloving, and friend or foe of all being, including himself. Who will Nancy be? What kind of unique destiny is she working out for herself? Will she be a unique instance of love or of hatred for God?

By our personal acts, then, we generate or beget our moral being. We have become the kind of person we are by our past willingness to do certain kinds of things--although, paradoxically, we might not be always quite willing to admit, even to ourselves, that this is what we have done and continue to do.

Acts are the fruits of the being. "By their fruits you shall know them." A thief is known by his acts of stealing. A murderer is known by his acts of murder. A saint is known by his acts of love. In and through his or her acts, a person is self-determining. As a fruit tree "determines" its destiny in the orchard by bearing good or bad fruit or no fruit at all, so a person determines his destiny in the community of creation by the *quality* of his or her personal *acts*.

People are obviously a mixture of good acts and bad acts (or not-so-good acts). A single act of deliberation does *not necessarily* determine one's *whole* destiny. Even many bad acts or many good acts do not necessarily do so. But they do count. Each act contributes to the fundamental attitude or life-direction of the person. Some contribute much more than others. But all are significant. Every personal act stays with the person for life, unless it is somehow revoked by other self-determining actions. Specifically human (personal) acts are--unlike those of simply material beings--states or dynamic conditions which last as long as the person lasts or until they are deliberately changed.

The fundamental life-direction of the person is crucial. This basic direction is an attitude that might be likened to the "attitude" of a space-capsule as it streaks from outer space toward the atmosphere of the earth. An angle (attitude) of too many degrees in one direction or the other dooms the astronaut. The capsule, upon striking the atmosphere, will either flip around and burn up or bounce off and be lost in space forever. Even the slightest forces in the right or wrong direction exerted upon the "attitude" of the craft can be decisive upon impact.

Similarly, the slightest degree of conscious, deliberate activity can be crucial in the destiny of a human
person. The impact of death can hardly be overestimated.
The mysterious and inscrutable character of his or her
personal life-attitude--known accurately only to the
person's Creator--is very likely critical at that time.
Even the slightest personal acts in the right or wrong
direction could alter the person's fundamental attitude
toward reality just enough to be decisive at death. (This
strictly rational reflection is supported by Christian
belief.)

In reflecting on the nature of a person and his or
her acts, one can readily see how the acts can all be
said to be *within* the person. The person is regarded
as the *whole* being, much greater than even the "sum" of
his acts. The acts can be thought to take place within,
and yet radiate from, the person.

But it is also true to say that the person is *within*
his or her acts--at least, within the personal acts:
those that emanate to some degree from knowledge and a
freely-directive will.

The person is present within his acts somewhat as
the soul is present within the body. The soul is not
"inside" the body, but within it in such a way as to
make the body *what* it *is*--this unique human body. In
fact, the *whole soul* is present, by its determining power,
in each cell of the body, not just in the body generally.
It is the whole soul that determines each cell to be a
human cell, not an animal cell, and to be John's cell,
not Nancy's cell.

So, too, the *whole person* is present within the whole
"body" of personal acts. The whole person (self) is within each one of his or her acts, making them to be what
they are as self-determiners. Thus, while it is true
that in knowing someone we know his or her self, it is
also true that we know this self in each self-determining
action.

The Moral Nature of a Personal Act

Every person's act is a moral act to the extent
that it is done freely and with an awareness of its relationship to what is right for a person to do. The person
adverts in some way to the goodness or badness of the
action. Before or during the action the individual realizes, however vaguely or clearly, that the action is something by which he or she is determining self for the

141

better or the worse. Every moral action is a commitment
to personal destiny.

But each deliberate act--no matter how weak or how
strong--is guided by two basic points of reference: natural structure and personal conscience.[1]

The ultimate point of reference in any moral act is
the natural structures, tendencies, and purposes of self
and others as they enliven the person in acting morally--
the Creator's dynamic, stable sources for intelligent
human action.

The proximate reference point is the person's knowing
power itself in so far as it judges that this particular
act is springing forth from these sources or thwarting
them. The person uses his or her power to know, in order
to evaluate whether or not a particular action would or
does enhance or diminish participation in the goods of
human and personal nature. This function of intellect
traditionally has been called conscience. It is the
proximate guide to moral action.

Part of what we call conscience is the remarkable
ability to encompass the total range of factors proper
to a chosen action, and to do so in an instant or a very
short time. The other part of conscience is the ability
to make a judgment, in the light of all relevant factors,
concerning whether the proposed act is morally good or
bad, and to what degree. Conscience also functions in
these ways after the act has occurred and is then the
activity by which one is reminded of the goodness or badness of the act, such that this act can serve as a model
for future acts or as the occasion for a change in behavior.

Every personal act, then, is designed or structured
with a built-in tendency to participate, through the mediation of conscience, in the fundamental goods of the human
person within which he or she dynamically exists. The
person's conscience is not the ultimate guide for right
or wrong action. It is the proximate guide. The individual act should be done in accord with conscience. But
conscience, which is the activity of the mind judging
the degree to which a given deliberate act is in accord
with absolute ecological laws, should be guided by these
laws.

A moral act is good or bad as it fulfills or rejects
the guidance of conscience. But, although it cannot be
itself good or bad in the moral sense, one's conscience

can be *true or false* to greater or lesser extents, depending on how it actually accords with the absolute ecological laws of creation. There is evidently a moral obligation to do what one can in order to enlighten one's conscience and make it as truth-filled as possible.

The moral nature of a personal act can be appreciated by considering a particular instance. If John and Nancy are married and they desire to engage in coital union, their action will be morally significant in so far as it flows from their conscious, deliberate choice to do so (even if that choice was made in the past and now constitutes a habit) and is at least vaguely realized by them as an action having some personally good or bad aspects. They realize that by this action they will be determining themselves, at least to some small degree, for better or for worse. Obviously, if the action is initiated under the heavy influence of alcohol or in a moment of sudden, uncontrollable passion it may not be entirely imputable to them as a moral act. Passion, fear, mental stress, illness, drugs, and the like can remove or reduce the moral goodness or badness of an action.

In so far as John and Nancy initiate the activity of intercourse with self-awareness and deliberate intention, they will be adverting, at least somewhat, to the two basic points of reference for a moral act--conscience and absolute ecological law. They will consciously determine whether this act is in accord with their nature as created *by God*, not by themselves.[2]

Every moral action has two sides. A healthy conscience respects these two sides of *one* and the *same* act: the self-determining and the pre-determining. The self-determining side includes all elements of the action which the person himself or herself--as a deliberative, freely-choosing individual--actually creates or causes. The predetermining side includes all elements of the action which constitute the givenness of the action--the natural structure of the action (its absolute ecological requirements)--independent of what the freely-choosing individual intends it to be. If a person is going to improve as a person, it is very important to examine and to analyze both sides.

In the area of special ethics concerning sexual behavior, overattention to one or the other of these sides is notorious. Past moral theory tended to exaggerate the predetermining side. Contemporary theory tends to exaggerate the self-determining side.[3] A careful look at both sides is needed if a person is going to

avoid many pitfalls to growth in sexual freedom and
friendship.

The Pre-Determining Side

The content of *any* action is just *what* the action
is--e.g., an act of walking, or sleeping, or shoplifting,
or marrying, or bargaining, and so forth--including the
proximate circumstances connected with it. The pre-
determining side of the *personal* act is the very content
of the action in so far as it is independent of what the
agent (the person doing it) thinks of it or intends it
to be. Growing from this core of the predetermining side,
certain proximate circumstances can be traced that are
likewise pre-determining and independent of anything the
subject or agent can do to change them.

For instance, John and Nancy contemplate engaging
in coitional intercourse. The core of this moral act on
its pre-determining side is simply the basic nature of
the act of coital union itself. Their being husband and
wife is a circumstance that is intimately connected with
the pre-determining core of the moral act that they are
about to perform. The pre-determined dimension to the
total moral act includes this circumstance and perhaps
others that could change its moral character significantly.

Every personal act has basic structural elements.
The predetermining side of the content of the act always
has three dimensions: physical, psychic, and spiritual.
These dimensions are not only objective, but essentially
indestructible. The moral agent cannot remove them or
prohibit them from determining behavior to a great extent.
(As one wag put it, nature bats last.)

The threefold structure of the personal act flows
from the threefold structure of the person's whole being.
Every moral act comes from the whole being of the agent,
not simply from the physical part, or the psychic part,
or the spiritual part. Every moral act is an act of
the whole person. While some personal acts are emphatically more physical than spiritual, they still have a
spiritual dimension and a psychic dimension because it
is a *whole*-person who acts, not just a part-person. Similarly, there are personal acts that are emphatically (but
not exclusively) psychic. Others are emphatically spiritual.[4]

The act of coital union is an emphatically physical
act, but it is not exclusively such. The action is also

144

an emotional and a spiritual activity. Even in an emphatically spiritual act when, for instance, someone
deliberately rejects his or her knowledge of the existence of God, there are bound to be emotional accompani-
ments and physical effects. The person himself or herself may not recognize or identify such effects. Others
may not be able to identify exactly what they are. But
there is an ecology to the human act. With every move
of the will, the interrelationship of all three energy
systems causes distinctive changes in every area of the
agent. An analysis of John and Nancy in their coital
act *as a moral act* must take into account the physical,
psychic, and spiritual tendencies built into their act
by nature.

In an act of coitional intercourse, the sperm and
ovum physically gravitate toward each other, even where
there is no ovum discharged in the Fallopian tube. The
ripening of the ovum prior to the next ovulation is *part*
of Nancy's nature as a woman to *tend toward* receiving a
sperm in the tube whenever it might be present. Even
after menopause, when there is no ripening ovum forthcoming, Nancy remains naturally--if not functionally--a
sperm-receiving kind of being.

Willfully blocking the *natural* potential for sperm
and ovum to meet and interact would be a moral act against
the nature of John and Nancy and thus against the laws
of human ecology, unless it were necessary to correct
an already-present defect in the genital system itself.
The contraceptive pills that purportedly prevent ovulation are not used normally to correct an already-present
defect, but actually to *cause* a defect. Thus, the act
of using them is anti-natural in its effect. Voluntary
acts of using pills that cause cervical mucus to block
the spermatazoa's natural attempts to move into and
through the uterus--when the cervical mucus would naturally allow and facilitate such penetration--are likewise
causing a defect in nature where one had not existed before.

But if someone were to take a medication that was
necessary in order to correct a serious defect anywhere
in the body, and yet it had the side effect of preventing
the natural gravitation of sperm and ovum toward each
other, such a person would not be *morally* producing a
defect in the genital-coital system. The real cause of
the defect would be the cause of the illness that was
honestly and accurately being treated. (The presumption
is that the illness or original defect is a serious one
and is not a sinus infection or the like.)

This case is something like a more dramatic one in the moral sphere: a killing in self-defense. If a person kills an unjust aggressor during an attack as the *only* way to prevent death (or probable death) to self, then the action is not murder but defense of innocent life. The assailant, in perpetrating an action with intent to kill another, has actually taken his own life, through the unwilling, but necessary, mediation of the potential victim. On the one hand, the intended victim *physically* (in an unwillingly instrumental fashion) killed the assailant, but *morally* protected his own innocent life. On the other hand, the assailant morally (though "unintentionally") killed himself.

In evaluating the total moral character of their personal act, John and Nancy must take into account not only the emphatically physical dimension to the moral act of coital intercourse and its particular circumstances, but also the psychic tendencies naturally structured in the act. Coital union is an action that, in itself, has a tendency to fuse the emotional lives of its participants--despite some couples' intentions to make it no more binding than a handshake. This bonding-inclination in the psychic life of coital partners is especially strong in the woman. It can be rendered dysfunctional, as in a prostitute; but it is, nevertheless, a natural inclination structured into the emotive forces of every person. The stable commitment of marriage seems to be the only proportional kind of circumstance under which this inclination should be freely exercised--especially when this bonding-inclination is considered in relation to the other dimensions of the action: the physical and the spiritual.

Coital intercourse also has a spiritual dimension. Coital communion is an activity of *knowing* another person in the most intimately physical way. It is not simply copulation. It is a profound personal experience for those who would let it be so. This spiritual dimension of any personal act is the most difficult to distinguish-- not because it is so little present, but because it is so all-encompassing. We cannot tangibly apprehend it. But it can be intuitively recognized and known, without precise verbalization being possible. (I will discuss it in Chapter 17 on Parentive Sexuality.) Perhaps one might simply say that the spiritual dimension of an act of coital intercourse on its pre-determining side is its potential for transcendent significance, good or bad. The meaning that it actually *does* have (including the predetermining) belongs to the self-determining side of the act.

The content of the pre-determining side of a moral act always involves the threefold energy and tendency in a person: physical, psychic, and spiritual. The brain is the main bodily organ of human coitional intercourse. Along with the penis and vagina, sperm and ovum, hormonal activities, and other elements, the couple's brains constitute the physical basis of the coital-genital interaction. This physical dimension of the one, total personal act is the most obvious and analyzable. Yet, in the ecology of the moral act (See Fig. 2, Ecology: General perspective, p. 148), there is also the surrounding atmosphere of the psyche and the unfathomable inner space of the spiritual dimension, within which the most readily knowable (the physical) part is like the planet earth nestled in the vastness of cosmic space. Every coital act, as a moral act, deserves consideration of the whole complex of relationships involved on its pre-determining side.

But that is only the "half" of it.

The Self-Determining Side

On the self-determining side of the moral act there is likewise a content to be examined. The self-determining content is strictly given by the moral agent himself or herself. It is entirely dependent on the intention, motives, attitudes, and subjective circumstances created by the person's own ability to determine self, consciously and freely, for better or for worse, in and through the act itself.

The self-determining content of any moral act is just what the action *means* to the moral agent. (What does he or she propose to do?) It is quite different from the pre-determining content, which is what the action is structured to mean by nature and nature's author. But these two sides are complementary and cannot exist without each other. A personal action not only is and means something in itself; it means something to the agent. The action not only does something, but it does something for an agent who intends something which is either harmonious or disharmonious with its pre-determining meaning. In other words, the action always means *both* what the agent can possibly mean for it *and* what it is and does in itself.

The core of the self-determining side of a moral act is the person's own meaning for it--including attitudes, motivations, and intention. (See Fig. 2, Ecology: General Perspective, p. 148.)

147

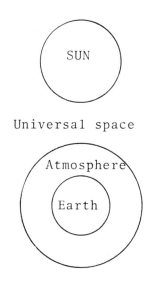

Universal space

(a) *Physical ecology*

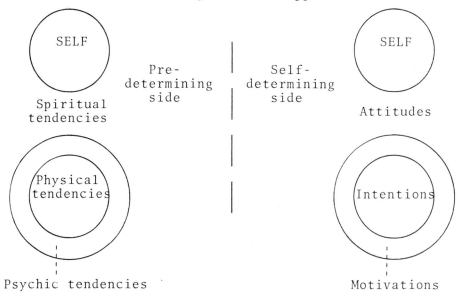

(b) *Ecology of the Moral Act*

Fig. 2. Ecology: General Perspective

In physical ecology (a) there is a threefold area of influence for the sun. In the ecology of the moral act (b)
there is a threefold core of action on both the predetermining and self-determining sides of a given moral act,
in which the self of the agent is always present.

148

Around this core one can find certain circumstances that the agent may or may not directly intend for the action, but which condition the act because of previous moral acts. A prime example of these self-determining circumstances is the area of unconscious motivation. If John consciously thinks he is making love to Nancy as the person she really is, then that is part of the self-determining *core* of the action. But if he has had an affair with another woman in the past, some of his motivation in the present love-making activity may unconsciously come from a desire to be with that other woman in this way. This unconscious motive is a circumstance that proximately conditions the action, even if it does not change its basic meaning. As a present fact, influencing the total moral act, it is an *objective* circumstance. As a fact which was caused by John, and therefore, in some sense is now being caused by him, it is a self-determining circumstance. However, it is not part of the core of the self-determining content.

The self-determining core has a threefold character. There are basically three dimensions to the agent's directly-willed meaning for the moral act itself: the intention, the motives, and the attitudes. They are, respectively, the "body, mind, and spirit" of the self-determining side of a moral act.

The intention of the agent is *what* he or she intends the act to be and do. It is the person's own objective or purpose for the act. It is the "body" of the act inasmuch as he or she is in control. The intention is the direction in which the person is "heading" the act. What does the moral agent want this particular act to accomplish? *Whatever* it is, that is the intention. Without the agent's intention, there is no moral act.

The word intention is often used ambiguously. So, it is important to point out exactly what is meant in this context. The intention is not what the act actually is structured toward, in itself. That would be the Creator's intention for the act. Intention in this discussion refers to the personal agent's intent as a directive force in the execution of the act. This intention flows strictly from the mind and heart of the agent. It is the *agent's* will for the act; not God's will. These two wills are *never* identical, but they are more or less harmonious or disharmonious, depending on the good will and intelligence of the agent.

Another possible difficulty with the word *intention* is that someone might confuse it with *motive*. Motives

149

for the given moral act are quite different from the intention. Motives respond to the question *Why* is the agent doing this act? What is moving him or her consciously, as a reason for performing the action? The concern is over conscious motivation--motivation which the agent deliberately lets enter his or her total meaning for the act. So, motivation is a second dimension of the self-determining side of a moral action. It surrounds the agent's intention very closely, but it has to do with the consciously causative factors.

Nancy's intention in the act of coital union with John might be to have an exciting and pleasurable time with John, as long as she does not get pregnant. So she uses a diaphragm or has taken a pill. *What* Nancy intends the act to be and do is her *intention*. But her doing it for the sake of pleasure--as well as because it is their wedding anniversary, or because John always feels better and acts happier the next day, or because she wants to try out a new "sex technique," or because she just wants to say "I love you so deeply"--is quite another dimension. *Why* Nancy engages in the act is her *motivation*. (Her motives may be many or few.)

The core part of the motivation is the conscious part. (As indicated earlier, some of the individual's unconscious motivation stands as a self-determining circumstance, which highly influences the act, but is not something that the person deliberately lets enter his or her input into the action.) What I am calling motivation can be termed the purpose or purposes for which the agent performs the action.

The problem is that Nancy can relate to the pleasure of her action as both an intention and a purpose. The pleasure is part of her intention in the act in so far as it is *what* she intends the act to be and do. She intends it to be a pleasurable experience. But it is a purpose in so far as it *consciously* motivates or moves her to engage in it. She does this act for the sake of pleasure.

Other purposes or motivations are more readily distinguishable from the intention. Doing the act because it is her wedding anniversary or because John feels better the next day is clearly different from part of the agent's intention or structural direction of the act. Different, but intimately related. Even though one cannot always pinpoint the difference in a particular case because of the often highly complex character of intentions and motivations, one can see *that* there is a definite difference between *what* one does and *why* one does it.

In the case of Nancy's self-determining behavior, this difference could be seen more readily if she always or frequently experienced pain during coital intercourse. On a given occasion, then, her intention in the act would include, as a part, the pain. But her motivation would not include the pain, unless she were being masochistic.

The motive or purpose of a moral act is sometimes called the end of the act. "End" is a word that, in this context, does not mean, "the last in a series." It means the purpose, that for the sake of which something exists or is done. But one must be very careful to distinguish the end of the agent from the end of the act. The end of the agent is a self-determining reason why the action is being performed. The end of the act is a pre-determining reason why the action is being performed. The agent's end for the act is not necessarily the same as nature's end for it. In the morally good act, however, these two ends may be the same. At least, we can say that the act is only as morally good as the agent's end or purpose approaches God's end for it. Or perhaps we could say, as in the case of intention, that the agent's ends or purposes should *harmonize with* God's or nature's--the absolute, ecological determinants.

A third dimension to the self-determining side of a moral act is attitude. Attitudes in a person are complex and run very deep within. They are extremely difficult to define. Yet, they are the most decisive factor of all in the self-determining area of a moral action.

For instance, John and Nancy could engage in coital intercourse without having a defect in their intention. Their intention might accord with both the open-to-love and open-to-life nature of the act. It might be good objectively. Furthermore, they could have only worthy motives consciously, such as saying, "I love you," and celebrating a family event. But if John's attitude were one of "let's get this over with soon, I've got a big day tomorrow," the moral quality of his act would be thereby diminished. Nancy's attitude in response to John's could raise or lower the quality of her moral act, too. If she were patient and understanding she would enhance the moral quality of the act, even though the action would not be as physically and psychically satisfying. If she were impatient or cynical in her attitude (or perhaps passive and masochistic) she, too, would detract from the moral value of the act, no matter

151

how satisfying it might be from a physical or psychic standpoint.

Attitude is an area that is extremely complex. Countless attitudes might be discerned as influential in a given moral act. The depth and breadth of self-determination is unimaginably vast in the area of attitudes. One might think of attitudes as constituting the universal inner space of the moral act's self-determining side. (Certain fundamental human attitudes will be discussed in Chapter 11.)

At this point, it is important to recognize that attitudes are the ultimate, self-determining conditions within which intention and motivations take place. Intention is *what* the agent intends the act to be and do. Motivation or purpose is the usually complex set of conscious reasons *why* the agent performs the act. Attitudes are the always complex and profound spiritual positions that the agent somewhat consciously assumes, which together determine *ultimately how* the action is performed.

If a friend says that John always treats Nancy like a queen, he may be referring merely to the mannerisms, customs, or even life-style involved in John's actions or he may intend to refer more properly to a feature of John's basic life-position toward Nancy. In so far as the manner in which John relates to Nancy comes from the depths of his mind and heart, it might be termed a moral attitude. It reveals something of the spirit of John's moral actions, with respect to Nancy and anyone else. Attitudes are universal moral conditions of the agent that he or she consciously creates to a significant degree and in the light of which he or she deliberately acts.

It is very important to realize that this third dimension involves only the conscious and deliberate portion of the person's attitudes. Like motivations, attitudes are largely unconscious. A person cannot be held morally responsible for the unconscious and non-deliberate depths of his moral action--except in so far as previous deliberate acts helped to condition these depths. The act is a moral act only to the degree that it is self-directive.

In the mystery of human personhood one can easily be intentionally keeping oneself from deliberating on a wider basis of alternatives and conditions than one is, at the time, directly conscious of. In so far as the agent, in the midst of the moral act, is deliberately refusing to see attitudes, motivations, and features of the act itself that might require a change of course, he or she *is* responsible for these self-distorting conditions.

There is a vast grey area in every moral action that cuts across the entire field of the person's inner self. The human person is probably freer than he or she thinks. The moral agent is so free that it is very possible to conceal, even from self, real motivation, attitudes, and intentions, and to do so freely and deliberately. Even though, in such a case, one does *not* know *exactly* what the hidden features really are (Am I really being understanding with this person by not showing anger, or would it be better to show it even though I might be thought to "lose my cool"?), one is responsible for them to some degree. The responsibility is indirect and not the same kind or degree of responsibility as the clearly conscious kind. But it is very real.

This condition of deliberately suppressing suspect motivation and attitudes is something like the situation where someone deliberately takes too much to drink at a party and then injures or even kills someone while driving home that night. The moral agent in this case knew he or she was exceeding personal limits and also knew he or she would be driving home. The maiming or killing of the victim is morally imputable to such an agent. The moral wrong is not of the same kind as it would be if the agent deliberately and directly ran the car into the victim. But the moral wrong involved is much more serious than the bodily and mental mistreatment of self in taking too much alcohol.

The contemporary practice of saying that an action is morally OK as long as you are honest and sincere can be understood as naive on at least two counts. First, it disregards entirely the pre-determining side of a moral act. But, more tellingly, this individualistic subjectivism tends to disregard the supreme complexity and depth of the self-determining side. When a person respects both the pre-determining character of a moral act, with its roots in the mind and heart of God, and also respects the self-determining character of the act with its incredible depths, complexity, and potential for self-deception, there is hardly room for egocentric morality. Espousing subjectivistic morality is tantamount to being a grossly egocentric and immoral act itself.

No one, of course, should attempt to judge *ultimately* either side of a moral act. No one *can* do so. Only the

Creator and Sustainer of all being can do that. But we can and must try to judge, more and more accurately, *both* sides of the moral act for the sake of ourselves and for the sake of others who may seek our help. The least we can do is to acknowledge the complexity of our moral actions, to learn basically what they are and how they work, and honestly try to live in accord with the truth as we increasingly know it.

The Unity of a Personal Moral Act

Every moral act is, then, like the person himself or herself. It consists of "a body and a soul." The body and soul are co-essential. The one cannot be without the other. (See Fig. 3, the Unity of the Moral Act, p. 155.) So, two extreme positions must be avoided.

On the one hand, a physical, psychic, and spiritual action flowing from a person spontaneously, without any deliberation, choice, or voluntariness, cannot be regarded as a personal act, but as an act of the person. Therefore, it is not a moral act. Nor is it the pre-determining side of a personal act. It is, morally speaking, a "body without a soul": a non-personal act.[5]

On the other hand, there is no such thing as a personal or moral act which lacks a pre-determining structure, independent of the personal power of the one doing it. An act is never just an intention toward doing something, accompanied by motivations and attitudes: a "soul without a body." There must be *something* which serves as the matter ("stuff") of the moral act, a pre-determining side: a "body."

Traditional terminology, such as *formal* and *material*, might be used to designate the two sides of a moral act-- the self-determining and the pre-determining. This usage, of course, could easily be misleading. The moral act is an act, not an entity. In trying to characterize these two sides of a single personal act, one is forced to speak analogically and somewhat metaphorically. With that proviso, I would say that the self-determining side is the formal side (the "soul" of the act) in making the act to be the specific kind of act that it is: a moral (personal) act. The pre-determining side is, then, the material side: a moral act is a knowing and willing *of* something--some behavior, such as feeding the hungry, stealing money, providing for a family, hating God. *What* is willed or chosen is the matter or "body" of the act *as a moral act. That* it is *willed* or *freely chosen* (and

154

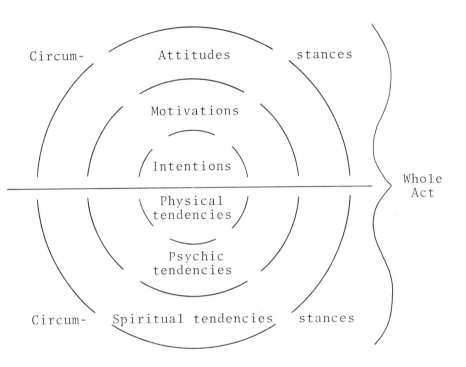

Self-determining side
"Soul"

Circum-   Attitudes   stances

Motivations

Intentions   Whole
                                         Act
Physical
tendencies

Psychic
tendencies

Circum- Spiritual tendencies stances

Pre-determining side
"Body"

Fig. 3. The Unity of the Moral Act

e moral act is an intrinsic unity of the pre-determining
de (body) and the self-determining side (soul). An act
nnot be moral (good or bad) without having both sides
 intrinsic parts. Even the threefold core of the one
de is analogous to the threefold core of the other.
ile the parts are not directly related (intentions are
t directly like physical tendencies; motivations are
t directly like psychic tendencies), they are propor-
onately alike. Attitudes :: motivations :: intentions
 spiritual tendencies :: psychic tendencies :: physical
ndencies. Circumstances radiate from and impinge upon
th sides of the one, whole moral act, but do not con-
itute its core.

155

not forced upon the person) is the form or "soul" of the act *as a moral act.*

In any event, the moral act, *as a moral act,* is *caused* by the person and no one else. Not even God is the specific cause of the moral action as such.[6] The moral agent works with the "matter" provided in nature by God. But he or she creates something that is entirel his or her work: the moral being of the self, the *desti:* of the person as a free and autonomous being. The person always enjoys or suffers the consequences of his or her moral behavior.

The moral agent can make something beautiful for God--or something ugly. The person's moral life as such will be the person's own creation--something unique, created out of the unique human nature (pre-determining side) that God gave to that person. But this moral work of art, which is entirely the work of the moral agent as artist, is open to evaluation. Just as in physical art there can be junk art--art that attracts or distract but does not inspire--so, too, there can be moral lives which are junk because they have perverted the "material and created obscene or commercialistic "figures and forms." These lives have been turned largely against their own nature (pre-determining side) through a misuse or a poor sharing of it and have created self-deceptive intentions or strictly utilitarian motives and attitudes (self-determining side).

In the history of moral thought there has been a propensity to become fixed almost exclusively on helping people "treat the materials" properly. Often theorists have grossly neglected the self-determining potential for morally beautiful lives. In our time, a great many moralists seem to be engaged in the opposite over-emphasis. They regard what people *think* about acting morally, but they do little examination of *what* is reall being done. Yet, a sound morality--a wholesome growth in freedom and friendship--requires that one "keep body and soul together." Both the pre-determining and the self-determining sides to the moral act are essential. Both are crucial to human sexual ecology.

NOTES

1. Cf. Thomas Aquinas, *Summa Theologica*, I-II, 21, 1.

2. There may be a legitimate sense in which we create our own tures. In determining our destiny we create a most important rt of ourselves. The art of *be*-ing the being whom God has given involves the great creation of our ultimate nature as a person--moral being. But this creation is a creation out of something--t of the unique, dynamic, and radically immutable (stable) nature--ven us by the Creator who creates out of nothing. I find no dif-culty in speaking of our self-creation, as long as we realize at the "stuff" of our "artwork" is our God-given being.

3. Many tend to use the terms *objective* and *subjective* for what am calling the pre-determining and the self-determining. I think is terminology is unfortunate mainly because "subjective" so readily nnotes arbitrariness--even capriciousness--and, in general, is garded as opposed to the "objective." Yet, subjective things, ch as a headache, are objective--they are really true, they really ist. Even a misinterpretation of a factual situation is itself uly what it is: a misinterpretation.
   In any event, "subjective" has come to mean something that is true or irrelevant. I am avoiding this connotation by using the pression that pinpoints the objective character of the moral ent's contribution to his or her own moral act: the self-termining dimension.

4. An example of a predominantly physical moral act would be hn and Nancy's coital action. An example of a predominantly ychic act would be their fantasizing how and when they would gage in their behavior. An example of a predominantly spiritual t would be a prayer that their coital union be blessed with a ild.

5. By non-personal I do not mean anything derogatory. The act generically personal, but specifically non-personal. The act neither good nor bad morally. It simply does not qualify as act that has moral significance.

6. The causality of God is quite different from the causality the moral agent. Of course, God can be regarded as the cause the *being* of the moral act--without God nothing at all would . And God is the cause of the intrinsic purpose of the action a total reality. But the human agent is the cause of the es-nce of the moral act as moral in a certain way--as *this particular* :ection toward self-destiny.

Chapter   10

SEXUALITY AND HUMAN VALUES

A personal act is any act done by the human being
in which there is knowledge and freedom of will. The
person directs the act by means of intellect and will.
The act is not something that just happens within the
person. Nor is the person simply the doer of the act.
The person is actually present in the action itself.

A person's presence in his or her personal acts
comes in degrees. The degree of presence is manifested
in the intensity with which the person engages all his
or her powers--especially the spiritual ones, intellect
and will. The more deeply the activity of the bodily,
psychic, and spiritual powers flows from the soul, the
more the action is an intensively personal one--for good
or bad.

Contemplation is the most personal kind of action.
It is human activity at its best. Contemplative activity
occurs whenever the person engages in a loving experien-
tial awareness of someone or something. The awareness
is so receiving and loving, so giving of self to the person or thing of which one is aware, that it tends to lead
naturally into a sense of the transcendent world, and
could even culminate in an intuition of God.[1]

The activity in contemplation is emphatically a giving kind of receiving. It is a female kind of sharing
and of being sexual. There is no need for any aggressive
or assertive kind of movements in the body, and yet the

159

senses are more open and active than ever. The whole emotional life is tranquil, but very much alive. And the spiritual life is afire with the goodness and the beauty of whatever is being so consciously received. There is little or no ego-involvement. The self is so present to the thing or person who is being experienced that one is not aware of oneself. There is an emphatic oneness with all being, and particularly with whatever is being consciously received.

Contemplative activity is the highest form of sexual activity. Contemplative seeing, listening, touching, holding, and enjoying the sheerly unique being of someone or something is sexually most fulfilling. When two people of different sexes enjoy each other in this giving kind of receiving--as well as receiving kind of giving--the potential for sexual fulfillment is greatest. As man and woman, they are structured to experience the world with co-relative emphases. The man is more inclined toward receiving kinds of giving himself; the woman is more inclined toward giving kinds of receiving him. She tends, not exclusively, but emphatically, to give herself by receiving him. He tends, not exclusively but emphatically, to receive her by giving himself. Authentic sexual behavior is primarily, but not exclusively, contemplative.[2]

In the context of this primary meaning of sexual activity, we can better appreciate how personal (moral) actions are necessarily sexual to one degree or another. Every personal act is, at its heart, a sharing of the gift of oneself with self and with others. The person participates in the essential structures of his or her personhood. How well the person participates in selfhood or personhood depends on how truly *shared* this selfhood is, in and through the particular act.

The degree of authentic participation in selfhood depends on two primary, reciprocal factors. First, how well does the person share in the gift of self by means of the total act in all its objective and subjective dimensions? In other words, is the person *receiving* well, from within, the rich gift of self while doing this particular action? Second, how well does the person share *(give)* self as a gift to others in this action?

Attitudes of authentic sharing--giving in a receiving way and vice versa--positively energize and enlighten one's whole being, including each individual act of participating in personhood. Attitudes of inauthentic sharing debilitate and darken both being and doing. One can participate in personhood very poorly by grabbing at the values of self or by exploiting others as one secretly exploits oneself.

Sharing self with self and others, as one lives very humanly in the world, begets further sharing and an opportunity to participate more deeply in human life by way of future personal acts. Such sharing activity determines or destines the person to a fuller and richer life. It is morally good. Reacting to, using, or exploiting self and others as one lives in this very human world begets more self-reaction, self-rejection, and exploitation. It lessens the opportunity to participate more deeply in human life by way of future personal acts. Even though it may be intensely personal, such self-*possessive* behavior determines or destines the person to a weaker and less meaningful life. It is morally bad.

The Eight Fundamental Goods of Human Personhood

People can *share* anything. Share an umbrella in the rain. Share a ride to work or a seat on the bus. Share a sunset. Share a meal. Share problems and difficulties in life. Share feelings. Share a home. Share children. Share values. There are as many things to share as there are unique people, unique relationships between them, and unique things. And whether others are present or not, the individual can share the thing with himself or herself.

Moreover, in every act of sharing a thing or an event or a feeling or whatever, one's *self* is also shared. In sharing *something*, one's own self is always shared with oneself. In the activity of the Giving and Receiving powers, the inner marriage of Adam and Eve is always celebrated.

But what is the content of our sharing activity? *What* is it about selfhood that we participate *in* or share *in* during a moral act? What does the act itself constitute in terms of self-participation and self-destiny? (In the preceding chapter, I indicated some of the essential elements in the structure of the moral act. Now, in order to get a basic understanding of the nature of self and human personhood, we turn our attention to the very self or person from whom and by whom this act flows.)

The *content* of our moral acts is *ourselves*. We participate in our human nature *by means of* individual acts.

This human nature is, first, God-given. We did not create it. Even if one holds that "man creates himself,"

161

it would be irrational to mean that man created himself as the kind of being that creates self. We did not freely decide to be the kind of being that creates self or the kind that does not create self. Our self-creation proceeds from a mystery-filled, *given* being with whose limits and potentials we are called to work in the art of being ourselves--the art of fulfilling our nature.

Human nature is, second, something common to all other such creatures as ourselves, whatever the time in history or the place on the planet happens to be in which they work at their personal destinies. While each person is unique and in no way the *same* as any other, there is a common *likeness* in basic structure, potential, and functioning, which is shared by every person. Common structures, potentials, and functioning of the physiological features of a person (such as those of seeing, hearing, breathing, remembering, and so many others) are but surface features when one begins to contemplate seriously the dimensions of our common human nature. Your eyes are not my eyes. Your dream life is not mine. Your intelligent response and capacity for wisdom is quite different from mine. But each of these features is common to our *kind* of being unique. Paradoxically, we are most alike in our deep capacities for being utterly unique. Such is our human nature, briefly and panoramically viewed.

When one surveys human beings, one can find many different kinds of commonality. In terms of ethical potential, we can cite certain fundamental areas in the structure of a human person. I suggest that there are eight primary areas in which every person attempts to work out his or her personal destiny. There are countless areas that are less than fundamental and that seem to stem from one or more of these eight areas. But there are certain areas that one must properly respect if one is going to *share* self with self and others, rather than simply experience this self.[3]

These fundamental areas for sharing in self and for sharing self with others are essential. They are basic human values that we need in order to have a healthy moral existence.[4] Just as in physical existence we have basic needs such as food, shelter, clothing, affection, personal space or territory, so we have in our moral existence certain basic human goods or values in which we participate throughout our life. These eight supreme kinds of human good are Life itself, Play, Aesthetic Experience, Speculative Knowledge, Integrity, Authenticity, Social Harmony, and Religion.[5] In any given personal

action an individual will be participating emphatically
in one or more of these Goods. But all of them are parts
of one's very personhood, which one can affirm or deny,
but which one cannot escape. These eight fundamental
Goods of being human and being a person are the basic--
not the only--human values in which we are all called to
share, no matter how unique and distinctive our individual
identities and personalities may be. They constitute,
in part, the basic anatomy of our moral existence. They
are as necessary to our moral lives as brain, heart,
lungs, liver, and other organs are necessary to our physical lives. These basic values are the values we most
profoundly share as human persons. They are true for
groups of persons or human communities, as well as individuals. To be human is to participate in these values,
individually and communally, for better or for worse.
They are the ultimate purposes for which anyone does
anything. They provide the basic ingredients of every
action that is a third-level act of freedom (self-
determination). One can participate in them well or
poorly, but one cannot avoid participating.

I will discuss the nature and meaning of each of
them briefly, indicating one or other aspect of sexuality
that especially illustrates our participation in the
particular Value itself. No one can comprehensively
define these Values because they are the major elements
of our total human environment. They form the basic
constellation of environments that it is the task of
human sexual ecology to understand. These fundamental
human Goods constitute the specifically human, uterine-
like environment in which all persons *as persons* live
and move and gestate their own beings.

Life

Everyone participates in the fundamental Good called
Life. All kinds of derivative purposes branch out from
this primary one: to preserve and to enhance life in
oneself and all other persons. The Value known as Life
includes a family of purposes, such as maintaining health
and safety, avoiding and removing pain, as well as keeping
oneself and others alive. (Even so simple an action as
brushing one's teeth is a participation in the Good of
Life.) Whenever a person is caring for the life of self
or others, he or she is revealing and participating in
a basic value that is an absolute good in itself--one
that cannot be used directly as a means to the attainment
of any other good.[6]

The most distinctive sexual dimension in this fundamental purpose of preserving and enhancing life is the
most obvious kind of sexual activity: the exercise of
one's genital and coital powers by which new life is naturally initiated on the planet earth in space and time.
Many members of the human community must include this
kind of sexual activity if human life is to be preserved
and enhanced in space and time. But the procreation and
education of children is not a *fundamental* or necessary
purpose for *individual* moral action. For the individual,
it is a secondary kind of purpose that stems largely from
the ultimate Value called Life.

Play

Every person in this world needs to do some things
just because he or she likes doing them. There is genuine
delight in the performance of the action. When people
play games and sports they are participating in this fundamental Good. Even if there is a struggle and stress
involved in the action, as long as it is done, to some
extent, as an end in itself, it is play. Unfortunately,
people often play games and sports in such a deadly serious way that they lose most of this sense of doing the
thing because they like doing it. The compulsive gambler
is participating very poorly in the basic Value of Play.
So, too, the puritan work-a-day mentality tends to vitiate
the fundamental Good of Play. When, for instance, coital
sex-play is engaged in by people who are doing it mainly
in order to procreate and who are even trying to suppress
the pleasure involved, the human Good of Play is being
poorly celebrated.

In matters of sex, we speak of "foreplay." Actions
of delight in each other done by a husband and wife, and
enticements to move into deeper genital arousal, exemplify
participation in the basic Value of Play. Coital intercourse with orgasm is an especially opportune activity
for sexually participating in this Good. There is a remarkable range of physical, psychic, and spiritual orchestration of the persons and their personalities in this
kind of activity within marriage. Outside of marriage,
the participants may feel as though they deeply participated in Play, but they cannot rightly mean it because
they have used another fundamental human good, the Good
of Life, directly as a *means* to achieving this experience
of play. Even within marriage, the most pleasurable and
exciting acts of sexual play are often not authentic
participation in the Good of Play, because the couple is
using the actions of play, and hence the fundamental Good

itself, directly *as a means* to another fundamental Good: Aesthetic Experience.

Aesthetic Experience

People want to do some things just for the joy of *doing* them. They likewise want to experience things that they have nothing to do about, just for the joy of *experiencing* them. Aesthetic Experience is the other side of Play. Play is exemplified by the artist who paints just because he or she loves the personal action of doing it. Aesthetic Experience is exemplified by the aesthetic admirer of the results of the painting, who views the painting just because of the delight that this experience causes in him or her. (The term *aesthetic experience* here does not mean necessarily something involving the fine arts. Even a common, pleasing experience such as enjoying a sports event on television could qualify as an aesthetic experience.)

Obviously, these two Values are intimately inter-woven in many cases. But there is a great difference in the orientation of the person inasmuch as he or she participates effectively in each of them. One can par-ticipate in both Goods simultaneously, just as one can participate in several or even all of the eight basic Goods simultaneously to some extent. But there is always at least a slight emphasis on one or the other of them.

The married couple who engage in coital intercourse both for Play and for Aesthetic Experience exemplify the intimate interrelationship of these two fundamental Goods. But if they engage in the action of foreplay and coital play rather as a *means* to get to the "pleasure part" than as a good in itself, then they are *using* the fundamental Good of Play directly as a means. Such action is bound to pollute the fundamental Play part of their personhood and by way of overflow will contaminate their participa-tion in other Goods, most notably Aesthetic Experience.

Aesthetic experience is authentic only to the degree that the participant delights in the experience as a good coming from an other-than-self. But if he or she is so intent on "getting to it!" the emphasis has been shifted to the ego-satisfaction rather than true self-satisfaction. Ego-satisfaction drains away much of the sexual energy-- the energy for sharing--which should be available to the deeper regions of the person in the depths of the self.

Aesthetic experience is a female kind of experience. Play is a male kind. In aesthetic experience there is a definite orientation toward *receiving* something or someone. In play there is the reciprocal emphasis on *giving* something to the world and to self. In fact, the specific kind of sharing activity involved when a person participates well in aesthetic experience can be characterized as a giving kind of receiving. It is an active and interested, self-forgetful receiving of someone or something. Play, on the other hand, can be characterized as an emphasis on a receiving kind of giving. It is the active and delightful projection or expression of self into the world--a projection valued as a good in itself. The major orientations of human sexuality in its depths are revealed in these two reciprocal kinds of basic human Value: Play and Aesthetic Experience.

Speculative Knowledge

Another ultimate kind of good for human persons is Speculative Knowledge. Any kind of knowing that is done as a good in itself, independent of whether it serves as a means to get something done, might be called speculative knowledge. In this kind of knowing we wonder what is the truth about something; we speculate on how something works, what it really is, or why it happens to be the way it is. We also enjoy the knowing process and whatever results are attained in response to our questions. If the knowledge leads to some practical gain for us--as it often does--that is incidental. In so far as we are participating well in this ultimate human purpose of Speculative Knowledge we are knowing for the sake of the knowing or the knowledge itself.

Exploring the mysteries of nuclear fission, learning about the depths of the human unconscious, and knowing or believing in the existence of God are instances in which this basic human Value is revealed and in which it is shared. But even learning about the newly arrived family down the street or getting to know the football scores from last Sunday's games could be instances of true participation in the fundamental human Good of Speculative Knowledge. As long as the knowing is enjoyed as a good in itself, this fourth fundamental Good is revealed.

Speculative knowledge is emphatically a receiving kind of knowledge. It requires a giving of oneself to a problem, in such a way that one is receiving knowledge simply, rather than doing anything with it. Speculative knowledge is a female kind of knowledge. It contrasts with practical knowledge, such as knowing *how to* fix an auto, parse a sentence, attract a mate, or prove the existence of God. Practical knowledge is knowing for the sake of doing. Practical knowledge is structured to produce something outward, even if only in the mind. Speculative knowledge is a doing of the knowing for the sake of itself. It is more inward.

A similar reflection is made in an analogous area of knowledge by other theorists on man and woman. Psychiatrist Karl Stern in his philosophical treatise, *Flight from Woman*, has tried to show that in every person intuitive knowledge is essentially female and analytic knowledge is essentially male.[7] Such a claim does not necessarily mean that women cannot be very analytic and men very intuitive. It does mean that women are naturally much more inclined toward intuitive knowledge and to occupations that emphasize it, and that men are inclined in the opposite way.

In any event, my suggestion is that both men and women are thoroughly giving and receiving, analytic and intuitive, practical and speculative in knowing.[8] In the depths of his nature, a man is essentially structured as a fundamental *emphasis* on celebrating all being, by way of a receiving kind of giving. Woman is the correlative kind of human orientation. Together they concelebrate and co-participate in all the fundamental Goods of life and in everything that they do.

Many men are functionally far more intuitive than most women. Many women are functionally far more analytical than most men. Many men are physically much weaker in lifting weight than some women. Many women are much less graceful than some men in physical movements such as ice skating and ballet. But the claim is that a man's way of being analytic or intuitive, of lifting weights, or of dancing is inherently different and complementary to a woman's way--even though we may not be able to point out this difference empirically or illustrate it graphically in many instances of male and female behavior.

One indication at a quasi-empirical level is that the men and women who are expert or who have reached the top of their profession in physical skills and arts show an emphasis with respect to giving and receiving, power and grace. In dancing and figure skating, when an artful couple are moving together one can readily tell who emphasizes power and who emphasizes grace. Both are very powerful and sure in their physical movements. Both are very fluent and graceful, too. But the man emphasizes power and the woman emphasizes grace in body movement.

Similarly, if one holds that body reveals soul and that there is a substantial unity of body and soul, then it is highly likely that there is a kind of mutual emphasis taking place in the structural depths of psyche and spirit proportionate to the emphatic bodily differences. Such a harmony would mean that a woman who is very analytic in her thinking, still does think analytically with an intuitive emphasis or leaning. And a man who is very intuitive in his thinking, thinks intuitively with an analytic emphasis in his intuitive act itself.

The rich personality is very adept at expressing both male and female traits, and can give and receive, emphasizing either one. Fixing an auto and attracting a mate are concrete actions that either a man or a woman can learn to do well, if he or she has some elementary facility with mind and hands. But the non-empirically observable depths of a man's way of going about either task suggests that he is celebrating life and all being-- unconsciously perhaps--by emphasizing the receiving kind of giving involved; and that the woman is approaching her doing either task by a reciprocal kind of emphasis.

Considering the basic Values which have been outlined so far, one finds that Play and Aesthetic Experience are correlative. Similarly, the fundamental Good called Speculative Knowledge can be seen as emphatically (not exclusively) female even as the fundamental Good called Life can be seen as emphatically (not exclusively) male.

Life itself, of course, is both male and female. But what is required in order to participate in the Value of Life does seem to involve an emphasis on the receiving kind of giving. We must perform in order to maintain our lives. We cannot simply receive our life. We must *do* something about it or else we lose it. Food, shelter, clothing, and other practical goods must be acquired. Proper health care requires the performance of innumerable tasks. In matters of life and death, such as when a person is about to drown in a lake, one does not properly counsel, "Give yourself to life, receive it just as it is!" That is the way to drown. One must *do* something, perform something, such as struggle to reach the capsized boat or *give* oneself to the *water* in an act of floating.

So far, I have briefly sketched four basic human Values. Two of them are emphatically male: Life and Play. Two, emphatically female: Speculative Knowledge and Aesthetic Experience. All four of these Goods can be called substantive goods. They form the basic content of all human action. They stand on their own and

168

do *not necessarily* place the moral agent in reference to self or to some other self. They are non-relational Goods.

But there are four other basic human Goods: Integrity, Authenticity, Social Harmony, and Religion. They are relational Goods. Integrity and Authenticity involve relationships within oneself. Social Harmony involves relationship with other creatures. And Religion concerns relationship with the Other, the transcendent, whom most people call God.

Integrity

Everyone wants to become a whole person. We want to be at peace with ourselves. But because we are so complex and need to grow in so many ways at the same time, we find within ourselves tensions and conflicts. The lack of integration of physical, psychic, and spiritual activity, and the lack of integration of many aspects within each one of these basic energy levels of the human personality is a primary concern for everyone. The right balance and proportion among all of our simultaneous activities is a fundamental human Good. We all participate in it with varying degrees of success at various times. Integrity is an essential need for moral development.

Much of our lack of Integrity comes from an inability or unwillingness to engage ourselves in times of stillness and solitude. We always seem to be so busy. There is often little chance for our powers and actions to become centered and fused. Integrity can occur only when the person affords self with periods of quiet, stillness, and receptive awareness. The person must learn how to *let being be*. Then the magnificent complexity of the self's structure can *be* itself, and personal activities can emanate from deeper and more centered regions in the mental, emotional, and spiritual life.

One cannot properly participate in Integrity as a fundamental human Good merely by piecemeal attempts to "get it all together." Of course, some kinds of practical work on this or that personality trait are necessary. But they are not the central activity that allows for effective participation in the basic Value of Integrity. Integration is emphatically achieved through intelligent attention to being still and being simply receptive to the total flow of life, without doing anything about it. As Anne Morrow Lindbergh indicates in her perceptive book on female integrity, the centrifugal forces, pulling

169

us away from ourselves in all directions, can only be balanced by taking ourselves in hand and receiving "gifts from the sea." These gifts are really gifts from the self.

Integrity, then, is a basic human Good that is emphatically female in nature. Integration of self comes emphatically, though not exclusively, through the exercise of one's Anima, the Receiving power within. Integrity comes through learning and practicing the art of centering. A person lets the inward sources and forces be themselves and they begin to find their own center.

Authenticity

Speaking and acting in accord with one's inner disposition is participation in the fundamental human Good of Authenticity. Act and attitude need to correspond. Authenticity is the more or less developed condition of living outwardly what we are meaning inwardly. Often this is quite difficult, especially when we are under pressure from parents, peers, authorities, clients, and others. Yet, no one likes a phony. We value people who have the courage to act out their convictions. Thinking one thing and saying or doing another is inauthentic behavior. All lying--the withholding or misrepresenting that which someone else has a right to know--is a violation of the fundamental human Value called Authenticity.

Efforts to participate effectively in this Good require doing something about our actions. Actions take us "out of ourselves" and into the world. From the personal interiority of attitudes to the external commitment of an outward action there is a vast territory to travel. One can easily lose the way. By the time an idea or attitude is externally conveyed it can be unfamiliar to the bearer himself or herself. People not infrequently think to themselves, "Why in the world did I do *that*, or say *that*?" An effort must be made to direc external behavior so that it accurately portrays inner disposition. It is not enough to know what you want to say and say it. One must learn how to say it accurately in accord with communication standards that exist outside the control of one's own personal desires.

Authenticity, then, is a basic human Good that is emphatically male in nature. It comes about mainly through an emphasis on exteriorizing interior disposition in accord with external as well as internal standards. Whereas the attainment of Integrity occurs largely by remaining still and being highly receptive like an ovum, the achievement of Authenticity emphatically involves going out from within and giving accurate representation of self to another, like the action of a sperm.

In the process of becoming more authentic, retardation occurs through lack of understanding how to communicate accurately and through weakness of will. Chronic patterns of self-deception also severely impede growth in authenticity. Many people suffer inability to deepen their participation in the basic Good of Authenticity because they persist in custom-laden actions which are not good, creative self-expressions of their own personal commitments as they concretely are. A man who insists on coital intercourse two or three times a week even during difficult times for his wife, late in a pregnancy, is not acting in accord with the commitment of heart that he has made through the marriage covenant. He exhibits a sexual impotence underlying his genital potency.

The inauthentic person, then, is an impotent person. In an individual person (male or female), authenticity is the primary sign of sexual potency, even as integrity is the primary sign of sexual warmth and responsiveness.

Social Harmony

The human being is a social being. We radically need other people and other creatures. We need harmonious relationships with them. While the fundamental human Good called Integrity involves harmonious relationships within the individual, the fundamental human Good called Social Harmony involves harmonious relationships with other creatures: especially people; but also animals, plants, and the whole environment of creation. (The word *social* is used very broadly here.) We participate in the basic Value of Social Harmony as we constantly attempt to develop sound, stable, and even intimately satisfying relationships with people and with all of the world's creatures. Social harmony is not merely a nearness or the fact of being in the same boat. Social harmony is ecological attunement--the attention to, and practice of, natural and harmonious interrelationships between all kinds of creatures.

This particular relational Good is like the substantive Good, Life, in that one must *do* something about it in order to participate deeply in it. Good ecology means constant practice--a going out to rectify, alleviate, and prevent environmental breakdowns. We cannot have the attitude, "Let George do it." Social harmony requires careful receiving (listening to) other creatures,

171

with the orientation of doing something for them and thereby actively supporting and improving our relationships. There is a critical dimension to social harmony that means receiving and letting nature take its course. But, if that is all that is done, the human ecosystem will eventually collapse. The life of creatures on the planet earth, like the life of the individual, is a constant struggle to maintain and enhance. In order to participate well in the Value of Social Harmony as in the Value of Life, a person must go out from himself or herself. Reaching out to touch other creatures is the only way to attain, secure, and ensure the beautifully human values of community and ecology.

Every family, civic group, nation, club, and other community of people in which there is a common good for the members greater than the satisfaction of any one of them and in which they each fulfill roles is an example of the fundamental Good of Social Harmony in action. This basic Good includes any relationship in which two or more people are voluntarily united for the sake of human values and not merely for the sake of achieving a goal. Every such community--no matter how simple or complex--can only be initiated and sustained by the active, outgoing participation of the members. When people stop fulfilling their roles, these communities grow weak and are susceptible to death.

The basic human Value of Social Harmony, therefore, is very similar to the Value of Life. In fact, it *is* the Value of *community* life.

Religion

Besides participating in their relationships with other creatures, the individual and the community have one other fundamental, relational need. People have some sense of a power which transcends them and over which they have ultimately no control. Their relationship to this power--even if the power is simply conceived as Nature itself--is a basic Value in human life. Generally, we call it Religion.

How one can best participate in this relationship is greatly disputed among the peoples of the earth. That it exists, however, is obvious from even a simple realization that we cannot ultimately prevent our death. Some power is great enough to overcome us in death, and is ultimately in control of everything in our life, except our freedom to say *yes* or *no* to what is happening to us

172

and the world. We can, of course, bless or curse the power that takes our life in the end.

In relating to the power which transcends every creature, our ultimate disposition must be a receiving more than a giving. What can we give to God that has not been given to us? Only our act of willingness to live as God created us to live. Even the *power* to make the affirmation of God's goodness and rightness, or to abuse it in an act of denial, is *given* to us by God. Our relationship with fellow creatures is primarily one of giving. But our relationship with God is primarily one of receiving. It is only in receiving that we are *able* to give. God receives our being, but emphatically gives it to us. We give our being to God, but emphatically receive it.

The fundamental human Good called Religion--participation in, and celebration of, one's relationship with God--is an emphatically female Value. The person's emphasis is definitely on a giving kind of receiving. The primary Jewish symbol of Isreal as the bride of Yahweh and the primary Christian sacrament of marriage, celebrating the Church as the bride of Christ, offer eloquent testimony to the particular sexual character of the basic human Value of Religion.

Correlatively, the fundamental Good which I have called Social Harmony--participation in, and celebration of, one's relationship with other creatures--is an emphatically male Value. True participation in the ecology of creation calls for us to emphasize as much giving as we can. Obviously, people who are gravely ill can only emphasize giving by intent. But that is the root of moral action anyway--intention. The spirit is willing. Willingness to receive from others--from people, animals, plants, the air, water, land, and so forth--is necessary for effective social harmony. Yet *willingness to give* to these other creatures makes the receiving authentic.[9]

The primary orientation in sharing the fundamental human Good of Social Harmony is *giving*: giving of ourselves, time, talents, and possessions. The *other* is the primary receiver in this basic ecological Value. While it is true that only in receiving from others--such as mother and father, teachers, and friends--are we able to give, it is even more emphatically true that only in giving to others--spouse, employer, employee, children-- do we receive the ultimate joy of *sharing* in the basic Good of Social Harmony.

173

The eight basic human Values are the wellsprings of
a sexually active life. People who not only participate
in them, but share deeply in them, are becoming sexually
fulfilled. Sexuality is part of the structure of each
of these fundamental Goods, and each one emphasizes either
the male or the female kind of sexual orientation as a
manner of sharing self within self and with all others.
In a very crucial way, human values are sexual values.

NOTES

1. This idea of contemplation is particularly consonant with the
perspectives of William McNamara, *The Human Adventure: Contemplation for Everyman*. On contemplation as the highest form of human
activity see Thomas Merton, *New Seeds of Contemplation*, rev. ed.
(Philadelphia: J. B. Lippincott/New Directions, 1972), especially
Chapter 1.
2. The performative dimensions of sexual behavior are also authentic, but not--strictly speaking--contemplative. Contemplation
is the deepest form of the activity of *receiving* someone or something.
3. The eight basic human Values are central to the general ethics
of Germain Grisez to whom I am greatly indebted. Cf. *Beyond the
New Morality*, pp. 64-74. In the characterization of these Values
below I follow his interpretation with some modification. The application to the area of sexuality is my own.
For another treatment of sexual morality in the light of fundamental human Values--but somewhat different from Grisez' general
theory and my particular application--see Peter Bertocci, *Sex, Love
and the Person*, especially pp. 25-71.
One might wonder, why eight fundamental Goods? These seem to
be irreducible Goods. Of course, someone might well use different
terms. But after reflecting on and discussing ethical literature,
one may find that all other goods or values can be best understood
as conditions for or derivatives of these eight. Goods such as
truth, beauty, freedom, and others are found to be *conditions* for
any of the eight. Goods such as marriage, fraternal societies,
nations, health care, sports, and many others are derivatives from
one or more of the eight fundamental Goods.
If a person is an atheist, he or she might well be willing to
acknowledge seven fundamental Goods, excluding Religion. Other
variations are possible. The justification for the eight is the
subject for a sustained treatise on values.
4. Again, I am using the term *value* as generally interchangeable
with the term *good*. *Good* stresses objectivity without removing
the aspect of subjectivity. *Value* stresses subjectivity without
removing the aspect of objectivity. *Value* also tends to suggest

174

a good that is somehow a means. This connotation should not be followed in the present use of the term.

5. I capitalize the first letter of these values in order to indicate their supreme objectivity. But I do not wish to imply anything like the supra-sensible Forms or Ideas in which Plato claimed the meaning of all transient existence was rooted. The intention here is to underscore the non-subjective character of these values and say that they have objective structural significance in our personal existence. I also wish to suggest that these values are the primary values from which all others flow and that no one can ever exhaust them, no matter how self-perfecting one becomes.

6. All of the fundamental human Goods are *absolutely*, not relatively, good in themselves. The juxtaposition of the word *absolute* with *good* in regard to these primary sources of ethical life does not signify God or the *Summum Bonum*—the *highest* (infinite) good.

7. Cf. Karl Stern, *The Flight from Woman*, Chapter 3.

8. I do not mean to imply here that analytic and practical knowledge are the same kind of knowledge. These pairings are inter-related analogously (not univocally).

Perhaps one way of conveying the point is by saying that, when an individual man thinks, he is inclined to be more analytic than he would be were *he* a woman. And when an individual woman thinks, she is inclined to be more intuitive than she would be were *she* a man. Similarly, if a man throws a ball, he is going to reveal more inclination toward power of movement than grace of movement than if *he* were a woman. And vice versa, for a woman.

9. These relational, fundamental human Goods find resonance in Jesus' summary of the Law: Love the Lord with your whole heart (Religion) and your neighbor (Social Harmony) as *yourself* (Integrity and Authenticity). All eight of these primary human Goods may be regarded as finite, indirect modes of participation in the infinite being of God—which is tantamount to being the eternal life for which all were destined (according to Christian theology). Yet these Goods can be known and delineated by the person's natural reason, working without any special revelation.

Chapter 11

LOVE AND MORAL HEALTH

The basic human values discussed in the last chapter constitute the womb in which a person acts as a person. They are the basic structure of the environment in which every moral act takes place. Every person as a human being in this world not only gestates in the womb of space and time as a physical environment, but also in the womb of goods that are necessary for spiritual sustenance and enrichment. The fundamental human Goods are the basic anatomy of the moral world-womb.

But if each one of us is morally nurtured by our participation in fundamental human Goods as children in a common womb, what about the structure of the children themselves? What are the basic moral "organs" of a person who is growing into a healthy life as a person?

We might distinguish two basic areas to the moral "organism." There is an autonomous area and a service area. Like the prenatal child, who has two areas to his or her physical self--the fetal and the placental--the morally acting person has an area from which each of his or her acts springs and an area which serves and sustains these acts as morally viable.

In this chapter we will consider the anatomy of the fetal*like* part of the moral self. In the next chapter we will consider the anatomy of the placenta*like* part of the moral self.

Today there is a strong inclination to regard the loving person as the moral person. One often hears that it does not matter so much what you do as long as you are loving. But what is it to be really loving? And what is the truly loving thing to do in a given case? Can rape be done with love? Can acts of genocide be done out of love? Genuine love brings truth with it. The truth of love--as a moral act or attitude--is predetermined as well as self-determined.

Love may be regarded as the *soul* of morally good acts. As the soul of these good acts, love is everywhere. It pervades, vivifies, and makes good the acts themselves right from within them. But love is not all there is to a good act, any more than the soul is all there is to a human being. Love is not everything. The particular moral act has a body as well as a soul. Good behavior is as necessary as good intention, motivations, and attitudes in constituting an act of love.

All of one's moral acts might be likened to the activity of the placenta that surrounds the fetal self. Moral actions taken together stand, like the placenta, between the autonomous part of the moral agent and the environment of basic human Values in which he or she participates. A person's love, then, can be only as vigorous as the effectiveness of individual moral acts in permitting him or her to be nourished by the primary human Goods. Anyone who says that love is enough is really attempting moral abortion, separating a person and his or her acts from the necessary womb*like* conditions that make it possible for acts to be morally good and for love to be more than a wish.

Love Is Sexual Superactivity

Love is not essentially a wish or a desire. Love is a will--a determined self. Love *is* willing the truest and the best for self and others, despite the cost. Love believes all things, hopes all things, endures all things. The one who loves believes that the truest and the best is really possible for self and others. Such a person continuously shares self with self and others, motivated by absolute Truth, Goodness, and Beauty. Love is God-centered, however weakly or poorly, or it is not love at all. The loving person is so willing to do what is truest and best in a given situation that he or she necessarily, if often unconsciously, attempts to commune with God in order to do what is right and good.

178

Love is always open to, and seeking, the best way to participate in the womb of God-given human values at every moment in the life of moral gestation. Love is the will to share oneself entirely with self, not closing off any of the fundamental human Goods by self-aborting behavior. Love is willing to die physically rather than to abort self or another from an existence rooted in the moral womb of fundamental human Goods. Love lays down its life, gradually or all at once, for its friends and its enemies. Love is making the attempt at fully sharing the gift of self. It is sexual superactivity.

The Person IS a Love

We speak of love in many ways. We can speak of an *act* of love, an *attitude* of love, a *sign* of love, and so on. But the most important level at which we can understand love is the level of *being*.

When one hears that God *is* love, love is being understood at the level of being. God's acts of love and God's being are really the same. But a creature's acts are not the same as his or her being. Acts manifest being, reveal being, even make being fuller or diminish it, but they are not the same as the creature's being.

Nevertheless, if the creature is created in the likeness of God--and every cause causes things to be like it in *some* way--then there is love right within the creature from the moment of creation. God is not the only love. God is a love: uncreated and unlimited love in being. Yet we, too, are each a love: a unique but limited love in being. God is a love. You are a love. I am a love. Love is not only an act of will, but also an act of being. To be John is to love. To be Nancy is to love. Each one of us is an act of being, which is an act of love.[1]

This act of being that each one *is* can be manifested in many lesser acts, such as talking, walking, giving, receiving, singing, enjoying, weeping. But *being* is our most important act. At any given moment we are engaged in countless acts, such as *breath*ing, *metaboliz*ing, *grow*ing, *know*ing, *lov*ing. But these are all branches of one, *super*unique and dynamic act of *being*, which we are always doing--well or poorly, consciously or unconsciously. We cannot not be. We cannot stop our act of be-ing. We may end our act of living in this world (suicide). But we cannot end our act of being--our act of be-ing at all, given absolutely by God in creating us.[2]

This act of being-at-all--the act of not being nothing, but actually being something--is the gift of self that we are called from within to share with self and with others in supreme gratitude to the Giver. It is love as sexual superactivity in its most intimate depths. Although it is difficult to understand and impossible to get a clear picture of our act of being, it would be foolish to deny its existence or to disregard its influence in moral behavior. So, I shall attempt to suggest that the ultimate anatomy of any individual moral act, flowing from the person, is the structure of our act of being as an act of love.

This way of viewing love implies that everyone is designed, at his or her ultimate depths, to *be* a unique love. The further implication is that since no one of us is loving to full capacity, we must be flawed beings. Since the human will is a free will, able to choose at every moment its *attitudes*--if not always its actions-- the great lack of love on our part must be the result of some free denial of the goodness of our being and the being of others, especially the Other who freely gave this gift of being to us. In the depths of our being, right now we are not saying full-heartedly YES to the goodness of God and all being, including our own.[3] If we were, our lesser acts would manifest it much better. But the most telling place that this lack of loving is revealed would seem to be our attitudes.

The Be-Attitudes

As I mentioned in Chapter 9, attitudes form the universal inner space of a moral act. They are the spirit of the self-determining side of a moral act.

We can indicate various kinds of attitude and several levels of attitude. One speaks of an attitude of despair, an attitude of gratitude, a cynical attitude, a lackadaisical attitude, a "sour grapes" attitude, a loving attitude, and so on. Attitudes are our inward responses to various aspects of living and being. They constitute the profound inner space of our very own unique being. Attitudes are largely mysteries to us. Yet we realize that people can and do change their attitudes.

In order to change one's attitudes and to have a singularly beneficial effect on one's entire personal life, it is very helpful to understand at least their basic inner structure or nature. I have already said that Values are the basic nature of the person's moral world. Attitudes, however, are the basic structure of the person *himself* or *herself* as a *moral* agent. And just as there are fundamental human and moral Values, so there are fundamental human and moral attitudes.

The basic attitudes of a *human person as an act of love* can be called Be-Attitudes because they constitute the God-given structure of our act of be-ing.[4] I suggest that St. Paul in his letter to the Corinthians was fairly singing these being-attitudes when he wrote of love. "Love is patient, kind . . . not puffed up" and so on.[5] In that discourse on love we might distinguish nine basic attitudes of love. They are Expectation ("Love hopes all things"), Anticipation ("Love . . . bears all things"), Confidence ("Love . . . rejoices with the truth"), Patience ("Love is patient"), Perseverance ("Love . . . endures all things"), Forgiveness ("Love . . . takes no account of evil"), Belief ("Love . . . believes all things"), Understanding ("Love . . . is kind"), and Humility ("Love is not puffed up, seeks not its own, vaunts not itself, not easily provoked. . . .").[6]

Some psychologists and moralists say that our personal life is essentially determined by the attitudes that we choose. They note that in a given situation where someone is annoying you, you can choose to be patient or impatient. You may not be free to get away, but you are free to be (more or less) patient or impatient with him or her. A person may be suffering a fatal beating or be tortured to the threshold of unconsciousness, but as long as he or she is conscious there is the freedom to love or hate the persecutor. The moral being of the afflicted is always free to determine self to be more or less loving or unloving in the depths of one's personhood.

This view of our freedom for self-determination contains a great truth. Patricipation at the third level of freedom involves choosing *to let* one's being be what it is called to be or choosing *not to let* it be. Therefore, it is not so much that in a given circumstance a person chooses either patience or impatience, understanding or cynicism, expectation or despair. The person does not so much choose a positive attitude rather than a negative attitude, or vice versa. Rather, the person can be said to be free in affirming or in failing to affirm, at the moment, his or her Being-Attitude of love called patience or understanding or anticipation. This affirmation is done with varying degrees of strength and weakness. Choice, then, is the specific and articulate way in which concrete action comes into existence as the result of a deeper activity of a particular intensity or

strength--the activity of affirming one's own be-ing at
the time.

Loving is the degree of true self-affirmation at
the heart of the gift of one's be-ing. It is not the
ego-affirmation that is so often advocated as self-
affirmation in psychology and in personal development
programs. Love is affirming the gift of self, *as a gift*
of an all-loving God, just as self was given to be in
the moment of creation and as this gift (self) can best
be shared in accord with its powers of attitude and action
at the particular temporal moment in question.[7]

The Organs of Love and Their Diseases

Love is the intensity of our unique act of be-ing.[8]
This be-ing who you are or this be-ing who I am is a
self-affirming, self-intensifying being. The more this
be-ing affirms self as good, the more it can give and
receive (share with) self and others.

The primary ways in which the love that you are or
that I am shares itself can be called Be-Attitudes. They
are the primary aspects or facets of love. Love, as the
gift of self, has a "body" to it. There are even special
"organs" which reveal the health and function of the
"body" and together help to make up the "body" itself.
The Be-Attitudes might be regarded as these "organs."

The nine Be-Attitudes might be compared to the organs
of the physical body in their basic functioning. The
"love body" that each one of us *is* may not be entirely
unlike the physical body that each one of us *is* as well.
Space does not permit me to define and show in detail
how each one of the Be-Attitudes is like a particular
organ of the physical body, but a brief identification
can serve to suggest the analogy. There is no intention
to imply a direct parallel. Making the analogy is simply
a way to celebrate intellectively the intimate union of
body and be-ing.

Faith, Hope and Love

The brain of our "love organism" might be regarded
as the person's powers of Faith, Hope, and Love. Traditionally these powers have been called the three theological virtues, because they are regarded as special
gifts that place us directly in the supernatural life
of God. Here they refer to the natural disposition in
any person for such gifts.

Faith may be considered as the activity in a person whereby he or she is implicitly or explicitly affirming the gift of self by saying, "I am!" This is a kind of superactivity or superattitude in which one is continuously grateful for being at all. The more the person wonders with delight and gratitude at his or her be-ing--in effect, saying, "I am!"--the more open the person is to the supernatural gift of Faith. Radical awareness of one's be-ing as a gift makes it almost impossible not to know God as a loving Father in whom one believes ultimately, no matter where family members, friends, and the whole world might stray in relating to him.

Hope may be considered as the superactivity in a person whereby he or she is implicitly or explicitly affirming the gift of self by saying, "I can!" This is the supremely interior root-affirmation of one's power to do. It opens one directly to the possibility of the supernatural gift of Hope in which one trusts God completely as a loving mother who wants to nurture him or her to maturity, no matter how difficult that growth may be. Every time that a person consciously and deliberately affirms the goodness of his or her be-ing ("I am!"), a new surge of power enters the heart and naturally leads to the affirmation: "I can!" "I *can* do more, despite my troubles and discouragements in life!" "I *can* be more patient with my roommate or spouse or children!" This natural superattitude becomes, in the life of God's grace, an "I *can* do all in the One who strengthens me!"

Love, in this context, refers to a kind of superactivity in which the person implicitly or explicitly is saying, "I will!" This affirmation of the gift of self is the root affirmation of one's power to intend to do. Willing is the root of loving. Love is not a wish or a want, but a will. "I will" is the heart of every moral act, because it is the inner life of *intent*. When *will* is present, good intentions *are* enough. They are enough to constitute a morally good act, even though one may be prevented from bringing it to physical fruition. Bad intentions, because of the will in them, are enough to constitute a morally bad act.

When a person spends time consciously willing his or her be-ing to be and to be its wondrous self as God-given, the person is much more apt to engage in truly-loving, concrete actions. This interior willing need not be very conscious and explicit. But the more conscious and explicit it is at times--meditative and contemplative times--the greater one's power to love becomes.

When affirming the goodness of be-ing by saying "I will!"--I will to *be* this being that is so ineffably given me!"--the person is naturally opened to the possibility of receiving the supernatural gift called Charity, in which the Spirit of God inflames the whole being with an everlasting, unlimiting love.

"I am!" leads naturally to "I can!" which, in turn, leads naturally to "I will!" Together they form a kind of supercenter for all the other attitudes of the person's God-gifted being.[9] The brain of the spiritual life is a kind of three-leveled structure made up of the natural powers of Faith, Hope, and Love.

"Love hopes all things"

The Be-Attitude of Expectation is the organ of spiritual hope on a day to day basis. It is the organ of vision in that the expectant person has a vision which he or she is constantly attempting to fulfill. By this Be-Attitude we are in contact with the horizons beyond ourselves. The organs of eye, ear, and nose place us in physical union with things physically distant. Similarly, the attitude or organ of spiritual vision puts us in spiritual union with conditions and situations spiritually distant, even eternally distant. By Expectation we "see and hear" realities we cannot yet "touch." We are sure that they are there even if we cannot yet embrace them. The greatness of a person is conditioned by the visions, dreams, and ideals which he or she really--though perhaps "darkly"-- sees and moves toward.

"Love bears all things"

Anticipation is the organ of spiritual providence on a day to day basis. By the attitude of Anticipation we can acquire and ingest spiritual food. Without this Be-Attitude being exercised we cannot taste the reality of a given situation to anticipate or surmise the prospective spiritual nourishment it may provide. Anticipation is the "mouth" of our spiritual life. By the attitude of Expectation spiritual nourishment is seen. By the attitude of Anticipation it is "tasted and chewed." All prospective physical nourishment is placed naturally first in the mouth, where it is taken in *just as it is*. There the beginning of digestion and transformation occurs. Similarly, all prospective spiritual nourishment is placed naturally first in one's Anticipation, where it is taken in just as it is, and then initially worked on in order to be received more fully into one's being.

As St. Paul says, love bears or covers all things.
ove side-steps nothing. It is intimidated by nothing.
t does not run away even from evil. All things work
oward good to those who love God. So, all things can
e received just as they are by someone who really loves.
healthy organ of Anticipation makes possible the "taking
n" and bearing of all things--all conditions and cir-
umstances in which we find ourselves--the bitter and
he sweet, the rough and the smooth.

Evil is a special point for consideration. The lov-
ng person exercises greatly the power of Anticipation
n regard to evil. Such a person prepares for evil every
ay. Evil, as well as good, is anticipated--neither
odged nor dawdled with. But the good is the key to
ffective anticipation. The lover knows and acts on
he assumption that all things are at bottom good and
an be *encountered as good, more than as evil.* All things
re spiritual food to the person who loves and whose or-
an of Anticipation is vigorously active.

Love rejoices in the truth"

Confidence is the organ of spiritual identity and
tability. By our attitude of confidence in ourselves
piritual food becomes securely our food. Without con-
idence we are insecure, indecisive, weak, and at times
ven vomitably lukewarm. We cannot hold our spiritual
ood. We ache in the pit of our being. We are even in-
lined to regurgitate whatever we have received as nour-
shment for our spiritual health. Confidence is the
stomach" of our attitudinal life. A confident person
s joyful over the truth of his or her being and receives
t fully.

A confident person can hold and process "spiritual
ata" without getting upset at the chaotic character of
hat is received. He or she can live well with confusion
ecause self-identity has been clearly achieved. Such
person *knows*--not just tastes--what he or she can do.
he confident person not only receives reality as it is,
ut digests it thoroughly. This digestion occurs in
nd through the person's Be-Attitude of Confidence. Di-
ested food, whether physical or spiritual, is food ready
or assimilation. By our attitude of confidence we can
ake situations or circumstances serve us and our being-
ul health rather than become a victim of them.

185

"Love is patient"

Patience is the organ of spiritual equanimity and
assimilation. By our Be-Attitude of Patience we keep
ourselves steady in the face of irritations and even per-
secutions. We also contribute a crucial internal element
that is necessary for assimilating the good of everyday
life. Spiritual food must not only be tasted, ingested,
and digested. It must be assimilated. In physical life,
it is *not* true that we are what we eat. We are what we
assimilate. Similarly, in spiritual life, an impatient
person is one who cannot assimilate the lessons of everyday experience, even though this person has been quick
and very apt at taking them in. He or she will not be
still long enough. An impatient person lacks the ability
to secrete a kind of spiritual insulin that "keeps the
blood sugar down." The person tends to get high. There
seems to be a deficiency in transforming, into assimilabl
experience, daily irritations of appreciable concentration. Impatience is an enzyme-like deficiency. The
Be-Attitude of Patience is, so to speak, the pancreas
of the spiritual life.

"Love endures all things"

Perseverance is the organ of spiritual endurance
and assimilation. By the attitude of Patience we are
able to *undergo* anything. By the attitude of Perseveranc
we are able to *go on*. We are enabled to go on and on
and on, enduring all things to the end of our tasks,
projects, commitments. We are long-lasting in our dedi-
cation and commitment. Also, through the Be-Attitude
of Perseverance we are able to assimilate the maximum
good from the spiritual nourishment of everyday life that
we ingest. Perseverance is a kind of "colon of the spirit" affording us this long-term assimilation of spiritual
nourishment.

Everyone has at least short-term patience, and can
stand some minor irritation. Everyone also has at least
a short-term perseverance, and can go onward toward a
goal in spite of obstacles to some extent. But the abili
ty to "endure all things" needs much development in persons generally. We "faint away" from our biggest tasks
so readily. There is great need to maximize the "long
organ" of our spiritual life, the Be-Attitude of Perseverance, so that we can attain maximum nourishment from
the sacrament of everyday life.

186

"Love takes no account of evil"

Forgiveness is the principal organ of spiritual de-
toxification. By our Be-Attitude of Forgiveness we process the poisons that are inevitably the results of in-
gesting and digesting reality "just as it is." Much of
what a person experiences each day and some of what is
actually, though unfortunately, assimilated turns out
to be poisonous to our spiritual lives. There is need
for a special power or organ that can neutralize the
"garbage coming in" and let it fluently become the "garbage going out." So, we all have a Be-Attitude of Forgiveness, somwhat as we have an organ called the liver
in our physical life.

Forgiveness toward ourselves is especially needed.
We tend not to forgive ourselves when we do something
wrong. This inability is, so to speak, a "liver disease"
called pride. (It also specifically affects the elimina-
tive process of the "skin organ" of spiritual life--
Humility.) When someone forgives himself or herself
there is released a poison or toxic condition that had
been inflicted upon self by impurities in thought or action. When one person forgives another, he or she is
releasing the poisons that the other's impurities and
hatred have inflicted upon self. This processing of poisons for release from one's spiritual system is a continuous one. The Be-Attitude of Forgiveness must be in
continuous "working order" so that daily poisons do not
"back up" too much and kill one's spiritual life.

"Love believes all things"

The Be-Attitude of Belief is "the lungs" of our
spiritual life. Believing is knowing--knowing things
unseen and benefiting from them. We believe somewhat
as we breathe. In breathing we take in something good
(air, oxygen) and feel it (know it), without seeing, hearing, tasting, or smelling it. By our Belief organ we
take in an unseen, untouched good from our environment.
We feel it (know it) without being able to prove it. We
believe in God's goodness and love for us with everything
that comes our way. A person takes in naturally and spontaneously this unseen, but somehow felt, goodness of God,
with which everything is surrounded (like the air).

But some believe much more deeply than others, just
as some breathe more deeply than others. The organ of
Belief can be exercised more and more effectively. Cynicism, despair, and indifference are some of the diseases
of the spiritual "lungs" that can result from shallow

believing. Deep believing can only come by being willed
and by being exercised patiently and perseveringly. Just
as air will not *fill* the lungs regularly without practice and continuous effort, so the goodness of the Other
surrounding all things and circumstances will not *fill*
our Belief nor catalyze our spiritual life-process to
its capacity without explicit acts of faith. Deep believing affords us the internal suffusion of God's goodness--
often called grace--so crucial to spiritual "metabolism"
and so critical for the "brain activity" (I *am*, I *can*,
I *will*) of spiritual life.

"Love is kind"

Understanding is the basic organ of kindness in one's
thoughts and deeds. Kindness, however, is not sentimen-
tality. Kindness is mindedness, rather than blindness.
It is not the mindless overlooking of the limitations,
faults, and sometimes outrageous practices of self or
others. Kindness is understanding. One who really understands is one who knows and accepts a person's limitations
as well as gifts, failings as well as successes, stupidity
as well as insight. Understanding is broadminded firmness
in knowing someone. Understanding (not simply knowing)
is knowing the person in his or her causes, and being
kindly toward that person because of this fuller knowledge. Love is kind because love understands ("stands
under") all of one's life--its processes of building up
and of tearing down (metabolism). Love is kind because
love pumps spiritual life-elements throughout one's whole
self--the diseased as well as the healthy parts of self.

Love's kindness, the Be-Attitude of Understanding,
is the heart organ of spiritual life. It pumps the blood
of kindness without fail to every one of the other spiritual organs. Without considerable understanding of oneself and others, one is subject spiritually to "heart
failure." If understanding falters or fails, patience
is no longer patience, confidence is no longer confidence,
anticipation is no longer anticipation. All attitudes
cease to function if they are not supplied with the constant rhythm of understanding. Knowledge of oneself
and others can be great or small in details, but the
"pulsing" of the Understanding Be-Attitude can always
become stronger through exercise. Whether an accomplished
genius of encyclopedic mind or a peasant leading the
simplest life, the person who knows with kindness is
understanding. Everyone's spiritual life is gifted with
a potentially strong heart.

"Love is not puffed up; seeks not its own"

Humility is another major "organ" of the spiritual life. Humility does not mean self-denigration. It is not a matter of running oneself down or putting on a sticky coat of false modesty. Humility is not a doormat attitude. It may be defined as the ability to *emphasize* the importance of other people.

Humility is an attitude springing from love by which we experience being one with other people and things. Others can become centers of the world for us through our Be-Attitude of Humility. The opposite of humility-- pride or conceit--closes one off from others and tries to make self the exclusive center of the world. False humility, such as an inferiority complex or passivity toward one's own worth, amounts to a leathery insensitivity to the being of others, as well as to oneself.

The Be-Attitude of Humility is the "skin" of the spiritual life. Physical skin is an organ of protection for self, and also an organ of touch--of continuity with and sensitivity to others and to the whole of one's differentiated environment. Humility is the attitude by which we are not only protected and conserved in who we are ("humility is truth"), but also united immediately with our spiritual environment and with the being of many others. A malfunctioning "organ" of Humility is like an insensitivity of skin and keeps us out of fluent touch with the importance of other people and things--our fellow creatures, in all their uniqueness.[16] Our physical skin is an organ of elimination (perspiration) as well as of sensation. Similarly, the Be-Attitude of Humility is notably exercised also as a way of letting out the poisons of pride and conceit on a regular basis, as well as keeping us united with others. It takes a humble person to excrete conceit, day after day.

Along with the superattitudes of Faith, Hope, and Love, these nine basic Be-Attitudes form the "organs" of our *be-ing as a love*. Each one of these Be-Attitudes is a fundamental and crucial power in the developing person, precisely as a person and as a moral being. We are morally dead without at least minimal use of them. Most of us might be said to be very undeveloped and sickly in our use of these Creator-endowed powers of our be-ing-- something like a weak and sluggishly living prenatal child.

But there is plenty of nourishment in the womb of human Values surrounding us. We are essentially free as persons. We can make deliberate efforts to change our immature and diseased condition. We can learn to exercise directly our fetallike, Be-Attitudinal self and to utilize our placentalike self more effectively.

How to utilize properly one's placentalike self through individual moral actions will be discussed in the next chapter. However, before moving away from these primary and irreducible attitudes of our be-ing, their relationship to what are traditionally called virtues will be suggested.

Virtues and Love's State of Health

The nature of virtue is important in any sound theory of morality. The virtuous person is one who, as a morally free individual, is able to act rightly with ease, rather than with difficulty. A person who is habitually courageous is said to possess the virtue of fortitude. A person who habitually makes sound practical judgments in everyday action is said to possess the virtue of prudence. Temperance is a moral virtue that enables a person to be moderate in the use of his or her basic appetites. Justice is the stable disposition in a person who is particularly sensitive to what is proportionate in the treatment of other people with their many and varied concerns.

These moral virtues are special strengths that persons can develop, either through long and persevering practice or all at once on a rare occasion of deeply acquired moral insight and change of character. Some people seem to be born with one or more of these particular moral strengths fairly well-developed. Virtue, however, does not really accrue to them until they consciously integrate their strengths into their lives of freely chosen attitudes and actions.

In the total spectrum of human and personal development, where do the virtues fit?

One way in which they can be understood is to recognize two kinds of virtues especially relevant to the moral life: theological virtues and moral virtues. (A third kind of virtue is intellectual virtue, which is not directly relevant.)

I have already noted how the three theological virtues of Faith, Hope, and Charity are supernatural gifts of God that no person can deserve by his or her nature, but which everyone has the natural disposition to receive. The brain of everyone's love-life--the affirmation-giving power of be-ing--is radically designed to receive these three special gifts and thereby become integrated into the life of God.

But, while the theological virtues are superattitudes and superactivities into which the great and mysterious life of all human attitudes and Be-Attitudes may become integrated, the moral virtues are natural strengths that accrue to the person as a moral agent, a doer of personal deeds. Justice, fortitude, temperance, and prudence are special kinds of strength that the loving person develops in his or her life of moral action. They directly relate to action and to the strengthening of positive, health-building patterns of moral behavior. But they are per-asively conditioned and toned by the Be-Attitudes.

For instance, the virtue of fortitude is a special strength that can accrue to the person because he or she acts regularly under the vigorous spirit of Perseverance. Justice is toned and conditioned particularly by Humility and Understanding. Prudence, which involves risk at times, is particularly conditioned by the aliveness of one's Expectation, Anticipation, Confidence, and even belief. Patience and Anticipation are special attitudinal conditioners in the development of temperance.

The moral virtues are crucial facilitators of the person's moral life. They mediate between the Be-Attitudes which inspire and condition them on the one hand and the particular moral actions which they directly regulate on the other. The freedom of self-perfection is effectively attained only by means of the achievement and exercise of the moral virtues.[10]

In summary, it can be said that the freedom of self-perfection, of which true sexual freedom is an important part, includes the basic elements of moral being. These elements are envisioned here as aligned in a certain way. First are the three superattitudes of Faith, Hope, and Love. These three attitudes superenergize the nine others discussed in this chapter (Expectation, Anticipation, and the rest). These Be-Attitudes, in turn, are perfected through concrete actions; and the result of the right kind of actions, imbued with these Be-Attitudes, is virtue. The moral virtues (prudence, fortitude, temperance, justice) stand between the Be-Attitudes and concrete actions as action-stabilizers and perfectors which establish one's moral character as significantly free and self-perfecting.

191

Love, then, can be mature or immature, healthy or sick. Moral virtue--attained through the right kind of care for, and exercise of, the "organs" of love (Be-Attitudes)--is the natural condition of mature and healthy love.

NOTES

1. This statement is not meant to deny the traditional distinction between essence and existence in creatures. I am not identically my existence or act of being. But then neither am I identically my essence. I am the whole being. "I *am* my *act of being*" is an assertion made here in much the same manner that I might say I *am* my body. My act of being, like my body, is not so much something I *have*--especially not as in having a watch or a shirt--but something I *am*. Be-ing is an act that is the most crucial part of my whole self. It is something I have been given preeminently to *do*--through God's act of creating me out of nothing. As an act of love, my be-ing is preeminently myself inasmuch as I am created by God who is the Source-Love. *I* do my be-ing love, which God gave me. Not God, nor anyone else. It is the *heart* of who I *am*.

2. God gave this act of be-ing to us without any strings attached. For further perspective on this way of understanding creation and our relationship to God, see R. Joyce, "A Christian Will to Meaning in Everyday Life," *Cross Currents*, 17 (Winter 1967):25-38.

3. The implication is that we are somehow personally responsible for original sin. My opinion is that Christian theology needs to develop in this area such that we understand better how there can be real suffering for innocent people in the presence of a God who is both all-powerful and all-good. Unless the person is, as Christians believe Jesus is, perfectly innocent yet freely willing to take on the sufferings of others in order to redeem them, it would seem to be contrary to the absolute power and goodness of God to let anyone who is innocent suffer.

I do not intend to deny orthodox teaching concerning the original sin of Adam and Eve and our inheritance of it. But I do intend to ask the question: Why would God allow us to inherit the consequences of that sin if he is all-good *and* all-powerful? If all-good, but not all-powerful, then God could be understood as not being able to prevent our inheritance of sin. Or if all-powerful, but not all-good, then it would also be perhaps understandable. But, then, in either case, we would not be speaking of God as Christians understand this Being.

In effect, I see no other alternatives. If one is to espouse the Christian view that God is both all-good and all-powerful, then either we deserve the evil and "hard times" that befall us in this world because of personal participation in original sin or we are, like Christ, innocent sufferers for the sake of healing and leading those who have sinned into a new life. (The latter alternative is interesting perhaps, but terribly presumptuous.) Actually, I see no incompatibility between the recognition of an original sin on earth that is inherited and personal responsibility for an original sin through poorly receiving our being in the extra-temporal dimension of free will at the moment of creation. One of our problems in this area seems to be that we have not taken seriously the possibility of our own unique being having existed from the moment of creation in another condition of things--not in this particular form of (space-time) existence, but totally in matter and in spirit--because we said fully Yes to God at that moment and hence needed no redemption.

4. The idea of the act of being having a structure is my own. In the traditional metaphysical interpretation, the act of being would not be thought to have structures, since that would necessarily signify it as an essence. But I would say that the expression "constitutes the God-given structure of our act of be-ing" simply signifies the essence of the particular, unique acts of be-ing that we call human--and tries to suggest the dynamic unity of the act of be-ing and its essence (the one that it actuates). Thus, it is rather a difference in manner of speaking than in substance. I wish to signify the super-dynamic character of both be-ing and essence in each one of us. Some philosophically inclined persons may find it more convenient to speak of the Be-Attitudes as dimensions of the spiritual part of a human being's essence.

5. The theological reflections that follow are not necessary to the moral philosophy of this book. They are a Christian elaboration to which this moral philosophy is open.

6. This idea of regarding as attitudes the qualities of love that were indicated by St. Paul to the Corinthians is suggested to me by a human relations and personal development program offered by Personal Dynamics, Inc. (Minneapolis). Robert Conklin, the creator of this widely used motivational program (called *Adventures in Attitudes*) distinguishes eight attitudes correlatable with St. Paul's discourse on love. I have added a ninth (forgiveness) and have called them Be-Attitudes--attitudes of be-ing--attributing to them an ontological, as well as psychological, significance and analogizing them to major functional parts of the human body. I do not claim that there are only nine attitudes in loving relationships. Nor do I claim that my analogy with our bodily organism has anything other than some inspirational, didactic, and possibly heuristic value.

7. The kind of self-affirming here is spiritual. But it does not in any way abrogate the need for affirmation by another person that is crucial to holistic psychological health. There is need for both self-affirmation and other-affirmation (affirmation of self by another) at the spiritual level. The latter affirmation is, first of all, given absolutely by God in creating us and in redeeming us. Secondly, it is given by other people when they affirm us in the wholesome ways suggested by psychiatrist Conrad Baars. (See, e.g., *Born Only Once: The Miracle of Affirmation*

193

(Chicago: Franciscan Herald Press, 1975). But, in any case, the person himself or herself must engage in the self-affirmation that the Be-Attitudes involve if he or she is going to *receive* the affirmational love of others, especially God. No one--not even an absolute Other--can make us loving persons by affirming us unless we affirm ourselves within as worthy of this other-affirmation.

8. Love is not essentially a feeling. There is no such thing--strictly speaking--as *feelings* of love. So-called loving feelings are extremely helpful but not absolutely necessary to an act of authentic love. The intensity of our unique act of be-ing is not specifically an emotional, but a spiritual, intensity. Very often there is a strong correlation between our feelings for someone and our love, but often there is not.

9. Of course, the fullness of contemplative activity lies not in self-receiving, but in other-receiving, particularly in *the* Other-receiving. Contemplative prayer is a non-verbal, rapturous "You are!" "You can!" "You do!"

10. For a creative interpretation of the moral virtues in the classical tradition, see Josef Pieper, *The Four Cardinal Virtues* (Notre Dame, Ind.: University of Notre Dame Press, 1966).

Chapter 12

EVALUATION OF A MORAL ACT

A person is a lover. The basic nature of a self-reflective, freely-willing creature is to be loving: to know and will the truest and the best for oneself and others, and to carry out this knowing and willing in creative and committed ways.

The preceding chapter describes some of the basic structure that is found in the person as *a love*. The person is *a being* who is *a love*. The core attitudinal powers that form the person's God-like being are found in us at various stages of growth and health (or disease). The person *is* his or her nature, which includes these irrevocable being-attitudes. This structure of the self cannot be basically altered; it can only be affected for good or ill. The morally good person is one whose loving nature is healthy, even if undeveloped; the morally bad person is one whose loving nature is sick, even if relatively mature.

The way in which a person specifically affects or modifies his or her personal self is through individual acts. These individual acts can be simple and concrete, such as giving a drink of water to someone who is thirsty, volunteering a day of work to help victims of a flood, or stealing a wristwatch from a department store. They can also be complex and intangible, such as delighting in the workings of Providence, choosing and planning one's future, or holding a grudge. Individual acts can likewise be complex and concrete, such as going to college for four years; or they can be simple and intangible, such as a momentary prayer for help. Sometimes acts with concrete results or acts having effects that can be somehow empirically apprehended are called *actions*, rather than acts, in order to distinguish them from acts that are intangible, such as acts of good or bad intention and the profound, complex activity of one's attitudinal life.

No matter how one distinguishes all these effluents from the person's soul--including the most concrete actions--they are all individual acts. One engages simultaneously in myriad, countless acts. One cannot begin to advert to each of them. But this inability need not incline one to conclude that the acts are simply one act. The cells of the human body are innumerable, dynamically active *individual* cells, all simultaneously being and acting. Similarly, the person's moral body--the whole body of activity and actions that simultaneously result from the exercise of intellect and will--is composed of multitudinous acts, simultaneously caused by the person and also exerting a "return" influence on that person.

Being a person is a magnificent ecological opportunity and responsibility. The art of be-ing demands that we take responsibility gradually--slowly, for the most part; in leaps of insight and good will, at certain times--for all of our personal activity. When we desire to see how we are doing in this creative process, the main thing we can do is to evaluate carefully a given individual act. The act that we evaluate is not simply a sign or symptom of our progress or regress in moral maturation and health. It is likewise, and more importantly, the *only* way we have to *determine* ourselves, our direction, and our destiny.

Obviously, some of our individual acts are much more decisive than others in creating and revealing our moral character. Someone may wish to focus on his or her action of giving a drink of water to a thirsty person. The evaluation of such an act can be helpful. But it is difficult to make because there is probably little content in it as a moral act.[1] Someone may desire to examine his or her rather habitual act of valuing all personal, goal-directed activities. Reflection on the moral character of this activity can also be helpful. But it is difficult to do because there is probably so much content in the act.[2]

In this chapter, we shall examine a moral act which involves considerable, but not overwhelming, complexity. The issue of premarital sex is often discussed. But all the talk about it, pro and con, does not mean very much if people are not comprehending even the most elementary principles of moral action. The more one recognizes and comes to know the essential ingredients of moral behavior, the more he or she can decide with reasonableness and certainty the proper course of action in any given circumstance.

In Chapter 9, I suggested that every moral act has two sides: a self-determining side that includes attitudes, motives, and intention; and a pre-determining side that includes the three levels of energy and of spontaneous inclination in the person--the physical, psychic, and spiritual. Both sides also involve various kinds of circumstances connected directly with the act itself and influencing one's determination regarding its morality. The self-determining side was called the soul of the act; the pre-determining side, the body. Now, we turn our attention to the nature of a morally *good* act. We will emphasize the kind of acts that are concrete, rather than attitudinal.

What constitutes a morally good action?

The Soul and Body of a Morally Good Act

The morally good act is the act of a lover. The love makes the act good, right from within itself. The act is as morally good as the person's loving presence within it *makes* it. The soul of the morally good act is love. But there is no such thing in this world as a soul without a body. What is the body of a morally good act?

The body reveals the soul. The body also affects the soul. The soul can only operate or be itself effectively in the world of action through the mediation of its body. The body is the tangible dimension of the one, whole living reality. In the sphere of morally good action, there is a tangible dimension to the loving action itself. There are certain general structures that can be examined to see how loving, how dynamic and healthy, a moral act really is. These structures arc modes of acting responsibly *as a human person* in this world.

These modes of responsibility are requirements for the person in attaining the freedom of self-perfection-- the freedom to become more and more healthfully and

maturely who one is created to be.[3] They are necessary
guides to developing the moral virtues, which strengthen
and consolidate the actions of good character. They are
utterly crucial structures that must be entirely respected
if an action is to be morally good. Morally bad actions
violate one or more of these modes of responsibility.

The modes of responsible action are the ecological
laws of our placentalike moral existence. In Chapter 11,
I discussed the basic structures of our fetallike moral
existence. They are the Be-Attitudes that I likened to
organs of the fetal or autonomous body. Now we are attending to the basic structures of our placental or service organ in moral life. These modes of responsibility
must be relatively healthy and active if we are to receive
the nourishment from the basic human Values which we need
to exist and through which we can grow healthfully as
moral existents.

We participate effectively in the fundamental Goods
of life only to the extent that we act in accord with
the modes of responsibility as guides for responsible
action. Every personal action is necessarily an act of
participating in one or more of the fundamental Goods of
life. The participation is basically good or bad as we
act in harmony or disharmony with all of the modes of
responsible action. If one of them is violated, the
action is morally bad and results in damage to our essential relationship with the basic Values of human life,
whether we realize it or not.

One cannot violate with impunity the ecological laws
of moral life. Lack of knowledge or awareness will diminish or nullify personal culpability, but some damage
will occur. Ultimately, ignorance is never bliss. If
a person violates the structure and function of the body
by eating junk food, bad consequences will be suffered
no matter how unintended the violation has been. Somewhat similarly, if a person violates the structure and
function of his or her moral body by acting in accord
with junk thought or junk guidance, bad consequences will
accrue, no matter how unintended.

In moral matters, of course, honesty and sincerity
do count to an extent. If they are present, the damage
will be much less than if the violation were fully or
partially intended. Nevertheless, we are often *not wholly*
innocent of an apparently unintended violation.

The modes of responsibility, then, are the necessary
conditions for effective participation in the fundamental

Goods of human life. They are, as it were, the dynamics of placental living in the moral life. They tell how to have a healthy "placenta." As the physical placenta is a vital part of the prenatal person, so the moral placenta is a vital part of the premortal person.

The Conditions for Responsible Action-- Laws of Human Ecology

The following are regarded as fundamental conditions for morally good action and can serve as criteria for determining whether or not an action is truly loving:

1. Develop a consistent commitment to a harmonious set of purposes or values.[4]

2. Never act directly against any of the fundamental human Goods.

3. Always act toward others as you would have others act toward yourself and those you care about.

4. Desire to help others develop and perfect themselves by realizing fully the goods of which they are capable.

5. Fulfill duties, both contractual and communal.

6. Efficiently pursue specific objectives which contribute to the realization of the broader, deeper purposes to which one has dedicated his or her life.

7. Be willing to lose or miss the good effects of action directed toward limited objectives (second-level action), if necessary, in order to participate in the human goods to which one is committed.

8. Practice creative fidelity in one's commitments to third-level goods.

These eight conditions for love are the primary practical attitudes that underlie both a good moral life and every individual act that is morally sound. Not every condition, however, represents a guideline that will be directly applicable to a given moral action. Some will directly apply, others will not.

In order to explain these modes of responsibility and to illustrate their varying applicability, I will

consider a particular kind of moral action--one that is
obviously sexual--and evaluate it in the light of the
foregoing principles.

The Situation

Jim and Janet are college seniors. They are engaged
to be married within six months. Jim thinks that they
are ready for expressing their love "sexually." He keeps
reminding Janet that they are deeply in love and are committed to each other for life, even now before the wedding. She agrees that they are committed and realizes,
too, that they have been faithful to themselves and to
each other by never having engaged in coital intercourse
with anyone. They have always lived by the ideal that
sex is somehow sacred and should be reserved for one's
lifelong partner in marriage.

Jim says that because they share so deeply the most
important values of human life, such as religion, children, how to raise a family, and the rest, they are,
practically speaking, lifelong partners now. "Besides,"
he points out, "we have known each other since freshman
year and we have always refrained from sex, even when
it was very hard to do so during recent months."

Janet is confused. She loves Jim very much and
desires, with all her heart, to be his partner in marriage. Both of them have grown as persons especially
in the past year and a half when they began going steady.
She feels sure that there is practically no end to the
growth that they can experience together in marriage and
as parents. But she seriously wonders whether sex before
marriage might have a retarding or damaging effect on
their relationship (even though, in their case, she cannot quite see what it could be). Some of her friends
have told her that this is so. Others tell her that it
all depends on *who* you are.

If Janet were to know and understand the eight modes
of responsible action, how would they apply in her situation?

The Issue: Whether ·Premarital Genital
Intercourse Is Ever Morally Good

Janet is faced with a difficult personal decision.[5]
Not necessarily because there should be doubt about what
is the right thing to do or not to do in this situation,
but because the right thing to do will inevitably cause
hurt to someone she loves.

Often people are confused regarding the meaning of moral decisions. They tend to think that such decisions must almost always be painful struggles because, they surmise, the morally right thing will be the hard thing to do. Actually, the right thing has nothing to do with the ease or difficulty of the action. Moreover, they do not sufficiently take into account that they are having conflict because of their personal relationships with others who are pressuring them in different directions. They need to distinguish attendant psychological conflict from the moral issue itself. They need to ask themselves, "But what *is* the right way to act in this situation, independent of what I or others now *think* or *feel* or *say* is right?"[6]

The nature of premarital genital intercourse is such that personal views, hang ups, or feelings do not ultimately count. Moreover, it is not an issue that can be decided for the good or the bad, depending on the total complex of many circumstances, such as whether Janet should practice her nursing profession after their marriage, and for how long. Genital intercourse and marriage *directly* affect the structure of both Jim and Janet *as persons* and as participants in *fundamental* Goods, such as Life, Social Harmony, and Religion. Therefore, the modes of responsibility will be decisive in evaluating what they or any other persons who are engaged to be married can do justifiably.

Our endeavor is not to evaluate Janet's personal culpability for undertaking premarital genital intercourse, if that is her choice. She may or may not be personally culpable, depending on whether she knowingly permits herself to act in violation of one or more of these guidelines for human ecology, by whatever wording or form she may conceive them. Through no fault of his or her own a person may not know the truth about a wrongful action and may be free of personal guilt--even though the action *will* have deleterious effects on his or her personal life. (Whether the person ever becomes aware of these effects is another matter.)

It is also possible for someone to engage in an action that is objectively sound and good, but to think that it is morally wrong. In such a case, the person would be culpable for an offense against nature that was thought to have been committed. The moral ill-effect, however, would not be that of the imagined offense itself, since such offense did not transpire. But the moral ill-effect would issue from the twisted disposition of the will which intended such an offense.

201

1. Consistent commitment to a harmonious
   set of purposes or values

   Is Janet's prospective action in accord with her
being consistently committed to a particular set of values? Let us examine the situation. She is consistently
committed to marriage as the way to ultimate sanctifica-
tion of the special love of man and woman. She takes
her engagement to Jim very seriously as a solemn promise
to marry him. They both claim to love each other until
death--and beyond, for that matter. Let us say, she
also believes that genital intercourse is *the* act of love
between a man and a woman. (This notion is challenged
in Chapter 16.) For Janet the significance of all other
acts of affection as love-expressions pales considerably
in the light of the coital embrace, wherein, she believes,
man and woman are called to give themselves to each other
in a *total* way. She feels entirely committed to Jim as
the man for her, the one person with whom she desires
to share her being as a woman for life.

   In the last few months, she and Jim have become very
sure of their undying love for each other. She asks herself whether she is perhaps not being open enough to Jim
by hesitating to give herself now in *the* act of love.
She wonders why she still feels insecure about doing so,
when Jim has promised to be faithful to her, no matter
what happens, until death. He has said even that he
would be faithful to her if marriage had to be put off
indefinitely, should she, because of some rare tragic
accident, become disabled in a state of paralysis or
unconsciousness. Why should she still be uneasy about
coital relations at this stage of their growing love?

   They both believe in having children some day,
when they are set up for it. Let us suppose that neither
of them desires to engage in contraceptive intercourse.
They plan to use a natural method of conception regulation. (The issue of contraceptive intercourse is taken
up in Chapters 13 and 17.) If a child should happen to
be conceived before their marriage they would gladly
adjust to the new circumstance and would reset the wedding for an earlier date. They both firmly believe that
a child needs a home and two good parents. They feel
that it would be an injustice to bring a child into the
world (to let one be conceived) unless one was able to
provide these basic conditions. Janet would like to work
for awhile in her nursing profession in order to build
up their financial resources before having a family. But
that value or purpose is far from an ultimate or absolute

one in her life, and she can easily see how they could make ends meet, if necessary, without her working.

But the chance of a pregnancy is so remote, Janet thinks, since she is quite knowledgeable in the techniques of natural family planning. (The nature of natural family planning is discussed in Chapter 13.) So, the risk of having a child before the time they both decide is right does not seem to compare with the exciting and fulfilling possibilities of sealing their undying love by an act of coital intercourse.

Obviously, the articulation of personal values is an involved and complex endeavor. It could be the subject of a whole book. But enough may be said here to point out some connection with this first mode of responsibility. The reader will notice that I did not say whether Janet's set of purposes are harmonious. I asked whether the action was consistent with her *particular* set of purposes or values. Often people overlook the requirement that the moral person establishes a *harmonious* set of purposes.

Anyone who is sufficiently intelligent can rationalize his or her values just enough so that almost any action will appear to be consistent with them. That is why the term *harmonious* is so important. The responsible person is one who is ever seeking to develop a genuine (not a manufactured or mentally confected) harmony among his or her values, such as the meaning of marriage, becoming a parent, supporting a family, expressing true love, living a sexually fulfilled life, and so forth. How is one's whole set of life-commitments and potential commitments organized? Is this dimension of his or her moral life a "blob of protoplasm," with little differentiation having occurred; or a mass of chaotically related growths; or a somewhat organized body of beliefs, but with certain distortions that might, on closer examination, evoke the term "monster"; or a well-organized, if yet embryonic body of personal beliefs, purposes, and values that are in reasonably good health?

The nurture and care of one's personal set of values, by which one is committed to in-depth participation in the fundamental Goods or ultimate purposes of human life, is a central area of moral responsibility. Individual acts that flow from a relatively harmonious set of purposes tend to nourish these purposes. Those acts that flow from a disharmonious set of purposes tend to reinforce the disharmony.

Every occasion for a moral act is an occasion to
examine and possibly rethink one's personal values and
their priorities. Janet's proposed action is a particularly apt occasion for this endeavor. Janet will be
fortunate if she is guided in her soul-searching by some
deeper and fresher perspectives than she presently possesses. Often people in this kind of situation do not
use the opportunity for deepening their insight into
values, but merely try to figure out logically what is
the "thing to do," based on present values and assumptions.

One of Janet's assumptions in this case is that "the
child will never know" that his or her father and mother
were not married when they brought him or her into the
world. Or else she assumes that if the child were to
learn of it later in life there would be no moral injury
involved. But even if the child shows no hurt feelings
at the time he or she is told, this child may be repres-
sing the hurt. Even if the child is not internally aware
of hurt at the time--perhaps having been raised in a
"liberated" generation regarding the role of marriage--
there is an objective, unconscious wounding of the child
involved, granted that marriage is the only secure place
in which children should be conceived and educated. If
marriage is not such a place, then, of course, Janet is
called upon to review her past and apparently present
meaning for marriage.

This mode of responsibility implies two levels of
harmony. A harmony between the actual purposes to which
one's life is already committed, and a harmony of all
of these purposes with the fundamental Goods of human
life. If a person is committed to shoplifting on the
occasion of "having that certain feeling," such a persona
purpose harmonizes neither with many of his or her other
basic purposes nor with certain of the fundamental Purposes or Values of life, such as Social Harmony, Authenticity, and Integrity.

Among other things, Janet's engaging in genital
intercourse at this time would not flow from a consistent
commitment to a *harmonious* set of purposes or values,
because the action would be flowing from her present stat
of disharmonious meanings and valuings of marriage and
child-care. One could say perhaps that she has a consistent commitment to a partially, but seriously, disharmonious set of purposes or values.

Janet should be encouraged to ask herself several
serious questions, not the least of which is, "If our

commitment *even now* is marital, why should we not get married *now*?" And then, "If we are not going to get married *now*, is our commitment to each other *really* that final?" Couples often seem to deceive themselves by not facing squarely this sort of question.

The particular disharmony between the values as Janet even now conceives them may not be evident because it all depends on how she does *actually* conceive them. Our characterization of these values is largely hypo- thetical. But, however she conceives and values marriage and child-care, the major disharmony is between her mean- ing for these particular values and the natural, God- given meaning structured into these values themselves and founded on the primary human Values. So, the moral reprehensibility of her prospective action may be seen better in the light of the following mode of responsi- bility, which deals with these primary Values themselves.

2. Never act directly against a
    fundamental human Good

Each of the eight fundamental Goods is supreme in its own way. Together these basic human Values form an absolute whole within which the Values themselves are similar to functions that cannot be dispensed with and cannot be substituted for one another. Like the necessary elements of uterine life that make continuance of the pregnancy possible and continuously serve the crucial needs of the child, the fundamental Goods of Life, Play, Integrity, Social Harmony, and the others are Values in which we participate for the sake of growth and survival as healthy moral beings. One's particular commitments, such as marriage, parenthood, civic and church involve- ments, and the like, are basic ways of rooting oneself in the uterine-like wall of these basic human Values, these ultimate purposes of life.

Because each of these fundamental Values is supreme in its own way, none can be used merely as a *means*. Each prime Value is an end in itself--a supreme Good of the human person. If a lover kills his beloved's spouse in order to maintain or enhance the Value of Social Harmony in which the two lovers endeavor to participate, the ac- tion is morally wrong. The fundamental Good of Life is being used strictly as a means to participate in another fundamental Good, Social Harmony (*and* for the sake of a non-fundamental good, a "love affair"). In cultures that have practiced child-sacrifice or virgin-sacrifice in the act of worshipping a supreme Being, the basic Value Life and the basic Value Social Harmony are being used chiefly as means to participate in the basic Value Religion. Such actions are objectively wrong, even though the participants do not realize that they are wrong or why they are wrong. The slavery of black people in the United States and elsewhere in the world was objectively wrong, despite the sentiments of many subjectively moral people who practiced it, because it directly used the fundamental Goods of Life and Social Harmony as means to some economic good.[7]

When any one or more of the fundamental Values of human life are used directly as a means to anything, then *persons* are being treated as means toward an end. These basic Values are part of the person's selfhood in the world. When an essential part of the selfhood of a person or of a group of persons is treated chiefly as a means to an end, rather than primarily as an end in itself, then the person is being so treated. The value of each one of these Goods or Purposes is inexhaustible and absolute. No one can exhaust the Good of Life, Play, Aesthetic Experience, Speculative Knowledge, Integrity, and the others. No class of people nor even the whole human race is above (or in control of) these Values. They are inviolable. When some person (or some society) acts against any one of them the action amounts to an attempt to abort not only someone else but even oneself from the basic conditions of moral integrity and development.

What can be said of Janet and Jim? Are they proposing to enhance or to hinder their participation in the womb of human values? Are they more openly and deeply rooting themselves in these Values or are they attempting (knowingly or unknowingly) a moral abortion of themselves?

Coital intercourse is the specific, natural action whereby another person receives the opportunity to enter this world and to participate in the fundamental Goods of human existence. It is also an action that is naturally designed to increase and intensify the relationship between a man and a woman. Such intercourse is a profound opportunity to participate rather directly in the fundamental Goods of Life and Social Harmony. Play and Aesthetic Experience are also very much involved as Goods in which people are called to participate through the act of coital intercourse. Can Janet honestly say that she and Jim would not violate any of these or any of the other fundamental Goods by engaging in premarital intercourse?

Janet may congratulate herself on the fact that they are willing, though not wanting, to support any child whose life might be conceived as the result of their action. They are willing to marry earlier and give the child maximum benefit of this close commitment were a pregnancy to result.

Moreover, they are not willing to engage in coital intercourse which acts against itself in the very act itself. Contraceptive intercourse would involve them in acting directly against the fundamental good of Life as a means to participating in the fundamental Good of Social Harmony. They would be using the life-giving potential of the act of genital intercourse in order to attain a better participation in the love-giving potential. Such intercourse is just the opposite of the old Puritanical approach in which people only engaged in the action for the sake of producing offspring and repressed or avoided participating in the pleasure and the love-giving potential.

Janet might say that they are open to both dimensions of the action and to both of the basic Values, Life and Social Harmony--not to mention their openness to the Values of Play and Aesthetic Experience in which they would participate through coital experience.

A closer examination, however, might reveal a way in which this complex human interaction does violate a basic Value by acting directly against it. Janet may or may not realize it, but her activity of coital-genital union with Jim makes her a parent-by-intent as soon as she engages in it. As she admits, a child could be conceived and she would be a mother. But she would be a mother whose relationship to the child at that time lacks the social commitment of marriage that every child inherently deserves.

Marriage is not simply the interpersonal commitment of two people to each other. Marriage is the mutual commitment of the two people together with the society. The society through its prime witnesses, especially the minister or priest or judge, receives the couple as husband and wife. Society promises to regard them as such and to protect them from the incursions of others into their sacred mutual trust. They, in turn, promise society that they will fulfill their promises to each other. Marriage is a primary social act, because by it a new cell (the couple) is formed in the social body. And that body is crucially involved in its own "cell division." (The

nature of the marriage covenant is discussed at length
in Chapter 16.)

Janet need not develop a highly sophisticated concept of matrimony in order to appreciate its social essence. Even very practical considerations can bring her
to the point of realization that she and Jim are not the
only essential participants in the marriage. Although
the form of marriage varies with different cultures, in
no culture can one *really* get married without complying
with a standard form. Even in lesser matters such com-
pliance is utterly necessary. In different societies
the form for making loans differs, but one cannot borrow
and lend without using a socially recognized form. Otherwise, even the parties to the agreement are not quite
sure what they are doing. Similarly, in the far more
serious commitment of marriage, the partners cannot really
be sure of the meaning of genital intercourse unless they
have actually committed themselves as members of the community. There is something basically disharmonious in
premarital intercourse with "marital intent."

The predicament of an unexpected child underscores
the disharmony. No matter how short the time between
discovery of a pregnancy and the actual marriage, that
period itself is an act of violating the fundamental Good
of Social Harmony because Janet's child, spiritually and
psychically, needs the social womb of a marriage for part
of his or her fundamental human security. Even if the
child never learns consciously that this violation occurred, he will know unconsciously through later interaction with his parents, whose knowledge of this fact
will definitely, if unconsciously, influence their attitudes toward him or her.[8] Even if the child dies in the
womb and never interacts with the parents in extrauterine,
developmental ways, the parents themselves know somehow
that they have violated directly and seriously--though
not massively--the basic Value of Social Harmony in relation to their very own offspring.

Considerations about possible future circumstances
can be helpful in revealing the actual character of a
morally good or bad action, but they are not quite the
point. One can speculate about the possibility that Jim
might leave Janet, should a pregnancy occur, despite his
obviously good intentions at present. Janet herself could
have a change of heart or mind about Jim being in her
life, with or without a pregnancy actually occurring.
Of course, with thoughts like these, premarital intercourse begins to look like adultery (displaced in time)
in relation to a *different*, potential future spouse.

The main point, however, centers on what Janet is *willing* to have happen to any child who might be brought into the world as a result of her free action with Jim. Even if she knew with medical certainty that either she or Jim is sterile and could not possibly conceive a child, her premarital coital union with Jim says--in itself-- that she is *naturally willing* that a child's right to Social Harmony be used chiefly as a *means* to her partici- pation in that very same Good. In effect, she would be saying through her action that she intends to deepen her participation with Jim in the fundamental Good of Social Harmony by *means* of suppressing her natural (if not func- tional) participation with a child in that same funda- mental Good. Also, she would be saying that she is natu- rally willing to *use* fertility (although it is function- ally defective), which is part of the fundamental Good of Life, directly as a means to participate in the Good of Social Harmony. But such participation would be there- by inauthentic and damaging to the persons involved, whether it *felt* like it or not.

The fact that Jim and Janet would be *functionally not able* to violate the Good of Social Harmony through the conception of a child would not take away from the fact that they would still be *naturally able* to do so. Moral good is rooted in the *nature* of a person and basic Values, not in how or whether they happen to *function*. In other words, moral good is an act of third-level free- dom, not second-level.

There would seem to be no way Janet could honestly rationalize coital intercourse with Jim as other than a moral willingness to wound a child and thereby herself, Jim, and all of humanity through directly blocking a natu- ral right of that child to begin life in the proper *social* womb. She may be psychically and spiritually unwilling to inflict on the child a faulty social beginning to his or her life.[9] But, if she decides to enter coital union, she is *morally* willing.

If Janet does engage in premarital intercourse with Jim and a child is conceived, the wound is inflicted and can never be taken back. But it surely can be forgiven. Obviously, it is not physically fatal to the child. Many such children recover very well and readily forgive their parents. Yet, at some level of consciousness or uncon- sciousness, Janet seriously impeded her own personal growth by directly acting against the fundamental Good of Social Harmony.

3. Non-exceptional action

The morally sound attitude includes another dimension. Do as you would have others do. For instance,
Janet could say to herself, "Jim and I are mature enough
for this action, but I surely do not think that Sally
and Tim are. They may be engaged to be married In June,
but they are so self-centered they probably couldn't
handle it." She might even believe that only a rare one
out of a thousand engaged couples can "grow by doing it"
and that she and Jim are such a couple. If her thoughts
would run along these lines, she would be violating this
particular mode of responsibility.

The point is not that this kind of discriminating
judgment about self and others is always wrong. In many
matters it might be part of true moral judgment. Moral
considerations such as when to have one's first child
or when to stop working during pregnancy involve just
this kind of thinking. Some people are ready for it,
others are not, at a given time. But, in the case at
hand, the issue really involves basic human Values directly. No one can morally make himself or herself an exception to the way in which these ultimate purposes of life
are lived. There are many human values that are far less
than ultimate and allow for great variability in fulfilling them. But the fundamental human Goods are common to
all persons under all circumstances and conditions. Making oneself an exception to the way in which they are
directly engaged is not homicide or genicide, but attempted personicide.

4. The fullest good of another

The eight modes of responsibility are so comprehensive in scope that a given moral action may be explicitly
encompassed by more than one of them. I have already
indicated that, by an act of premarital genital intercourse, Janet would be naturally violating her possible
child's right to marital nurture and protection. Another
way to view the action is to say that she seems unwilling
to act with the fullest good of the other in mind. A
mother or father who has a morally mature attitude desires
wholeheartedly to give a child the best start in life and
to provide such a good growth-experience for the child
over the years that he or she comes to the fullest exercise of talents and powers, even surpassing what the
parents have achieved.

Janet does seem to be very concerned about doing
something that will truly foster the fullest growth in

Jim. Such a concern is commendable in itself. But a
sound moral attitude includes doing what is simultaneously
the truest and the best for self and *all* others, no matter
what it costs in criticism and trouble from those who
do not understand or do not care. Janet may be in need
of exercising this particular mode of responsible action.

5. Duties

One's duties are a complex lot. They arise naturally
from all of the interpersonal relationships in life. Basically they are of two kinds: contractual and communal.

Contractual duties are strictly second-level choices
and actions. Jim and Janet may agree to pay an artisan
a certain amount of money for designing wedding rings
by a particular date. They have a duty to pay for the
work they contract. The whole thing is largely a means-
to-an-end proposition. These duties derive their moral
content from the fact that they implement and support
commitments, which are third-level choices--such as marriage to each other, and helping others (including the
ring-maker) earn a *living*.

Communal duties are those which arise from participation in third-level social relationships. Marriage is
a third-level commitment that is initiated and put into
practice voluntarily. Being the son or daughter of particular parents is a third-level relationship that is
initiated (or at least occasioned) involuntarily, but
it is gradually put into practice (through the years of
childhood development) to an increasingly voluntary extent.

Janet has duties that arise from these and many other
relationships in the human community. Such duties spring
from the variety of social roles that these relationships
naturally involve. Each of the communities to which Janet
belongs is bound together by a shared commitment on the
part of the members for the sake of realizing some basic
human Value or Values. By nature these communities tend
to structure themselves in such a way as to participate
well in the Values concerned. The activity of the members
can be regarded not simply as individual actions but as
a common act. Inappropriate behavior on the part of a
member violates the natural, third-level bond of the community, in particular, and the basic Value of Social
Harmony, in general.

Sometimes, however, one's duties in life conflict.
A wife, for instance, may be able to fulfill her duties

toward one community and, at the same time, not be able to fulfill them toward another. If her parents, whom she has not seen for two years, are planning to have her bring the children to visit them during her father's one-week vacation, yet her husband needs her to help him with his business that same week, she may have a serious conflict. In this area of moral action, circumstances play a great part. If her parents--now residing in Chicago--are moving the following week to Australia where her father is being transferred by his company, the conflict escalates. She must act, of course, by choosing to do what she can honestly see is the most responsible course of action. She is not obliged by the community whose needs she fails to fulfill, *if* they cannot be met in this instance and *if*, under the circumstances, the responsibility to the other community is greater.

Let us suppose that Janet's parents are very strongly opposed to premarital coital intercourse. That they would be terribly hurt by Janet's proposed action is not a genuine reason to refrain. Sometimes, one cannot avoid hurting other people when one does the right thing, if these people do not realize how right it was. But since the action of premarital intercourse is a free act and would be done to please Jim and herself, rather than to fulfill some moral obligation, Janet is called upon to weigh seriously her natural duties toward her parents--even though she is "of age"--and her natural duties toward Jim, to whom she is solemnly engaged and with whom she has a special love-commitment.

In this particular case, independent of other modes of responsibility, Janet has a rather serious conflict of duties arising from these two natural communities. One could also suppose that Janet's religious affiliation is with a church community that disapproves of her prospective interaction with Jim. Obviously, Janet must try to reconcile this conflict as honestly as she can for the sake of all the communities concerned, including the one she forms with Jim.

6. Pursuit of limited objectives

Janet may regard an act of premarital coital intercourse with Jim as a very practical way *to show* her undying love for him. The act is, then, the pursuit of a limited objective. Certainly, such an objective is ordinarily proper in assessing part of the value of coital intercourse in itself. This kind of intercourse can and should help the partners fulfill various specific objectives, such as expressing love emphatically, increasing the personal bond of the couple, or trying to conceive a child. These objectives constitute some of the particular ways in which people can participate in the fundamental Goods of Social Harmony and Life.

The pursuit of limited or specific objectives is a very necessary thing. In general, it is a positive moral good. In particular, however, it depends on whether this pursuit is a proper way to forward one's participation in the ultimate purpose of life. The pursuit of limited objectives is always a second-level action that is only as good or bad as the third-level action which it embodies. Second-level actions help to put flesh on the bones of third-level action.

The utilitarian principle of doing the greatest good for the greatest number of people is an instance of this particular mode of responsibility. Within the proper context of responsible choice at the third level, it makes good sense. On this basis, Janet might be inclined to reason that refraining from coital union with Jim before the wedding might well be doing the greatest good for the greatest number of people, including her parents and family, all of the faithful members of her church, and any possible child she and Jim might conceive. But, within the strict confines of this mode of responsibility alone, she might argue that if they kept their actions private they would not hurt anyone and yet would increase their love and union with each other, which is a very great good in itself.

Such an exclusivistic approach would only serve to illustrate how this mode of responsibility is not enough.[10] All of these guidelines together form a proper whole from which one can receive sound direction in any moral action or attitude.

7. Detachment from second-level
   action and goals

This mode of responsibility for one's attitudes and actions is often bitterly experienced. A person can be sailing along toward the attainment of very noble purposes. Then a tragedy strikes, and all of his or her means to the end are washed away.

If either Jim or Janet should become paralyzed and comatose through disease or an accident in the next few weeks, the goal or purpose of their wedding preparations would cease being realistic and their actions toward it would be terminated. But their participation in the ultimate purposes for which they had been living could continue. Janet could still continue to participate in the fundamental Goods while relating to a hospitalized and comatose friend. She could still love him and deepen her participation in the basic Values by caring for his health as a nurse (Life), appreciating their nearness to each other (Social Harmony), enjoying the doing of little things to make him comfortable (Play), and so on.

The critical test of authenticity in third-level action is whether and how one participates in the ultimate Purposes that encompass the specific purposes of second-level perspective, when this perspective is drastically changed or reduced. In regard to premarital coital union with Jim, Janet might well ask herself (in accord with this mode of responsibility) whether she is sufficiently detached from this kind of union with Jim. What is her moral attitude toward it? Would she still love Jim-- even more deeply perhaps--if an accident deprived Jim of his physical ability to engage in such intercourse? Would she still regard Jim as her man, and herself as his woman? If not, then she is probably deceiving herself now when she claims that this kind of action would foster greater love between them as man and woman. Coital intercourse is not a *basic* human Good or Value. It is a great good and value, but it is not fundamental to personhood and moral perfection.

The big question that should arise in determining whether premarital coital intercourse is ever morally justifiable is this: Whether coital intercourse is basic to *sexual* fulfillment and *sexual* love. Can Janet and Jim genuinely love each other as man and woman, as male and female persons, without ever engaging in genital interaction? Even beyond that, can they be *fully* loving as sexual beings without this kind of union?

Most people would emphatically deny that a man and woman can have *full* sexual relations without coital-genital intercourse. Very likely, Janet would do so. How can she and Jim love each other as persons in a *totally sexual* way by leaving out the exercise of the most obvious and exciting way of doing it? A response to that question more properly fits under the final mode of responsibility, which specially complements detachment from second-level, means-end action.

8. Creative fidelity to commitments

Detachment from second-level action is intimately related to "attachment" to third-level action.[11] The person's commitments are all third-level action, which is done as good in itself and as a direct way of participating in basic human Goods. Fidelity to these commitments, such as marriage, parenthood, scholarly work, memberships in various community organizations, and so forth, is a necessary characteristic of responsible moral behavior. Considerable set-backs to one's goal-striving behavior should not necessarily be reasons for ending one's commitments, which the goal-striving behavior is naturally designed to sustain and support. There is an inherent power in the person for creatively continuing to participate in the underlying Values by reassessing and adjusting his or her ways of fulfilling commitments.

In her situation, Janet has ample opportunity to think into the meaning of her commitments more deeply than ever before. She may be defining sexuality by confining it to the genital area. At the very least, she may be thinking that sexuality is consummated in genital activity, even though it pervades the rest of the personality. She may not realize that every act is a sexual act; that is, it has a definitely sexual dimension, just as every cell in the body does. She may not regard the very essence of sexuality as sharing the gift of self with self and with others. It may never have occurred to her that she and Jim are having *physical* sexual intercourse all the time, by seeing each other, hearing each other, touching each other, and even smelling each other.

What would genital intercourse with Jim really do to make their sexual sharing more *physical*, more *real*, more *meaningful*? Coital intercourse would make their sexual sharing more *dramatically* physical, because it is much more elaborate as a physical action. But it would not make their sexual sharing more *dynamically* physical than any other act of physical tenderness and love. Coital-genital intercourse is, specifically, but one dramatic form of one kind of physical interaction, namely touching. It is a dramatic act of touching each other. Seeing, hearing, smelling--and maybe even tasting--each other are normally involved. But the action is *specifically* a kind of *touching*--not specifically a seeing, hearing, smelling, or tasting--and the most dramatic result of that act of touching is another human being in physical creation.

As I indicated earlier, however, the parents are not ultimately responsible for the care of this new human being and for the care of the generations of offspring that this child might eventually help to propagate. The ultimate receiver of the act of conception is the society. Coital intercourse, therefore, is a personal action in a limited sense. It is social, above all. The *specific*

215

good of this action is ultimately procreation. The general good--as with all human actions, especially those
in which persons "face" each other--is unification and
love.

Janet may come to realize that her genital union
with Jim would necessarily be two things at once: a personal interaction in society, and a society-interaction
through persons. As much as she might like it to be just
a personal interaction between Jim and herself (as friends
and lovers) she can come to see that somehow this interaction is *primarily* an action of society done in and
through the two of them. Society has the primary right
to specify general conditions under which this kind of
action should be performed. That is done in the social
covenant of marriage. Janet's radically natural membership in society would seem to prohibit her from engaging
in the action before marriage. Her responsibility to
be faithful to the natural commitment to society that
each member of society sustains by reason of conception,
birth, nurture, and education demands a more creative
approach to her love-making with Jim.

Janet needs to reflect on the nature of genital
union. She can be creative in her approach to love-
making only if her efforts are based on a firm understanding of the difference between personal organs and
social organs.

Eyes, ears, nose, and skin represent personal organs
of physical receptiveness to people and things. They
are specifically *personal* organs that facilitate interpersonal, physical love-making. But the person's genital
organs are not specifically personal, since the specific
good of their action is not something received only by
the person involved (as are color, sound, flavor, odor).[12]
The *specific* good of genital organs in action is a child.
Genital organs are specifically and primarily social
organs. They are (physical) *social* organs by which society maintains and enhances itself. They do not fulfill
a specifically individual good.

Genital organs *can* fulfill a generally individual
good: man-woman love. But this latter good can just as
well--and often much better--be fulfilled by simpler acts
of tenderness, care, and sharing through touching, seeing,
and listening to each other. Such actions are just as
real and often much more *meaningful* than coital intercourse. (And, in accord with the definitions of this
book, these actions are just as sexual.)

216

Coital-genital intercourse is, therefore, not necessary to *personal* sexual fulfillment. It *is necessary* for
society's sexual fulfillment. But individual persons
are essentially free members of society and not so structured that they *must* share the gift of self with self
and others in a genital or coital way. Sharing the gift
of life with another person (a child) is a very fulfilling
way to be sexual. But it is designed to be a *personally
free* way.

If there is no genuine choice about whether I can
attain total sexual freedom, except by engaging in at
least one coital-genital act, then acts of this kind
are not free. Yet, unfree acts, such as nutritional consumption, defecation, and the like, cannot be, as such,
acts of love--although they can be done by people with
loving attitudes. Freedom is the heart of loving. Therefore, Jim and Janet's coital union, *as such*, would not
be a *personally* loving act. Janet's prospective action
would involve contradictory motivation inasmuch as she
would be desiring to express *love*--a free act--by means
of an act that, in effect, she would be regarding as
practically necessary to increase or manifest their love
at this time.

Creative fidelity to her commitment as an individual
member of society acting freely and responsibly means
that Janet will refrain from loving Jim at this time in
a coital way, but that she will love him all the more
tenderly and firmly by saying no to his request for this
kind of intercourse. A thoughtful and convinced response
on her part will raise her own self-esteem as a person
and as a woman. It may also occasion a new respect for
her in Jim, even though he may grumble and react negatively at first. It could be the start of a new horizon
in their friendship as man and woman.

In any event, challenging Jim on the authenticity
of his love would seem to be necessary if the couple is
to grow. The depths of male chauvinism may be seen in
the widely held, largely male assumption that it is the
woman's responsibility to "keep the man in line" on sex.
Male irresponsibility in the control and integration of
sex drives is a direct and overwhelming cause of the
sexual energy crisis and its major forms of pollution.
The time may have come for women in Janet's position to
accept their own responsibility while asserting themselves and insisting on a *single* standard of sexual responsibility for both sexes, based on the common requirements for responsible action (attainable by any reasonable
person) which we have considered in this chapter.[13]

All of these requirements for personal responsibility
serve to provide the necessary perspective for an ever
more deeply meaningful participation in the basic Goods
of human life. They are guides to self-love and love
for others. Once discovered, they instruct the person
in the general ways to discipline his or her moral attitudes and moral actions so that in the light of their
truth his or her deepest self is discovered and loved.

NOTES

1. Of course, there can be immense content in such an act, if
it is done with consciously loving affirmation as though it were
the most important thing one were doing at the time. Jesus once
said that a person would not go unrewarded for giving even so little
as a cup of water in his name. Giving something in Jesus' name,
consciously and deliberately, may be an act of considerable content
because of its motivation, if not because of the simplicity and
habituality of its behavioral dimension.

2. Perhaps it can be said that moral acts are of differing kinds,
something like body cells. Our simplest and most concrete moral
acts might be likened to individual body cells, which in great numbers constitute body tissue or complexes of cells. What might be
called our more complex and intangible moral acts would then seem
to be like specialized groups of cells of various kinds. Thus,
there are various kinds of moral acts such as vocational decisions,
occupational decisions, inter-racial attitudes, religious affiliation decisions, etc. that are somewhat like the various kinds of
body tissue and complexes of cells such as muscle tissue, organ
tissue, glandular tissue, brain cells, skin cells, bone cells, etc.
These complex and specialized moral acts are very numerous in kind
and are each composed of multitudinous acts or actions that help to
constitute them, just as in the case of the many kinds of body tissue composed of the individual cells which comprise them. In both
areas of our being--moral and bodily--the more complex is not simply
the sum of its individual parts but constitutes a thoroughly unique
kind of part within the whole.

3. "Modes of responsibility" may sound strange to some ears. On
the undermining of responsibility in the contemporary world--effected
largely by the individual's powerlessness over his destiny in the
nuclear age--Rollo May is particularly insightful. See *Love and
Will* (New York: W. W. Norton, 1969), especially pp. 183-89. May
believes that the contemporary "lack of will" is much more than an
ethical problem: ". . . [T]he modern individual so often has the
conviction that even if he did exert his 'will'--or whatever illusion
passes for it--his action wouldn't do any good anyway. It is this
inner experience of impotence, this contradiction in will, which
constitutes our critical problem." p. 184.

I would add that this problem highlights our impoverished sense of what ethics is about. We are conditioned to think that responsibility means having the power to get things done--to achieve second-level goods (goals). This is the soul of the anti-ethical utilitarianism that has poisoned Anglo-American culture. On the contrary, one only becomes functionally capable of ethical growth and maturity when one is *willing* to relinquish the products of empirical human production, and wills the good--anyway. The good-- ethically relevant good--is attained over and above any overtly beneficial results. Of course, the ethically good person will endeavor to effect concretely good results in everything he or she does. But that is only *part* of a wholesome, ethically valid intention and desire. The modes of responsibility concerned with detachment and creative fidelity discussed later in this chapter are particularly relevant to this point.

4. These eight criteria are essentially the same as those offered by Grisez and Shaw in *Beyond the New Morality*, but involve some modification and interpretation. Someone else might formulate criteria that are fewer or greater in number but that, nevertheless, adequately express the substance of any morally responsible attitude or action.

5. The issue is "genital intercourse" rather that "sexual intercourse." Sexual intercourse is going on all the time. Also, in formulating the issue, I do not say "coital intercourse" because I wish to include more actions than actual coition and orgasm. Any deliberately intended stimulation of each other's genital organs is included.

6. What I *now* regard as morally right may well be so. But genuine moral evaluation always involves readiness to go beyond present positions because of new meaning or evidence that is always independent of my limited grasp of it. My mind is dependent on truth; not truth, on my mind.

7. I have said that it is immoral to use one fundamental Good *directly*, *merely*, or *chiefly* as a means to participate in another fundamental Good. Obviously, it is morally permissible and necessary to use one Good for the sake of the other indirectly, partially, or secondarily.

For example, the friendship or social harmony of two people permits one of them to utilize this condition in asking the other for help to maintain health or life. When someone assists a blind person to cross a busy street, the fundamental Good of Social Harmony is being indirectly, partially, or secondarily used as a means to participate in the Good of Life (through safe passage). But when someone borrows money from a friend, with no intention of paying it back (stealing), then the fundamental Good of Social Harmony is being used directly, merely, or chiefly as a means to participate in the Good of Life (through money for higher quality housing, nutrition, etc.) or the Good of Play (through money for vacations, recreation, etc.) or some other fundamental Good.

8. In this post-Freudian age, it is interesting to see how little attention most moralists give to the effects of unconscious motiva-

tion in evaluating the consequences or meaning of an action. Of course, unconscious motivation cannot have the same significance as conscious motivation. But it should likewise be obvious that unconscious motivation must be carefully taken into account when making a moral decision and when reflecting on its meaning.

9. That is, prereflectively and spontaneously she may be very loving toward her potential child.

10. One cannot really keep the effects of an act of coital union private--except at the relatively superficial level of rational consciousness. The effects of such an act are profoundly influential subconsciously on each other and on everyone they meet--for good or bad. Thus, it would be extremely naive for Janet to think that they can effect only good by such an interaction if they keep the *fact* of the intercourse a secret. The essence of a good moral choice is that it is made with an inclusivistic attitude. One must be open to *all* criteria for moral evaluation, not just any one or a special few. Exclusivistic use of such criteria itself presupposes "bad faith" or inauthentic and unintegrated behavior. On the essence of inclusivistic and exclusivistic choices and their moral significance, cf. Grisez, *Beyond the New Morality*, pp. 85-95. On the nature of this utilitarian mode of responsibility and how it is abused by many moral theorists, see pp. 113-114.

11. Actually, one is never really "attached" to a good. One is only attached to goals. One has no hold on a good as a good, only as a goal--and, in that case, it is not being treated as a value or good but as an objective or acquisition. Values or goods cannot be grasped. They can only be enjoyed, participated in, experienced. What appears to be *attachment* to value in a saintly person is rather a profound *commitment*. People do not grasp values or goods. The goods or values grasp people. And people let or do not let themselves be "taken in" by them.

12. Genital organs are, rather, *multi-personal* in the sense that they specifically pertain to the whole human community, as is explained below.

13. Derivation of these requirements for responsible action and attitude in human behavior--as well as discernment of the fundamental human Goods in which they make participation possible--is the work of philosophical anthropology and metaphysics more than of ethics. Ethics receives its fundamental principles from these basic philosophical disciplines.

Part   IV

SOCIOSEXUAL IDENTITY

Chapter   13

FERTILITY AWARENESS

The evaluation of a moral act is often difficult because of the extreme complexity of personal and interpersonal ecology. One cannot always be sure that one has addressed all the relevant criteria for making a sound judgment on whether the act is good or bad, virtuous or vicious. The depth and complexity of human nature evokes wonder and admiration, but also causes concern that we do not overlook some mode of responsibility--naturally inherent in each person--that helps to constitute the basic moral ecosystem.

In the last chapter, I discussed eight moral criteria that work together ecologically. The voluntary exercise of one's coital-genital powers is subject to these intrinsically interrelated standards. The evaluation of an individual genital act is made all the more difficult at times because of the nature of human sexuality. The supremely social character of human sexuality is so readily obscured by the intensely personal feelings and emotions it normally evokes. Because the satisfactions and frustrations of coitional sexual desires so forcefully impinge on the ego, most people seem to be little aware of the definitively social meaning of these desires.

The history of most couples' coital-genital relations seems to be only faintly colored by an awareness of the gift-sharing nature of their actions. Partners tend to unite for the sake of mutually rewarding experience. A reward is not a gift. A gift is not basically a reward. Coital-genital relations often amount to giving-and-getting sessions. Little distinction is made between the giving-and-getting of a mutually rewarding experience and the giving-and-receiving of authentic sexual activity. Sexuality is buried alive in their sexploits.

Because little distinction is made between mutual reward and mutual sharing in coital-genital relations, the great difference between genitality and sexuality is not acknowledged. Genitality and sexuality are not only seen as more intimately related--which they are-- but as practically identical--which they are not. Frequently, people seem to settle for the attitude that "sex is sex."[1]

The opposite attitude, however, seems to be threatening the immediate future of sexual awareness. As women move more assertively and self-consciously into all of the professions and into much of the total work force, many have the tendency to separate sexuality from genitality. As individuals, they may say, "I am a woman, a sexual person, not a sex thing or a baby-maker; my womanhood has little to do with my anatomy or my fertility." They will have the inclination to regard genitality, the power to share life, as an impersonal *function*. In other words, they will not really see it primarily as a power to *share a gift*, but simply as another power to produce. Sexuality may be considered a personal quality; but genitality will remain outside the limits of effectively personal responsibility.

Other women, of course, will assert their rights as individuals while still denying that sexuality is personal. Their denial effectively amounts to this: "I am not a woman at all, except anatomically and physiologically." Both sexuality and genitality are evaluated as something less than personal.[2]

A Breakthrough in Logic

Why are so many women today--not to mention ever so many men--considerably constricted in their sexual self-concepts? When insight fails, logic is never the ultimate culprit. But an inadequate kind of logic, as well as an inaccurate use of logic, can be a great obstacle.

Women today, as they stand at the threshold of a long-desired and much-needed freedom, individually and socially, suffer from the male-dominated, two-valued logic

of the Western world.[3] At least since it was developed
by Aristotle, either-or logic has been over-valued in
Western civilization. We all have difficulty seeing
that two things which are quite diverse can be quite similar and can have many of the same kinds of things said
of them. So, for instance, the great diversity of man
and woman is often denied because they are so obviously
quite similar and because we can say almost everything
about the one that we can about the other.

The logic to which we are heir is important and
necessary. It is the logic of yes-or-no. A thing cannot
be true and not true at the same time under the same respect. I cannot be in this room, here-and-now physically,
and not in this room. I can be in this room and not in
this room at the same time in different respects--physi-
cally and mentally--but not in the same respect. And,
of course, I can be in this room and not in this room
at different times under the same respect.

This two-valued kind of logic is practical.[4] It
serves the attainment of any kind of truth--physical or
mathematical, theoretical or practical. But it has its
limitations and it can be readily abused.

Besides this yes/no logic on which all of our compu-
ters are based, the human person needs to operate with a
yes *and* no logic. Anyone who has ever taken a true-false
test on a subject of depth and complexity is very probably
in a position to understand the need for yes *and* no logic.
Some questions, no matter how carefully worded or qualified, cannot be answered adequately with a yes or a no.
The mind attains levels of depth and complexity that can
be honored only by saying *both* yes *and* no to the question.
One is inclined to say, "Yes, it is true in *this* way and
to *this* extent." The person may be inclined to go on,
adding qualifications to the qualifications. At the
same time, he or she will want to say very definitely
that it is false to *this* extent, inadequate in *such and
such* a way, and so forth.

The human mind needs *both* a logic of problem-solving
(an either-or logic) *and* a logic of mystery-participating
(a both-and logic). Even this last sentence reveals the
need for a both-and logic. The question is not: should
we have *either* an either-or logic *or* a both-and logic?
The question is: do we not need *both* an either-or logic
and a both-and logic? The logic of mystery and paradox
encompasses the logic of separation and identity. When
issues are deep and complex it is very often easy to

225

overlook this truth and to function only at the level of
either-or in a pragmatic effort to "get somewhere."

So, when human sexuality is in question, it is not
surprising that people have their capacity for insight
blocked by our culturally developed reflex of relying
on a narrow-frame logic. A woman, for instance, might
have difficulty in regarding herself as *both* sexual *and*
genital in the depths of her personhood. She might be
heavily inclined to think that if her personhood is distinctively *sexual* (having the power to share self as a
gift, with self and with others) then it *cannot be* distinctively *genital* (having the power to share the gift
of life with another). She might well think that, after
all, brute animals "share" the gift of life with other
members of their species, so this power of genitality
is not part of being a *person*. Her propensity for either-
or thinking could readily keep her from seeing that only
persons can *share* the gift of life with another of their
kind and that this sharing of the gift of life is a mode
of sharing *within* the sharing of the gift of self. In
other words, sharing the gift of life is an exercise of
both sexuality *and* genitality; it is not *either* one *or*
the other.

Both Sexuality and Genitality Mean Sharing

Careful attention to the basic meanings of sexuality
and genitality can help to preserve a balanced sense of
their relationship.

Sexuality is the personal power to share the gift
of self with self and with *every* other. This personal
power is always present in the person. But it is so
often operating at a very low level of effectiveness.

People do share themselves naturally with others,
even though they are not aware of doing so at the time.
The sharings may be healthy, unhealthy, or practically
non-existent. A woman, for instance, selling merchandise
to a customer in the course of her everyday duties is
sharing herself not only with the customer to some extent,
but also with her husband and children whom she is helping
to support through this work. Yet, in instances of cold-
blooded murder or rape there would seem to be a complete
cessation of sharing activity. Lack of exercising sexuality in healthy ways twenty-four hours a day leads to
crimes of violence--not only in physical deed, as in
murder or rape, but in mental desertion and hardness
of heart. Low-grade daily sharing culminates in cruelty.
High quality sharing is a kind of heaven on earth.

Genitality is the personal and social power to share the gift of life with another person. Genitality is *not only* a power for personal sharing *but also* the power by which society is created and maintained in its membership. It is a specifically *social* power. Not only does a person share life with a child by the exercise of genitality, but *the society shares* its membership with a new individual, in and through the exercise of this power on the part of that new individual's parents.[5]

Life in this world is a very personal gift that we receive through our parents. So, when our parents exercise their genital powers they are doing something very personal. They are procreating a person. Persons generate persons--not blobs of protoplasm or products of conception, as the rhetoric of a viciously technocratic culture often suggests.[6] Even though many people exercise it so impersonally, genitality is a supremely personal power. Parents give us life in this world. Few things could be more personally meaningful to us than the gift of this life. While all good things are ultimately the gift of God, life in this world is a special gift of our parents. They are the particular agents of this giving, this sharing. God *alone* can give us the gift of self. But other beings, creatures like ourselves, really do cooperate in giving us the gift of life.

In sharing the gift of life with someone else, a person is likewise sharing himself or herself. Life and self are not at all the same, but they are intimately related. Genitality is an intimate form of sexuality. Parents are sexually intimate with their children in exercising the power of genitality. In doing this, they are acting like God who is sexually intimate with every creature, by sharing Self with the creature in the act of giving the creature a self.[7]

Being careful to retain the use of a both-and logic, we can now turn our attention to fertility, the main functional dimension of human genitality.

Fertility Awareness: an Important Part of Self-Awareness

In Chapter 5, I suggested certain clues toward understanding the difference between male and female sexuality in the depths of the person. The behavior of sperm in contrast to ova, the structure and placement of genital organs, and other features were cited in developing the notions of male and female as involving a receiving kind of giving and a giving kind of receiving. I suggested that the surest way to know sexuality is to meditate upon the structures, functions, and interrelationships found in genitality and coitality.

The contemporary movement known as natural family planning offers a dramatic case in point. Thousands of couples in various parts of the world are regulating the exercise of their genital powers by means of fertility-awareness techniques.[8] Knowledge of one's fertility--not the same as natural family planning, but a potential base for it--is a special kind of knowledge of one's genitality. Reflection on the nature and meaning of fertility can, therefore, lead people through a heightened sense of genitality into a deep and rich knowledge of their sexuality--from fertility to genitality to sexuality. A knowledge of one's personal fertility is a concrete beginning in knowing oneself as a deeply sexual person. It likewise provides a solid base for achieving sexual identity and self-confidence as a sexual person in society.

The natural family planning movement today is concentrated on two main approaches in the use of fertility awareness. One approach is called the Ovulation Method and the other is known as the Sympto-thermal Method.[9] Neither of these methods is directly associated with the Rhythm Method that involved calculation and prediction of the times of ovulation based on the actual pattern of previous menstrual cycles. Such a method, sometimes called Calendar Rhythm, was reliable for those women who had strictly regular cycles, but was not reliable for those whose cycles were often or occasionally irregular. The latest methods are, for the properly motivated couple, as reliable as any contraceptive method.[10]

The Ovulation Method, developed mainly by Drs. John and Evelyn Billings, through more than twenty years of research, is based on a woman's direct observation of cervical mucus.[11] A woman can be taught to check for mucus at the opening of the vagina. Under initial guidance of a well-trained instructor--usually another woman, who need not be a physician--she can learn to monitor the changes in characterisitcs of the mucus when it occurs. The mucus is a natural discharge that occurs before and during the time of ovulation. It changes the vagina from an acid condition to alkaline, which is favorable to sperm life. It nourishes sperm which happen to be present by providing nutrients to keep them alive, and it facilitates their migration toward the ovum.

228

When the mucus first appears it is usually thick, clotty, opaque, whitish or yellowish, scant and sticky. There is usually a feeling of stickiness. As its consistency begins to change, the mucus is cloudy. But it gradually becomes clear. It also becomes thinner, more fluid, transparent, and elastic. As ovulation approaches, the mucus is thin and clear, watery and slippery, fluid and stretchy. Most women agree that at this time the mucus has the consistency of raw egg-white and tends to be discharged in "threads." After a peak period of wetness, the mucus either disappears or decreases sharply in amount and becomes thick and sticky again.[12]

Learning how to read her fertility in the language of mucus puts a woman in direct contact with her fertility-infertility cycle. She is able to be in control of her body by knowing her body. She can know when she is fertile, within a matter of hours in most cases. She can decide to have coital intercourse at that time in order to increase her chances of conceiving, if she so desires; or she can refrain from intercourse during the several days before and after the time of ovulation, if she does not desire to conceive.

The method must be communicated by a competent instructor. It cannot be put into practice effectively simply on the basis of hearing or reading about how it works. Even reading a thorough and detailed explanation of any natural method will not be sufficient to practice it on one's own. Unlike contraceptive *measures*, the practice of natural family planning is truly a *method*-- as well as a philosophy--and as such it must be learned from a qualified teacher who initiates the couple into the *art*. Yet, a woman of any age and socio-economic background can be taught the method in a simple, direct manner. It is working for thousands of illiterate couples, and is growing steadily in the developing nations.

The Sympto-thermal Method is a combination of detecting the mucus characteristics and other signs of fertility, along with recording the basal body temperature (the temperature of the body at rest). The signs of fertility include a gradual opening of the cervical os, as well as a softening and a rising in the position of the cervix about the time of ovulation.[13] But these characteristics of the cervix are secondary to the observation of mucus and the rise in temperature. Besides these major signs, there are many auxiliary signs that can be used by individual women.

By taking her temperature with a specially designed thermometer immediately upon wakening in the morning, a woman can daily monitor a major sign of fertility-infertility. Once ovulation occurs, a woman's body temperature rises and remains at a higher level until the end of the cycle.[14] There are definite rules for interpreting the use of the thermometer, as well as the monitoring of mucus signs, so it is necessary to receive instruction.[15] But once competent, individualized instruction has been received practically any woman can be confidently in control of herself with respect to fertility.

When couples are first introduced to one of these natural methods of conception control they often wonder whether they can tolerate the periods of refraining from coital intercourse that are part of the method and of the underlying philosophy. The overwhelming sentiment of those who faithfully practice the method is that these periods help to strengthen the bond of love on which this method is based.[16] Natural family planning is the co-operative way to regulate one's response to fertility. Many have pointed out that it is the only non-sexist method.[17] NFP, as it is called, places the responsibility for conception control on both partners. They must *share*. One can say, therefore, that it is the "sexyist" method of family planning, too. It challenges man and woman to participate in their shared genitality with the mutual understanding that is essential to authentic love.[18]

People who use NFP often point to several beneficial psychological factors in the practice of periodic continence. Some have observed that regular orgasm tends to get monotonous and loses meaning. Routine is the deadliest enemy of coital sex enjoyment. It has been compared to the practice of frequent lunching, such that one is never hungry enough to enjoy a good meal. Cyclic continence, on the other hand, tends to heighten desire and renews the appeal of intercourse. NFP users often refer to the time at which intercourse is renewed as "the honeymoon."

Times of coitional silence are really a natural part of genital love-making. For love to grow there must be spaces in the couple's togetherness. Their coitional togetherness is no exception. Not engaging in genital intercourse even when they feel the urge to do so can be a sexual, and even a genital, expression of their love. Behavioral performance is like a vocal performance, so that keeping silent under appropriate circumstances is part of communication, and can be a very expressive dimension. Proponents of contraceptive intercourse often ignore this crucial element in the development of coital sex love. Married couples actually reveal and foster love by restraint as well as by performance. They need to develop a creative pattern of love-making which integrates (rather than negates) the natural pattern of their fertility and their interpersonal desires for conceiving or not conceiving another person at the time.

Fertility awareness itself is not simply an instrument-for natural family planning. Awareness of when one is fertile and infertile is an important dimension of self-awareness as a man or woman. *Every* woman should be encouraged to learn her fertility-infertility cycle to some extent. Some unmarried women have come to realize that becoming skilled in observing the main signs of ovulation can be rewarding. They can better understand their own changes of mood as these changes relate to phases within their menstrual cycles.[19]

But a woman ought to know her body not simply in order to control her body. When she begins to know her bodily signs of genital fertility she can begin to know something rather definite about her sexuality and her being as a woman. She can know her genitality in order to *be* her sexuality with greater intensity. Body and soul are one. They are not two things, but two mutual parts of one being. Anything that a woman can know about her pattern of fertility-infertility will be itself a knowledge of her being as a woman.

Men, too, can learn about their own fertility, and in that way increase their knowledge of themselves as men. Generally, it can be said that men are fertile all the time. They do not dramatize fertility as women do by definite cyclic patterns--although men may have indefinite cyclic patterns, at least with respect to times of peak fertility.[20] Their ever-ready kind of fertility points again to their natural emphasis on manyness and other-directedness, in contrast to the female emphasis on oneness and inward-directedness. Above all, men need to learn respect for the very different kind of fertility in the sexes. The relative simplicity of a man's genital fertility is *both* quite diverse *and* quite complementary with respect to the relative complexity of a woman's.

In their ecologically toned little book, *Joy in Human Sexuality*, John and Nancy Ball suggest that a woman's fertility cycle is like the earth undergoing the seasons of the year. They portray her cycle as a passage from the autumn of menstruation, through the winter of

vaginal dryness and lower body temperature, to the spring
of ovulation, and then into the summer of lush uterine
build-up and higher temperature.[21] Perhaps, a man's fertility could be likened to the steadiness of the atmosphere through which seasonal fluctuations are sustained.
The atmosphere is ever ready to contain a new season. A
man continuing to be fertile long after the age of a woman's menopause is a dramatic illustration of the different emphasis in a man's very being. He is ever ready
with more.

For both men and women, fertility awareness is an
important part of self-awareness.

Fertility Awareness and the Basic Human Values

Several of the fundamental Goods of human life are
distinctively enjoyed when a person grows in fertility
awareness.

The rapid growth of natural family planning is a
striking example of people gaining an opportunity to enrich the quality of their participation in the basic
Value of Life. Knowing when they *can* most likely conceive
and working with that knowledge makes a couple ready for
the life that they *may* conceive largely through their
own choice. Life itself is celebrated much more intelligently when a person comes to know and respect the
cycle of life's possibilities.

The basic Value of Social Harmony is prominent in
the effective practice of a natural method of conception
regulation. Natural family planning challenges the two
people to become friends as well as lovers. Their communication almost inevitably becomes deeper and richer.
Regular sharing regarding the concrete details of the
couple's fertility cycle often leads to conversations
about the meaning of their life together and to a mutually
developed philosophy of marriage and family life. As
amorous mates they are free only to react to their fertility condition. But as friends they are free to share,
with Nature and their Creator, the responsibility inherent
in the only ecologically sound way of participating in
genital life.

The genitality of every person needs to be integrated
with all other parts of the self. Fertility awareness
is an important aspect of personal integration. When a
person can engage in self-control by respecting his or
her fertility, he or she participates deeply in another
basic Value: Integrity.

Personal fertility needs to be integrated, not "controlled." Practically speaking, there is no such thing as "fertility control." The pill user, for instance, is one who is trying to control fertility by suppressing it and releasing it. But fertility is not being controlled. It is being squelched. Conception is being regulated by means of a lack of fertility control and a lack of self-control.

Fertility is not so much something to be controlled; it is rather something to be integrated through knowledge and love. NFP is used very effectively to achieve or to avoid pregnancy. The time of conception is determined through a cooperative knowledge of one's own particular fertility and thereby through a richer participation in the fundamental Goods of Life and Integrity.[22]

A fourth basic Value that is experienced and celebrated by those who achieve a measure of true fertility awareness is Speculative Knowledge. Knowing one's genitality better is a good in itself. As with all the other Goods, such knowledge increases one's being by enriching one's selfhood. Fertility awareness that is designed *only* to make it possible to achieve or to avoid pregnancy cheapens and degrades the fundamental Good of knowing one's personal power to share the gift of life. Such knowledge is a value in its own right, independent of any use to which it validly may be put. Knowing periodically when she is functionally able to share the gift of life is something that is good for any woman as a person.[23] Sound education in fertility awareness helps a person to become joyful over being *able* to share the gift of life, whether he or she ever chooses to do so or not.

Psychic and Spiritual Dimensions of Fertility

Everyone is somewhat familiar with the close connection between the fertility cycle of a woman and her mental or emotional states. The powerful hormonal changes that quite naturally occur during the fertility cycle are bound to have an ecological effect on her psyche and even on her spiritual life. These effects in the psyche and spirit are the effects of specifically bodily conditions.[24] The body exerts considerable influence on the mind. However, all changes in body or mind that are associated with a woman's ovulation and menstruation processes are part of her physical fertility. They should not be confused with what might be called psychic and spiritual kinds of fertility.

Physical fertility may be defined as the person's functional ability to conceive a child. It includes very complex hormonal and physiological sets of conditions. It is the physically functional aptness of the person for sharing the gift of life with another person. But there are psychic and spiritual dimensions which must be taken into account if one is to assess adequately the individual's *basic genitality* (capacity for "having" a child, for *sharing* the gift of life).

Psychic fertility may be defined as the person's functional ability to give the child a warm, nurturing, stable, emotional atmosphere. It includes an extremely complex and profound set of personality characteristics. It is the psychically functional aptness for sharing the gift of life with another person. Genitality, like sexuality, has a psychic level as well as a physical level.[25]

Genitality also has a spiritual level. Sharing the gift of life with a child is a spiritual action as well as an emotional and physical one. Although the parents' spiritual dimension is often shared poorly with a child, some sharing does occur. If the sharing is low in quality, the child is as bound to suffer from that spiritual weakness as from weakness in the genetic structure of sperm and ovum, or from the emotional ineptness of the parents. Spiritual fertility may be defined as the person's functional ability to provide moral and spiritual care and guidance for the child. Often this kind of guidance is best given through example and role modeling. But it is inevitably given--for better or worse.

Although they are just as essential to genitality, psychic and spiritual fertility are quite different from physical fertility. One might note that these psychic and spiritual dimensions can be supplemented by the action of foster parents and other people in the care and guidance of offspring. Yet the exercise of the psychic and spiritual qualities of child-care by surrogate parents are, strictly speaking, not parentive but parent*like* behavior. Parenting--the fundamental exercise of genitality--is one whole act (physical, emotional, and spiritual). This activity can be retarded or become crippled at one or more levels. Parent substitutes do an inestimable service to the child who is deprived by his or her parents in one or more of these three dimensions of genital exercise. But they cannot *be* the parents. They cannot *do* the sharing of the gift of life that the parents do. They can only do *like* it, and make up greatly for the lack.[26]

Psychic and spiritual fertility are not the same as sexuality. They are special modes of sharing the gift of self with others. These non-physical dimensions of fertility are special functional aptnesses for sharing the gift of *life*. Life is not authentically *shared* if sharing stops at conception. Genitality, without its psychic and spiritual components, would not be the personal and social power to *share* the gift of life with another. Sharing is a totally personal activity and presupposes all three levels of the human person. Genitality is a thoroughly personal (as well as social) power.

Genuine fertility awareness recognizes and rejoices in this truth.

NOTES

1. Once genitality is carefully distinguished from sexuality, it can be seen to relate quite definitely to certain human goods--most notably to the basic good of Life. This relationship, which is quite clear, straightforward and unalterable, explains to a considerable degree the definiteness of Christian sexual morality. In this respect, sexual (genital) acts are much more readily discerned as morally good or bad than many other kinds of acts.

2. Ti-Grace Atkinson, Germain Greer, and others have "inspired" this concept of a flat sex society. See, e.g., Greer's *The Female Eunuch* (London: MacGibbon and Kee, 1970). In his book, *The Prisoner of Sex* (New American Library/Signet, 1971), Norman Mailer attempts to show its absurdities. He scores points, but seems to lack both empathy with women's needs and a truly revolutionary perspective for fulfilling them.

3. Cf. Mary Rosera Joyce's discussion of the logic of identity and separation and some of the unfortunate consequences of its misuse in the field of human sexuality: *The Meaning of Contraception*, pp. 107-109.

The exclusive exercise of this two-valued logic inevitably results in revolutions that are only that--revolutions, going around and around a common, false premise. For instance, the so-called sexual revolution of the 1960s had no real leverage philosophically. An avid women's liberation advocate, Susan Cohen, puts it succinctly: "What the much-touted sexual revolution has accomplished is to deprive women of their former protections while leaving them as much at the mercy of men as ever. Still a sexual object, she is expected to enjoy being one." *Liberated Marriage* (New York: Lance Books, 1971), p. 22.

4. It is based on the principle of non-contradiction. But it is also founded on other principles such as the principle of the excluded middle (of two contradictory propositions one or the other

must be true) and the principle of identity (a thing is itself and not any other). It is basically a logic of identity and separation. Two words stand for things that are either identical or separate. There is no middle ground, because this Aristotelian logic is geared to action and practical results. A charming and lucid description of the character of our two-valued logic and its purpose as a logic of decision is given by Donald Nicholl, *Recent Thought in Focus* (New York: Sheed & Ward, 1953), pp. 135-38.

Aristotelian logic does not, in itself, involve any defect. It has been used by Aristotle and other thinkers--notably Thomas Aquinas--with great dialectical flexibility. The general philosophical problem with its use is twofold. On the one hand, there is the confusion of logic and metaphysics, which began with Medieval "realists" and blossomed into the vast modern rationalist/empiricist tradition with Descartes, Spinoza, Locke, Hume, et al. On the other hand, there is the rather complete lack of a complementary logic of paradox (a union of opposites) in non-poetical thought in the Western world.

5. Another area of unparadoxical thinking on the part of most people seems to be concerned with genitality itself. People tend to be fixed *either* on the obviously and immediately social dimension of the coital-genital partners themselves *or* on the eventually and consequentially obvious social dimension of the parents with a resulting child. Coital-genital relations are social relations *both* in regard to the couple themselves *and* in regard to the potential or actual persons generated by these relations. I am asserting here that society shares--through the parents--more emphatically with the child than the parents do.

6. A blatant case of logic blockage in the contemporary mind is the widespread inability to recognize the paradoxical nature of abortion. Abortion is not only the "termination of pregnancy" but the extermination of a human being. Many people seem to be using our either-or logic as a foil in defending a so-called reproductive freedom.

7. The idea is that genitality is a power through which we can symbolize God's sharing with us by giving us our being in creation. Procreation is a symbol of creation. The gift of life to another celebrates in a radically unique and dramatic way the gift of a self that God has given to each of us. The exercise of genitality is designed to be a free exercise of our power to share self with others, very much in the likeness of God who freely shared Self with us by creating us. The exercise of our sexuality, however, symbolizes our likeness to God within the Godhead, independent of creation. According to traditional Christian teaching, the Persons of the Triune God necessarily share with one another in an eternal and infinitely-full interrelationship. So, one might say that each Person in the Godhead necessarily shares with the others. Our sexuality (as distinct from genitality) is a specific likeness to this Divine sharing of Self with Self and with the Others that each Person does in the Trinity. Exercising sexuality is necessary in God

and in sexual creatures. But creating and procreating are special, freely-willed overflows of sexual being.

8. Complete information on the natural family planning movement and on fertility awareness can be gained from the Human Life Center, St. John's University, Collegeville, Minnesota 56321, U.S.A. The Human Life Center publishes a Newsletter and the *International Review of Natural Family Planning*, a quarterly journal of professional perspective on all dimensions of NFP. The Center also offers instructional seminars for teachers of NFP. Practical information on where instruction is avilable in the United States can be obtained from the Human Life Center and from the Couple to Couple League International, Inc., P. O. Box 11084, Cincinnati, Ohio 45211.

Primary clinical research and teaching of the Ovulation Method in the U.S.A. is conducted by Dr. Thomas Hilgers, M.D., and associates at the Creighton University Natural Family Planning Education and Research Center, Creighton University School of Medicine, 601 N. 30th St., Omaha, Nebraska 68131.

General reading on the natural family planning movement in the U.S.A. is found in two books published by Rawson Associates, New York: *Natural Sex*, by Mary Shivanandan; and *No Pill, No Risk Birth Control*, by Nona Aguilar.

9. For a comprehensive treatment of these methods, see John and Sheila Kippley, *The Art of Natural Family Planning* second ed. (Cincinnati: Couple to Couple League International, 1979). This book thoroughly explains natural family planning. The publisher's address is given in note 8.

10. This claim is now being made by experienced researchers and clinicians, as well as by leading instructors. An example of the latter is Ingrid Trobisch, whose beautiful book *The Joy of Being a Woman: And What a Man Can Do* (New York: Harper and Row, 1975) contains one of the best introductions to natural family planning available anywhere. See Chapter 3, "Living in Harmony with the Cycle."

Information on the clinical and scientific research done by Bonomi, Klaus, Marshall, Rice, Roetzer, John and Lyn Billings, Hilgers, Brown, Keefe, Dunn, Vollman, and others is available from the Human Life Center--address given in note 8. Dr. Josef Roetzer, M.D., has many years of clinical experience with the sympto-thermal method and has reported a failure rate of .7, considerably less than the actual figures for oral contraceptives.

It is important to realize also that a woman can use NFP effectively for thirty to thirty-five years--all of her fertile life. But the rate of couples abandoning the use of the pill by the end of the *first year* is reported to be as high as 50 to 60%. Robert A. Hatcher, M.D., et al., *Contraceptive Technology 1978-79* ninth ed. (New York: Irvington Publishers, Inc., 1978), p. 20.

11. The Billings were not the original researchers, but they have been the main developers and educators. Evelyn L. and John J. Billings, *Atlas of the Ovulation Method* (Melbourne: Advocate Press Pty. Ltd., 1977). Also, John J. Billings, M.D., *The Ovulation Method: Natural Family Planning* (Collegeville, Minn.: Liturgical

Press, 1978). A brief historical-philosophical perspective on NFP is given by John Billings, *The Control of Life* (Dunedin, New Zealand: New Zealand Tablet Co. Ltd., 1975). Publisher's address: P. O. 5449, Dunedin.

12. For further detail, see Paul Thyma, *The Double-Check Method of Family Planning* (South Deerfield, Mass.: Marriage Life Information, 1978), pp. 9-18. This is an expanded edition. Publisher's address: 115 Sugarloaf St., South Deerfield, Massachusetts 01373.

13. One of the earliest professional approaches to NFP was initiated by Edward Keefe, M.D., of New York City. He is the developer of the ovulindex thermometer, the most widely used thermometer by practitioners who include basal body temperature in their knowledge of the cycle. Keefe is the pioneer medical expert on the cervical changes associated with fertility. See, e.g., his article, "Cephalad Shift of the Cervix Uteri: Sign of the Fertile Time in Women," *International Review of Natural Family Planning*, 1 (Spring 1977):55-60.

14. Some of the most important work concerning temperature in relation to fertility is being done by Josef Roetzer, M.D., Vocklabruck, Austria. His main work in English on NFP is *Fine Points of Sympto-Thermic Method of Natural Family Planning*, 2 vols. (Collegeville, Minn.: Human Life Center, 1977). Volume 2 contains a supplementary article by Dr. Edward Keefe on how physicians can make NFP work.

The renowned Swiss expert on the menstrual cycle, Dr. Rudolf F. Vollman, has done outstanding research. See, e.g., his article "The Premenstrual Phase of the Menstrual Cycle," *International Review of Natural Family Planning*, 1 (Winter 1977):322-30. His recent monograph, *The Menstrual Cycle* (Philadelphia: W. B. Saunders, 1977), is an authoritative source.

A comprehensive, succinct manual of the Sympto-thermal Method, presenting a creative integration of the practical signs of fertility is that of Carman and Jean Failace, *The Joy in Planning Your Family* third ed. rev. (Smithtown, N.Y.: The Family Life Promotion of New York, Inc., 1978), available from the Human Life Center (Collegeville, Minnesota).

15. Competent instructors are those who know thoroughly the empirical facts and treat NFP as a way of life, rather than as merely another way to prevent conception. True and false attitudes are communicated just as effectively as are true and false information. Moreover, the information necessary for practicing NFP effectively needs to be fitted into knowledge of the particular woman's physical, biopsychic, and attitudinal conditions. Individualized instruction is imperative.

16. Unfortunately, periodic continence as an integral part of NFP is a foreign idea to many people because of popular indoctrination by sexologists, clinicians, and other professionals. The "establishment mentality" in our culture includes the negative assumption that a healthy man and woman, living in the intimate relationship of a good marriage, could not--and should not--refrain from coital intercourse. One is almost forced to conclude that the

238

popular idea of a good marriage (or even any healthy man-woman relationship?) is: the less uncopulated, the better. The following comment on continence is typical of sex manuals: "In marriage, continence or refraining from sexual intercourse, despite a desire for it, is not ordinarily feasible or advisable, if the partners are in normal health. It is one thing for the unmarried to live a continent life for lack of opportunity or out of moral or religious conviction, and quite another for a married pair to avoid intercourse while living in close proximity, unless the marriage is no marriage but rather a state of emotional divorce." Jerome and Julia Rainer, *Sexual Pleasure in Marriage* (New York: Pocket Books, 1959).

This common attitude is thoroughly countered by psychiatrist George Maloof in his two-part article, "The psychology of Sexual Decision-Making," *International Review of Natural Family Planning*, 1 (Fall, Winter 1977):207-14, 297-309; and in his article, "Psychology of Sexual Relations and Natural Family Planning," *Marriage and Family Newsletter*, 8, Nos. 10-12 (Oct.-Dec. 1977):6-24. Also John E. Harrington, "Psychology of Family Planning," *Marriage and Family Newsletter*, 5, Nos. 10-12 (Oct.-Dec. 1974):3-13. This international newsletter is a professional resource, available from the publisher, P. O. Box 922, Peterborough, Ontario, Canada, K9J 7A5.

Lutheran missionary Ingrid Trobisch encapsulates the attitude of a great many people in the developing countries when she tells about a group of African men, who were asked whether they thought African males could practice periodic abstinence. They replied indignantly: "Who do you think we are? We are men. A child wants what he wants when he wants it. A man knows how to wait." One might simply add that the self-pampering males of technocratic cultures are the ones—of all kinds of people—who need the most help in human sexual development.

17. Notably Margaret Nofziger in her clear and simple introduction to the main methods of NFP, *A Cooperative Method of Natural Birth Control*, second ed. rev. (Summertown, Tenn.: The Book Publishing Company, 1978). Nofziger is a member of a well-established hippie community of over 1100 members. This book is available from the publisher (Summertown, Tennessee 39493) and from the Human Life Center (see note 8).

NFP is likewise not a "Catholic method" of birth control. Nofziger—not a Catholic—came to her knowledge of NFP through research in medical journals and her experience with members of her community, known as "The Farm." Some of the most articulate practitioners and advocates of NFP are not Catholic, e.g., Overduin, Trobisches, Ernst, and Christensons. See, e.g., Larry and Nordis Christenson, *The Christian Couple* (Minneapolis: Bethany Fellowship, Inc., 1977), particularly Chapter 8, "Contraception: Blessing or Blight?" Also see Siegfried Ernst, M.D., *Man the Greatest of Miracles*, trans. S. Margretta Nathe and Mary Rosera Joyce (Collegeville, Minn.: Liturgical Press, 1976).

18. As I have indicated earlier, sexuality (as sharing self with self and others) is the heart of loving action. Truly loving people are, therefore, really "sexy" people. Those who become devotees

of erotomania are prohibiting the growth of love and sexuality by fostering in themselves and others genital and coital congestion. Pseudosex is not sexy. On the nature of pseudosex, Germain Grisez says, "Masturbatory sex, which we might call 'pseudosex,' is a displacement activity not integrated into the personality, which permits frustrated energy to be used in a manner that yields easy and certain gratification." "Natural Family Planning Is Not Contraception," *International Review of Natural Family Planning* I (Summer 1977):121-26. The psychological difference between sex as displacement activity and mature sexual (genital) activity is well-stated by Claire Russell and W. M. S. Russell, *Human Behavior* (Boston: Little, Brown, 1961). See, e.g., p. 277.

19. Teaching fertility awareness to high school and junior high school young women in the context of sound moral values would be a refreshingly positive form of sex education. It is a keenly needed form of body awareness and a significant way to raise the self-esteem of women entering puberty. Showing her how to control her body by knowing her body is much more helpful to a woman than showing her how to be controlled by the cultural imperatives toward denial of her body (specifically her fertility) through contraceptive intercourse.

20. This idea of cyclic pattern assumes a fluctuation of sperm count between periodic, involuntary emissions of sperm, with no voluntary intercourse intervening. Peak fertility might then be regarded as the time just prior to involuntary emission.

21. *Joy in Human Sexuality*, (Collegeville, Minn.: Liturgical Press, 1975), pp. 51-54.

22. One can readily appreciate how persons can participate very deeply in these fundamental Goods by studying the excellent treatment of NFP by John and Sheila Kippley, *The Art of Natural Family Planning*. This book is the most comprehensive volume in the field, comprising both detailed, practical knowledge of the methods with the finest intangible values of NFP as an art. The Kippleys take a directly ecological approach to NFP, and integrate what they call "ecological breastfeeding" with NFP as a means of child-spacing. Their philosophy of NFP is entirely consonant with *Human Sexual Ecology*. The Kippleys are founders of the Couple to Couple League International--already mentioned. See note 8.

23. Again, I wish to distinguish functional ability from natural ability. Menopause marks the cessation of a woman's functional ability to have a child. However, her natural ability is not substantially altered. This kind of distinction is helpful in developing and maintaining a healthy self-concept as a woman.

24. Specifically bodily conditions can exert an effect on the spiritual life, although the effect itself, in so far as it is bodily, is not spiritual. Perhaps we could say that the bodily condition influences or conditions spiritual activity, but does not produce a spiritual effect as such.

25. The same is true regarding coitality. Both genitality and coitality essentially involve all three levels of human energy--physical, psychic, and spiritual.

26. Some people who are adopted offspring, as well as some who are adoptive parents, may find this claim disconcerting. Again, we need to see and honor the real difference between the natural and the functional. Adoptive parents are functionally--and usually quite effectively--parents of their adopted child. But they are not naturally parents of this child. The condition of not having one's natural and functional parents as the same people is bound to have (unconsciously at least) a negative influence on the child, even though the care of loving adoptive parents beautifully compensates for it.

Chapter 14

VOCATIONAL IDENTITY

While the first three parts of this book are concerned with general principles in human sexuality and in ethics, Part IV begins with an outline of a practical way of becoming sociosexually integrated. Awareness of fertility enables a person to integrate and freely relate to his or her society-forming power (genitality). Becoming aware of one's present state of fertility or infertility is likewise a practical way to prepare for personal commitment within a freely chosen vocational identity. The self-awareness gained through personal knowledge of fertility can be helpful to men and women in each of the vocations of life.

The present chapter takes us into a direct consideration of sexuality itself as it is lived socially--with or without the deliberate exercise of genitality.

There are three basic vocations: celibacy, marriage, and parenthood. They are the three basic ways of living sexually. The gift of self can be shared with self and with others in three major modes: as a single person, as a spouse, and as a parent. These radically natural ways of sexual living represent potentially deep *calls* from within one's personal nature. That is why they are known as *vocations*.

Vocations are closer to one's personhood than they are to one's personality. They are not life-styles, but life-commitments. Life-styles correlate more closely with personality. There are various life-styles within a given vocation.

What kind of life-commitment do you most desire to lead as a sexual person? Your response to that question is your vocation. Vocations are calls; but they also involve a choice--at least once in a lifetime. In the healthy person all three calls are present; all three vocations seem to be good ways to live. But one must choose. One cannot choose what kind of sexual *being* he or she *is*. But one can and must choose what kind of sexual *life* he or she will *lead*.

Vocational Identity: a Form of Sexual Identity

Vocation, then, is a matter of sociosexual identity. A vocation is a way of committing oneself to live in the world as a sexual person, relating to self and others in a stable and predictable way for the good of the entire human community.

Vocations should be freely chosen, especially when they are undertaken in a formal manner, such as religious vows or marital vows. Many people, however, seem to slide into their vocations with little reflection on the meaning of the particular, objective way of sociosexual functioning in which they find themselves. Often vocations are not lived well. The unmarried young man who makes a cult of promiscuous sex behavior is a Playboy celibate, acting as though he were a parent--a procreator. His way of living sexually is being-a-celibate, but this vocation is being lived poorly.

The idea of a vocation does not necessarily imply that God is calling a person to one and only one vocation. It does not mean that the person would do well to choose that "right one" or else a bitter life will follow. Everyone should hear and respect all three calls from his or her radically God-given nature. The person should seriously consider living in any one of the three. A person who cannot lead a healthy celibate life is hardly able to lead a healthy life as a spouse or as a parent. Someone who would make a good parent is one who would also make a good celibate. Of course, practically speaking, one will have a personal preference and a particular aptitude for a certain vocation.[1] (One also may have a special call from God which involves one particular vocation.)

Vocational identity, which involves the three ways of living sexually, is a community-determining commitment, and should be a matter of free choice. Freedom is limited when a person thinks that he or she *must* get married or *must* have children or *must* be a celibate. The vocational choice should be made freely with the best insight available concerning what is good for society, as well as for self.

Willingness to foster participation in the primary Values of life is the most crucial aspect of sound vocational commitment. How can I help myself and all others whom I meet participate most effectively in the fundamental Goods of human life? Society's needs at the time of vocational choosing are a basic consideration for the sexually mature person. Such a person is as inclined to live for others as for self. This inclination is a mark of personal freedom, and is required for a healthy vocational choice.

Not infrequently it happens that a person finds himself or herself with a vocation which arose without considerable reflection, such as a hasty marriage, an unexpected pregnancy, or an enforced celibacy. Yet, having many options is not essential to free choice. There remains the free choice of accepting or rejecting the condition in which one finds oneself.

A person can make a fundamental commitment freely by *accepting* a condition, as well as by *projecting* a condition. Everyone is called, as an adolescent, to *accept*--at least for a time--the vocation of celibacy. Receiving is the radical center of human sharing, and is the base on which one can project authentic alternatives for action. (Christians can reflect on the fact that Jesus' redemptive act was less a human project than a commitment of total acceptance of his Father's will).

Vocation within a Vocation

Unfortunately, people often think of vocations as social boxes into which we put outselves or in which we find ourselves. Such a conception entirely overlooks the organic relations of these vital forms of sociosexual organization. If we reflect deeply enough on the nature of celibacy, marriage, and parenthood, we can see how one vocation differentiates itself and grows *within* the other. The three vocations form a very important area of human sexual ecology. I will briefly trace the contours of vocational ecology in this chapter and then discuss in some detail each of these remarkably interrelated systems of sexual living by devoting single chapters to each.

Celibacy, the Roots

Celibacy is the root vocation. We all start out as celibates. People at three years of age, at ten, at fourteen, and so on, are called to lead celibate lives.[2] The specially committed form of cohabitation with one person of the other sex is anti-natural to their lives. Coital and genital interactions are likewise disorderly conduct for the single person.

Celibacy may be regarded as the root vocation because even parenthood is intimately concerned with it. Parents procreate and raise little celibates. Parenthood initiates the vocational cycle that begins with celibacy.

The celibate person is one who lives *alone* sexually. The word *celibacy* comes from the Latin word meaning *alone*. Aloneness (not loneliness) is the call of the celibate person. The aloneness is a sharing kind of aloneness; it is *not* a withdrawing--either mentally or physically. Celibate persons are able to share with others in a way that is unique to their stable way of living. And the virtues developed in living well celibately are crucial to the person who would choose to become a spouse. Healthy, periodic aloneness is grounds for a good marriage; not grounds for divorce.

Marriage, the Stem

If celibacy is the root vocation from which all others receive their nourishment and support, marriage is the stem or trunk. Becoming a spouse is a free choice in which a person chooses to regard for the rest of his or her life--or the spouse's life--one particular person of the other sex as the primary (not exclusive) center of his or her social relations. This centering is exclusive in that the intention is to share at least bed and board, and much more, it is hoped, with this one person, until the death of one of the parties. Marriage is a special kind of commitment called a covenant, in which the two persons vow before God and the human community that they will live as two in one flesh. The flesh that they are two within is not necessarily a genital bond--although very likely it will become that as well. Genital bonding is another vocation that calls for an implicit but actual covenant with a wholly other person or persons, the couple's offspring.

The marital covenant is made before the human (and religious) community's appointed witnesses who act on behalf of society, in which a new cell is being formed. The parentive covenant, however, is made in the act of coital union (privately) but with the specific use of generative organs that naturally tend toward the production of a totally new member of the human family.

The intent of the marital covenant includes *openness to receive* the vocation of parenthood by engaging in generative activity with each other exclusively. But the intent is directed *specifically* to the celebration of the goodness of being man and woman together. Marriage is the sacrament of man and woman, in which *this* man and *this* woman vow to live in fidelity to each other as sexual persons, sharing the one flesh of all their earthly possessions, personal talents, achievements, frailties, and social conditions in order to celebrate the goodness and fidelity proper to any and every man-woman relationship.

While celibacy chiefly symbolizes the inner fidelity in *every* person, by which self is faithful to self, marriage chiefly symbolizes the "outer" fidelity of *everyone* with *every* person of the other sex. Marriage celebrates the face-to-face goodness and power for sharing with which every man and every woman are endowed by their Creator.

Marriage is a vocation *within* the vocation of celibacy. It is within celibacy, but not *of* it. Marriage is structurally quite other than celibacy, but not separate from it. The spouses continue to celebrate the inner marriage within each person as they begin to change their emphasis. They change *emphasis* from sharing self with self to sharing self with *one sexual other*. They form a new kind of celibacy--the social celibacy of being two alone. By their unique kind of commitment spouses are, as individuals, no longer specifically celibates, but they are organically related to celibacy something like the stem to its roots.

Parenthood, the Branches

The branches on the tree of sociosexual life are formed by all the people who choose to be or come to be parents. Parenthood and the parentive act (coital intercourse) are the most obvious ways of living sexually. Just as the branches and foliage of a tree are all that is seen from a great distance, so parenthood and genital union are often all that people acknowledge as sexual. The roots are hardly glimpsed by people who view a tree,

247

even at close range. Similarly, celibacy as a way of living sexually is rarely recognized.)

Becoming a parent ought to be a free choice in which a person elects to establish a new kind of covenant-- *other* than that made with the spouse in marriage, but *not outside* it. Parenthood is a covenant within a covenant. This covenant should be a covenant *within* marriage, but *not of* marriage. Parenthood can and most certainly does, in many cases, exist without marriage, but always in a paralytic way. Parenthood is naturally designed to be sociosexually a vocation freely chosen within the man-woman vocation of marriage. The parent-child vocation may be regarded as the most obvious, though not the only, way of sexually participating in the structure of society, since through it the actual "building blocks" of society (its members) are provided and fashioned.

Parenthood is a society-making covenant by which one engages his or her generative powers which are uniquely physical. These generative powers are personal social powers and are not specifically personal individual powers. They are *within* the individual, but *not of* him or her. (They are *of* the individual personally, but not specifically.) Generative powers and organs are physically related more to one's children than to oneself. Therefore, they are more properly called *genital*, rather than sexual, powers and organs.

Not infrequently, parenthood occurs unintentionally even within marriage. The so-called "rhythm baby" or the "contraceptive failure" speaks plainly of this kind of occurrence.

Unintended parenthood can happen in two ways.

The partners may simply lack a specific intent to conceive a child at that particular time. The couple is willing to accept a baby, but is not trying to have one. The conception is unintentional through a lack of specific intent.

But a quite different situation, morally speaking, occurs if the couple intends *not* to have a baby. In this condition, the couple is acting against the prospect of a child. The attitude is contra-intentional, not simply non-intentional. The actual intention involved in the act of intercourse is contra-parentive, not simply non-parentive. It is related to the systematic use of contraception and leads to the idea of the "unwanted child." This phrase is used often to cover up the idea of the

"unwanting parent" or the "unwanted parenthood." It is
not, however, the child that should be unwanted, but
this kind of intention: to have coital intercourse while
not being willing to receive a child. The perennial
"unwanted *child*" mentality amounts to what should be
an "unwanted *mentality*."

In any event, the vocation of parenthood is like
celibacy in that it can be readily unchosen. Unlike
marriage, which cannot exist without a basically free
act of mutual choice, parenthood can happen thoroughly
against one or both of the partners' will. Although
unchosen parenthood is undesirable, it is nonetheless
real. This vocation comes *in* and *through* the *genital*
bonding of a man and a woman. Parenthood is a *new* bond-
ing--a bonding with a child in and through that genitally
bonding action. Under good conditions, it is a freely
covenanted action, done by a man and woman who *thereby*
enter a new vocation.

Parents are people who procreate celibates. So,
the sociosexual cycle of the three vocations is completed
in the relation of parents to their celibate offspring.
The tree of sociosexual life culminates in the area of
"seed-bearing" branches. Coital union is a specifically
life-giving activity by its very nature--as well as being
generally love-giving. As soon as a man and woman engage
in coital intercourse, with or without the willingness
to have a child at some time in their relationship, they
have become virtually parents. Once conception occurs--
the formation of at least one individual human being
through the interaction of sperm nucleus and ovum nucle-
us--they are naturally constituted as parents. Whether
they know it or not, they then become sociosexual members of a new covenant. Their sexual being has taken a
new *emphasis, other than* their own union as man and woman.
They are beyond-themselves-within-themselves by reason
of their parentive activity. They are no longer a couple,
emphasizing specifically the goodness of man and woman;
they are a family, emphasizing the goodness of a new
celibate. When one is married, he or she is a spouse
for life. But when one becomes a parent, he or she is
a parent forever.

The Sociosexual Tree

By using the image of roots, trunk, and branches
for the three vocations I do not mean to convey the idea
that every healthy individual member of society should
move through all three kinds of vocational identity.
I simply intend to suggest that there is a kind of organic

249

character to the sexual life-structure *of society as such*. We have need for ecological conditions in socio-sexual identity. At any given time, a healthy adult population should have significant numbers of these three kinds of people: celibates; spouses committed to spouse-hood, but not necessarily to parenthood; and spouses committed to parenthood.

By the middle vocational identity I do not mean married people who engage in coital intercourse but do not want children. My thesis is that if people engage their coital-genital powers they are thereby committed to at least one child--if possible. However, a certain proportion of the population--and it need not be more than a small fraction, depending on population needs, and other conditions--ought to be committed spouses who do not engage their coital-genital powers for reasons somewhat similar to celibates, such as special work in the world or a special way of doing that work (practically or symbolically). From this perspective, one might claim that society today--and generally in the past--is practically trunkless, if not rootless.

Celebrating the Nature of Self

Vocational identity is the primary kind of socio-sexual identity. What is my basic relationship to society as a sexual being? What is the fundamental orientation of my way of living, through which I serve the needs of society and celebrate the life and growth of the whole human family? These are questions about celibacy, spouse-hood, and parenthood. They have basically a social bearing, but they have a radical foundation in the self-hood of the individual who asks them.

The threefold character of vocational identity is naturally rooted in the three dimensions of self-consciousness. The following analysis may be sufficient to outline this analogous relationship.

A person is a self. This self is conscious of it-self. And this self is even conscious of its being conscious of itself. I (self) know things, and I also *know* that I know them. (Animals know things, but do not know that they know.) For purposes of this reflection, one can think of self as the preconscious interior source of freely radiating energy coming from one's depths and spreading in all directions. Without the self, this radiating and continuously thrusting energy could not even *be*.

250

But a person is not simply a self which emanates energy. The person can know and receive this energy in a certain way. I am *conscious* of my self. I am aware of myself. I am not simply a self. This ability to be conscious of oneself (and of others) is a second dimension; it is within the self, but is not simply the self.

There is a third dimension to one's conscious self. The human individual is not only able to be conscious of self, but to be conscious *of* that consciousness of self. We are engaging our power to be conscious of our self-consciousness (or of our consciousness of others) as we write or read these lines. The human individual is not just an individual entity. The human being knows things, including self. But the human being also *knows* his *knowing* of things. I do not simply know that I am typing this sentence, I know that I know it. You not only know the sentence that you are now reading, you know that you know it.

So, there are three basic dimensions to yourself as a knower: yourself as self; yourself as knower of self and others; yourself as knower of your knowing of self and others. Any further "knowing of your knowing of your knowing of something" can be regarded as basically an intensification of the third dimension and not a new dimension to the self. There are just three basic kinds of reality involved: a *self* which, as a self, has no object; a *consciousness* of self which, as such, has self as its object; and a *consciousness of* this *consciousness* of self, in which there is a new kind of object, namely, a consciousness. Any supposedly further act of reflective consciousness would have as its object the very same kind of reality that the latter has--namely, a consciousness. The natural structure of the individual self is essentially triune.[3]

This triadic structure of consciousness within every individual person can be seen analogously when one considers the structure of vocational identity in a society. Society is a self. Not surprisingly, then, one finds a resemblance between society itself and the individual members who constitute it. As the individual's consciousness (by which he or she can share self with self and others) has three basic dimensions, so the society's sexual identity (by which sharing is fundamentally organized) is quite naturally threefold. And any individual will necessarily find his or her socio-sexual identity in one of three basic ways in which society knows and expresses itself.

The individual's sociosexual identity is, then, a special celebration of a particular dimension of society's ways of being sexual. And this identity is rooted ultimately in one of the three primary areas of human selfhood.

Celibates celebrate self as self, with no special object--the first of the three dimensions. They emphasize the radical virtues of being a self. They celebrate the self of society as well as the self of themselves. Self is, after all, the beginning and the end of self-consciousness. The self is the agent that *does* the act of being conscious of self or of anything else. And the self is the *ultimate* object of any act of self-consciousness, including the consciousness of consciousness of oneself. (As I have indicated, parents *ultimately* do not engage in genital union for the sake of themselves or their marriage, but for the sake of celibacy in the form of a new celibate--a new self--on the planet earth.)

Spouses celebrate, in their very being as spouses, the second dimension--the self as object of self. They emphasize the radical virtues in being self-conscious. They celebrate society's self-consciousness, as well as their own individual powers to be self-conscious. In commitment to a person of the other sex as the primary center of his or her social otherness, the spouse becomes the special focus of a sexual other and through that other person the focus of all society. In marriage, the person *is known* by someone and by the human community in an emphatically personal and social manner. A spouse is no longer a single other, but a self-known other in an intimately social way.

From another point of view, one can consider the spouse as a person who does not only radiate outward to all other persons as does the celibate celebrating selfhood. The spouse is one who is conscious of one other person in a centered and sustained manner. In being so focused on his or her spouse, the married person is celebrating self as being *conscious* of something. And one is never just conscious. One is always conscious of *something*. (The object of consciousness may be self or it may be a particular other person or thing. But one is never simply conscious in general. Because there are innumerable acts of consciousness formed by the self at the same time, one may not know *what* one is conscious of--and one certainly does not know all of the things that one is conscious of at a given moment. There are as many acts of consciousness as there are things to be conscious *of*.)[4] Every act of consciousness is a marriage

252

between a particular knower and a particular known. The
covenant of marriage, then, is like *each* of our acts of
consciousness. It is directed to a particular other in
an unqualified way.

Parents celebrate the union of the knower and the
known--the third dimension, in which there is a new kind
of object. Parenthood is society's way of knowing its
knowing of something, particularly the knowing of self.
Parenthood and the parentive act are designed to celebrate the marriage itself in a special way. That is why
the act of coital union is often called the marital act
or the conjugal act. This action is designed to be a
renewal of the marital covenant. But it is specifically
the establishment of a further covenant, the covenant
with new celibates--children, actual or potential.

So, in the parentive act (the act of coital union)
marriage is celebrated immediately, but celibacy is celebrated ultimately. Coital union is a knowing of one's
knowing of self. As a knowing of one's *knowing*, coital
union is celebrating marriage. A knowing of our knowing
has as its immediate object the knowing act of which it
is a knowing. But, ultimately and radically, it is a
knowing of what is known in the first place: the self.

Parenthood and its distinctive act of initiation
(coition) constitute a union of celibacy and marriage,
just as one's consciousness of consciousness of self
(inner parenthood) is itself a union between the self
that is being conscious (inner celibacy) and the act
of consciousness (inner marriage). Parenthood is a vocation in which society (as a self) knows its knowing of
itself (marriage) and celebrates the relationship between
celibacy and marriage by procreating celibates right
within the marital union itself.

From another point of view, the unitive meaning of
the parenthood vocation can be more readily understood.
If we regard the knowing that the self is doing as a knowing of something other than self, this aspect of the
third dimension and of the third vocation becomes clearer.

When one is conscious of a book on the desk, the
consciousness or act of knowing the book is a reality
that brings the self into a special kind of union with
the book. That is what marriage does for a person as
a spouse. The spouse is brought into immediate and direct
union with one person of the other sex, even as the self
is brought into direct union with the book as another
'self." But, as the person *realizes* that he or she is

253

knowing the book--that is, as the person is more distinctively *conscious of* this act of knowing the book--another kind of union emphatically occurs. In this reflective act of knowing, the direct *act of knowing* the book is reunited to the self from which it (the direct act of knowing) emanates. (See Fig. 4, Consciousness and Vocational Identity, p. 255)

This reunion happens because the reflective act of knowing is not just an act of knowing one's knowing act, but also an act of knowing oneself. The ultimate object of my consciousness of my knowing the book is *both* the book *and* myself. Without both the book and myself actually existing, my knowing of this book now--this particular, direct act of consciousness whereby I know this book--could not even exist. So, the *reflective* act of consciousness is a radical way of knowing the necessary causes and ingredients of the *direct* consciousness-- namely, the book and oneself.

Similarly, the personal act of being a parent is a social act in which the marriage of the two people is reunited with celibacy. The knowing of one particular other person (marriage) is reunited with the causes and ingredients of this knowing act, by the symbolic action of procreating and educating offspring--celibates. Children may physically resemble their parents in various ways. But, more importantly, as the celibates all of us originally and ultimately are, children symbollically stand for their parents.

Celebrating the Nature of God

To Christians who believe that God is three Persons in one nature and that the individual person is made in God's image and likeness, it is not surprising that there are three basic dimensions to the individual self and three basic vocational identities possible to persons in society. A reflection on the Christian teaching concerning three Persons in one God may help to support the idea of these natural, triadic interrelationships. It may also help to suggest the necessity for all three vocations and for their equal value to the human family. (The following speculations are offered very tentatively.

The Christian teaching on the Trinity is often explained in this way. The Father knows and loves himself. With this activity, eternally and co-equally the Word proceeds from the Father. Together the Father and the Word know and love each other. The Holy Spirit is the

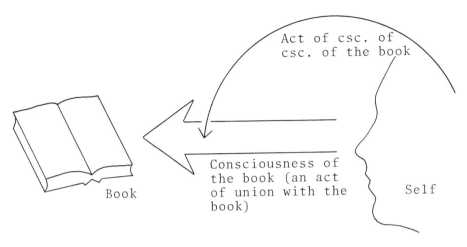

(a) *An act of reflective knowing*

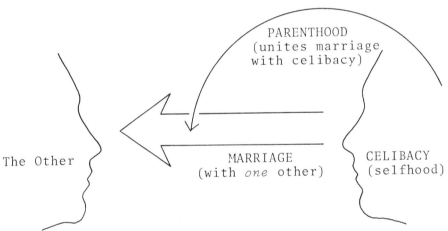

(b) *Analogous representation of sociosexual identity*

Fig. 4.   Consciousness and Vocational Identity

An act of reflective knowing (a) done naturally by an
individual person is suggested as a primary analogue for
understanding the threefold sexual identity exercised
naturally by a society. Parenthood is portrayed as unit-
ing marriage and celibacy somewhat as one's consciousness
of his or her direct consciousness of a thing unites that
direct, outward flowing act with the self from which it
originally flowed (b).

Person that proceeds co-equally and eternally within this mutual love of Father and the Word.

One could say that the Father is the Self Person of the Trinity. The Word is the Consciousness-of-Self Person. The Holy Spirit is the Consciousness-of-Consciousness-of-Self Person. Each one is real. All three are equal in being-value. But there is a procession of the second and the third Persons. The second Person "comes from" the First Person, and the third Person "comes from" both of them.

In accord with the philosophy of sexual ecology, one could make a case for the intersexual nature of this procession. God the Father is the Supreme Emphasis on radiating energy and thrust. All maleness is distinctively rooted in God the Father. God the Word is the Supreme Emphasis on receiving energy, a word formed from the energy of the Father to which Eve may be likened as a person formed from the rib of Adam. God the Word in the Divine Nature can be regarded as female, even though in his human nature Jesus, the Word, was a man.[5] (What has been called the hypostatic union of the Divine and human natures in Jesus might be regarded as another *marriage*--between Creator and created in a single Person.) God the Spirit is the Supreme Emphasis on the *union* of the Giving emphasis of the Father and the Receiving emphasis of the Word, the Mother. (This Third Person may be regarded as emphatically androgynous.)

In relating vocational identity to the Trinity, one could then say that celibates celebrate God as Father more than as Mother or as Spirit. Spouses celebrate God as Mother emphatically. And parents celebrate God as Spirit emphatically. Celibates are the roots of the energy in the sociosexual community. Spouses are the intermediate, receiving persons in the human family, who engage in the radical kind of receiving of another (the spouse) that relates to the other as one flesh. Parents are the branches of the energy in the vocational community, proceeding from both the stem and the roots.

Society cannot survive without the distinctive contribution of all three vocations. Together they make up a whole society in the image and likeness of God. They are sociosexual relationships. Celibacy is social maleness and fatherhood. Marriage is social femaleness and motherhood. Parenthood is the child of both celibacy and marriage, even as the Spirit is the Eternal Child in the Divine Family. Parenthood means initiating and sustaining both males and females (children), even as the Spirit Person in the Trinity proceeds from both the maleness and the femaleness of God. Parenthood *gestates within* marriage, the mother-vocation.

No person can live more than one of these primary vocations at the same time, any more than the Word can ever *be* the Father, or the Spirit *be* the Word. Despite their equality, they are not equivalent, in the sense of *one* being *both*. They are radically other in themselves. Once a person chooses to be a spouse and becomes one, he or she cannot remain simply a celibate. A person cannot be alone-with-another and alone-without-another (a special sexual other) at the same time. Likewise, once a person chooses to be or comes to be a parent, he or she cannot remain primarily a spouse. The person remains spousal and celibate in his or her roots, but takes on an entirely new *emphasis* in living sexually.

Parenthood involves an entirely new emphasis in sharing the gift of self. In marriage, the emphasis is on sharing the gift of *self* with one special person of the other sex. In parenthood, the *emphasis*--not the total life--is shifted to a sharing of the gift of self with one or more special persons of either sex, through the power to give life in space and time. The parent primarily celebrates the goodness of the Holy Spirit, the Child of God, even as the spouse primarily celebrates the goodness of the Word, and the celibate primarily celebrates the goodness of the Father. Each one celebrates all three Persons. But, in likeness to these Persons who can be *only themselves* even in their infinitely mutual activity, each vocation is necessarily a radically natural emphasis on one specific Person.

Celibacy, marriage, and parenthood can be viewed as natural revelations of the inner life of God.

NOTES

1. Actually, considering the conditions of many people's lives it seems that they could not flourish in any vocation but one. For example, someone might find living well in a celibate life practically impossible and would seek to marry shortly after the death of a spouse. Another person might be quite unsuited to marriage, such that he or she would do well to turn down even very attractive opportunities. These abilities or disabilities, however, stem from people's varying *functional* capacities and have more to do with the

inevitable *life-style* of the vocation than with the basic character of the vocation as a radically natural way of living sexually.

2. People at three years of age are hardly capable of responding to the call by making it a matter of choice--making decisions, deliberately developing appropriate attitudes, and so forth. However, they are called to celibacy or a single way of sexual living for many years in the future by their natural needs and by their socio-sexual position of requiring growth in extensive self-knowledge. Their response to the celibate call gradually comes forth as they grow in self-reflection and functional ability to make choices.

3. A fuller explanation of the triadic structure of consciousness and its social applicability is given in an article on the nature of discussion. See Robert E. Joyce, "Toward a Philosophy of Discussion," *Improving College and University Teaching*, 16 (1968): 8-11.

4. So, my act of consciousness of this paper might be regarded as a "tissue of acts of consciousness"--consciousness of the paper's color, of its texture, of its shape, of its lines, of its upper half, of its lower half, etc. (all of which supernumerous acts of consciousness form a unitary consciousness of the paper). The consciousness of the paper is itself a component of a supernumerous variety of other simultaneous acts--such as my acts of being conscious of the light in the room, the sound of the heating system, of my hand moving the pen, of my breath, etc. (all of which multitudinous acts of consciousness form a unitary consciousness of "the world"). My consciousness is like an organic body made up of inexhaustibly numerous simultaneous acts of being conscious of diverse things and parts of things.

5. This speculation receives little direct support from traditional sources. A notable exception, however, is Julian of Norwich, *The Revelations of Divine Love*, trans. James Walsh (St. Meinrad, Ind.: Abbey Press, 1974). In Chapters 58-63 the second Person of the Trinity is explicitly regarded as the Mother Person of the Godhead.

Chapter 15

CELIBATE SEXUALITY

Everyone comes into life a celibate. Being a celibate is a very positive condition. The celibate person conducts his or her life in such a way as to emphasize the uniqueness and otherness of every being. No being is the same as any other and the celibate shares himself or herself in every activity by emphasizing this beingful (ontological) truth. A person does not have to be aware that this is the kind of sharing he or she is doing in order for it to occur. Most people have little awareness of the meaning of their sociosexual identities.

Who are celibates? Children, and all other people who have never been married and who are not parents.

There are two major kinds of celibate people. Those who are permanently committed to living this way for life, as in religious life where vows are taken; and those who are not so committed. Among the latter we can distinguish two kinds: those who are preparing themselves for permanent commitment and who *intend* to be celibates for life, as in the case of temporary religious vows preceding final vows, or those who make promises for a special period in life; and those who have no particular intention of being single either for life or for a particular period of life. Generally, therefore, we might speak of committed celibates, precommitted celibates and uncommitted celibates.

In the fundamental ecological sense, no one who has ever parented or married is a celibate, though he or she may lead a celibate style of life. Widows and widowers are people who are called to a celibate style of life since they can no longer lead a marital style of life and their children may be grown, distant, or deceased. Unwed parents are called to a celibate life-style, even though they have taken on the vocation of parenthood. They also have a special obligation, on behalf of the child, to seek a marital style of life through valid marriage--but not necessarily to the other parent.

Celibacy is not the same as virginity. A virgin is one who has never deliberately engaged in coital-genital intercourse. But there are many people who have deliberately engaged in coital intercourse and yet not conceived. These people are not virgins. They may be actually celibates, although virtually parents. Also, anyone who has married validly but has never engaged in coital-genital intercourse is a virgin, but not a celibate.

Celibacy is a radically natural and largely unconscious orientation in sharing the gift of self--in being sexual. The celibate is one who is called to share the gift of self both with self and with others, but emphatically with self. Twenty-four hours a day this person is called to live as a unique, unbonded sexual being. The person's very life and life-style bespeak an *aloneness* that should be an emphatic *all-one*-ness. The celibate speaks loudly and clearly by his or her actions--for anyone who wishes to hear--that it is good to be unique and "utterly other" than any other being. The celibate celebrates by attitude and action the uniqueness of every blade of grass, of every drop of water, of each new sunset, of every person who will ever exist.

This attitude and action of the good, wholesome celibate life is the natural basis of any special reasons for celibacy, such as being celibate in order to serve the kingdom of God or in order to devote one's entire life to science or scholarship. These and other purposes constitute worthwhile motivations for the person who would lead a celibate life. But they are not enough. Along with entertaining these useful purposes, the more a person can engage in celibate living as a good in itself and as a special, fundamental expression of the uniqueness of all God's creatures as well as of the Persons of God, the healthier his or her moral life can be.

Nothing so vitiates moral life as a utilitarian attitude toward the radically natural ways of sharing self. Religiously committed people often seem to suffer from a very subtle and pervasive kind of spiritual utilitarianism, such that their primary conscious motivation for leading a celibate life is *not* to share self with self emphatically and, from that, overflow freely to others. Their primary motive for celibacy is to let themselves be *used* by others, including God. Since God never violates his own natural gifts, the motive of God *using* them in anything but a figurative way is a specious one and can do considerable harm to their whole moral and religious life.

The Celibate Union

Celibacy is not a life of selfishness. When conducted in a morally sound way, it is a life of self-fullness. The healthy celibate is one who can readily and happily be alone with self and share deeply with self. In the overflow of that self-sharing-with-self, others are freely and non-compulsively celebrated and served. Everyone is called to this kind of growth early in life. If marriage is eventually chosen it will be done out of this healthy self-with-self sharing and not out of a desparate need to live parasitically from the life of somebody else. Such an ideal kind of marital sharing is often impossible.[1] But people who choose celibacy-for-life dramatically reveal the importance for everyone in becoming whole and all-one within.

Often one hears about marital union. There is also a celibate union. Celibates do not simply emphasize the union of male and female within each person. They also participate in a special, global kind of union with *all* other persons. Celibacy should be lived not only for the sake of dramatizing the inner marriage of Adam and Eve, but also for the sake of all other persons. Even as marriage is an emphasis on the specialness of one person of the other sex, and parenthood is an emphasis on the specialness of certain other persons of either sex (one's offspring), celibacy is an emphasis on the specialness of *every* person who exists.

We can speak of the social act of celibate union. This act has both a specific, co-creative purpose and a general, unitive purpose--a specific nature and a general nature. The *specific* nature of this act of celibate union is to establish a sound, true-to-self freedom and capacity to live alone in the service of anyone and everyone. The *general* nature of this act is to be unitive by expressing

love and affection between the celibate and any other
person. A celibate should be not just a "man for all
seasons" but a person for all *people*, in a fundamental
way that is not possible for spouses and parents.

Within Self, Female; with Others, Male

In order to understand the radically natural identity
of a celibate, we can turn our attention to the structure
of the vocational ecosystem. There is a balance between
the sociosexual vocations of celibacy, spousehood, and
parenthood. They intimately interact with one another
in many ways. In this general study, I can hardly begin
to suggest all of them. But the crux of their mutual
balance and relationships as fundamental modes of living
sexually can be indicated briefly.

There are essentially just two directions in which
a being can relate. To self and to others. The paradox
of vocational identity is such that each vocation is sexually the opposite when regarded in accord with these
two directions. Celibacy, spousehood, and parenthood
are sexually both male and female--but male in one direction, and female in the other. Here I will consider this
mutual balance of sexual identity within the vocations
as it occurs in the celibate part of the total sociosexual
ecosystem. (The other identities will be discussed in
the two chapters to follow.)

When one regards the celibate as in relation to
himself or herself, one finds a definite emphasis on the
female side of sexual identity. The celibate (male or
female) is one who emphasizes inwardness and the sheer
receiving of self, so characteristic of Anima and the
Eve within. The ability to be still and let being be,
including the whole being of oneself, is a radically
receiving kind of activity. Sharing the gift of self
with self is both a giving and a receiving on the part
of oneself, but emphatically a receiving, in a giving
sort of way.

When the celibate is regarded in relation to others--
to any one other or to the whole world of others--there
is a distinct emphasis on the male side of sexual identity. The celibate (male or female) is a person who goes
out in all directions and is not bonded to one person.
The celibate is spermlike in relation to others. There
is an emphasis on manyness, differentiation of relationships, and a flowing outward to serve others.

This natural orientation to manyness does not mean
that the celibate should not have one or two close
friends. It simply means that there is no bonding to a
special one as in marriage, where there is an emphasis
on the female attitude of oneness with, and centeredness
in, the *one* other. The celibate, in relation to others,
emphatically lives with the male attitude of the *otherness*
of everyone, in contrast to the spouse who emphatically
lives with the female attitude of the oneness or *togetherness* (with self) of every other.[2]

The celibate receives others, but not as emphatically
as the spouse receives the special sexual other. The
celibate emphasizes giving to the other, more than receiving from the other. Also, while the spouse (in his or
her basic sociosexual orientation) does dramatically
give self to *the* other, the celibate is called to give
self to *any* and *every* other. Celibacy is male with respect to others, but female with respect to self.

Centering and Genital Integration

Celibacy is the sociosexual vocation in which centering of one's genital-erotic drives and impulses ought
to occur. Marriage and parenthood need the maturity
that comes through the centering process, in which one
deliberately lets one's drives and impulses *be*, without
doing anything about them. The celibate is sexually
committed, first of all, to self and the sharing of self
with self. This kind of sharing is impossible without
some degree of ability to center one's genital and coital
urges. If one's drives and impulses are disorderly and
impetuous, there needs to be much opportunity to let one's
drives find their own center, before they become functionally activated in relationship to another person.

If the person marries and engages his or her genital
and coital drives, without first having them adequately
centered within self, then it will be extremely difficult to recover from the loss of centering. There is
a crucial ecological balance (a mutual centering) involved
in a healthy intergenital relationship. The erotic and
genital inclinations of both persons should be centered
within themselves. When they come into an erotic and
genital relationship with each other there is an additional centering of these inclinations within--not upon--
the other.[3] The tendencies are then doubly centered and
balanced between self and the other, with an emphasis
on the other.

263

But in a person who has failed to let his or her genitality become centered within self, there eventuates only one "center" for these drives in marriage: the other person. The gravitational force of the other's erotic attractiveness is likely to be so strong and so unconsciously operative that the person will find it very difficult to do any kind of centering within self until some kind of crisis arises in the relationship and some of the romantic finery is frayed. But, even then, the force of genital habit may have become so strong that the loss of erotic attractiveness is covered over by an even greater compulsion to be genitally satisfied in and by another. Erotic love-making becomes something more like a clinch than an embrace. It becomes a powerful force in keeping the person off-center sexually. A celibatelike period in the partner's lives is practically essential if each of them is to acquire the much-neglected art of centering their own genitality within themselves. (Incidentally, problems of coital-genital dysfunction in sex therapy are not infrequently being dealt with by methods that include no intercourse for a sustained time.)[4]

A sexually healthy person is one who respects his genital and coital drives and knows how to let them be. The stillness of *being*, required for effecting the centering and the inner sharing toward which it naturally tends, is at the heart of the celibate vocation. Celibate sexuality is for everyone.

Masturbation and the Use of Self

Masturbation is the key symptom of lack of centering one's coital-genital drives. While it is practiced by some people who are spouses and parents, it is a primary sexual defect associated specifically with celibate sexuality.

Masturbation may be defined as the deliberate stimulation of oneself in order to experience specifically genital (venereal) pleasure. In this way of defining it, masturbation may be partial or complete. Complete masturbation involves self-stimulation to the point of having an orgasm.

Venereal pleasure may be defined as a particular kind of sensual pleasure that can only be found associated with activation of one's genital organs. It is impossible to state clearly when a person is necessarily having venereal pleasure. But each person can tell by adverting to the question: Is this sensual pleasure I am experienc-

ing something that could not be had in the use of any
other organ? Young people, when first capable of experiencing this distinctive kind of pleasure, may sometimes
confuse it with other good feelings of a tactile kind,
such as smoothness-of-skin or warmth-of-body feelings.
Venereal sensation is a particular kind of good feeling
that can only be experienced in connection with the partial or total erection of genital organs. (Erection of
genital organs does not necessarily, of itself, cause
venereal pleasure. But it does place the person in a
condition that is immediately preparatory to such pleasure.)

Individuals vary greatly in their sensitivity to
sense pleasure generally and to venereal pleasure specifically. This factor makes it sometimes difficult to
see how the definition of masturbation applies to a particular individual. But guidelines can be given. One
is that self-stimulation need not be done with the hands.
That is why the term self-manipulation is not being used
here. Self-stimulation can occur by simply moving bodily
in relation to something else, such as one's clothing
or bed.

A very important consideration is that masturbation
is defined as a deliberate action. Self-stimulation can
readily occur at times--especially in men--without deliberation and without any intention, direct or indirect,
to allow it to happen. Occurrences of solitary genital
stimulation that are not intended (directly or indirectly),
such as what have been called nocturnal emissions in men,
should not be considered as instances of masturbation.

Masturbation can be effected without appreciable
physical stimulation. In some persons the genital drive
is so strong and sensitive at times that seeing erotic
subjects or even imagining them can cause specifically
genital pleasure, even to the point of orgasm. If such
activity occurs with some measure of deliberation or
intention, it is an act of masturbation.

Intention is crucial to what is being called masturbation. Unintentional stimulation of oneself in which
venereal pleasure occurs may be regarded as inevitable
and natural. In some people it may never or rarely occur.
In others it may occur with some frequency. The key is
whether it is intentional or unintentional.

Venereal pleasure is good, and it should be experienced in activity that is intended for coital intercourse.[5] If it is experienced at any other time, the

morally proper thing to do is to recognize the pleasure just as it is--as venereal pleasure--but not consent to producing it. A person who intends this pleasure apart from attempts at justifiable coition violates the integrity of the coital act of intercourse, with which the pleasure is (by nature) specifically associated.

On the one hand, it is important not to repress venereal pleasure, if it unintentionally occurs. One should not pretend that one is experiencing something non-pleasurable when it is very pleasurable. That would be self-deception. On the other hand, consenting to a pleasurable action that is specifically structured into the power to give life through coital union, when one is not engaging in this unitive action or is not validly engaging in it at the time, constitutes a misuse of one's power to give life (genitality) and of the power to make love genitally (coitality).

In a situation where no venereal pleasure has been directly intended but where its involuntary presence gives occasion for enjoying it indirectly (such as in partially awake seminal emissions) the moral act largely consists in one's ability to receive the pleasure without "willing" it to be there. One ought to learn how to acknowledge fully the pleasure, if or when it ever occurs, without even partially willing it.[6] Genital respect and reverence for the integrity of the life-giving action of coital intercourse, as well as a full receptivity to the basic goodness of all physical and psychic passions and pleasures, will carry one a long way in developing strength of character and a generous personality.

The moral act involved in responsiveness to an occasion of venereal pleasure is primarily dependent on how well the person has already received his or her erotic and genital drives in themselves. These drives are within the person at all times and are important not only in the specific exercise involving coital-genital union, but also in the whole development of one's personality. These drives are an important part of the person's whole power to give life, which needs to be thoroughly integrated into his or her personality, whether or not it is ever functionally activated toward its specific good. The erotic and genital inclinations are radically natural and good in themselves, even though they are never deliberately activated. Persons suffering from a utilitarian attitude--and all of us are greatly influenced in this direction by our culture--are bound to find it difficult to let these strong and vital inclinations just be themselves without interacting with them or performing with them in some way.

Masturbation is a sign that proper centering of these drives has not yet occurred. It is also an activity that makes centering more difficult. When a person deliberately stimulates his genital drive in order to experience the pleasure that is, among all the inclinations of the person, proper only to coitional activity, he or she is engaging in an anti-centering activity. Taking the pleasure away from its natural center within the coital-genital drive and making it available for obviously noncoital-genital purposes seriously damages the person's participation in the fundamental Good of Integrity. The deliberate misuse of genital organs also acts directly against the fundamental Good of Life, because genital organs are specifically life-giving organs and are, as such, intrinsically a part of the fundamental Good of Life.

Masturbation may be *normal* behavior for many people. But it is *not natural* behavior. What is normal is what most people or the average person in a society *does*. What is natural is what everyone in every society ought to do, because it is positively good for everyone. Masturbation would not be good for anyone, even though it were practiced by everyone. Claims that it causes acne, V.D., or whatever, are not being made. Even if they were true--which they are not--such physical harm would be secondary to the moral harm of this anti-centering activity.

Masturbation, as the intentional stimulation of oneself in order to experience venereal pleasure, is the attempted separation and isolation of a specifically human pleasure from the power to share the power to give life (coitality) in which it naturally inheres. No matter how seemingly valid a person's motive may be, such a separation cannot be deliberately attempted without a distortion of his or her personal perception of the good of Life and of genital sexuality itself.

A person may be motivated by a desire to feel comfortable with his or her sexuality. But feeling comfortable is beside the point. One may have to feel very uncomfortable for a long time (or at times) in order to fulfill the truth about self and his or her sexuality.[7] Moreover, the motive of feeling comfortable is hardly the kind of motivation of which healthy personalities are made. It is simply the opposite extreme from the motive of having to feel miserable if an action is going to be virtuous.

Even where the motive *seems* to be very respectable, such as masturbation for the sake of integration, the person is intending an action that does exactly the opposite of his or her apparent motivation. Masturbation is really a self-disintegrating sort of action. In this action one separates oneself from one's body, making the body an object. There may be an apparent integration experienced inasmuch as tension is greatly relieved and a pleasurable feeling is achieved. But this integration is *only* an integrationlike *feeling*.

Actually, such action produces a much more serious tension and condition of alienation--a tension between one's consciousness and one's body, and a sense of alienation from one's body as really part of oneself. A dualism is created between mind and body. The body is regarded as subordinate and as a mere instrument of satisfaction for a subtly imperious mind. Further exploitation is inevitable. The body is *used* by one's consciousness instead of being properly revered and judiciously served.

In so far as people sincerely act in ignorance of the disparity between what masturbation is and what they want it to be, they are not guilty of what is called--theologically--sin. But they do make it ever more difficult for themselves to become sexually centered and genuinely integrated. Just as a person who unknowingly consumes contaminated food does not sin, even though it severely harms his or her physical health; so, a person who unknowingly engages in masturbation, without realizing its anti-natural character, does not sin, even though it severely harms his or her psychic and spiritual health, and undermines to some degree the basis for moral development in the area of sexuality.

Masturbation is always morally wrong. The objective wrong does not consist simply in its being a "misuse" of self or of part of self. Strictly speaking, a person should *never be used*. No part of a person should be used simply as a means to an end. In solitary venereal pleasure one's genital power is being *used* as a means to an end outside itself. The masturbating person is engaging in genital pleasure, not for the sake of coital-genital intercourse, but for the sake of tension-release or entertainment.

Genital powers should never really be *used*, but exercised or engaged. Even our food-consummatory powers

or our defecatory powers are not strictly to be *used*.
The actions of all vital powers of a person are goods
in themselves and ends-in-themselves-along-with-other-
ends. To the extent that they are morally significant
actions, they are direct participations in the good of
health, and ultimately in the Good of Life. But genital
powers have a still greater reason to be treated as ends-
in-themselves. They are not specifically individual
powers but social powers with which each person is gifted
in order to share, at least non-directively (as in the
case of celibates), in the procreation of other human
beings.

Problems Concerning the Meaning of Masturbation

Masturbation is perhaps the central issue in the
morality of coital-genital sexuality. Many special problems can be raised in the effort to understand this
complex phenomenon.

I will discuss two particular areas. First, there
is today a growing attitude of acceptance toward masturbation among many proponents of the women's liberation
movement. Second, a generally permissive attitude concerning masturbation seems to be widespread in medical
counseling. These two developments will be given some
consideration.

One special problem is the growing practice of female
masturbation. Women are told that they can "become the
sexual equals of men." Since men have orgasmic pleasure
at their beck and call, some people argue, women have
the right to explore and develop ways to achieve self-
induced orgasm. Many seem to think it is a duty to attain
a facility in masturbation that rivals the speed at which
it is attainable in men and that supersedes the quality
and orchestration of the relatively simpler male orgasm.

Women who hold to a "free female orgasm" perspective
are not likely to see or admit that female venereal pleasure is an integral part of the power to give life. Yet
the pleasure that they seek is located specifically in
certain genital organs, the clitoris and vagina. Even
though one may argue that the clitoris is not specifically
used in effecting coital union or in generating a child,
it *is* essentially a genital organ. *Use* should never
be a decisive criterion for designating the nature and
function of any vital power. The clitoris does serve
as an auxiliary source of genital pleasure during coitus.
But its nature and function in naturally generative union
is more celebrational that useful. Intentional stimulation

269

of the clitoris, apart from action that is directed toward
coital union, attempts to separate and isolate clitoral
pleasure from its naturally intended function of celebrating the union of man and woman in an integral act
of coital intercourse.

Some women even argue that vaginal orgasm is uncon-
nected with their genital powers because a woman can
have genital intercourse and give birth to a child without any such pleasure. But this argument suffers from
the same utilitarian attitude. The idea is that, since
the pleasures of vaginal orgasm are not particularly
useful in getting the woman's side of genital activity
accomplished, they can be treated as though they did not
inherently belong to a woman's genital powers and activity. Sheer use or necessity is the sole criterion being
addressed by such argumentation. The human person is
being treated as a high class mechanism--something that
is only as good as it is efficient. The ownership concept of mind-body relationship is the key to this kind
of perspective. The mind owns the body. The body is
treated as a beast of burden upon which the mind can
thrust its projects and plans for "getting somewhere."

This utilitarian attitude is functioning as the decisive criterion for responsible moral action. In Chapter
12, I indicated that the pursuit of limited objectives
is one of the modes of responsible action. But there
are at least seven others that need to be taken into
account before an action is morally sound.

Female orgasm is not necessary for effecting coital
intercourse. Even male orgasm is not always necessary.
Orgasm is a basically superfluous, yet highly desirable,
outcome within the activity of coital intercourse. Female masturbation, as well as male masturbation, directly
violates the fundamental Good of Integrity because it
attempts to *separate* a pleasure from the vital act in
which it is naturally centered.

One must clarify the difference between separating
something and distinguishing something. In separating,
one does not keep the item intact. In distinguishing,
one simply notes the difference and lives with it. People
who try to justify female masturbation are not simply
noting the difference between coital functioning and
orgasm, yet keeping the relationship intact. They are
separating--or attempting to separate--venereal pleasure
from coital action. They are not letting the act be
intact. The action of genital (venereal) self-stimulation
is thereby anti-centering and anti-self. It treats the

fundamental Good of Life, through its specifically participating organs--clitoris and vagina--as simply a means to
the end of personal pleasure.[8]

A second special problem concerning the meaning of
masturbation arises from the concern of counselors. I
noted earlier the anti-centering effect of masturbation,
even in cases of apparently high-quality motivation. It
was likewise pointed out that normal behavior should never
automatically be regarded as natural. But what I have
said about masturbation applies only to self-stimulating
action that is undertaken with freedom and deliberation in
order to experience venereal pleasure and release from
tension apart from coital-genital union with one's validly
married partner. We have not considered the question of
self-stimulation that is undertaken for other reasons,
such as obtaining semen in a male in order to effect artificial insemination, or under other conditions, such as release from pathological anxiety and repression in psycho-
therapy.

The latter consideration is too complex to be adequately treated here. But a brief analysis of masturbation related to artificial insemination can be made. Many
counselors today advise artificial insemination as a matter of course in cases of demonstrated infertility problems. (Some naively regard *in vitro* fertilization as
ordinarily free of moral problems. But we shall confine
our consideration to the common genital behavior connected with artificial insemination.)

In the case of self-stimulation for the sake of obtaining semen, an obviously presupposed deliberation exists. The person is not engaged in the action through a
fit of passion, but after consideration and counsel.

When the action is examined in itself, it is evident
that it is being used as a means to an end outside the
action's natural result. The motive may be admirable.
Perhaps it is a case of the male sperm-count being normally too low ever to eventuate in a pregnancy from the
natural act of intercourse. Yet, the means taken to
assist nature's action goes against that action itself
by separating the action from the natural conditions
under which it can achieve its end.

The natural conditions that are essential to a given
act of generating a child include the interposition of
penis and vagina. Without such conditions, and others,
no natural activity of human conception can take place.
Anything that facilitates the interposition of penis and

271

vagina or of sperm motility and penetrativity, without interfering in the natural dynamics of the action, yet actually assisting the course of nature in the act itself, is morally sound. But self-stimulation in order to obtain sperm, which are then transferred to the female partner by extra-natural means, is an action that directly violates the generative powers of both persons. The *achievement* of a pregnancy is not theirs at all, even though they are the parents of the child, once conceived. The *achievement* of a pregnancy has been stolen from them as agents of nature.

Who has done the stealing? If they were willing for the artificial insemination process to occur, as they most likely would be unless they were, perhaps, forced at gun-point, then they were the ones who did the stealing through the help and instrumentation of therapists and scientific means. The couple, as natural agents of conception in the act of giving life, were robbed of their natural powers to *give* life. The fact that they *wanted* to be robbed makes it nonetheless a robbery. The fact that *they* did the robbing makes it no less anti-natural. One might say that nature was robbed, not the couple. But when it is one's own nature that is being harmed or exploited it is oneself that is being so treated. The essence of the damage consists in the separation of self from nature through the given activity or attitude. The attitude that my body is my plaything or my tool, and the actions that reveal and reinforce such an attitude, are serious attempts at separating self from self, rather than sharing self with self. They are anti-sexual actions.

Artificial insemination is not wrong because it is artificial, but because it is anti-natural, and specifically anti-genital. It treats the genital organs and their power as less than good in themselves and in their natural activity. They become means to an end that is outside themselves. A third-level act of freedom, the loving expression of self in sharing the gift of genital life, is being turned into a strictly second-level act of freedom involving a goal extrinsic to the action itself, which (action) is only a means to that external end.

Homosexuality, Homogenitality, and Hemoeroticism

Another issue specifically associated with celibate sexuality is whether people of the same sex can love each other sexually. In the context of the philosophy of human sexual ecology there can be only one answer to this question. Yes. Sexuality is the personal power to share the gift of self, with self and with every other person, not just persons of the other sex. In the "Copernican" sexual perspective, there is an inevitable recognition of the value of homosexuality as well as heterosexuality.

The meaning for homosexuality in an ecologically sound, sociosexual world is not, however, what the popular advocates of homosexuality have in mind. Because of the "Ptolemaic" frame of reference from which people have always suffered and from which even the most ardent gay liberationists continue to suffer, there is bound to be a grave distortion in the meaning of both hetero-sexuality and homosexuality.

In the parlance of the past, the term *homosexuality* necessarily connoted something bad and perverted. No allowance was made for meaning something healthy. The word *heterosexuality* usually evoked suggestions of some-thing healthy. Generally, neither *homosexuality* nor *heterosexuality* has been used in a morally neutral way, allowing for both good and bad forms.

Today many are presenting homosexuality as an option for sexual behavior that is essentially good--an alter-nate "life-style" on a par with the normal genital pref-erence for persons of the other sex. They see little room for meaning something unhealthy by the term. Yet, they share an underlying premise with those who regard homosexuality as bad: sexuality is basically equivalent to genitality.

In the past and in the present, the term *homosexual* has been applied, for the most part, to behavior that is really *homogenital*--genital interaction with a person of the same sex. This usage clearly indicates lack of awareness of any significant meaning for sexuality deeper than the genital. The person is not regarded as capable of sharing indefinitely, *as a man or woman*, with persons of either sex without necessarily sharing in a genital way.

As a result, people who want sexual fulfillment and for some reason cannot find it with members of the other sex are frustrated. Thinking that sexual fulfillment--affirmation specifically as a man or as a woman--is nec-essarily genital, they are not infrequently inclined to turn to members of the same sex. Homogenitality seems to have a higher incidence in prisons, for instance, because under such confinement people do not have, as the mechanistic idea of sexuality expresses it, "hetero-

sexual outlets." (Most often persons who resort to homogenital relations under these conditions return to normal,
heterogenital relations once they return to the outside
world.)

When a person makes a breakthrough in seeing the
deeper dimensions of sexuality, then it can become apparent that homogenital relations represent a functional
incapacity to *share* self as *man* or *woman* with either sex
and that they constitute one particular form of compensation for this inability. Everyone unconsciously wants
sexual fulfillment. Everyone should want it, consciously,
too. But people who know that there are numerous ways
other than genital to experience their manhood and womanhood with people of either sex are not inclined to fall
into homogenitality (a distorted form of homosexuality)
any more than they are inclined to be trapped in unsharing
forms of heterosexuality. This is especially true if
they experience their personal sexuality as a gift, not
just as a given.

Homosexuality--the sharing of self as a gift with
persons of the same sex--is a good thing. Sharing as
man and man or as woman and woman is a common, positively
necessary human interaction. The possibility of sharing
between members of the same sex is structured into everyone's physical, psychic, and spiritual being. (Even
physically a person is bi-sexual. There are male hormones
in the woman and female hormones in the man.) The person's Animus and Anima, as well as the inner Adam and
Eve, do not simply interrelate dynamically within the
individual. They relate with their counterparts in other
persons. In any given interpersonal encounter, the Animus
of one person relates spontaneously with the Anima of
the other.

When a man and a woman interact in a conversation,
there occurs a particularly complex interfusion of their
respective inner sexual resources. A natural psychic and
spiritual embrace results from their opposite orientations
as Giving and Receiving Emphases in being. But, even
when a man and a man or a woman and a woman interact,
a simpler interfusion occurs wherein the receiving kind
of giving power of the one relates directly to the giving
kind of receiving power of the other. These crossfusions
of sexual energy constitute the essence of the homosexual
response which transpires naturally--at an almost exclusively unconscious level most of the time--between persons
of the same sex.[9]

Homogenitality is essentially a disorientation of
a person's erotic drive. Everyone has an erotic drive,
which is both powerful and delicate. It needs to be
understood in relation to the person's sexuality.

Erotic love is a condition of possessing and being
possessed by someone. It is a special kind of sexual
love.[10] If it is authentic, erotic love is centered in
the sharing activity of sexual love. A person can share
with someone whom he or she desires to possess (and to
be possessed by). As long as the sharing dimension of
their love is primary, the erotic dimension is balanced.
But when the desire to possess is stronger than the desire
to share, all kinds of distorted behavior may follow. The
person possessed has become primarily an object, rather
than a person, and the third-level freedom to participate
in fundamental human Goods with him or her is neglected
for the sake of treating that person as a goal.

Autoeroticism is one of the behavioral distortions
that often results from a lack of centering one's erotic
drive within one's sexual (sharing) being. Autoeroticism
is a distortion of the natural power to *share* self with
self and to be in possession of oneself in a healthy way.
People who are mature and self-possessed--who know and
respect their deepest powers to be human--might be regarded as autoerotic in a positive sense. Autoeroticism,
however, is a pseudo self-possession in which the person
tries to compensate for his or her lack of self-control
by manipulating part of the self--such as fantasies or
venereal capabilities--as a means of "self-mastery."
The person enslaves part of himself or herself--largely
unconsciously--as a means of achieving the *feeling* of
being in possession or command of self.

Besides autoeroticism, which is a distortion of the
power to share self *with self*, we can distinguish homoeroticism and heteroeroticism. The latter are similar
attempts to compensate for a lack of functional capacity
to share self *with others*. Homoeroticism is a pseudo-
possession of another in which the person tries to compensate for his or her lack of sexual centering by manipulating part of a person of the same sex--emotionally
and/or venereally--as a means of "possession." Heteroeroticism is the counterpart attitude and activity in
relation to someone of the other sex.

There are natural, healthy attitudes and activities
that might be called homoerotic and heteroerotic. People
have a natural inclination to feel possessive toward certain persons of either sex whom they like. These feelings

of holding and being held by friends of either sex actually serve to support and enhance the core activity of sharing in these relationships. Erotic or possessive feelings toward someone serve to heighten and channel particular acts of sharing somewhat as the banks of a river serve to direct and protect the flow of the water.

True homosexual relations are natural and largely unconscious, just as true heterosexual relations are. People really need to be more intelligently conscious of these kinds of relations which are present in every interpersonal exchange. The dynamically operative powers to give and to receive in opposite ways, even between persons of the same sex, make participation in the fundamental Good of Social Harmony a real possibility. But every homosexual relationship that becomes a homogenital one short-circuits the sharing of self with the other, no matter how good the partners may *feel* about their relationship.[11]

Homogenitality, popularly known as homosexuality, is the attraction toward a person of the same sex in which genital pleasure and satisfaction are taken. Persons who are attracted in this genital way may have been the victims of improper childhood conditioning and education, or may have suffered some earlier traumatic experience that helped to set in motion the present sexual (genital) orientation.

Such persons need not be ashamed of this orientation in so far as they were not responsible for it. But they do have an obligation to attempt to attain the natural attraction toward persons of the other sex. This reorientation may be practically impossible in many cases, even for those who make serious and prolonged effort under the guidance of skilled professional counselors. In any event, all homogenitals--like all heterogenitals-- are particularly obliged by the nature of specifically human freedom to refrain from any genital interaction with a person to whom they are not validly married.[12]

Often people seem to confuse homogenitality (the disorientation of nature which they call homosexuality) with what might be called homoerotic feelings. Within the naturally functioning human being, there seems to be a psychic and physiologic eros toward persons of the same sex. Such an inclination is not the same as the inclination toward genito-centric activity. It is ordinarily nonpathologic. It might be characterized as a modality of consciousness not unlike the sense of appeal of an attractive person of the other sex. A kind of

erotic attraction to persons of the same sex flows naturally from the mutual structure of each person as both
male and female within.[13]   One should not be surprised
if this metaphysical condition of every person is felt
at times when one is in the presence of an attractive
member of the same sex.

Young people particularly--but also people of any
age--ought to acknowledge their feelings of attraction
for people of both sexes. Both kinds of feelings can be
integrated into one's personality in a similar way. A
woman, for instance, who finds another woman erotically
attractive in certain ways can help to integrate her feelings by thinking of this person as a sister (if they are
close in age), as a daughter (if she is considerably
younger), or as a mother (if she is considerably older).
These attractions can be recognized as invitations to
grow much closer to people of the same sex--all such
people--through the mediation of this carefully and intelligently cultivated relationship.

Homoerotic feelings are basically good. They are
not necessarily, though they can be, disorientated. They
can--unlike homogenital feelings--lead to an enrichment
of personality and a joyful celebration of the Good of
Social Harmony. It is unfortunate that young people are
so readily confused by these feelings and often tend to
repress them. (Repression is not good. Suppression,
however, may be quite good and necessary at times.)[14]
A young man, for instance, may find homoerotic urges in
himself unduly disturbing and sometimes or always repress
them, leading to a vicious and cruel attitude toward
people whom he stereotypes as "queers."

Homogenital feelings--as feelings--are good, even
though they symptomatize an erotic disorientation. It
is the homogenital intention that is morally bad--the
intention to put these sick, disordered feelings into
action which necessarily violates the fundamental Good
of Life (through its powers) by using this Good chiefly
as a *means* toward the achievement of the fundamental Good
of Social Harmony. Yet even the Good of Social Harmony
is violated inasmuch as it is treated as a goal, rather
than simply as a good. Homogenital interaction is a kind
of mutual masturbation. Two people are engaged in genitally stimulating and satisfying themselves by means of
each other. The organs of life are being exercised for
a manifestly *unprocreative* purpose (definitely incon-
sonant with their specific nature) and the other person
is being *used* (with his or her consent) specifically as
a means to venereal self-gratification.

277

The freedom to be a sexual self alone--*all one*--with others is being cut down. The freedom to choose homogenital interaction as a way to express appreciation and love is a second-level choice that is necessarily cut off from the freedom to choose life and deeper sharing through the life-potential of the action itself. Homogenital relations--as distinct from homoerotic inclinations--are symptoms of failure to live well the sociosexual vocation of celibate sexuality.

Sexual Virgins

The short-circuited sexual actions of masturbation and the misdirected sexual energy in homogenital relationships underscore the need for a radical vision of celibate sexuality. The question of virginity needs to be reopened. What is the value of virginity in attitude and action?

The world needs virgins--virgin sexuals as well as virgin forests. Virgin sexuals are an important part of the human community's sexual balance. The ecological stability of sociosexual life requires that some people commit themselves to the root vocation to which everyone is called at first and in which basic sexual maturity is to be found. Once the commitment of marriage or parenthood is made, any attempt to develop sexual maturity is doubly difficult, because one then has more than one center in his or her sociosexual life.

Virgins, and other celibates who live their sexuality well, give crucial witness to the possibilities of sexual maturity and freedom. One is not really sexually free until he or she can honestly say, "I am always free to deepen and intensify sharing myself with others and I never *have to* express it in any one particular way, including a genital way."

We are not free to become more and more fully who we already are by refraining from sexual intercourse. We *must* engage in *sexual* intercourse. Sexual intercourse should become deeper and richer in all our relations, with both men and women. But we are free to refrain from genital intercourse or any other kind of intercourse that is not in accord with our basic life-commitment or the particular circumstance. We are free to *be* genital and to *be* coital, without ever functioning in these ways. Celibate sexuality is the root of sexual freedom and love.

1. Parasitical kinds of living in marriage (or not in marriage) are often necessary. When an individual is physically or emotionally ill, or is advanced in age, such attachment is positively good. But moral parasitism--not thinking and deciding for oneself in whatever circumstances of social dependence or independence one happens to be found--is never good. Yet, it is often the case; and it needs to be changed. Both before and after marriage, persons need to grow in their personal power to be morally autonomous and to share their authentic selves.

2. The ecology of these relationships is difficult to discern and describe. The healthy spouse emphatically lives with the female attitude of togetherness with every single other precisely in virtue of receiving the sacramental power of marital union with *one* other. Thus, in the mature spouse every person is met with a special feeling of closeness as an overflow from the dramatic, symbolic and very real marital encounter with his or her spouse. My observation is that married people generally are not mature enough to perceive and effectively sense the specialness (marital*likeness*) of each interpersonal encounter. Yet they have the grace (help) for living it--to the extent that they grow healthfully in the intimacy of the special relationship with their spouses.

3. Centering is an internal activity even when it is mutual. Unfortunately, a person who is not sexually mature will inevitably center his or her erotic and genital inclinations upon the sexually attractive other. Part of the business of treating someone as a sexual object is the possessing and clinging reflex toward another person as an unconscious attempt to compensate for uncentered sexual feeling within self. The mature person, who is sexually centered within, lets his or her erotic and genital inclinations toward another find a place within the other's life that is proportioned to their respective life-commitments in the condition (or at the stage of) their mutual friendship.

The devastating conditions of sexually objectifying and being objectified are well expressed by Masters and Johnson when they write about sexual responsibility. See, e.g., William H. Masters and Virginia E. Johnson, in association with Robert J. Levin, *The Pleasure Bond: A New Look at Sexuality and Commitment* (New York: Bantam, 1974), pp. 1-15, 267-85. Their comments are all made within the "Ptolemaic" frame of reference. Nevertheless, they offer many insights into effective genital-personal communication.

4. Masters and Johnson have developed a kind of "philosophy of touch." They regard touching as an end in itself. In my opinion, this is an important feature of sexual ecology. See, e.g., *The Pleasure Bond*, pp. 244-55. Touching as an end in itself is a centering activity that is very helpful during periodic continence.

5. The reason for this statement is that venereal pleasure is the *specific* pleasure afforded by the act of coital intercourse. The intentional separation of such pleasure from the act which it is specifically designed to encourage and facilitate violates the

integrity of the act and, ultimately, the agent. Just because the pleasure *can* be readily experienced apart from coitional or pre-coitional interaction does not mean that it *should* be intentionally so experienced. In morality, *can do* is certainly not equivalent to *should do*. A person *can*, for instance, experience great pleasure in possessing attractive merchandise once displayed in a department store—either by purchasing it or by shoplifting.

6. The English language does not have distinctive words for all of the various kinds of significant volition involved in moral activity. In the case of unbidden venereal pleasure, one should naturally *will* that it occur—obviously, nature "wills" it. And one should naturally will that it be *what* it is—a pleasurable sensation, not an unpleasurable or neutral one. But one is called to refrain from taking advantage of the presence of this pleasure in order to enjoy it as though it were a kind of unconscious substitute for coital union.

The important point is that one does not, practically speaking, *bring about* the pleasure—either by directly choosing or proposing that the pleasure occur, or by omitting to forestall a cause of that pleasure occurring when one can and should, or by being *willing* to choose this pleasurable occurrence again on another occasion, and so forth. The same basic volitional structure applies to other appropriations of pleasure that do not belong to the individual at the time and under the circumstance—such as owning an extravagantly appointed automobile when such ownership is disproportionate to one's income and ability to care for one's family.

7. The moral situation is very similar to that which faces one who is tempted to engage in premarital genital intercourse. Both situations are a challenge to one's authenticity and self-esteem. In dealing with the pros and cons of premarital sex, Paul Popenoe distinguishes between feelings of frustration and feelings of deprivation. The person who refrains from coital intercourse as a means of preparing for something better in the future is, in some sense, deprived of an experience, but not frustrated. The feeling of deprivation does no harm because the person sees a reason for it and because the sense of self-esteem is not threatened by it. A person whose self-esteem is low, however, may feel frustrated and engage in coital intercourse out of this feeling of frustration and as a compensation for an assumed lack of "sex appeal." The latter reaction can only lead to even greater frustration and deeper self-alienation. See *Are Virgins Out of Date?* (Baden-Baden: Editions Trobisch, 1968).

The reason for greater frustration and deeper self-alienation in the case of masturbation is that the desired integration of one's sexuality that is supposed to occur cannot possibly be attained in that way. True integration unites all powers and aspects of the person, and puts consciousness and body in mutual service rather than mutual exploitation. Instead of being dissipated in masturbation, the bodily energy involved needs to be brought, by one's consciousness, into the service of life, of daily work, and of creating community with others.

280

8. The *powers* of generation are violated--not necessarily the organs. Here I hold the traditional position of the natural unity of organs and powers. The organ of sight, e.g., is really different from the power to see; and at the same time this organ (eyeball, optic nerve, etc.) is *one with* the power to see. Damage to the organ can result in the functional incapacity to see and does *affect* the natural *power* to see, but it does *not take away or destroy* this natural power.

The organ is related to the power as body to soul. It would be morally wrong, therefore, were a person to damage deliberately his own or another's eyeball. Not only because it could render the person functionally sightless, but also because the person has a natural right to see which is inherent in his or her natural *power* to see.

Violations of body are always direct violations of soul. But some violations of soul do not necessarily affect directly the body and its functions. Thus, preventing someone physically from seeing something he or she has a right to see would be morally wrong and a direct violation of the person's natural power to see, even though no damage at all was done to the person's physical eyes. For instance, a mother has a right to see whether her child is playing safely or is getting into danger. But if someone holds her hostage in her home and keeps her blindfolded, she would be deprived of her natural right to see--not to mention other natural rights. Yet her power's organs would not be directly violated. Similary, in the case of genital powers and artificial insemination, the natural power to generate one's child is being directly violated even though the physical organs (such as penis, testes, vagina, etc.) are not being damaged or directly affected in an adverse way.

9. There is a spontaneous, magnetic-like attraction of Animus in the one for Anima in the other. Animus and Anima can be conceived (partly) in terms of polarity--opposite poles attracting, and the same poles repelling. If two men were "all male" they could not tolerate each other. Also, if one meets someone whose dominant *psychic* polar element--at a functional level--is the reverse of his or her sex, one is, initially at least, repelled. Such is the case in meeting "effeminate" men and "butchy" women.

10. According to C. S. Lewis, the genital sex drive looks primarily to justification by way of physical pleasure and release of tension (and can be with any "body"). But eros is the state which is called "being in love." Erotic love looks primarily to the person--a desire to possess the person as a particular individual. Eros is a love that can take possession of a person and become a god, independent of genital consideration. *The Four Loves*, (New York: Harcourt Brace Jovanovich, 1960).

11. They can *feel* good about their relationship because they are relating in virtue of the natural crossfusion of Animus and Anima between them. But inasmuch as the relationship is homogenital they are violating that crossfusion itself. The bodily counterparts of Animus and Anima (e.g., penis which is both male and female but emphatically male and vagina which is both but emphatically female)

are being misused. In the case of two males, the penis of each is being specifically activated without any complementary and proportionate receptivity in the other. They may not *feel* that this is happening, but only a rationalization of their own disregard for their bodily (coital and genital) integrity as persons can cover up the spiritual wounding that inevitably occurs.

Contemporary moralists are especially prone to overlook the bodily dimension of homogenital intercourse in their efforts to stress the *soul* of the action--good motives, fidelity, spirit of generosity, and so forth. Their moral evaluations are "bodiless souls"--all focus is placed on *how* the action is done and none on *what* is being done.

12. For a basic orientation to the psychological and moral aspect of counseling the homosexual (homogenital) regarding his or her behavioral patterns, see John F. Harvey, "Chastity and the Homosexual," *The Priest*, July-August 1977, pp. 10-16. See also, "Treatment of Homosexuality," a section in William E. May and John F. Harvey, *On Understanding Human Sexuality* (Chicago: Franciscan Herald Press, 1977), pp. 57-67.

13. Our society has largely repressed the positive features of homosexual sharing in its past efforts to abhor the intergenital and mutually erotic aberrations. Nevertheless, the practice of men inevitably congregating in one area and women in another at the usual social gathering not only seems to indicate insecurity with regard to healthy heterosexual interaction but also a kind of healthy enjoyment and sharing of one another's commonly structured, sexual being.

14. Repression means unwillingness to admit one's feelings to consciousness. Suppression involves dismissing certain feelings already acknowledged, and can be good or bad, depending on the circumstances. If one has a strong urge to punch his or her employer in the nose, one might want to admit (to self) the feeling, and then suppress it--for the time being at least--until one's anger subsides. If, however, one really admires his or her employer and some special accomplishment or characteristic of this person, but on a given occasion suppresses the urge to say something (perhaps out of an irrational fear of being regarded as an "apple polisher"), such an occurrence could be detrimental to personal growth.

Chapter 16

MARITAL SEXUALITY

Marriage is the middle vocation. As a vocational identity, it tends to become submerged. Basic consideration is often given to celibacy as the time of growth and preparation for marriage and family. Under the guise of talk about marriage, parenthood receives an enormous share of vocational attention. But marriage, as a good in itself, is hidden by utilitarian concerns about having sex, and having children.

Marriage is regarded primarily as a utility vocation. It is thought to be the only way to preserve natural family relations and to keep a man and woman working at loving each other when the going gets rough. It is considered to be the "go ahead" for coital intercourse. No matter how valid they may be, each one of these and other motives for marriage, taken separately or together, tend to be excessively utilitarian and functionalistic.

An in-depth understanding of marriage can never be attained until this vocation is seen as a good in itself, alongside the two other vocations and quite distinct from them. Just as celibacy is primarily a celebration of the male-female union within each person, marriage is primarily the celebration of the male-female union between individual persons.[1] The intersexual nature of every person-to-person relation is celebrated when a man and a woman vow to be faithful to each other until death. Their action is a primary symbol of the fidelity to the intersexual union all persons should have with

each other. Every person has a unique intersexual relationship with every other person, man or woman. When
one man and one woman vow themselves to be faithful to
each other for life, they are sociosexually singing the
praises of the mystical body of a marriage underlying
all other relations among creatures (and between creatures
and their Creator). This remarkable act of marital commitment is taken seriously in the Judeo-Christian culture
by its recognition as being a symbol of God's union with
his Chosen People and of Christ's union with his Church.

Marriage is the sacrament of man and woman. It is
the sacred sign of interpersonal sexuality. In marrying,
two celibates of different sex offer to each other a life
in which the Animus and Adam of the one are committed
to integration with the Anima and Eve of the other by
way of a qualitative character and intensity comparable
to the inner marriage itself within each person.[2] Marriage should be, therefore, monogamous not only because
it is good for the children and good for the emotional
security of the partners, but primarily because it celebrates interpersonally the prototypically monogamous
marriage within the partners themselves and within every
created person.[3]

Marriage is a vocation *within* the vocation of celibacy, but *not of* it. The vocation of celibacy is the
direct celebration of the creational marriage (within
each person).[4] Marriage as a vocation is a special am-
plification of that primordial "marriage" vocation within
celibate life. In vocational marriage two celibates
become no longer two only, but also one.[5] Marriage is
a new celibacy: the celibacy of a uniquely constituted
social entity, sharing within itself the dual polarity
of the Animus-Adam of the one partner with the Anima-
Eve of the other. In marriage, the partners sociosexually
and culturally dramatize (as well as symbolize) the androgynous unity that every single person experiences
within himself or herself.

Like the celibate, the spouse is one who is called
to a distinctive orientation in the depths of his or her
sexual life. The celibate is one who is naturally invited
(from within) to share the gift of self with self and
with others, but emphatically with self. The spouse is
one who freely chooses to share the gift of self with
self and with others, but emphatically with *one* other.
Both celibate and spouse share emphatically with *one* person. The celibate, with self; the spouse, with the chosen
marital companion. The celibate, with a person of the
same sex; the spouse, with a person of the other sex.

In the heart of their different vocations, the celibate
and the spouse are as similar, yet as opposite, as man
and woman.

Within Self, Male; with Others, Female

In the preceding chapter, I observed that the celibate is related within himself or herself as female,
and is related to others as male. The spouse is related
in the opposite way. The spouse is called to a way of
living in which he or she is no longer *simply* himself
or herself. The spouse relates to self as more than self.

Even in the inward relationship of self with self,
the spouse emphasizes not the simple self alone--as does
the celibate--but the *other* self as well, with whom he
or she is sociosexually one. So, in relation to self,
the spouse emphasizes otherness and differentiation,
which are emphatically (not exclusively) male characteristics. The spouse is emphatically *giving* to self
right within the self. The spouse is giving to self the
self of the other.[6] Naturally, there is a profound receiving activity as well. But, relative to the celibate,
the spouse is, with self, emphatically engaged in a receiving kind of *giving*.

When we regard the spouse in relation to others,
there is a distinct emphasis on the female side of sexual
identity. The spouse is one who relates emphatically
to one special other, and not to all others. The spouse
is ovumlike in relation to others. There is an emphasis
on oneness, on the unification of a particular relationship, on the centrality of the marriage as the center
of all social relationships.

This natural orientation to oneness does not mean
that the spouse should have only one or a few good
friends. It simply means that in the marriage covenant
there is a bonding to a special one--a bonding which
expresses specifically the female attitude of emphasizing
oneness and centeredness in the *one* special other.

The spouse gives to many others, as does the celibate. But the emphasis is just the opposite. The spouse
gives selectively, though dramatically, to the special
sexual other. Yet, the basic relationship of the spouse
to any and all others is emphatically a receiving. Most
dynamically, in the marriage covenant itself the spouses
receive, from the human community, the right to be and
act as spouses. The spouse is, then, emphatically (though
not exclusively) a giving kind of *receiver* in relation

to others as a whole. Like an ovum, which receives emphatically and dramatically the attention from a "world"
of spermatazoa but selectively gives itself only to one
of them; so, the spouse, in the sacrament of marriage,
receives emphatically and dramatically from the whole
human community the functional power to give self selectively to this single sexual other.[7]

The spouse is primarily female with respect to
others, but male with respect to self. In the vocational
ecosystem, the celibate and the spouse sexually balance
each other. They are male and female in opposite ways.
Later I will indicate how the vocation of parenthood
simply adds a richness and fullness to the harmonious
relationship between celibate and spouse.

The Marital Union and the Marital Act

There is a marriage within each person. Likewise,
there is a kind of underlying global marriage of each
person with every other person, man or woman, by virtue
of being created intersexual. Upon this ontological
(beingful) base, vocational marriages are covenanted and
contracted.[8]

Marriage, then, is a special social structuring of
the community in which two people of different sex, by
their whole way of life, participate in certain inner
mysteries of human sexuality. They present themselves
to the human community as one social unity and are received by the community as being so united and as serving
its needs in some way. Usually, the most dramatic way
in which the married couple serve the community is by
undertaking a further vocation, that of parenting new
members. Nevertheless, a married couple--simply in them-
selves--are a new celibacy, and together they can serve
the community somewhat as the single celibate does.

Marriage is in no way a private commitment. It is
not simply a personal act (or co-act) on the part of the
couple. It is a socio-personal act, necessarily involving
a public proclamation that this man and this woman freely
choose to constitute themselves in the community as husband and wife, living together and sharing all their
earthly possessions in common, as well as their minds and
hearts. Before the wedding ceremony there is no marriage,
no sociopersonal act. Because marriage requires reception
by the community in the person of the witnesses, anything
that the couple does that is preceremonial is also premarital. The two people do not simply vow themselves to
each other. They vow themselves as a couple to the

community. They promise--at least implicitly--that they will live in the community as two in one flesh. The community in return promises--at least implicitly--that it will honor and protect them as husband and wife. In marriage, couple and community are united somewhat as the man and the woman.

Marital union begins, then, not with a first act of coital intercourse, but with the covenant proclaimed before the official witness of society. The pronouncing of vows is a definite external sign of an internal event, the union of minds and hearts--of understanding, intention, and determination. No further physical sign of the couple's intent is necessary in order to make the union known to the public. By their words, the partners impregnate each other's souls and the soul of the socio-sexual community into which they are being received. Anything further may be important, but not necessary.

Coital-genital intercourse is, then, not *the* marriage act. It is *a* marriage act, along with many other free acts of loving which the couple shares daily. Coital intercourse *cannot specifically* signify the kind of commitment a man and woman make in marriage. But their mutual words can. Coital intercourse speaks its own language concerning the natural intent to be a parent, to receive a child.[9]

We can, therefore, speak of the social act of marital union. Like the social act of celibate union, this act has both a specific, co-creative purpose and a general, unitive purpose--a specific nature and a general nature. The *specific* nature of this act of marital union is to establish a "home" and a special man-woman covenant for life which will uniquely and properly celebrate the relationship of God and his people, of Christ and his Church, of Animus-Adam and Anima-Eve. The *general* nature of this act is to be unitive between *this* man and *this* woman by a total life of mutual affirmation and appropriate love-expression. The marital act is not at all the same as engaging in coital-genital intercourse or in raising children.[10]

The marriage covenant of a man and a woman is a good in itself, a vocation all its own. This covenant is worth being lived just as it is, without necessarily adding to it the vocation of parenthood. Yet, as soon as the couple engages in coital union, they are beginning to participate in another vocation. They are engaged in *the parentive act*. They are beginning a new covenant: a covenant with a child or children. They are exercising

their distinctively social powers and organs designed
specifically for the generation of new community members.
They are committed to the community and to each other
in a new way.

When a couple engages in coital union on their wedding night, the vocation of marriage as a good in itself
has not lasted a full day. (This is a matter of fact,
not necessarily of regret.) Marriage is the sacrament
of human sexuality, not of human genitality. Human genitality is itself so sacred and serious that it, too,
should be expressed, like marriage, only in a free and
responsible way. Many people apparently marry with the
idea that human coital intercourse *must* transpire within
a loving marital union. But the very necessity or urgency
about coition occurring renders the coital union in such
marriages thereby less free and less responsible. The
marital union so readily becomes largely a function of
coition and children.

Traditional thinking on the nature of marriage tends
strongly to identify marriage and parenthood, or marriage
and "sex." Only the "Copernican Revolution" in human
sexuality will make it possible for a differentiation
(not separation) of the two vocations to become well
established. The sexual revolution that is needed will
afford people the opportunity to distinguish radically
between the marital act and the parentive act.

The parentive act is the act that initiates parent-
hood--coital-genital intercourse. This kind of intercourse has two primary purposes or ends, the unitive and
the procreative, neither of which should be acted against,
and both of which must be accorded its place in the intentions of the mutual agents.[11] But the marital or conjugal act is a different and much more pervasive act
than the genital or parentive act. The marital act is
the act of giving oneself to, and receiving, this one
person of the other sex as the *primary* center of social
otherness, for richer or poorer, until death. The purpose of the marital act is, in its own way, both unitive
and co-creative, love-giving and society-giving. Marriage is specifically designed to be a sign of God's
love-giving and society-creating. All of the acts in
a marriage are meant to be love-giving and society-
creating, including any coitionally parentive acts. Marriage is society-making. The society that marriage makes
is the two in one flesh--the couple. (Parenthood is
society-continuing, society-adding).

Marriage is also the Sacrament of society. For Christians, it alone symbolizes and participates specifically in the union of God and his creature, and of Christ and his Church. God would be all-good and all-powerful even if he only created a single creature with whom he intimately related. Jesus would have died even for a single person in need of redemption. Similarly, the efficacy of the marital union is the union of spouse with spouse, one single person with another single person of the other sex. Children, then, are *not of* the essence of marriage, but are (or should be) *within* the essence, something like the truth that more than one creature is not of the essence of creation but within the essence of creation, and more than one member of Christ's redemptive body is not of its essence but within it. In special social otherness, marriage celebrates *the one*; parenthood celebrates *the many*.

Marital Fidelity

The marital act must be a free act. The vow is made by two relatively mature persons who know what they are doing. They do not know what the consequences will be in detail. No one can foresee much of the future. But they freely desire to express their love for each other in such a way that, however devastating their conditions of life might become, they will be faithful to each other as this one person of the other sex with whom life is primarily shared. That is the kind of solemn promise that constitutes marriage.

If one or both partners does not intend to be faithful basically as *the one* sexual other until death, then a marriage has not taken place, despite how close they feel. Marriage is specifically a moral union, not a physical or a psychic union. It is a moral union that includes all three sexual-energy areas of the persons involved. The energies of the individuals are fused morally by their own free choice and thereby a third entity is created: the marriage.

This marital union that is effected by the mutual will of the parties, in accord with the will of the community, begins a zygote*like* existence the moment it is conceived. A new life is conceived in the womb of society at the moment the vows are validly pronounced. This life will grow healthfully or ailingly until the death of one or both persons. Because the choice of each other was freely undertaken, this special social union was conceived. Each person can only be a party to *one* of such unions by the very nature of marriage as a sociosexual emphasis on the one special other.

The question obviously arises: Can this social zygote or embryo be aborted? Can one or both spouses take its life by "changing their minds"?

If marriage were merely a contract, set up by the mutual agreement of the parties involved, then the marriage could be dissolved by mutual consent. But even then it would take agreement by both members, not just the faintheartedness of one. Society cannot allow its members to break official contracts simply by individual changes in intention. The other party's mind is equally important in the contract, and social justice demands that it be equally regarded should a change be made.

Another consideration is that marriage is not a solemn agreement simply between the man and the woman. The covenant includes both the couple and the community. Marriage requires the willingness of the community as well as the promises of the partners. The community promises to treat the couple as a couple for life and to support them and their offspring should they later not be able to support themselves. Even if marriage were merely a contract, the community's interests would have to be considered seriously.

But marriage is *more than* a contract. The marital act is a covenant. In religious terms, it is a vow before God (as well as before each other and the community) that this union will be lived faithfully until death. Even from a more secular, philosophical point of view, if the people really mean what they say--and the presumption should be that they do, in most cases--then there is *no* later act of will on their part that *can* revoke this solemn promise. The promise is not made with any conditional clauses--implicit or explicit.

If, at the time of making the vows, there is no real intention to be faithful (no matter what the cost), then a marriage is not being entered. In such a case, all subsequent activity of the couple is really not marital activity--including coital union and the rearing of children. From an objective point of view, all such activity involves a moral wrong, since the man and woman have not really been received by each other as the primary center of sociosexual otherness in space and time until death.

Today, on the one hand, there are probably many non-marriages in most communities. The situation is particularly unfortunate for anyone who has attempted to receive the sexually other person as a spouse, but was not really so received in return, and may not even know it thirty years later. Perhaps we could reasonably surmise that many divorces are not really divorces (that is, attempts to dissolve a marriage bond) because there was no marriage bond present in the first place.

On the other hand, a free choice to live as husband and wife until death can and often is made by both persons who do know what they are doing and yet who are very weak in their determination to carry out this vow. Weakness of ability to carry out the responsibilities of the covenant should not be misinterpreted as a conditional mindedness about the vow itself. The person may well intend to be faithful to his or her spouse for life, and then fail miserably to live up to this commitment.

The vow is really quite simple to understand, but quite complex and, not infrequently, quite difficult to fulfill. Any intelligent adult with sufficient emotional stability to hold a job is likely capable of valid marriage. He or she can understand the meaning of living together as husband and wife, sharing all of life's goods and possessions. The person can likewise understand that there will be ups and downs, possibly ecstatic joys and possibly severe setbacks or disillusionment. What death basically means is evident to all adults. Death means the cessation of all personal life in this world, including the physical. A psychic or spiritual "coma" in the couple's relationship does not qualify as death, any more than a physical coma does. Unfortunately, when a marriage becomes cold and when there is little or no hope for recovery from this condition, some people start rationalizing it as a death, rather than as a coma.

Nevertheless, the covenant of marriage involves a particular kind of will act. Each person wills the marital relationship in an irrevocable way. Built right into the marital act of will is the intention that no subsequent act of will by anyone (self or spouse or society) can violate it. So, years later, when someone who has made such an act of personal will at the marriage ceremony decides to retract it, he or she is attempting to act *against* his or her own will. But such an act of retractive will cannot be successful, since by it the will is contradicting itself. The latter act is really a non-*will*, although it may be a definite want or desire.[12]

291

Marriage is not simply a contract, such as one makes in buying a house. A person may sign a contract for deed and agree to pay so much a month for so many years until the house is paid, when he or she will receive free and clear title to the house. Such a contract or agreement can be broken by the mutual consent of the parties. If it is broken by the installment buyer, there may well be penalties to be paid. But the contract can be broken. One did not enter into a *covenant* with the owner of the deed. One did not will his life to the action of purchasing a house, even though it may feel like that at times of financial hardship.

Contracts are second-level actions that should be done in accord with third-level commitments and purposes. But covenants are themselves third-level actions. They are special third-level actions in which the person constitutes a whole new relationship with another. Contracts can be broken or violated. Covenants cannot be broken, but can be violated.

When it is said that a covenant is broken, the meaning should be that it was violated. Spiritual *entities*, which a covenant specifically is, cannot be literally broken. Marriage, which is a covenant, cannot be aborted or killed, because it is a moral union that is essentially spiritual. It is neither psychic nor physical in essence, although its fullness demands emotional and physical intimacy.

Moreover, the marital covenant is an act in which one promises to be faithful to those to whom he or she will *not* be married. It is a solemn promise to the whole community. The idea of making another such covenant while repudiating the first one is a futile one. The attempt to make a second covenant, while the first spouse is still living, renders the "second" one incredible in itself. One can hardly promise sincerely to live with a second person as husband or wife, for better or worse until death, if one has refused to do it with a first person. The person perjures himself or herself in the very attempt.

In the original marital covenant such a person had already promised that he or she would be faithful to the spouse by living together lovingly for life. This kind of promise implies a fidelity to *every* person of the other sex. One is vowing not to attempt such a union with any of these others. Therefore, the vowed commitment to live with the first partner implied a vow to the second partner that they would *not* live together.[13]

292

Keeping one's marriage vows means being faithful to *all* of one's friends, who are part of the community in which one has been received as the spouse of *this one* person.

Creative Separation

According to the preceding perspective, divorce is impossible. A valid marriage act cannot be aborted, as a child can, because the marriage act is a specifically spiritual and moral entity.[14] The mental and physical act of disregard taken by most people who engage in legal divorce proceedings can only be morally damaging. The neglect of caring *primarily* for the well-being of the person to whom one once committed his or her life in body, mind, and heart is bound to be a major source of sexual pollution in one's subsequent personal relationships--whether it is acknowledged or not.

Divorce violates, but does not dissolve, a relationship that, in some sense, even God cannot sever. Human beings are created with the freedom of will and of choice such that they *can* be taken seriously in this life and in the next.

With respect to individual sexual identity the person has no choice. He or she is naturally male or female. (Not even a transsexual operation can fundamentally change that identity.) But in the matter of vocational identity there are three main choices. A person is free to choose committed celibacy, marriage, or parenthood as his or her primary vocational identity. Of course, the person is also free not to choose, and thereby may live in uncommitted celibacy for life.

The *marital* act--as distinct from the coital act--is the free act of covenant made in the marriage ceremony. With the mutual consent of partner and of society, the person causes the existence of a new social entity--the marriage itself--which not even God will take away. Spouses co-create with God in the marital act a unique social creature. God will not annihilate any creature.

Once a person is a parent, he or she is always a parent, because God will not annihilate the new person. Similarly, once a person is a spouse, he or she is a spouse for life, because God will not be divorced from creation. God is always faithful to the covenants of creation.

What, then, can a couple do when it is obviously impossible to live together? Is not separation the gate-way to divorce?

The often necessary legal divorce is not a matter for question here. Such a measure may be practically necessary, especially when the other partner demands it or when one partner is very abusive. How to separate in bed and board and property and even children, and yet to regard seriously the separated spouse as one's primary sexual (sharing) partner challenges the person's ability to be continuously and creatively faithful.

Creative fidelity should start in the marriage before the break-up. There is a great difference between slavish fidelity and creative fidelity. The one is hardly a fidelity at all. No one is called to be another's door-mat. Masochism is personally destructive in all sexual relationships--including the genital. Fidelity flows from integrity. The faithful one is the person who re-lates with another in a truly loving way, no matter how the circumstances have changed. A person is always free to will the truest and the best for one's spouse, no matter what the cost in creative energy.

The loving thing to do is not always the most pleas-ant or that which *seems* to be loving. Sometimes the best thing a separated spouse can do--at least for awhile-- is to let the other go and be himself or herself, with-out direct communication. Even though one partner is doing practically all that he or she can do to make the separated marriage a viable arrangement, the other part-ner is often unwilling to cooperate and lets his or her interests stray. At certain times, it may be necessary to make special efforts to establish basic communica-tions--even with the strong possibility of total rebuff. If the other person has entered a legal marriage with a third party, constant communication may be difficult or practically impossible. It may not even be wise, though possible, in some instances. Nevertheless, the possibilities and circumstances for creative fidelity in a separated marriage are numerous.

Creative separation involves any way of loving the alienated spouse that can be reasonably justified in terms of both the undying commitment once made and the practical necessity to live apart. The very fact of separating can be the first step toward a creative solution to one's marriage problems. But it can only be a step. Fidelity to a freely chosen life-commitment is, for most people, rarely easy, often difficult, and sometimes nearly impossible. But since no one can take away the person's freedom of choice, the faithful spouse is one who chooses to continue regarding the estranged partner as his or her primary sexual other, despite the fact that this choice is not reciprocated. One who perjures his or her own will on the occasion of a partner doing so is not acting in fidelity.

Creative separation does not mean that the abandoned spouse cannot have friends of the other sex. In such situations, there may be greater need than ever for these friends. Man-woman loving friendships are always desirable, for marrieds and singles alike. Marriages themselves would be much healthier if they would or could sustain special, caring relationships of the partners with other members of the opposite sex. In times of separation from the person of the other sex to whom one is committed for life, there is a great need for friendship with one or more people of the other sex who can handle the relationship in a way that is itself creatively faithful to the marital and celibate commitments of all concerned. (Chapter 18 discusses the possibilities of loving friendships between man and woman, independent of any marital relationship.)

In a time of marital separation, the natural strength of celibacy, which the person should never have abandoned, can sustain him or her through the change of life-style such a circumstance demands. Unfortunately, in our society there seem to be many married persons who do not have enough self-confidence in their innate celibate natures. They are not widowed and thereby they are not free to marry. They are espoused in body, mind, and heart to someone by whom they have been deeply wounded and whom they may have injured in some way as well. Self-pity is a common attitude. Such persons are poorly conditioned to handle a deeply caring relationship with a person of the other sex who might well be their friend. Therefore, while loving friendships with people of the other sex can be supportive to a separated spouse, they are often very dangerous. Creative separation is another moral position which cries out for the support of a "Copernican Revolution" in human sexuality.

NOTES

1. Between individual persons of the same and of different sex. I have theorized earlier (Chapter 15) about the androgynous, cross-fusions of Animus and Anima in persons of the same sex. Marriage *generally* symbolizes the unique sexual fusion of any two individuals. It *particularly* symbolizes the unique sexual fusion of any man and woman. And it *specifically* symbolizes and celebrates the unique heterosexual fusion of this man and this woman (the spouses).

2. This commitment to integration of the psychic (Animus Anima) and the spiritual (Adam and Eve) of the spouses includes the more obvious commitment to integration of the physical (body, material goods, and relationships). They belong to each other--as well as to themselves--on all levels of human sexual energy (hormonally, emotionally, and spiritually).

3. This idea is a key insight of Mary Rosera Joyce in *Love Responds to Life*, p. 21. The ultimate natural foundation for monogamous marriage would seem to be the relation of male and female within each spouse. The supernatural foundation might be regarded as the relation of the Father (Animus Person) and the Word (Anima Person) in the Trinity. See speculation on the sexual life of the Trinity, Chapter 14.

4. By creational marriage I mean the inner union of male and female definitively structured in the physical, psychic, and spiritual being of each person from the moment of creation--a marriage that is for better or for worse forever.

5. In the past, much of the cultural wisdom concerning the nature of marriage seemed to encourage the idea that the individuals were somehow no longer two individuals but a single moral entity. Most unfortunately, this "unity" was treated in such a way that the wife's identity was engulfed by her husband's. I would suggest that an over-extension of the Aristotelian either-or logic is particularly evident in this area. The claim of Jesus (Matt. 19:4-6) that the spouses are "no longer two, therefore, but one body" seems to have been taken with this logic exclusively operative. But being "no longer two" can mean that they are no longer only two. It can readily be understood as a way of emphasizing the definitiveness of the additional identity and its indissolubility. Jesus was mainly speaking of the ontological or beingful character of the marriage relationship with reference to divorce. Thus, we might be wiser to make sure we read such a text while using a *both-and* logic. The spouses are *both* two individuals with their own personal identities and autonomy *and* they are no longer two *only*, but *also* one body.

6. By the inner will in making the marital vow, the spouse is continuously called to present within himself or herself the needs and desires of the marital other as *one* with those of his or her own. As Paul proclaims to Christians, "I live now, no longer I [alone], but Christ lives in me" (Galatians 2:20), so a spouse has a call to exercise the natural aptitude created within each of us to say of some special, real and symbolic person: "I live now, no longer I alone (celibately), but my beloved spouse lives within me."

7. The idea is that the *giving* of self to one's spouse is sub-dominant with respect to the emphatic receiving of power from the whole human community of *others* to do this giving. The interrelationships here are extremely complex--especially if we enter the different orientations on the part of a spouse who is male relative to one who is female. The limitations of this book--which is more synoptic with respect to the whole field of sexuality than it is analytic with respect to any one area--prohibit further refinement in understanding the ecology of these relationships.

8. Marriage is a consent that is embodied in a contract. The marriage consent is a consent to enter a primary way of living. V. A. Demant, for instance, calls marriage a state that is brought about by the instrumentality of a contract. Unlike a contract, a state of living cannot be cancelled. He says that while many human relations in civilization are contractual there must be some kind of relation in which a human being is respected for what he or she is and not simply for what he or she does. Children, for instance, have a "status" in the home and a natural right to a certain kind of treatment and affection because they belong there. "In marriage a man or woman enters voluntarily into a new status, like, but different from, the status they enjoyed as the young of their original families. To have some part of our life as status is paradoxically a condition of freedom; because human beings, not being pure spirits, must have settlement in some part of their existence in order to be free in others." *Christian Sex Ethics* (New York: Harper and Row, 1963), p. 63.

9. But it is, nonetheless, a very confirmatory sign of the marital covenant. An excellent discussion of coital union as a renewal of the marital covenant is found in John Kippley, *Birth Control and the Marriage Covenant* (Collegeville, Minn.: Liturgical Press, 1976), pp. 105-24.

10. Although the social act of marital union is not the same as married coital union, they are very closely related, such that in the Roman Catholic Church a marriage that is not consummated (definitively begun) through coital intercourse can be dissolved. It may be regarded as valid, but it is not regarded as consummated until coital intercourse occurs. According to this traditional teaching, a valid marriage cannot occur unless both parties are open to exercising their rights to procreate, whether or not they ever choose to do so.

11. The inseparable connection between the unitive and procreative purposes of genital intercourse are thoroughly treated by Mary Rosera Joyce, *Love Responds to Life*, pp. 67-81.

12. Freedom comes only in willing, not in wanting or desiring as such. The latter can be aspects or forms of will (which is a spiritual power) but they can also be aspects or forms of emotional attachments that represent compulsive or impulsive conditions which the person rationalizes as *will*.

13. Not as husband and wife, at least; and therefore, not as father and mother--which is what coital intercourse naturally involves. Nevertheless, in the case of someone who is unfortunately

297

but reasonably forced to live apart from his or her spouse there would not necessarily be any reason to forego close living with someone else of the other sex in the same dwelling. If these friends were mature enough--and if scandal would not be given--they might be able to live an authentically spouse*like* life; without the commitment, without formally shared property and possessions, without any genitally active relations, etc. This idea concerning close living with someone other than the spouse is admittedly visionary in its perspective and requirements. It is likely that the percentage of people who could live this kind of relationship in a morally sound way is very small.

14. Nor can the spiritual dimension and moral destiny of a pre-birth child be aborted.

Chapter 17

PARENTIVE SEXUALITY

A celibate is a person who is called by nature and
social circumstance (chosen or not) to emphasize specifically the uniqueness and otherness of every being--
God and creatures. A spouse is a person who is called
by nature and by chosen social circumstance to emphasize
specifically the unique togetherness and oneness of every
being in relation to every other being--God and creatures.
A parent is a person who is called by nature and social
circumstance (chosen or not chosen) to emphasize specifically the unique power and creativity of every being-with-
being relationship--God with God, God with creature, and
creature with creature. The parentive emphasis is dramatized in the conception of a child and in conception-
orientated activity.

As parents, man and woman look emphatically beyond
each other. Just as they look beyond themselves as individuals in order to become spouses, in coital interaction
they look beyond themselves as a couple to become parents.
The looking-beyond may be largely or totally unconscious.
It is thoroughly compatible with the obvious looking-
toward each other that coital union also entails. But
it is as naturally present as the looking beyond self that
the covenant of marriage requires. (People can engage
in marriage with a largely self-centered motivation at a
conscious level, overlooking the essentially other-directed
character of marriage itself. People likewise can engage in coition with a largely couple-centered motivation

at a conscious level, overlooking the essentially other-directed character of the coition itself.)

When a man and a woman deliberately engage in coital intercourse they have virtually entered the vocation of parenthood, even though they fully intend to avoid or to prevent conception. They are engaging in the parentive act, the act that, of itself, bespeaks conception of a wholly other.[1]

In their very action, nature is saying that they must be open to the possibility of conceiving a new person. Sperm and ovum tend naturally to gravitate toward each other. Unless the partners deliberately act against their own fertility, conception could occur. Their intimate interaction in coital union is essentially an action in which nature is saying *both* "love each other" *and* "be open to new life."

In general, like all interpersonal actions, coital union is designed naturally to be an act of love. It is a very dramatic way of expressing man-woman love. But the main source of drama in this particular manner of love-expression is not the genital and emotional excitement, which last for brief periods of time; nor is it the psychic bonding that is increased quite naturally and may last as long as they live. The main source of drama--largely unconscious, but very real--is the imminent possibility of initiating the life of another person, whose individual existence will last forever and whose progeny may extend throughout the world, influencing generations until the end of time. Therefore, the specific--as distinct from the general--purpose of the coital union is the affirmation of the good of a new human life that might be conceived as its most dramatic and telling effect.

People who are *de facto* parents--whether they are married or not--*as parents* exist for the sake of the other(s). Their lives are forever changed by the new, real relationship (with a child or children) that they have--or that they intend (implicitly at least) by their willing the coital interaction--independent of their desires and subjective intentions.

Parenthood is obviously a sociosexual vocation. The parent is one who is called to share the gift of self, with self, with self and with others, but emphatically with many others (not just with one other). By saying *many others* here I mean that this person is one who is structured in society for the stable and dynamic cele-

300

bration of the being of *spouse plus at least one* other.
I also mean to imply that while a person can morally
have only one spouse he or she can have more than one
child.   Parenthood emphasizes something that is open
again to the pluralness of being--the "branch vocation"
is like the "root vocation."   But unlike the celibate,
the parent's "many" are a very special many that flow
from him or her in union with the special sexual other
who ought to be one's spouse.

The celibate's attention to many is not directed to
many as a procreative flow from himself or herself.   The
celibate's many is a non-family many, a kind of "absolute
many."   The celibate draws his social identity as a celibate from being related to the many of the common world,
something like the roots of a tree draw their sustenance
from being related to the openness of the common ground.

The parent, on the other hand, expresses a manyness
that comes from the common flow of interpersonal energy
generated by self together with a genital other (normally
one's spouse).   The parent's many is a special family-
many.   The parent draws social identity as a parent from
being related to the particular many of his or her actual
or potential children, something like the branches of
a tree draw their sustenance from the energy flow through
the stem or trunk into the leaves and fruit, which the
branches specifically produce.

Woman As a Parent; Man As a Parent

Being a parent would seem to entail fundamentally
opposite relationships for a man and a woman in the
depths of their sociosexual orientations.

A mother, on the one hand, is a person who is most
emphatically female in her relationship with others--
especially with her children.   She bears them in her womb.
She gives birth and, perhaps, breastfeeds them.   The bonding of a mother with her child is emphatically and dramatically (especially in the very early years) a unitary
flow of nurture and attention.   She is continually receiving them in an unqualified way.   She lives a radical
kind of receiving life with her offspring.

A father, on the other hand, is a person who is most
emphatically male in his relationship with others--
especially with his children.   He is obviously, and rather
dramatically, *other than* his prebirth child.   For the
most part, his protection and care for the prenatal and
neonatal child occurs in and through the mother.   The

father tends to relate to the infant in an emphatically and dramatically giving sort of way, by providing, in a rather measured way, the physical, economic, and emotional support that both the mother and child need. He also is called to receive them as they are. But his emphasis is on providing and protecting mother and child during this time of special vulnerability.

In the early years the father has a considerable influence on the self-identity of his children, especially the boys. His stability and other-directed inclination help children go out to the world more effectively. He has a better opportunity to reveal the realness of the world outside the home than the mother, who carries the child within her and at her breast for the first year or more of the child's life. Although any mature mother can also point to the world for the child, and do so better than many men in certain respects, the man has a natural inclination to emphasize this kind of education as best he can.

A woman is much more inclined--not just by her culture, but by her nurturing nature--toward keeping the child centered in the home. *Both* mother *and* father need to help the child develop the natural forces within--some centrifugal and some centripetal--by which he or she becomes a person who is well-integrated in the sociophysical world. But *each* has an emphasis by nature, even though any given individual man or woman may not be as effective in realizing his or her dominant sexual emphasis as well as a person of the other sex.

Now when one turns to regard the mother and father as they relate to themselves *within themselves*--rather than as they relate to others, especially their children-- one may detect a reciprocal and balancing emphasis.

The mother is, in relation to her self, male in emphasis. She is, *as mother*, continuously leaving herself for the sake of her children. In order to receive them fluently, she is naturally giving her self away within herself.

In relation to the children, she emphasizes receiving. But in relation to herself, she is an emphasis on giving to others. Her inner self has a natural outgoing quality in so far as she is specifically a mother--not in so far as she is a woman. A mother naturally is subjected to multitudinous centrifugal forces as she cares for her children. The mother *as a mother, in relation to herself*, is called to emphasize a receiving kind of

302

giving. As a mother, she is male within, as well as female in relation to others.

The father, however, is, in relation to himself, female in emphasis. He is a father by emphatically *being* himself--that stable, self-unified, self-contained human being with whom the child needs to identify at the same time as he or she is being received by the nurture of the mother. In order to give himself firmly and protectively to his children the man needs to be continuously receiving his own inner strength. The man *as a father* is stable and self-contained within. The father *as a father*, *in relation to himself*, is called to emphasize a giving kind of *receiving*. As a father he is female within, as well as male in relation to others.[2]

The complexity of sociosexual ecology is quite evident in the vocation of parenthood. Parenthood itself is highly complex within its own nature. But the most obvious manner in which parenthood reveals the ecology of sexual identity is as the androgynous counterpart to the male-female polarity of celibacy and spousehood. In both directions--in relation to self and in relation to others--celibacy and spousehood stand as reciprocally opposite sexual emphases. I have noted this polar emphasis in the two previous chapters. But parenthood rounds out the polarity by being--as I have just indicated--both male and female in *each* direction, depending on the sex of the parent. Vocational ecology is resplendently evident in parenthood.

The Parentive Union

The importance of distinguishing the marital act from the parentive (procreative) act was discussed in the previous chapter. Once this distinction is understood, it becomes easier to see that there is a special, parentive union radically different from the marital union. What psychologists sometimes call parent-child bonding is a development of this specifically parentive union, which can only be discerned philosophically.

The individual who is a parent has a special union with his or her child. It is a direct union that comes with the act of conception in which a parent (along with the other parent) is the direct cause of the child's being in the world. Parents do not create their children; they procreate them. They *cause* them. They cause them to be here--in this world at this time.

Causing a child to come to be in this world is not the same kind of act as causing a tree to be planted in the backyard. Every child is a person of inexhaustible value. Moreover, the child usually grows to adulthood and procreates others who do the same. The child that a person causes to be in this world may very well influence the destiny of countless individuals and families over many generations. The parentive union not only branches into the child and into subsequent generations, but into the human community as a whole. The coital act is not simply a personal act. In itself it is a social act.

In addition to its community-building significance, the parentive union stems from and reinforces the marital union. Every act of marital coition is meant to be a renewal of the marital covenant. It is a unitive act as well as a procreative act. The parentive union is intimately related to the marital union, but it is not the same. We need to take a closer look.

In a loving marriage, genital communion is a renewal primarily of the parentive covenant, and secondarily of the marital covenant. This parentive act of coital union is a particular kind of renewal that constitutes, and participates in, a whole new vocation--beyond marriage, yet within it. The parentive covenant is the vocation of living together no longer simply as this man and this woman, but as this man and this woman for another, for a child or children.

Whether the first act of coitional union of the married couple comes at sixteen or sixty it naturally marks them as parentive together. They are parents together virtually, even if not functionally. The whole emphasis of their lives necessarily shifts in the moral sense. Once coital intercourse occurs, they continue to live *basically* with and for themselves as this man and this woman, but they live *specifically* with and for certain others--their potential children. Their union as parentive spouses is consummated. (Consummated does not mean that it is finished, but that it has definitely begun.)

The love-giving character of their genital union is fundamentally interpersonal and intersexual. In virtue of their marriage, it is basically interspousal. But it is *specifically* and emphatically interparental, not interspousal.[3] The marriage and parenthood relationships are a matter of vocational difference based on moral and spiritual emphasis. One cannot *emphasize* both.

Because parenthood is forever, it necessarily places the relationship of the partners into a new emphasis--beyond themselves, within themselves.

If one is a parent he or she can never again *be* emphatically a spouse--although one can live an emphatically spousal *style of life*, as when children are raised and the parents return to the style of life before they were functionally parents. Even should one's child die, one will always be specifically and emphatically a parent together with the sexual other, rather than specifically and emphatically a spouse. (The significance of the terms *specifically* and *emphatically* entails complementarity. *Specifically* signifies that something is of a certain special character or kind that is not reducible to anything else--a rose, for instance, is specifically one kind of flower and cannot be a geranium. *Emphatically* signifies that something is continuous with something else and shares a common base but is decisively structured or empowered to reveal a particular feature of that which is commonly shared--for instance, the left lobe of the human brain is emphatically, but not exclusively, oriented toward analytic functions and the right lobe is emphatically, but not exclusively, oriented toward global and poetic functions.)

Even where two people who have children are very wholesomely and beautifully committed as spouses, they are still emphatically and specifically not spouses but parents. They can certainly be said to *function* practically as spouses and to be spouses basically, but they can be said to be specifically and emphatically *only* parents. These people are living sociosexually as celibates and as spouses, but emphatically (dramatically) and specifically as parents.

The parentive act starts with coitus and continues through pregnancy, childhood, adulthood, and eternity. Parenthood is a radically distinctive vocation. While marriage is a commitment until death, parenthood is a commitment forever.

Parentive union or coital union (like marital union and celibate union) has both a specific and a general purpose. The *specific* purpose of parentive union is procreating offspring. The *general* purpose is to be unitive: to express love, affection, and care between two people of different sex who are committed for life to a home which they *are* to each other as man and woman and to their offspring as members of their love. (As noted in the previous chapter, the general purposes of

305

marriage and parenthood are very similar.) These purposes determine the nature of the act itself and serve
as the necessary context for a morally good act of coital
intercourse.

Contraception

Contraceptive intercourse is an ancient practice.
People have always had inclinations to limit family size
and to keep the number and care of children from interfering with genital pleasure.[4] Since the 1960s the oral
contraceptive known as "the pill" has been heralded as
a breakthrough in sexual freedom. Women have been told
that they were now equal with men in controlling their
own fertility. Both men and women have been led to believe that through use of "the pill" they can be liberated
for all the spontaneous sex they desire.

Disillusionment has not been long in coming. The
severely adverse side effects of "the pill" on many women
are becoming widely known. This contraceptive treats
a woman as though she were suffering from a serious af-
fliction. It is difficult to believe that women are
thereby achieving sexual equality with men. People somehow realize that women cannot be "saved" by a pill.

There are many adverse side effects of "the pill"
other than physical. One of them is that a woman no
longer has the same freedom to say no to genital expression. If she claims to love the man sexually, then he
is inclined to believe her refusal of "protected" intercourse represents a slackening in that love. Women in
marriage and in non-marriage relationships experience
considerable social pressure for impulsive intercourse.[5]

Many men are also feeling the unliberating effects
of "contraceptive liberations." They are being called
upon to perform genitally at more frequent intervals.
Women who think that they should use their contraceptive
armament to greatest advantage tend to be overly demanding
and even threatening to men. Male impotence can readily
result as a psychic effect of imperious female desires.

Why was "the pill" once so widely characterized as
a revolutionary turn in man-woman relations, promising
sexual freedom to rich and poor alike? And why has it
not even begun to fulfill this promise? "The pill" and
all other forms of contraception have been employed as
sex liberators because sexuality is still regarded as
centered in the pelvic regions of human beings. Contraceptives have not liberated and cannot begin to liberate

en and women because they simply perpetuate the conscious
r unconscious myth that sex is genito-centric. The
Ptolemaic" view of human sexuality is nowhere more ob-
iously inadequate than in the field of birth control.

The contemporary movement into contraceptive birth
ontrol is especially tragic because it has taken so
any good-willed, intelligent people into a dead end in
uman sexual development. They have operated from a
Ptolemaic" point of view on sex. The promise of free
ntercourse, unburdened by prudery and by the fear of
regnancy, was a consummation of many people's fondest
opes. They did not see that the longed-for sexual free-
om was merely a means-to-an-end (second-level) freedom--
 sterile condition depriving the self of deep partici-
ation in the fundamental Goods most influential in sexual
rowth and health. The eventual consequences of such an
xclusively utilitarian approach to sexual liberation
re now startling to many who, with every good intention,
nce entered into the practice of contraception.

The move into abortion as a "back-up" means of birth
ontrol is dramatic evidence of the failure of contracep-
ives and of the contraceptive approach to birth regula-
ion.[6] Women cannot honestly be said to be controlling
heir bodies by killing their babies.

Another serious consideration in regard to what are
ow called contraceptives is that these instruments of
arfare against one's own fertility may be actually work-
ng by killing human life itself.[7] The IUD (intrauterine
evice) is certainly a case in point. As is the case
n the use of the various kinds of pills, the *exact* way
n which an IUD works is unknown. But it is unreasonable
o suppose that it always works by suppressing ovulation.
t is quite reasonable to assume the contrary, that it
ever or rarely works in that fashion and that its main
ffect is to make implantation of the new tiny human being
mpossible. The IUD must be regarded morally as an
bortifacient device, one which does not necessarily
ill fertility at all, but which kills human life itself.[8]

The oral contraceptives marketed in our society to-
ay must be suspected as being abortifacients, too.[9]
he trend toward the manufacture of pills with less and
ess ostensible side effects for the woman means that
he ovulation-suppressing effect of these pills should
e called into question. If a pill does not always sup-
ress ovulation, then there is a chance that it works by
bortion. One can deduce the abortifacient possibility
f the pill by realizing that there are three main ways

in which it can be regarded as producing its effect: suppressing ovulation, so that fertilization does not occur; producing a deleterious effect on the lining of the uterus, so that a developing baby does not implant; and causing mucus blockage of sperm at the neck of the uterus, so that sperm cannot reach beyond that point. There are a few other, secondary suppressant effects, such as affecting the motility of the ovum.

Pregnancies, however, can occur even when the oral contraceptive method has been followed accurately. Therefore, one can conclude that none of these intended biochemical mechanisms always functions. At times, the pill may cause neither blockage of sperm nor suppression of ovulation. In these few (or many.) cases the conception of a human life could occur and then, because of the hostile condition of the uterine lining caused by the oral contraceptive, this new life would be sloughed off at the point of implantation in the womb. The effect is like that of locking someone fully alive and well in a room with no means for attaining oxygen and nourishment. Whatever the subjective state of mind of the moral agent in such a case, the objective action is an act of killing The anti-life consequences of using common contraceptives is a serious matter.

Some advocates of abortifacient "contraceptives" are inclined to attempt justification of their use by saying that, after all, nature sloughs off a significant percentage of early embryos. They seem to overlook the *moral* significance of human care for fellow human beings, especially the most vulnerable. We persons are capable of love and even heroic care. We are not simply parts of the impersonal forces of the cosmos. Nature eventuall "kills us all."

But the problem with contraceptive intercourse, ever for married people, does not simply reside in some of the consequences. Sound moral judgment comes not only from analyzing what an action *does* and what its practical consequences are, but from understanding what the action *means*. The good or bad value (the value or disvalue) of an act is centered in the act itself. This act, independent of its practical effects, *means* something to the person and for the person. The action *says something* about the person who is present in it. Moral acts are personal acts and thereby *say who* the person *is*, as well as *what* he or she is *doing*.

In her book, *The Meaning of Contraception*, Mary Rosera Joyce gives considerable attention to what the

ction of contraceptive intercourse means as an act of
free communication between the couple. She says that
the issue is not just what contraception does, but especially what it means. A comparison is made between coital
intercourse and verbal dialogue. The similarity of coital
intercourse and verbal intercourse is sketched:

> Both forms of human intercourse are voluntary or
> personally chosen actions. Both result in concep-
> tion. Coital intercourse is fruitful in the con-
> ception of a child. Verbal intercourse is fruit-
> ful in the conception of ideas and the development
> of these ideas in the womb of the mind. The words
> expressed in verbal dialogue are physical sounds
> produced by physical organs, and are voluntarily
> spoken. Once the words are physically uttered,
> the physical aspect of the movement of sound takes
> its own course, just as the generative substance
> takes its own course once it is voluntarily ex-
> pressed in coital union.[10]

The author further elaborates the comparison by noting:

> In both forms of communication, not all acts of
> intercourse result in conception. One person may
> try to express an idea to another repeatedly before
> the other understands. The generative power of
> the mind is not always ready for activation. Simi-
> larly, not every act of coital expression is ac-
> tually generative.[11]

One could add here that the generative effect in
verbal dialogue would be the receiver's conception of a
new idea as the result of being stimulated by the giver's
words. Most verbal intercourse is not so stimulating
that it is specifically generative of new ideas. People
are usually content with the give and take of the verbal
exchange as a way of being friendly. Banter about the
weather is typical. Much verbal intercourse is intended
to communicate one's own feelings and thoughts to another
without necessarily inducing a new idea in that other.
Despite obvious differences that exist between verbal
intercourse and coital intercourse, there are many such
likenesses, all of which together can be instructive in
seeing what an act of contraceptive intercourse really
means.

Physically dramatized, the act of contraceptive
intercourse is like someone using ear plugs so that the
sound of his partner's voice does not reach his or her
hearing and result in the conception of a new idea. Or

it might be likened to taking a drug that affects the auditory nerves so that they cannot function properly for a time.

In any event, the essence of contraceptive intercourse is its attempt to separate internally the coital act from its generative power. Without the use of a contraceptive, the coital act would be functionally united with its generative power. The contraceptive morally separates one of the natural human powers from a natural human act. A human (personal) action is being intentionally separated from one of its fully human powers.

Contraception is very similar to lying. Lying is an internal separation of a communicative act from its power to express and to generate judgments truthfully. Mary Rosera Joyce describes it this way:

> As a communicative act, speaking is a sharing with another person who has a right to know what the speaker judges to be true, false or doubtful. When separation is offered under the guise of union, or falsity under the guise of truth, the lie comes into existence. Where there is no communal relationship as in a case where the other person has no right to such a relationship, and where force is being used, the articulations of statements and other signs to express as true what is judged to be false does not fulfill the definition of a lie. Such speech is as different from interpersonal or communal speech as copulation under the force of a rapist who has no right to union is different from the coital act.
>
> . . . In verbal communication, then, lying is an act which prevents the conception of truth right within the very act of presenting something as true. In coital communication, contraception is an act which prevents the conception of life right within the very act of presenting that which conceives life. These definitions and descriptions of lying and contraception reveal their basic similarity.[12]

The author sees a particular application to the contraceptive pill. In so far as this pill chemically manipulates the germ-producing processes in order to produce its anovulant effect and even in so far as it chemically produces a defect in the uterine lining or in the consistency of the cervical mucus, it acts very much like the internal form of lying known as rationali-

310

zation. Rationalization prevents the conception of truth in one's own mind by logical manipulation.

Moreover, the use of a diaphragm is comparable to closing one's mind while pretending to listen. The diaphragm allows a woman to pretend she is receiving the conceptive substance of her husband while she remains internally very inhospitable to it.

Perhaps the essence of what contraception really means can be shown by exposing the action as strictly contradictory and self-deceptive. The partners are engaged in an act that contradicts itself, and they thereby contradict themselves and each other at the same time. With their bodily actions they are saying to themselves and to the world, "We will the *possibility* of a conception." But with the contraceptive usage--whether it be physical or chemical--they are saying, "We do not will the *possibility* of a conception."

A contradiction occurs when something is said to be and not to be at the same time and under the same respect. It is not a contradiction if the yes and no come at different times or under different respects. In the case of contraceptive intercourse one and the same thing is being affirmed and denied at the same time. It must be said that, in the very instant of the interaction of intercourse, the contracepting partners are *willing* (*not* "intending," *not* wanting, but willing) that a child be conceived as a result of *this* action, and they are *not willing* that a child be conceived as a result of this same action. The action implicitly, but actually, contradicts itself.[13]

If coital intercourse in human beings were a basically involuntary act, such as the reproductive process in animals, then the action would not be regarded as contradictory. A defect--too many children, like too many puppies--in the operation of the genital system could be regarded as remedied by the contraceptive positioning. But a veterinary solution to a human problem is not morally responsible.

The coital act is designed in human beings to be a special act of man-woman love. It is, therefore, a free act. Love cannot be communicated by impulsive, compulsive, or any kind of unfree action. Such action is bereft of the meaning that makes it a specifically personal act.

311

People who do not realize the spiritual-centeredness of human sexuality usually regard abstinence from coital activity as an intolerable deprivation of what they regard as the only way to show man-woman love for each other. Therefore, they are inclined to fall into the practice of producing physical defects in themselves in order to prevent conception. Contraceptives do not rectify an already present defect in the person, such as failure to ovulate, irregular cycles, low sperm count, and the rest.[14] They *produce* a defect in already-healthy organs. Contraception is like trying to cure a headache by cutting off the blood supply to one's hand.

Furthermore, contraceptive intercourse is a distinctive form of anti-life behavior. With *every* act in which anyone would use a contraceptive it is assumed that a baby might otherwise result, and this possibility is firmly *rejected*. The significance of this rejection can be clearly seen when one realizes that human life is not simply a collection of individuals but is also a physical continuum--life *really* is handed on. Therefore, one must admit that contraceptive intercourse attacks and cuts off life at its point of transmission, even though it does not destroy the life of an individual. Actually, it simultaneously projects and rejects a definite, possible person.[15]

The contraceptive binds from which people often find themselves suffering represent failures to do the ecologically sound thing: keep all sexual systems open to each other, within and outside the individual. Closing off one system against the others can only lead to psychic and moral difficulties.

The great closure that produces most couples' major difficulties is their unawareness of the sexuality of the soul and of the psychic and spiritual depths of every person. Natural family planning works with the knowledge of these deeper resources of sexual energy. The knowledge may be largely implicit. But effective users of natural family planning methods are people who know they can express their man-woman love in a variety of satisfying ways other than coital intercourse.

Natural Family Planning

When the question of natural family planning arises, an assumption is often made that NFP is also a form of contraception. Most couples who practice NFP are using this approach to avoid conception. So, many people think that NFP is really just a more subtle and particularly devious means of birth control. They are inclined to distinguish NFP as *natural* contraception and the use of chemical and physical instruments as *artificial* contraception.16

Important differences, however, between NFP and the use of contraceptive means of birth control (more accurately, conception control) can be determined.

First of all, contraceptive intercourse is not morally wrong because it is artificial, but because it is the use of artifacts in an anti-natural way. There is nothing wrong with the use of a drug or a physical instrument that helps the person act more in accord with his or her nature. If, for instance, a person should take a drug that would lessen--not eliminate--the strength of his or her genital drive, the action could be done with moral justification. The artifact would be aiding the person in coming to the point where his or her will could effectively handle the erotic situations in which he or she normally and reasonably is found. Contraceptive drugs and devices, however, are employed in order to put some crucial part of one's totally natural fertility temporarily out of commission. They are used as a means to temporary sterilization, in which fertility is violated and nullified. The fact that these chemical and physical methods are artificial has nothing essentially to do with the morality or immorality of the action.

A second very important distinction between contraceptive intercourse and NFP is that in contracepting a person is *preventing* conception, but in the intercourse that is authentically NFP the person is *avoiding* conception, if a child is not desired at the time.17 NFP respects the natural patterns of male and female fertilities and works with them. But contraception takes decisive measures to block the natural patterns of fertility in order to ensure the non-occurrence of conception. NFP is *always* open to conception as the natural result of an act of intercourse. Contraception is *never* open to conception.

An important point, however, can be made about the actual attitudes of those who use NFP. People can merely use NFP as a method to eliminate pregnancy. This attitude is most common when the method is used outside of marriage. But even within a relatively stable marriage, people can engage in NFP methods with a contraceptive mentality. This mentality is formed by the intention to avoid conception at all costs, so that if the couple felt NFP would not work for them they would use some anti-NFP method. In such a case, they are only *appearing* to be engaged in NFP. They are already, by intent, practitioners of contraception. In its essence, contraception is a moral act. In its functioning, of course, it can be *emphatically* physical or chemical or psychic or spiritual.

NFP is not simply a method. It is a way of living with one's fertility somewhat like living with a faithful friend. A friend is one whom a person can trust to be himself or herself and to tell the person where he or she "is at." A friend is not someone like a pet dog whom one may periodically leash. A friend is autonomous and someone from whom one can always learn, no matter how much, at times, disagreements arise.

Authentic NFP cannot be practiced successfully and satisfactorily by people who are unwilling to develop their philosophy of life and of sexuality. It requires sincere attempts at basically good communication between the couple, and it implies growth toward a vital communion of the one with the other. Respect and even reverence for the person of the other--including his or her pattern of fertility in its regular or irregular movements--is the mark of success in the practice of NFP. Contraceptive intercourse strongly tends to let people escape from the challenge of growing genitally mature, as well as sexually and personally mature, because it is itself an escape from the meaning of being a freely-living bearer of the power to give life.

Perhaps the difference in attitude and meaning involved in genital intercourse through contraceptive usage on the one hand, and genital intercourse that is authentically NFP, on the other, is sufficiently illustrated by the following example. (In her book, *The Meaning of Contraception*, Mary Rosera Joyce suggests this difference in a similar way.)[18]

Suppose you owe someone a considerable sum of money which you are not able to pay at this time. You see this person at a distance coming down the street. Since you do not want the embarrassment and inconvenience of having to explain in detail why you cannot pay now, you turn and walk the other way, going a few blocks out of your way to reach your destination. Your creditor might, after all, take you to task and, on the occasion of seeing you, might decide to take you to court the next day.

Persons who are authentically using NFP are doing that kind of thing. They are *avoiding* at a particular time a conception which might be quite inconvenient or even a great burden.

The contraceptive way of reacting to the situation is something very much like the person who would continue toward the creditor and knock him out in order that the unwanted subject not be raised on that occasion. The person who contracepts is treating his or her fertility in a quite inhospitable way. He or she is violently avoiding conception.

The NFP practitioner is non-violently avoiding conception. If, in the terms of the example, the creditor were to catch a glimpse of you walking away or going another way and were to take determined steps to confront you anyway, you would presumably not render him or her unconscious in that case. In other words, if you had the attitude of NFP, you would accept willingly the conception of the child and all of its consequences, even though one could not expect you to leap for joy immediately upon hearing the news.

Since persons are fully present in their free and deliberate acts, the choice of a contraceptive act of intercourse is an anti-personal choice. In the example, you could not simply say that you were knocking out the person's *power* to speak to you. You would have to say that you were knocking *him* out in order to prevent him from speaking to you. Somewhat similarly, when action is taken against one's own or another's power to give life, the action not only renders the *physical* system dysfunctional but also renders the moral self dysfunctional. In traditional religious terminology, one might be said to be killing the life of the soul.

However one wishes to express it, the action of deliberately disrupting one's own power to give life is a pointed attack on one's whole self. When someone else attacks my fertility he attacks me. One can only wonder how it could be essentially different if *I* attack my fertility. Life and the power to give life are fundamental human Goods of the person. They cannot be violated by anyone, including the person himself or herself, without considerable damage to the person, as well as to the power.

NFP, however, preserves and builds up the fundamental Goods of Life (and its powers), Play, Aesthetic Experience, Integrity, Authenticity and Social Harmony.

315

Each one of these basic Values is increased in an authentic act of coital union. More specifically, when the coital act is honestly and sincerely open to the gift of a new life then coital play can be freer and more vigorous; the delight and intense pleasure of this emphatically bodily activity can be more deeply received; one's power to give life is more thoroughly integrated with one's power to give love and with other features of the whole person; one more fluently expresses the absoluteness and interiority of the gift of self through the genital sharing in this act of behaviorally unrestricted communion; and the abiding mutual friendship of the couple is broadened and deepened by the openness to the family or potential family that the activity primarily celebrates.

An act of contraceptive intercourse not only says *no* to the presence of oneself and one's partner through the violation of personal fertility, it also says *no* to the potential child or children that might well result. If a given act of intercourse would have resulted in a child, but did not do so because a contraceptive prevented the new life, then the action denies life to this child and to any potential grandchildren through this child. A given act of contraceptive intercourse is effectively a *no* to potential generations of persons. It is thereby society-negating--an intimately anti-social act.

NFP intercourse always says *yes* to the coital partners and *yes* to every life which this love-giving act might initiate. It is done in private. But it is a pro-society act--even when the couple are engaging in it without the particular desire to conceive and are simply renewing their covenant as parents and as spouses.

In summary, contraceptive intercourse can be distinguished from NFP by noting the basic movement of thought behind each of these morally different ways of parentive sexual expression.

Morally speaking, contraceptive intercourse begins from at least two assumptions: (1) coital intercourse is *necessary* (for love, personal fulfillment, sexual fulfillment, or all of these) and (2) a baby (too many babies) must be *prevented*. It concludes: (3) effective preventives must be used.

NFP is morally quite distinct in that it works on at least these two assumptions: (1) at times there are various goods to be enjoyed (participated in) by coital intercourse, but (2) at times (for a whole variety of reasons) one would be acting wrongly to engage in this kind of intercourse. It concludes: (3) so, when there is reason to engage in coital intercourse--and no reason not to--we will; but, when there is a strong *moral* reason (of any sort) not to engage, we will not. *One* such reason is that we *ought* not to have a child (or another child) at this time.

NFP is a necessary condition for ecologically sound parentive sexuality.

Adultery

The word *adultery* commonly applies to an act of coitional intercourse in which a married person engages with someone who is not his or her spouse. This common use of the term is inadequate, because it assumes that coital union is *the* marriage act. But, as I have suggested, coital union is the parentive act. So, what is called adultery is specifically a violation of the partners *as parents together*, rather than as spouses.

Of course, such an action does violate marriage. It certainly *adulterates* the strength of the marital bonding. This kind of intercourse, however, might be better called extra-parental than extra-marital. Like the concept of homosexuality, the popular concept of adultery stems from a lack of realizing new horizons in the sources of sexual energy.

As a violation of the parentive act, adultery specifically demeans the child and the family (or the potential family) of the spouses. In an act of adultery, the father or mother attempts (unconsciously, in most cases) to head a new family simultaneously with the original. But a head with two bodies is a gross social anomaly and is a violation of the original body. As long as the spouse of the person is living, the original family cannot be rightly incorporated with another one through another spouse. Only if one's spouse is deceased is there the possibility for a union of families under one couple as head. Of course, then coital intercourse would not be adultery, if the partners were married.

Coital union with a third party does *not* act directly against *the* marriage act, but against *the* parentive act. Nevertheless, it does violate the marriage of the adulterous person.[19] The innocent spouse is wounded indirectly as a spouse, directly as a parent. The adulterous spouse is renewing the marital covenant with the wrong

person. The covenant is in no way destroyed, but it is
adulterated or weakened considerably, whether the offended
spouse realizes it or not. The effects of adulterous
action within the adulterer are bound to inflict themselves really, if indirectly, upon the violated spouse.[20]

Engaging in coital interaction with a person to whom
one is not married can be regarded as the most obvious
form of positive adultery. But there are many other ways
in which a marital union can be weakened. Any friendship or liaison with a person of the other sex--or with
someone of the same sex--in which the marital bond is
truly neglected is an instance of positive adultery.
Flirtations that are really playful may not harm a marriage, but often such occurrences are self-indulgent
escapes from the appropriate spousal attitude and orientation. In general, any activity in which the person is
not in some way enriching or supporting his or her marriage is an adultery.

Men and women who are married really should develop
friends of both sexes. These friends need not always
be friends of the couple. A husband or wife who develops
a special friendship with someone of the other sex to
whom he or she is not married may be enriching and deepening his or her whole life. This special relationship
can be a positive benefit to the marriage, as well as
to all other interpersonal relationships. Care must be
taken in the development of such a relationship, since
it is especially easy to deceive oneself when erotic or
romantic aspects play a part.

The other side of the coin is what might be called
negative adultery. When a person is unduly fearful about
developing friendship with someone of the other sex and
leads a rather closed life, centering around his or her
spouse as the one-and-only sexual other in life, negative
adultery has occurred. It is adultery by default. A
failure to enrich oneself sexually through relationships
with members of the other sex beyond one's spouse necessarily weakens the marriage bond, even though it *feels*
quite the opposite. People who are very insecure about
their own sexual and marital identity often tend to weaken
it further through passivity and lack of suitable contact
with both sexes. Negative adultery may be the starting
point for positive adultery. It tends to choke off fresh
sexual air that every marriage needs to live authentically
in a world community.

The term *adultery*, then, should actually refer to
any violation of the marriage covenant. The marital bond

318

is a delicate· one that can be injured in many ways, not simply by coitional intercourse with an outside lover. It can be gravely harmed by rapelike intercourse with one's spouse. Therefore, the health of parentive sexuality depends on the self-control developed in a celibate condition, as well as on the fidelity to one person developed in the marital covenant, growing through the years. Parentive sexuality is a vocation within a vocation within a vocation (parenthood is within marriage, which is within celibacy), calling for more complexity, if not more depth, than either of the others.

NOTES

1. Being parentive is not the same thing as parenting. The suffix (-ive) indicates intentionality, not functionality. The term is used to express the *natural* directedness of every coitional (or even every deliberately venereal) action toward the conception of another human life. Again, *natural* is not the same as *functional*.

2. Father and mother are, within themselves, both male and female as parents. Again, the *emphasis* is the determinant.

3. *Interparental* means between themselves *as parents* (by the *nature*, if not function, of the act), not simply (nor specifically) as spouses. Thus, respecting the traditional view of marital consummation, one can say that the partners consummate their marriage as parentive spouses—not simply as celebrative spouses (celebrating the unique union and covenant they have undertaken).

4. On the history of contraceptive practice in the context of moral teaching, see John Noonan, *Contraception* (New York: The New American Library, 1965).

For an analysis of the arguments in favor of contraception, see Germain Grisez, *Contraception and the Natural Law* (Milwaukee: Bruce, 1964). Also, M. Joyce, *The Meaning of Contraception*. A third philosophical defense of the traditional position against contraception is that of Elizabeth Anscombe, professor of philosophy at Cambridge University, in her pamphlet, *Contraception and Chastity* (London: Catholic Truth Society, 1977).

5. The tyranny of the new pseudofreedom afforded women by means of contraception has not been seen by most sexologists. Their obtuseness may be explained partly by their failure to recognize that freedom of choice over alternatives (second-level freedom) is not really freedom at all unless it includes the primacy of freedom within primary Values. For instance, in an interview for *Playboy* Virginia Masters says that through the use of contraceptives women have a new freedom of selectivity. "They now have more freedom to say no than they ever had before." She suggests that today the young woman is free to make her choice, pick her time, her place, her circumstance, without the old fears. She apparently does not

perceive--or did not do so at the time--not only the new fears
and anxieties which revolve around the medical and psychological
pollution in the use of the pill, IUD, and sterilization techniques,
but also the moral pollution involved in treating sex activity mainly
as a goal to be chosen rather than as a good to be received. Her
unawareness of authentic human freedom is encapsulated in a remark
about the efficacy of a freedom of alternatives: "With all the
druthers now available to her, we have a hunch that the intelligent
girl tends to be more sophisticated in her selection--simply because
it is her selection." Quoted in Nat Lehrman, *Masters and Johnson
Explained* (New York: Playboy Press, 1976), p. 168.

6. Actually, leading proponents of contraceptives knew the "necessity" of abortion before it dawned on the people at large. Many
of them have been asserting as much for several years. For instance,
Christopher Tietze said in 1974: "Even if the woman uses adequate
contraception, there is likely to be a significant number of contraceptive failures within a year or two of the first abortion."
Family Planning Perspectives, 6 (1974):148.

7. Unfortunately, today there is a movement among certain medical
authors to "redefine" conception as implantation rather than fertili-
zation--an obvious "scientific" ploy to keep the IUD and the pills
that may not always prevent fertilization from being classifed as
abortifacients.

Many moralists are only too willing to rationalize the use of
pills and IUDs as morally permissible by means of this unwarranted
shift in definition. Even some Catholic moralists are outspoken
in their claims that individual human life could not occur in the
first two weeks after fertilization. An example of this claim--
which is superficially and speciously defended--is in *Sexual Morality: A Catholic Perspective* (New York: Paulist Press, 1977), pp.
136-37. The author, Philip S. Keane, works from an ethics of the
proportionate good. According to this view, there is no action
of a human being that is evil in itself, although all human actions
contain some ontic evil--lack of fulfilling their potential. An
action is, therefore, regarded as good and morally viable if there
is a proportionate reason for doing it. Keane's position and that
of Catholic moralists such as Fuchs, McCormick, Dedek and others is
really consequentialism--the consequences determine the goodness
or badness of the action. But consequentialism is essentially utilitarianism, in which the good to be done in various alternative concrete actions is weighed (put on a "scale"). This is a sheer means-
to-an-end (second-level freedom) approach that dehumanizes the
ethical enterprise by oversimplifying it in the midst of its claim
to be taking concrete circumstances seriously.

8. See the well-documented study by Thomas D. Hilgers, M.D.,
"An Evaluation of Intrauterine Devices," *International Review of
NFP*, 2 (spring 1978):68-85. Or see "The Intrauterine Device: Con-
traceptive or Abortifacient?" *Marriage and Family Newsletter*, 5
(Jan.-March 1974):3-24.

9. For documentation, see the newsletter, *Love/Life/Death/Issues*,
Special Issue, August 1977. (Available from the Human Life Center,

Collegeville, Minnesota 56321.)

10. M. Joyce, *The Meaning of Contraception*, p. 25.

11. Ibid., pp. 25-26.

12. Ibid., p. 27. Permission of the publisher, Liturgical Press, Collegeville, Minn., is gratefully acknowledged.

13. How contraception violates marriage at both natural and supernatural levels is incisively treated by Paul M. Quay in *Contraception and Married Love* (Washington: Family Life Bureau, 1962).

14. Many doctors have been known to prescribe "the pill" for the purpose of "regulating the woman's cycle." Presumably, even these physicians did not know that the pill does not produce or induce a menstrual period, but a pseudo-menstrual period--one that produces mock symptoms of menstruation. If the pill actually did "regulate the cycle" then there would not necessarily be any moral objection to its temporary use, if the woman really needed it for that purpose (to "regularize" ovulation) and was not rationalizing its use to cover for anti-conceptive purposes. The moral objection to contraceptives has nothing to do with their being artifacts, since artifacts may well be used to assist nature. It is the anti-natural use of artifacts that is objectionable.

15. Cf. Germain Grisez, *Contraception and the Natural Law*, pp. 76-106.

16. Even some teachers of NFP, who actually do not mean what the expression implies, habitually use the term *artificial contraception*.

17. Many moralists seem to be unable to distinguish between avoiding and preventing conception. For example, in making a critique of the Papal Encyclical *Humanae Vitae*, philosopher Carl Cohen says: ". . . [I]f all control of sexual intercourse with the deliberate intention of *avoiding* birth is dishonest and disorderly, it is so whatever the method employed to reach that end." "Sex, Birth Control, and Human Life," in *Philosophy and Sex* (Buffalo: Prometheus Books, 1975), p. 162 (emphasis added). He then claims that the "rhythm" method is susceptible to the same criticism that is leveled at contraceptive methods. But this claim fails to take into account that conception regulation through fertility awareness (without any use of contraceptives)--while it *can* be *used* with a contraceptive mentality, and is, in such cases formally a contraceptive method--can be undertaken in order to *avoid* conception without attempting to *prevent* it. That undertaking is what Paul VI regards as a morally sound approach to family planning, even though the argument and language of his Encyclical could be clarified and expressed more forcefully.

Philosophy and Sex is an anthology of recent articles in philosophical literature on the many different aspects of sex behavior and abortion. It contains a very helpful introductory chapter written by the eidtors. But the majority of the material is what I regard as anti-ecological thinking on human sexuality. The book is recommended to the reader as an example of "the other side" of sexual morality from that developed in the present volume and as a source of philosophically oriented literature (its bibliography).

18. Cf. p. 129. Concerning the practical difference between contraceptive intercourse and NFP, as well as the requirements for moving from the former to the latter, see the sensitive article by John Hamlon, "Through the Eye of the Needle," *International Review of Natural Family Planning*, 2 (Winter 1978):299-307.

19. See, e.g., Kippley, *Birth Control and the Marriage Covenant*, especially pp. 114-15.

20. Subconsciously, e.g., the adulterer cannot be as authentic in his or her enthusiasm for sex play and intercourse unless or until he or she rejects as wrong the adulterous action--in heart, if not in word, with respect to the offended spouse and others.

Part   V

INTEGRATED SEXUALITY:
HERE AND HEREAFTER

Chapter 18

THE LOVING FRIENDSHIP

As Barry Commoner has succintly described it, ecology is the science of planetary housekeeping. In this physical science one studies the interrelationships between living beings and the processes sustaining them within the physical and chemical environment.

In the philosophical science of human sexual ecology, one can study the dynamic interrelationships of male and female (within and between human persons) and the environmental conditions for good man-woman relations. If, at the present time, the term human sexual ecology means nothing else, it should suggest loving, man-woman friendships. Loving friendship is the only sound environment for all the obvious and subtle, simple and complex, incidental and profound, human relationships. Not all of one's friendships can be particularly loving. But everyone greatly needs one or more relationships of this kind.

Loving friendships, especially between men and women, form a rich base for marital and parental relations. As John McGoey says in his book, *Through Sex to Love*, young people need to engage in premarital love, not premarital sex.[1] One could also add that there is much need for extramarital love between people of different sexes who are strongly attracted to each other. So often, people either avoid each other for fear of being overly tempted or they rationalize themselves into an adulterous liaison. Loving friendship is a difficult art, requiring patience and perseverance. But it is an immensely beneficial

atmosphere embracing the entire planet of human relationships.

One of the main reasons for the grave threat to our
physical environment is the inability of man and woman
to relate well with each other. The rape of the land and
the rape of a woman are not unrelated.[2] Passivity and
indifference toward the mounting ecological crisis today
goes hand in hand with the traditional lack of self-
assertiveness in women who are being physically or culturally abused. If the men and women who face each other
in a physically intimate way every night would be challenged by this tremendous opportunity for growth in interpersonal relations, they could face more creatively the
dawn of a new day in caring for the motherly environment
of nature all around them. Loving friendships are the
basis of a healthy life for all creatures on the planet
earth.

Special Friendship

The loving friendship can be characterized as a
friendship in which there is mutual affirmation and a
kind of specialness or intimacy. In Chapter 7, I suggested that friendship has four basic qualities: equality, esteem, affection, and value sharing. By the expression *loving friendship* I wish to include all of these
qualities plus some kind of regard for each other as special. Such a relationship can exist between people of
the same sex as well as between man and woman.

Usually, and quite naturally, a loving friendship
includes freedom in touching. We do not seem to have
this freedom with everyone we might regard as a friend.
A person can think of many neighbors, for instance, whom
he or she regards as equals, esteems, feels affection
for, and with whom he or she shares many values of government, politics, religion, and so forth. Such people
are friends, not enemies. But they are not considered
as special friends. Obviously, the degrees of specialness
are practically unlimited; so, precise definition is
impossible. But in *our* society one practical criterion
might be how free one feels in touching--even momentar-
ily--these neighbors, other than to shake hands. How
free is one *when* touching them?

Touching is highly related to intimacy. One of the
practical, though not infallible, signs of intimacy is
the freedom to touch someone with one's eyes. Seeing
is a highly refined form of touching something or someone. When two people who genuinely participate in the

four qualities of friendship are likewise rather free to look each other in the eye without having to speak or gesture, then there is good reason to believe they are experiencing a degree of specialness or intimacy that might be called a loving friendship.

The kinds of touching that are morally sound in expressing one's loving friendship for another person differ greatly depending on the vocations of each and their basic life-commitments, as well as on sex, personality, and temperament. Genital touching, for instance, is morally or ecologically sound only for married persons who have a commitment to parenthood. Depending on how they are defined, petting may be wrong and necking quite acceptable for non-married people under certain circumstances. The important point about a loving friendship is that it is an interrelationship of people who mutually affirm each other in a holistic way, with their beings turned toward each other. Such relationships essentially include a well-developed emotional spontaneity, in which *each* person is being affirmed by the other in an emotionally secure environment. They express the degree of intimacy in their hearts by the way they touch each other with their eyes, their hands, their tone of voice, and their manner of listening to each other.

Sexual Affirmation

Unfortunately, many people seem to be psychically dysfunctional in respect to this kind of relationship. Not having been affirmed early in life by parents or guardians, they have never really *felt* loved as the unique, whole persons who they are. They may have been *told* countless times that they are loved. Parents and peers may have been good to them in the *things* they *did* and continue to *do*. But the words and deeds of love are not quite enough. The *feelings* of love must come along with the deeds and the words.

Words are important and deeds are necessary. Yet, the words and deeds of love are inadequate without the lover's feelings being expressed within them. Sexual ecology requires activation of emotional energies in the human ecosphere.

Anna Terruwe and Conrad Baars are psychiatrists who have developed what they call affirmation therapy. They write tellingly concerning the growing percentage of unaffirmed people in our society. People need affirmation from other people who themselves have been affirmed. One cannot genuinely affirm himself or herself.[3] Many people

try to be self-affirming, self-starting, or self-actualiz-
ing. But they cannot become authentically fulfilled
until they have learned, from experience with another
person, how good it is to *be* loved *and* to *feel* loved.
Without such experience their most determined efforts
at self-affirmation largely serve to cover up the emotional hurt and impoverishment from which they really
suffer.

In his book, *Born Only Once*, Conrad Baars points
to the fact that there are very many people in the world
who have achieved fame, fortune, and renown, and yet have
not had feelings of being worthwhile and significant.
He singles out Marilyn Monroe and Adolf Hitler as examples
of two different kinds of unaffirmed achievers. During
their lives no one was sufficiently interested in them
as unique persons. They had no one to whom they could
ever open up the depths of self. Without such a person
in one's life it is, in the view of Terruwe and Baars,
impossible to discover and experience one's own great
worth as *this unique person*.

In order to see the ecological significance of affirmation and its crucial part in loving friendships, one
needs to reflect deeply on the causes and conditions of
human happiness. No one can be happy if he or she is
not himself or herself. You first have to be *you*. Yet
you cannot be you until you "become you." Becoming the
great being that you already are can only be done by
first receiving the *gift* of yourself. But the inward
morning of receiving yourself deep within can dawn only
if someone moves the planet of your being toward the
master-light of your very own soul. In order to receive
this gift (yourself) there has to be another who *gives*,
without taking or demanding anything. This person gives
you what is not his or her own. The person gives you
what is yours, your own goodness in itself.

Conrad Baars says that another person can do this
kind of giving only when he is already happy with himself,
and thus open to the goodness of all else. The other person must be an affirmed person. Af*firm*ation--feeling
firm and strong, possessing oneself in joy, and feeling
worthwhile--starts with, and is dependent on, another
human being. The affirming person:

1) *is aware of, attentive, and present to* your unique
   goodness and worth, separate from and prior to
   any good and worthwhile thing you may do or can
   do, and

2) *is moved by, feels attracted to, finds delight in* your goodness and worth, but without desiring to possess you, or use you, or change you, and

3) permits his being moved by and attracted to you *to be revealed* simply and primarily by the psychomotor reactions--visible, sensible physical changes-- which are part of his "being moved."

. . . Anything more--helpful deeds, words of advice, gifts, acts of kindness or support, silence, patient waiting, and so on--is the concrete expression of affirmation, but not its essence. Affirmation is first of all affectivity, a matter of *feeling*. Only secondarily is it *effectivity*, a matter of *doing*.[4]

Mothers are very important people in their power to affirm even the smallest child. Young babies can literally *feel* the difference between being loved unselfishly, for their own sakes, and being loved possessively, for the sake of gratifying a mother's need.

What can be done, if one did not receive affirmation as a child? According to affirmation-theory, such a person can only desire it, be open to it, and wait for someone to come along who discerns his or her goodness and unique value and who graciously gives the person to himself or herself. This gift involves an opportunity to grow. It is an invitation to grow that creates the unconscious realization: "If I am considered lovable in my presently imperfect way, how much more lovable will I be when I outgrow my imperfections."[5]

Dr. Baars says,

It is in this process of affirmation, this process of *knowing and feeling, without doing*, that I give the other to himself. I do not give him his physical existence as a human being. I give him his psychic existence as this specific unique human being. As the popular song expresses it, "You're nobody until somebody loves you!"[6]

When a person is truly affirmed, he or she finds real delight in personal goodness. The person is revealed to himself or herself as good. The other has given the person *who he or she is*. This unique person is no longer alone.

329

I have been linked to another human being in this
process of affirmation not by communication of
what I have, but by the revelation, the communion
of what I am. In friendship the greatest gift
my friend can give me is himself. In affirmation
I receive an even greater gift: myself.[7]

This gift of myself that I receive from another
person is a kind of sexual consummation, and it is the
distinctive feature involved in a loving friendship when
it is mutual. Warmly expressed, unqualified affirmation
of two persons for each other is the essence of sexual
consummation. Unlike genital consummation, it can occur
between persons of the same sex as well as persons of
different sex. It is always one with one. It is never
a group phenomenon. Nevertheless, several people can
be together on occasion, between each of whom there is
this loving affirmation and friendship, and then the
joy becomes all the greater in this mutually intimate
sharing.

Throughout this book sexuality has been defined as
the personal power to share the gift of self with self
and with others. Now we are in a position to understand
the consummation of this power. Sexual consummation is
a relationship in which each person is exercising his
or her sexuality to such a degree and in such a way that
the sharing of self becomes *both* a sharing of oneself *and*
a sharing of the *other* self with the other person and
with oneself. While such sharings can and do occur between persons of the same sex, they are more dramatically
experienced with persons of the other sex, precisely because the self of the other that each affirming partner
gives to the other is *sexually other*. In the act of
affirming a woman, a man is giving to her a self (female)
that is sexually other than himself, not only a self that
is sexually common. The woman is doing something proportionately similar with the man.

This loving friendship-consummation has nothing
essentially to do with coitional consummation--although
coital union is a beautiful symbol of it. Man and woman
were made for loving friendships, not necessarily for
coitus. Loving friendships are not mutually exclusive
relations, such as married coital-genital union. These
friendships are warm, loving, open and vulnerable. They
are non-possessive. They do not establish a family circle, but they do constitute a point, between a man and
a woman, from which the circumference of such a circle
may healthfully develop.

330

These relationships are thoroughly and freely sexual.
They are among the most fulfilling relationships a man
or woman can experience in this world. All the power
and dignity of one's personal sexual self is enriched
and magnified by the sexually-other self that it tenderly
confers on the beloved. In such loving relations one
can find not only redemptive healing and personal growth,
but the celebration of all being and the contemplation
of God for which every heart was primarily created.

Unlike genital consummation, sexual consummation is
never a dramatic activity. There is no empirically identifiable moment when it occurs. It happens specifically
in the spiritual dimension of interrelationship, enlightening and warming all of the special friends' concrete
interactions. Sexual consummation is a once-beginning,
but never-ending *mutual* affirmation that can be richer
or poorer through the opportunities and limitations inherent in the life-commitments and everyday circumstances
of the two people involved.

This consummation--inclusive of other such consum-
mations--may be largely unconscious. Becoming conscious
of it, however, will greatly increase the joy and sense
of sexual fulfillment as long as the new awareness is
not *used* as a *means* to *achieve* deeper levels in the relationship or to *acquire* other such relationships. The
delicate life of sexual fulfillment is extremely susceptible to abuse. It needs supportive kinds of awareness.

The PAC of Sex

Though a man and woman may consummate their friendship in the communion of loving affirmation, they still
need to develop the art of communication with each other.
Communion is the ground and the atmosphere of healthy,
consequential communication. But communication is a task
all its own. Awareness of the psychosocial ego-states
can assist in this communication endeavor. Parent,
Adult, and Child are ever active in the healthy interpersonal relationship.

These basic parts of the human psyche are thoroughly
sexual. An awareness of psychic sexual needs in each
other can be developed by becoming familiar with the PAC
of sex. I have already indicated the general psychic
relationship of Animus and Anima. The PAC of sex might
be regarded as its basic anatomy. Each person has an
inner Father and Mother (P), an inner Boy and Girl (C),
and an inner Man and Woman (A).

The Parent of both men and women is the basic psychic inclination to protect and nurture. The person's inner Father is a protector-nurturer inclination that is emphatically protective. It is "programmed" to say things such as, "Be careful of the dark stairway so you do not trip and fall," or "Don't be so lazy and irresponsible, go out and get a job." The person's inner Mother is a protector-nurturer inclination that is emphatically nurturing. Often one is internally advised, or spontaneously advises others, by saying things such as, "You poor dear, you'd better stay home today with that miserable cold," or "Take another six-pack in case company comes tomorrow." Statements like these come out of the psychic instincts of both men and women.

Some Parent statements may be difficult to classify as paternal or maternal in emphasis. But there are plenty of statements that clearly lean more toward protectiveness than toward nurturance or vice versa. In any given transaction a man may be actively nurturing a woman or a woman actively protecting a man. For instance, a man might say to his lady-friend, "Come here, Honey, you can cry on my shoulder." Or a woman might say to her male companion, "Better take that higher paying job or our engagement is off." Each one is coming on Parent. But this man has an inward-drawing, ovumlike character to his suggestion. This woman has an outward-thrusting, spermlike character to her demand.[8]

The Child of both men and women is the basic psychic inclination to act immediately as one feels. The Child is curious about, and reacts to, inward and outward experiences just as they happen without the mediation of any social norms. The person's inner Boy is a curious-delighting attention to both outward stimuli and inner feelings, with an emphasis on a curiosity about outward stimuli and how they work. The inner Girl is a curious-delighting attention to both outward stimuli and inner feelings, with an emphasis on a delight over the way things feel. The Boy is an inclination to say things such as, "Wow, look at the size of that elephant," or "Isn't that a four-cycle, two-speed washing machine?" The Girl is an inclination to say things such as, "How bitter this salad dressing tastes," or "Isn't the sound of Mancini's orchestra divine?"

In any given transaction between a man and a woman, the man may speak more from his inner Girl than inner Boy, and vice versa. The man might say, for instance, "Say, these pancakes really are filling!" And she might reply, "I really get excited by the chance to use my new

electric range with the special timers in preparing them!"
Each one is coming on Child. But the man has an inner,
attentive delight over the way things feel, and the woman
reveals an outer, attentive intrigue about the way things
are working. The female emphasis of receiving in a giving
sort of way is celebrated in the man's emphasis on the
inner-flow of feeling. The male emphasis of giving in
a receiving sort of way is celebrated in the woman's emphasis on the workings of outer-occurring stimuli. Generally, however, a man will tend to come on more Boy-
Child; and a woman, more Girl-Child.

The Adult of both men and women is the basic psychic
inclination to integrate the data from the inner Parent
and Child and from the outer world, and to direct one's
action on a rational course. Essentially, the Adult
is the psychic source of integration and of determination,
based on the total input from within and outside the
person who acts.

The inner Woman, then, is the psychic source of
inclination to integrate all of the many forces and influences, from within and without, into a unitary whole.
It includes the male inclination to determine or decide
a course of action, but it emphasizes *integration* of
data. The inner Woman of the Adult psychic ego-state is
disposed to say things such as "Jim and I have many values
that we share deeply," or "Why is sexual ecology an important kind of study?" As a part of the *Adult*, the
inner Woman "speaks" factually, with an emphasis on integration.

The inner Man is the psychic source of inclination
to direct personal action in a rational way by choosing
the most fitting course of action. It includes the female inclination to integrate all the many forces within
and outside the person into a meaningful whole. But it
emphasizes the inclination to *determine* or *decide* a course
of action. The inner Man is disposed to say specifying
things such as, "The most important feature of Judy's
personality is her joy in being alive," or "I will no
longer be so shy when I am introduced to strangers."
Both the inner Man and the inner Woman are very active
in men and women. As in the other ego-states, the healthy
male personality will emphasize the male side of the
Adult and the healthy female personality will emphasize
the female side.

One should never confuse these dynamics of sexual
personality with any sociocultural role. There is no
male *thing to do* as opposed to a female *thing to do*. Men

can change babies' diapers just as well as women if they
decide to learn and apply themselves. Women can do garbage removal just as well as men if they decide to learn
and work at it. Allowing for some advantage generally
that women have over men in manual dexterity and that
men have over women in muscle strength, these jobs are
basically interchangeable. But a healthy man will still
do either job with a physical, psychic, and spiritual
orientation that is *correlative* to that of a healthy
woman. The way in which the work is performed will be
attitudinally distinctive, even though the difference
might not be empirically measured. This correlative
orientation is extremely important if a man and a woman
are going to develop a loving friendship and are going
to deepen the consummation of their intersexual relationship in the midst of sharing life's most mundane, as well
as noblest, endeavors.

One might ask whether there is also an inner Brother
and an inner Sister. Actually, this sexual differentiation would seem to be an underlying one at all three
levels. We are all brothers and sisters as sons and
daughters of God and of the progenitors of the human
race. Every father and mother and every husband and wife,
as well as son and daughter, are brother and sister first
of all, before they relate in these more specifically
sexual ways. The sexual Adult (the inner Man and Woman)
includes the sexual concept of brother-sister, but really
focuses upon the spousal relationship, which is the proto-
type of love.

How to Integrate Romantic-Erotic Feelings

In a friendship with a particularly attractive person of the other sex an individual's erotic and genital
feelings can readily become a problem. What can be done
about it?

In Chapter 8, I discussed the importance of centering
in the life of the young celibate. Centering (within
oneself) these feelings and drives is a necessary part
of personal integrity, and it is crucial to the development of loving friendships. But there is another centering that occurs in loving man-woman friendships--one
which complements the inward centering of the individual.

When faced with a highly desirable person to whom
one is coitally attracted there is a way of perceiving
that person so that one's feelings for him or her are
given their proportionate expression. In these stimulating situations involving persons who are not married to

each other, each one needs to receive the other as good in himself or herself, no matter how much or how little this good flows toward oneself. There is a simultaneous detachment from anything that the relationship might produce for oneself and a creative fidelity to the funda- mental Good of Social Harmony, no matter how it may be celebrated in this relationship. Genuine love includes the good of the beloved--and the good of the whole world in relation to the beloved--as well as the good of one- self. This perspective of seeing the beloved as a great good in himself or herself--independent of any personally gratifying experience which this relationship might bring--is absolutely necessary for a healthy, loving friendship.

If this beingful perspective is present, then there is the opportunity to sink the roots of one's strong feel- ings for the person in a warm, soft, rich soil of unlimit- ed depth. Every interaction can be a good in itself that does not necessarily have to lead to something more or something further. Every common project is immediately buoyed up by deep commitment to third-level purposes or values that are capable of nurturing and protecting the relationship, spontaneously and naturally. Two soli- tudes are, in Rilke's words, "protecting, touching, and greeting each other."

A painful period in a loving, man-woman friendship usually occurs through which the two people need to be purified of their impulsive desires to engage themselves genitally. But the beingful perspective, if it is genu- ine, will inevitably see them through. Tenderness and firmness with oneself and with the other are always ap- propriate, and especially in a time of crisis such as that of deep desire to consummate their sexual inter- action in a genital way.

Yielding to such desire, outside of a proper time in marriage, makes genuine *sexual* consummation much more difficult later and, in fact, sometimes practically im- possible to achieve. The coital union of people who are not married to each other--and, not infrequently, of some married couples--is never an occasion of sexual consum- mation. It is never a genuine instance of the one per- son giving the other to himself or herself. It may simply be a situation in which the two people have made an im- pulsive (or compulsive) attempt to share the gift of self with another. In such an action, self is used large- ly as a means to self-gratification, and is hardly a gift.

Two people may deliberately *choose* to share themselves in a coital way many hours or days before they actually do so. But that does not make the action non-compulsive and free. People engaged in morally wrong choices or morally bad states of life can exercise considerable "self-control." Playboys can do so if the stakes are high enough and if the anticipated "pay off" is intensely gratifying. But such "self-control" is an unintegrated kind. The self is really not *in* control but out of control and is merely being driven in the direction of the latest, most attractive course of action. Particularly in their erotic-genital drives, people are often like the driver of a moving automobile in which the ignition is on, the gas pedal is stuck in a depressed position, and the gear-shift is locked in high.

A person needs to learn how to unblock the programming that he or she has received from childhood regarding the "overpowering" character of the sex drive. As long as that false conception still dominates unconsciously, there is little hope for genuine self-control. Great feats of ego-strength in holding back the floodgates of passion are not necessary for one who is integrated in his or her power to share the *gift* of self. When self is perceived as a true gift to self and others, one's whole world of relationships changes--from opportunities to be used into invitations to share. The invitation and the sharing are marks of the freedom already attained.

Because no one is totally integrated as a person and as a sharing being, there may be times of strong attraction in which one's passions might seem to want to take over. These passions are like children within us. They are good and beautiful. But they still do not know how to control themselves. Yet they really do not want to become wild. They really want discipline and restraint.

Our passions, like children, want gentle but firm direction and guidance. Our intellect and will are the inner parents of our passions. These passions will be ordered and regulated in their expression by what we understand and *know* to be true through our intellect and by the strength of our self-empowerment toward what is good through our will.

All emotions, feelings, and passions are good. Not one of them is bad. They all need, within us, the affirmation that they are good. Occasionally, we should spend time with them directly by appreciating them in our minds and hearts. This conscious dwelling with our feelings

is a kind of interior, spiritual-affirmation activity
that lets them know our control of them is with love.
Just as good parents take their children aside and love
them, so the intellect and will ought to be turned to
one's passions so that they can be known directly and
immediately and willed to *be* and be *themselves*. Children
need much touch. Feelings and emotions do, too.

Through our intellect and will we can give our instincts, feelings, emotions, and passions not only a
share in our spiritual life, but we can *give them to*
themselves. This gift is the basic act of loving affirmation. When it is given to one's own inner psychic self
in which the dynamism resides for the most intense kinds
of anger or erotic love-making or fear or heroism, all
compulsiveness and impulsiveness are immensely softened
and begin to become naturally harmonized in the depths
of the unconscious. The attractiveness of a person of
the other sex is then able to be appreciated and enjoyed
without being exploited by *unruly* passions or emotions.

Nevertheless, this inner personal activity of
emotion-affirmation can only be as effective as the person himself or herself feels affirmed by another person--
preferably from his or her mother's breast. An unaffirmed
person can simply wait and be open to being affirmed by
another.[9] Because so many people are, as Baars and
Terruwe point out, unaffirmed, a loving friendship between
a man and a woman cannot occur until both persons are
affirmed persons. If one person is affirmed and the other
is not, such a relationship cannot develop unless the
unaffirmed person lets himself or herself be affirmed.
Under the often-considerable, erotic stimulation found
within the relationship, affirmation is not readily received by the unaffirmed, no matter how affirming the
other person is. But it would seem to be possible. In
the case of two unaffirmed persons, loving friendships
between them--whether the same or different sex--would
seem to be impossible.

In any event, the two friends need to be particularly cognizant that naturally their relationship is
destined to go through three overlapping stages: the
romantic, the pragmatic, and the celebrational. These
stages have been discussed (using similar terms) in Chapter 7. It should be noted that even in the romantic
(first) stage there are or should be traces or intima-
tions of the other two. And similarly for the other
stages. In the celebrational (third) stage, all that
is healthy and pleasing in the romantic stage is integrated and actively appreciated through the maturation

of love. In this stage, the pragmatic features of the relationship are still very active, but hardly a chore. The dissillusionment process so characteristic of the second stage has practically disappeared.

The insight into, and anticipation of, these three natural stages in a friendship are the specific results of intellect and will, the spiritual powers of the person. As parents of the emotions they make all things possible in coming to healthy man-woman love.

One might coin the phrase, "control your emotions by knowing your emotions." The intellect can be regarded as the spiritual *mother* of all the powers within us-- psychic and physical. The crown of intellectual activity is wisdom, a loving kind of knowing and a knowing kind of love. We need to understand our emotions and passions, not repress them or exploit them. A good mother nurtures and centers her children. A good intellect nurtures and centers one's emotions and feelings.

Another important phrase in attaining romantic- erotic integration would be, "direct your passions by loving them." Loving them means willing the truest and the best for them. The unconditional best for them is that they--like persons--be given the gift of themselves. A feeling of anger so needs to be affirmed as a good in itself. A feeling of erotic possessiveness so needs to be affirmed as a good in itself. They do not need to be affirmed for what they can *do* for you, but for what they *are*. When they are consciously so affirmed at times, then they naturally become centered and *are* themselves in a non-impulsive way. Willing the *being* of one's pas- sions is the fatherly act of the will. Passions do not become unruly through over-attention, but through lack of attention and of loving care.

The person who thinks he has to discharge his emo- tions or passions when they occur is really one who acts like a permissive parent, not caring about the good of the child himself. Parents who "love" their children by giving them things and "things to do" while mother and dad go their own way to do their "adult things" are bru- tally neglecting their children. The neglect of passions is similar. A person who thinks he or she is being good to passion and emotion by letting them do whatever they want is really neglecting them and treating them merely as means to his or her gratification.

Passions are like persons, because every person is a passion for God. There is one total good for all persons and their passions and that is the ultimate Good. In Augustine's often-noted way of saying it, "Our hearts are restless until they rest in You." When people have the vision of God's glory and his infinitely good Will in mind, and are also willing to move toward that Good, then all other goods and temporary gratifications find a proportionate place in their lives. The right sense of priorities about life united with God (in the present world as well as in the next) is the most important, but not the only, element in healthy integration of romantic-erotic drives and energies. Knowledge and love of God is the supreme Good of all persons and passions.

Friendship of the Unmarried

A discussion of the two kinds of non-marital man-woman relationships may yield further perspective. One kind is the relationship between two people, neither of whom is married. The other is the relationship between two people, one or both of whom are married to another. Because of the marital relationship involved in the latter kind, special considerations would seem to be necessary, and will be made in the next section.

When two people who are not married begin to develop a presumably loving friendship, their behavior receives a challenge. How can their acts of touching be warm and non-possessive? Expressions of affection such as holding hands, kissing, and embracing need to be done in ways that celebrate (joyfully express) their special and intense liking for each other without signifying any specific intention to activate their genital powers. This kind of touching can be done freely and can help each person to grow in spontaneous regard for the other as a beautiful individual worthy of respect and reverence. These acts of affection can say to the sexual other: "You are so good, simply as you are, without necessarily being related to me as a genital partner." In this way, the partners develop a capacity to relate beyond the point of consciously or unconsciously regarding each other as a sex object.[10] It is this kind of loving discipline that prepares them for possible coital intercourse later with each other, or with someone else, in the definitive community of marriage. Whether the persons ever marry or not, the inner discipline they develop is very valuable in strengthening personality. This discipline crucially involves relating sexually, without relating coitally or genitally, with sexual others.

Two general guidelines would seem to be reasonable in evaluating the interactions of the unmarried man and woman in their attempts at developing a genuinely loving union. First, they should do only those things that foster their present vocation of celibate sexuality. Second, they should refrain from any action that is *specific* to the other vocations (marriage and parenthood). The first guideline is fulfilled by any behavior which increases their dignity and self-concept as personally complete sexual persons, who freely share themselves with each other without any necessity of living mutually parasitic lives. The second guideline is a "keep out" injunction that requires elaboration.

Any action that is physically, psychically, or spiritually intimate in a way that is proper *only* to spouses would violate the integrity of marriage--any and every marriage, not just potentially their own. Premarital and non-marital genital interactions violate all marriages--not simply marriage in the abstract. They take away from the specialness of the action which people committed to marriage practice as unique to their vocation and to their manner of serving the community and celebrating sexual values.

Sleeping in the same bed, locked in an embrace, even without any specifically genital sharing, would probably be an instance of violating the marriage covenant at an emphatically physical and psychic level.[11]   In these circumstances, the individual's body becomes specially sensitized to the body of the sexual other and the emotional life is inclined to become considerably less than non-possessive.

Also, any promise of a solemn nature to relate in a special sexual way for life *only* with this other person would seem to be a violation of the marital covenant. Perhaps this kind of promise would violate the covenant at an emphatically spiritual level.

The promise *to marry* that constitutes an engagement is not the kind suggested here. Persons who are unmarried and are free to marry can beautifully express their loving friendship at the time in which they promise to marry--that is, they promise that they *will* make solemn vows to each other in the foreseen future, unless something entirely unforeseen develops in their relationship before the time of the covenant. But it is a considerable disorder of understanding and intention when a couple promises privately to live as husband and wife from that point forward until death. They would seem to violate the whole human community in that action, because the community must be an explicit party to that

340

kind of commitment. They also violate the vows of married people whom they purport to be joining without risking the effects of public commitment.

Any act of love-expression between unmarried persons that is even partly *intended* to stimulate genital activity, such as an erection of the penis or of the clitoris, violates the vocation of parenthood. Specifically genital action and venereal pleasure are proportionate only to the exercise of the organs which are activated in coital intercourse. Of course, it is very important to distinguish genital stimulation that is not even partly intended, but happens, and genital stimulation that is part of the intention of one or both partners in an embrace. It would be unreasonable to expect that people of different sex who were strongly attracted to each other could always touch or kiss or embrace without any genital stimulation occurring.

The point is that they do not engage in their expression of affection or even in their thoughts of each other partly or wholly *in order to* receive such stimulation, venereal pleasure, or both. In effect, they do not mentally adopt a proposal to be stimulated genitally. In a truly loving expression of themselves as non-parentive people they *do intend* or propose to share themselves with each other *sexually, but not genitally*. If some incidental genital stimulation occurs, even regularly, one's generative powers are not being misused. They are not even being used. They are simply acting of their own free accord, somewhat as they do in the activities of ovulation, menstruation, spermatogenesis and periodic (involuntary) seminal emission.[12]

If a young man kisses a young woman goodnight, very tenderly and affectionately, sharing himself as a man with her as a woman, and he does not have an erection, there *might* be something wrong with him. Even thinking about someone very attractive can readily be the occasion of a genital stimulation. Such occurrences are normal and natural. What is normal in many circles, but not natural, is to engage in a kind of fantasizing which is partly or wholly the execution of a proposal *to stimulate* genital reaction. Pleasure is not simply taken in the image--which *might* be quite innocent enough--but also in the accompanying pleasurable sensations which happen to be of a specifically genital (venereal) kind. Such action does not let one's genital-erotic nature be itself, but exploits it. It is a common sign of sexual immaturity and a compensation for an inability to love rightly self and others (who are always, at least indirectly, involved in one's fantasies).

Erotic emotions are as natural as emotions of anger or fear. But the *deliberate* stimulation of erotic emotions (with accompanying physical erection) is as irrational as the *deliberate* stimulation of anger (with accompanying redness in face or neck) or of fear (with accompanying tremor of hand and sweat of brow). Such stimulation for the sheer pleasure of the erotic experience is as anti-natural as stimulation of anger or fear for the sheer pain of these experiences. The pleasure . or pain is being severed from the natural act in each case. The experience is rather neurotic than erotic. The stimulation of the erotic emotion in this case is done neither by an object other than the stimulated person nor by the person for the sake of others, as in acting a role calling for emotions of eros, anger, or fear. The stimulation is a part of an insular, self-enclosed attitude that inevitably pollutes the individual's ability to love and stifles growth as a person.

Fantasies are also natural to the human person, but they can result from abuse of one's personal power to know through images. Deliberate fantasies can be morally good or bad for the person, depending on their content and the person's intent.

If someone fantasizes or imagines a scene in which someone of the other sex suffers brutality, and this fantasy is done partly for some delight it causes--whether genital arousal occurs or not--then he or she is violating the fundamental Good of Social Harmony. Such an action-- although simply a mental action, without intent to put something into physical practice--degrades the dignity of all persons of the other sex in the mind of the daydreamer. The fantasizer is engaged in mind-pollution.

Sadism is, first of all, an attitudinal debasement of all sexual others. When physically executed, such acts are only secondarily directed to the victim who may be willing (masochistic) or unwilling. They are primarily directed against one's *inner* sexual other (Animus or Anima). Antipathy toward intrasexual integration is also a direct violation of the fundamental Good of Integrity.

If, however, the deliberate fantasy is done in order to see or appreciate what such sadistic actions are really all about, with no intention to delight in them but simply motivated by speculative knowledge and, perhaps, by

342

practical purposes such as more effectively counseling persons who are attached to such behavior patterns, then this fantasy might well be regarded as morally good. In the first example, one is actually--even if unwittingly-- moving toward an increase in the amount of sexual violence in the world. In the latter example, one is moving toward a reduction of it.[13]

Imagining oneself engaged in coital intercourse with another person--whether the partner is known to be real or strictly figmental--is morally right or wrong depending on the motivation, attitude, and intention. If it is done--except by a person in reference to his or her spouse--so that one might receive some of the particular delight proper to the act of coital union, it is morally wrong because it is an engagement in the act itself, by intent. Such a fantasy is not morally wrong because there is something unclean or immoral, unworthy or less human, about coital union. It is wrong because the action is so good and worthwhile, so morally sound and intensely human, when undertaken with conditions that can occur only in a loving marital union.

The particular kind of activity that a man and woman engage in, and the particular way in which they do it in a loving marital union, is so special and unique to them, that the public display of such an action represents an invasion into the privacy of every such loving couple. Coital union in marriage is not just any kind of action, such as sharing a meal or sharing a conversation. It involves specifically sharing their genital powers and organs, which are private to the person even though they are ultimately social in their nature. A person who fantasizes about himself or about someone else engaging in such action without serious reason to do so-- such as mentally preparing for doing it in a loving marriage--is violating the natural privacy of self *and others*. He or she is making "public" what should be done only in private communion.

Again, as in the case of imagining some activity of sexual abuse, if the person fantasizes about having intercourse with someone--no one in particular--in order to identify with his or her own power to do such activity as a man or woman, independently of whether the future presents any morally good opportunity for it, then it is probably morally sound. As long as one does not *propose* to experience delight proper to such activity, he or she may rightly attempt to imagine what such activity involves. The *intention* to experience delight, even partially, constitutes an inner personal pollution, not because the pleasure intended is itself wrong, but because it is proper only to acts that move intentionally (structurally) toward genital fulfillment within the coital embrace.

Genital fulfillment can occur naturally only through coition. Genital fulfillment (in this context and in many others throughout this book) really means coital fulfillment. Coital fulfillment is a specific kind of genital fulfillment. It specifically includes venereal pleasure and orgasm. (Everything coital is genital, though not everything genital is coital.)

So, the beginning of a coital-genital act, with its accompanying pleasurable sensations, should not be separated from its end--coitional intercourse. Deliberate delight in the beginning of an act is morally responsible only if it includes the specific intent to follow through to the end of the act. Otherwise it is self-deceptive activity. Since a person who is not married cannot morally follow through, he or she cannot genuinely intend the beginning of the act. To do so is to sever-- or to attempt to sever--a deeply personal action.

This moral severance occurs because venereal pleasure is *specifically* coital pleasure; though it is *generally* genital pleasure. Of course, many things that are specifically genital are not coital: spermatogenesis, the tension produced in the seminal vesicle, and the spontaneous seminal release in the man; and ovulation, menstruation, lactation, warmth through nursing, and so forth in the woman. But *venereal pleasure is specifically found in coitally-oriented action and nowhere else.* Thus, any deliberately induced or permitted venereal pleasure constitutes a *part* of human coital activity. If such pleasure is *deliberately* experienced apart from coitional union itself it is being severed from its natural whole. The coitional act is being removed (by its deliberately intended non-existence) from what *is* there: the venereal pleasure, which is a natural *part* of this whole action.

Extramarital Friendship

There is much talk about extramarital sex. Little has been said (or even thought) about extramarital love. The giant supposition seems to be that a healthy and sexually vigorous man and woman who are attracted to each other will need to restrict their personal contacts considerably lest they end up "having an affair." Moreover, many counselors would say that, in some circumstances, "having an affair" can be a healthy outlet for marital

344

oredom. The latent assumptions are that sex is ulti-
ately too strong to be controlled without severe repres-
ion, that loving motives will inevitably be thwarted
y sexual attractiveness, and that sexual attractiveness
ignifies potential satisfaction only in genital (coital)
atiation.

A man and woman who are married, but not to each
ther, have just as much right to be friends as anyone
lse. Special friendships between them can responsibly
ccur within the parameters of their respective commit-
ents to spouses and to their other relationships.

Ideally, the spouse or spouses who are not involved
hould be friends with the special friend of their spouse.
hey certainly should not be (or become) inimical. But
ecause of the considerable insecurity in most marriages,
ealousy on the part of the spouse or spouses who are
ot involved makes loving friendships of this kind very
ifficult.

How to preserve a marriage as well as the rights of
ne's own spouse, while giving special attention to some-
ne else of the other sex, is a very important and dif-
icult matter. The difficulty is not removed by assuming
hat it cannot be done or that one ought to "let well
nough alone." The existence of such attitudes not only
locks the personal potential for extramarital friend-
hips, but prevents genuine growth in marital friendship
s well. Yet, one should not underestimate the difficulty
n cultivating an extramarital relationship that is truly
oving and deeply meaningful in the midst of a society
hat cynically presupposes its impossibility. In addi-
ion, the two friends themselves are often inclined to
verlook signs of disorder in their relationship, because
f their defensiveness in protecting it and because of
mperfections in their motivation.

One of the great advantages of a leisure society--
society that is more or less removed from the daily
truggle for family subsistence through labor on the land
nd in the sweatshop--is the opportunity to develop deeper
nd richer friendships within and outside the family.
he person who is serious about developing and living
thoroughly satisfying sexual life will want to cultivate
is or her relationships with various people of both
exes.

If a special relationship naturally develops with
married person of the other sex, then one should want
o let the relationship develop in the unique way in

345

which this relationship would best benefit *all* concerned. Those most notably concerned would be not only the two people involved in a loving friendship, but the spouse of one or both of them and any children either of them might have. This kind of loving relationship is much more complex than that between two celibates. If both persons involved are spouses and parents, the relationshi might have to entail very limited time together (alone or with others) because of the needs and reasonable desires of the close family members of both of them. Yet, quality time can be provided in most situations. Few people in our society do not have the leisure for special friendship--inside and outside marriage.

Loving affirmation of another person does not necessarily require long hours in this person's physical presence, although it might be important at times, and in some cases.[14] The crux of loving friendship is the quality of the total relationship and of every interaction. This quality can be evaluated somewhat in the way that one can evaluate a moral act. The predetermining and self-determining sides of the relationship can be examined in regard to their physical, psychical, and spiritual dimensions. *What objectively* is occurring between the two people? Does it totally harmonize with human nature generally and the nature of human sexuality specifically? Also, circumstances such as the amount of time available for developing the relationship, the particular needs of the spouse or spouses who are not directly involved, the needs of any children, and many more factors must also be considered very carefully.

If a man and a woman do have such a relationship, and if they have the time and circumstance to cultivate it, one of the most prominent questions in the back of people's minds is: how far can they go physically? Do the standards proposed for a loving friendship between two celibates readily apply in the case of one or both parties being married to someone else?

In view of the spousal commitments already made by one or both of them, it would hardly seem that the standards should be exactly the same. In the case of the two people who are celibate but free to marry, a phenomenon that might be called "alienation of affection" does not occur. Some of the ways of embracing and kissing that a married couple commonly engage in might be justifiable in two celibates--assuming definite intent to preclude genital pleasure. They could be saying by those actions that they are seriously regarding each other as potential partners for life. But between two people,

346

at least one of whom is married to another, such embracing and kissing could readily be contradictory to their communication with their own spouses.

A physical expression of affection which is tender, warm, and caring between two married people (who are not married to each other) can be morally sound. A kiss or an embrace can be a man-woman--rather than simply a brother-sister, father-daughter, or mother-son--encounter. Of course, it may not be done with even a partial intention to stimulate genital arousal in either oneself or the other.

Particular ways and styles of affection-expression between persons in such circumstances are many and varied. The two people themselves can develop in these ways spontaneously, much as they would in other (non-marital) circumstances. But the affection of each one's own spouse must be kept primary. Any action that would tend to take away, rather than increase, the genuine feelings of affection one has for one's spouse would be ecologically (morally) unsound.

No one, however, can be *required* to *feel* what he or she does *not feel* for someone--even one's spouse. If the non-marital friend evokes stronger feelings of male-female attraction and affection than one's spouse, that should be admitted consciously to oneself. But, then, expressive acts of affection for the non-marital friend should be guided by this circumstance.

If one could *honestly* say that a kiss or embrace on this or that occasion will tend to increase, rather than decrease, the affection one feels for one's spouse, as well as increasing the affection for the non-marital friend, then perhaps such an action is justifiable. But if the action is honestly seen to tend toward dampening one's affection for one's spouse, then it would be morally wrong. The action would constitute a real alienation of affection.

Some would say that a good rule of thumb is never to express affection to a non-marital friend that one would not express in the presence of one's spouse. While this guideline is practical in many cases, there are many others in which it would seem to be too strict. There are many spouses who are too possessive, jealous, and immature to appreciate even the slightest show of physical affection given by their mates to attractive persons of the other sex. As in all moral decisions, the individual agent must take into account all sources of practical

and theoretical evaluation--including especially significant others in his or her life--but must make the decision
for action based on the best reasons (which do not *necessarily* include *all* of the feelings of one's spouse,
one's friend, *and* oneself).

Prudence (practical wisdom) is a key virtue in this
kind of moral decision-making. Even though a course of
action would seem to be morally responsible under normal
circumstances, it might be imprudent to engage in it because of the particular circumstances (such as an "unreasonable" spouse). Prudence might require refraining
from very innocent expression of affection if others
might be truly scandalized, due to severe cultural inhibitions. Or prudence might require the risk of alienating
or "scandalizing" some people for the sake of affirming
the unique goodness and particular needs of a friend.
In each moral decision one needs the inspiration of a
power that provides unique insight into how the contem-
plated action can best effect deeper, authentic participation in the fundamental Goods of human life. No book
can offer the decisive comment on the efficacy of a given
act of self-determination. Prayer, however, can be the
occasion for receiving decisive inspiration.

A Good Broader Than Marriage

A loving kind of friendship is a good broader than
marriage. The healthy friendship of man and woman is
the most crucial environment for wise choice in (and
mature development among) marital partners. It is not
enough for men and women to be intensely attracted to
each other. Their mating-attraction needs to be rooted
in love that can sustain commitment. Nor is love alone
sufficient. In addition to love, the mutual attraction
and passionate attention to each other (so often called
"love") of which men and women are capable constitutes
the fabric of everyday sexual life in the vocations of
marriage and parenthood. A loving kind of friendship
before marriage is the only sound ecological base for a
marital choice and commitment which will creatively integrate persons and passions for the good of the whole
human community.

Loving, mutually affirmational friendship between
persons of either sex is not simply--like marriage--a
commitment which deeply facilitates participation in one
or more fundamental human Goods. Loving friendship is
the paradigm of participation in one particular fundamental Good: Social Harmony. Man-woman friendship, in
turn, is the heart of this supremely human Good that forms

the ecological base for the entire human community on the planet earth.

Mature loving friendship between any man and woman incorporates the insight into human sexual ecology expressed by the poet Rilke:

> . . . [O]nce the realization is accepted that, even between the closest human beings, infinite distances continue to exist, a wonderful living side by side can grow up, if they succeed in loving the distance between them which makes it possible to see the other whole and against a wide sky![15]

NOTES

1. McGoey, *Through Sex to Love*, Chapter 12.

2. This idea is an underlying theme of Alan Watts, *Nature, Man and Woman* (New York: New American Library/Mentor, 1958). The book culminates in a remarkably insightful section entitled "Consummation," in which sexual (coital) communion is illuminated by contemplative perspectives from Taoism, Buddhism, and Zen. See especially pp. 160-61. See also Karl Stern, *The Flight from Woman*.

3. Not, at least, in the holistic way necessary for full human, and specifically *emotional*, development.

4. *Born Only Once*, pp. 23-24.

5. Ibid., p. 26.

6. Ibid., p. 27.

7. Ibid., p. 28. Permission of the publisher, Franciscan Herald Press, Chicago, is gratefully acknowledged.

8. This point underscores the ecological complexity of Animus-Anima in men and women. No man is all-male in any part of his personal identity (including his penis). Nor is any woman all-female. Men and women are extremely fluent, yet perfectly firm, in their inner sexual orientations (natures).

9. Baars, *Born Only Once*, Chapter 6. Here I am agreeing with the idea of Baars and Terruwe that one cannot authentically affirm oneself. Elsewhere (Chapter 11) I have referred to a kind of self-affirmation where one affirms the goodness of parts of oneself--notably the Be-Attitudes as organs of spiritual life. This affirmation of a part by the whole is very therapeutic at all levels of the person. For example, one can affirm one's feet mentally and by touch, "telling them" that they are good--thus helping to restore circulation and vitality. Baars and Terruwe, however, are referring to an affirmation of one whole person by another whole person. This kind of affirmation cannot be given to oneself--at least not in the

emotionally fluent manner that is essential for healing and personality growth.

10. In some senses, they become for each other *sex subjects*--
man and woman subjects, not coital-genital subjects. (A subject is
someone *who* is a source of life, knowledge, energy, and spiritual
destiny.) Their shared acts of affection--which are manifested
in deeds as well as looks and touches--help each one to regard all
sexual others as subjects (not objects) precisely as sexual.

11. The marriage covenant is not regarded here as a genital act,
but as the covenant itself, initiated at the marriage ceremony.

12. John McGoey writes cogently on the meaning of a loving kind
of celibacy in his book on love and sexuality for celibates, *Dare
I Love* (Toronto: Scarboro, 1971). His insightful work includes
the following passage on the celibate who cares for the whole world's
needs and "dares to love": "Moving into this need, he is assured
of fulfillment as a human being by loving well. The sexual feelings
experienced in the beginnings of friendships, and with which he
lives so maturely, make him aware of the responsibility to love
well, assure him of his masculinity (or her, of her feminity), and
afford evidence of normal emotional health. The prostate, Cowper's
and Littre's glandular secretions (or their equivalent in the female,
Bartholin's, Skene's, etc.) stimulated by the tenderness of love,
challenge him to a moral maturity by integrating the normal sexual
feelings accompanying genuine love and affection honestly manifested.
The emotional calm of tranquil love dominates the sexual emotions
of the celibate whose attention is diverted from his genitals to
the good of the whole person loved. Experiencing how secondary
the sexual emotions remain under the dominance of genuine love, the
celibate learns more quickly than do married people, how very completely sex can be subjected to the over-all direction of love."
p. 104.

13. Nevertheless, bombardment of oneself by means of viewing
pornographic films, with the intention of getting a firm grasp on
what potential clients or advisees are experiencing, would seem
to be morally indefensible. Sexual attitudes reassessment programs that claim to help professional people understand sado-
masochists, beastialists, prostitutes, pimps, et al. by "desensi-
tizing" them through exposure to "flesh flicks" are deceptive. Any
counselor whose imagination is *incapable* of reasonably representing
the conditions that people experience when suffering from such
erotic aberrations is not intelligent enough to do effective counseling. The intention to remove the sexual "hangups" of professionals
seems to be inspired by a much more repressive and degrading hangup:
a fanatic fixation on genital orgasm as sex itself. The fact that
such films are presented in the context of what is called values
clarification can have little redeeming value since one of the assumptions behind such a procedure is that there is no objectively
true set of values for everyone--at least not when it comes to
sex. These programs in sexual attitude reassessment seem to be
value-centered in an unacknowledged way. They promote the pornographic industry by buying, distributing, and popularizing some

350

of its wares, and they inevitably leave the strong, but perhaps unstated, impression that homosexuality, masturbation, mutual sadism, et al. are morally acceptable for some segments of the population and that they ought to be outside the moral judgment of competent people in the helping professions.

14. For example, persons who are legally divorced or separated, but validly married to their estranged partners, are often in great need of loving affirmation from members of both sexes. Such people need considerable support in their celibate life-style. In many cases, they are victims of the sociocultural assumption about the impossibility of loving man-woman friendships between people not married to each other. I do not wish to imply here that a divorced person may live with a member of the other sex in a quasi-spousal relationship, but that a divorced person--more likely than others-- might well need some kind of sustained and more frequent attention, due to the extra burdens of perhaps raising a family without the marital partner or just getting through a period of depression over the rupture in the marital relationship from which he or she is inevitably suffering.

The danger of unduly scandalizing others by frequent or "intimate-appearing" contacts should not be dismissed. Yet, the need for mutually supportive, heterosexual affirmation on the part of all members of society is very great. Unless individuals take prudent risks by engaging in such relationships, the "Copernican Revolution" in human sexuality is little more than a dream. What is prudent risk and what is impulsive rashness in these matters can only be discerned through open-minded attention to past experience (in the light of sound practical and theoretical principles) and a considerable degree of genuine self-knowledge (under the inspiration of one's Creator).

An emphasis on the necessity for a deep spiritual life in man-woman friendships--quite consonant with the reflections on loving friendships in this chapter--is provided by philosopher Dietrich von Hildebrand, *Man and Woman* (Chicago: Henry Regnery, 1966). See his chapter on "Friendship Between the Sexes." He tries to show how man and woman have a special "spiritual mission" toward each other and how they "enrich each other in a way which is not possible with the same sex." p. 64.

15. Quoted in Lindbergh, *Gift from the Sea*, p. 98.

351

Chapter 19

THE CHILD WITHIN

We are living in what might be called the age of
the prenatal child. Ever since Lennart Nilsson shocked
us with his photographs in 1965, dramatically detailing
human life in the womb, this society has steadily grown
in awareness of the personality and meaning of prebirth
children.[1]

Dr. Albert W. Liley, the researcher responsible for
the first successful intrauterine blood transfusion and
often called "the father of fetology," says that the
human fetus is the master of the pregnancy. As early as
1967, he described in breathtaking terms the dynamic life
of the prenatal person, claiming very effectively that
the fetus is "not a passive, dependent, nerveless, fragile
vegetable, as tradition has held, but a young human being,
dynamic, plastic, resilient and in very large measure
in charge of his environment and destiny."[2] So alive,
active, and adaptive is the child in the womb that, as
Liley puts it, "In many respects it would be more appropriate to consider the adult as a poorly functioning foetus than the foetus as a poorly functioning adult."[3]

There are many forces still bent on keeping a shroud
of darkness over the uniqueness and human vigor of life
in the womb. Legal and moral protection for this life
has been relinquished widely at the very time that its
humanity is becoming increasingly acknowledged. Archaic
sexual fixation on genital orgasm, combined with the
heady wine of technocratic power, has temporarily eclipsed

353

the personalities of prenatal children and their profound, symbolic message of sexual freedom to their parents and the world-at-large. But the meaning of prenatal child- hood is an idea whose time has come. And the loving friendship of man and woman is an important part of that meaning.

In this chapter I will discuss the symbolic meaning of the prenatal child and point out how this book has attempted to reveal some of the implications. A few of the earlier references to this theme will be brought into sharper focus. Consideration will likewise be given to the way in which the chapters of the book unfold the message of the prebirth child as the central figure in human sexual ecology.

The Child Within That We Are

I have already suggested that each person in this world can be regarded as a kind of premortal child, ges- tating in a cosmic space and time, heading for a new birth at the moment of death. The womb in which we ges- tate might be regarded as eternity or God, into whose presence we come much more directly after death. The environment of space and time is like the amniotic sac in which we developed during the many weeks before birth. When we die, it is as though this spatio-temporal sac breaks and we are ushered into a much wider world of timeless truth, beauty, and goodness (or, perhaps, decep- tion, ugliness, and evil) in accord with our self- determined destiny. At death, our premortal "placentas" are buried like the "afterbirth," and our fetal*like* selves live onward, experiencing the new and fuller life toward which we were rather unconsciously growing in this world.

This image of human beings as premortal persons is suggested as a contemporary symbol of Christian self- consciousness. While the basic ethics of human sexuality that we have been developing in this book is not depen- dent on the Christian worldview, it finds particular support and inspiration from Christian revelation. If a person can see how remarkably like a fetal individual he or she is, human sexual ecology will make good sense philosophically. If the likeness is not seen or is re- jected, the principles and guidelines discussed in this book will be much less meaningful as part of one's phi- losophy of life.

In our age we are witnessing a growing interest in what might be called the vestibule phenomenon. People who have been clinically declared dead or who have been very close to death have reported dramatic experiences of leaving their spatial bodies, viewing them from a distance, being drawn through a kind of tunnel to another world of light, seeing relatives or friends who have died come to take them, meeting a Christ figure, and other such things, before returning to their bodies. Although this phenomenon is not unique to our times, some observers speculate that the contemporary medical ability to resuscitate victims of accidents and seizures has produced a much greater potential for experiencing the "threshold of death." Whether one believes in the literal significance of vestibule experiences or not, one is probably well advised to consider such reports carefully. In any event, they do tend to reinforce the potential fruitfulness of imaging ourselves as now engaged in a largely placenta*like* life which is preparing us for "rushing through the birth canal" at death into a life of wider, freer movement of mind and heart "on the other side."

For some years now, as the space programs have progressed, people all over the world have become accustomed to the image of the astronaut attached to his spacecraft by an "umbilical cord." The likeness of astronauts groping in outer space, critically attached to mother earth may not be lost on a generation that is becoming more intent on inner-space travel. One must give serious consideration to the idea that the "road to immortality" is really a gestational orbiting within the "inner space" of time and cosmic matter, waiting to be drawn by superior forces into the wider world of universal being.

The Child Within That We Mother

Symbolically, there is another Child Within. Not only is each one of us a child within the womb of eternity, groping for eternal life; each one of us is mother (and father) to a child within the depths of our very own self. This inner child has various forms. The psychic Child of transactional analysis has been mentioned in this book. Moreover, in Chapter 18 it was suggested that our emotions are like children within us who need the motherly and fatherly care of intellect and will. But, in the last analysis, it would seem to be our very self that is a Child Within. The self within our self-- waiting to be born in myriad ways--is a child with whom we are pregnant as long as we live. It would seem to be this Child Within to which Jesus referred when he said, "Unless you become as little children, you shall not enter the kingdom of heaven" (Luke 18:17).

This Child of Self-identity is the gift that we share
with self and with others in the activity of being sexual.
Sexuality is the personal power to share this gift of
self (this Child Within) with self and others in joy
and sorrow--joy over the goodness of being the unique
gift that we are and sorrow over the considerably adverse
conditions under which this gift often struggles to be
born. Everyone is called to be a loving parent to the
Child of Self-identity gestating within the Anima (Eve)--
the womb of our be-ing.

As an introduction to human sexual ecology, this
book has been concerned specifically with the Child Within
that we mother--the Child of Self-identity. We have been
studying the basic relationships involved in growing
healthfully as men and women. Human sexual ecology is
the systematic study of sexual "homemaking."

We can now briefly review our study of ways to make
a home for the Child of Self-identity.

Sexuality and Liberation (Part I)

Our reflections began with the basic meaning of
sexuality and with an elucidation of its primary aspects.

Sexuality, I claimed, means sharing. A person is
exercising well his or her sexual power to the extent
that true sharing is occurring. *What* is being shared
in the central activity of sexual life is one's very own
self. A person's unique self is a gift to be shared with
self and with the world. This self *is* the Child Within.
So sexuality may be regarded as the personal power to
share the Child Within that each of us experiences in
our beingful depths.

Genitality, then, may be seen as a specialized personal power to share, with self and with the world,
another kind of Child Within--a whole physical person,
who, for a time, abides literally within the physical
body of the mother. Genital sexuality is a natural power
enabling a person--whether man or woman--to share (not
so much oneself as) another person in space and time.
The parented child is a special symbol of the parented
inner self which is fused with a sexual other (the
spouse).

After defining sexuality and its most obvious, specialized expressions (genitality and coitality), I described, in Chapter 3, the nature of sharing in terms of
sexual energy. The mutual relationship of giving and

356

receiving was focused upon because it is the essence of sharing and because it serves to define the being of man and woman. The protection and nurturance of oneself (self-fathering and self-mothering) depend on the degree of implicit, if not explicit, attunement to the proper structural dynamics of giving and receiving as a man or as a woman. The exquisite care that the *gift* of inner self needs comes from one's inner fidelity to one's nature as man or woman. The Child Within thrives on the creative intimacy and intimate creativity generated by the person who is deeply in harmony with his or her sexual identity-- which entails an emphasis on either a giving kind of receiving or a receiving kind of giving.

The definition of man and woman given in Chapter 5 was prepared for by the delineation of stages in human liberation discussed in Chapter 4. Passage from the state of relative non-identity (watching images and shadows) through many phases of struggle with self-identity and self-direction (struggling with the light) into a state of integration and relative maturity (adapting to the sun) is the gestational history of the Child Within--the Child of Self-identity discovered, lived, and celebrated.

Freedom and Friendship (Part II)

The second part of the book dealt with the basic meanings of freedom and friendship (Chapters 6 and 7). I delineated how one can begin to develop his or her deep potential for being free and being a friend, especially in view of the need to integrate genital drives and erotic feelings (Chapter 8). The process of letting oneself become centered was indicated as the paradoxical stillness leading to dynamic activity and growth. The person was encouraged to "have a date" with self by spending times of solitude, in which the inner Adam and Eve can naturally become integrated and intimate with each other, without the individual "doing" anything about it. This interior intimacy was said to be the opposite of what Karl Stern has called "the flight from woman." At times of loving solitude with one's own being, the inner Child can play and grow in freedom.

Love and Morality (Part III)

Love and morality was the theme of the section dealing with basic ethical theory. The eight fundamental human Goods, the eight modes of responsible human action, the nine Be-Attitudes of love, and the nature of a moral action were all described and put into the perspective of the theory of human sexual ecology. The Be-Attitudes

357

(expectation, anticipation, patience, perseverance, forgiveness, and the others) were characterized as the fetal-
like body-organs of the Child Within (the Child of Self-
identity). This Child was said to have a placental*like*
life (consisting of moral actions in space and time),
the health of which is governed by regard for the eight
modes of responsibility. The absolutely essential nutrients for authentically human growth and development
were called the eight fundamental human Goods. These
basic Values were seen as the practically unlimited source
of moral and spiritual life for the Child Within. Participation in *these* values is an initial participation
in the life of the womb (eternity) inasmuch as they are
all ends in themselves, irreducible to one another, and
necessary ways for limitedly, but ever more abundantly,
growing in union with the unlimited Creator and Source
of all truth and value.

In this part of the book I analyzed and evaluated
a particular moral action in order to appreciate how a
person can, through a single deliberate action, increase
or decrease in love and moral well-being. In other words,
we were learning how to become our own best parents of
the Child Within by means of the concrete practice of
this inward art. In every personal action we mother the
Child of Self-identity by letting this inner self receive
directly, in a giving sort of way, one or more basic human Goods; and, at the same time, we father this Child
by assuring its allegiance, in a receiving sort of way,
to all of the basic modes of responsibility.

Sociosexual Identity (Part IV)

Part IV was undertaken only after the basic structure of the Child Within was given in considerable (though
far from complete) detail. How to share oneself as a
man or woman and the need for liberation (Part I) was
followed by discussion of the nature of human freedom
and friendship (Part II), which are primary attributes
and conditions of genuine sexual love. The nature of
love and the essential powers of the Child Within for
expressing love authentically (Part III) were then treated
in preparation for considering the sociosexual identity
afforded by vocational commitment (Part IV). I emphasized
that, while people have no choice regarding the kind of
sexual *being* they are, they do have (to an appreciable
extent) a choice regarding the kind of sexual *living* they
will do.

The section concerning sexual vocation began with
a chapter on fertility awareness. The knowledge gained

about one's physical power to give life is crucial in forming a healthy self-concept as a sexual person and in integrating one's bodily, emotional, and spiritual powers as they are brought into the service of one's chosen sociosexual identity. After indicating the importance of knowing the basic patterns of both male and female fertility and after discussing the application of this knowledge to natural family planning, I delineated the three primary vocations of celibacy, marriage, and parenthood. Each of these three forms of sociosexual identity were then discussed in separate chapters.

Celibacy, marriage, and parenthood were viewed as mutually environmental--structured to nurture and promote the growth of one another. I suggested that celibacy was a kind of absolute sociosexual environment which is necessary for all healthy growth in socializing one's sexuality. Married people need celibacy as an abiding environment in their lives even after they take on a new, proximate environment for their sexual relationships: marriage itself. When a man and woman become parents, then, they really do not (authentically) leave either celibacy or marriage. These two sociosexual identities are necessarily supportive environments for parenthood, which is the new environment created by relationship to an actual or potential child.

Celibacy, marriage, and parenthood are three intimately related ecosystems in the sociosexual life of human persons. From the standpoint of the individual, they represent three basic ways in which the gift of self (the Child Within) can be shared with the world. A person might think of these primary ways of sexual self-commitment as the three basic ways in which the Child of Self-identity can be rooted in the womb of eternity. The person had no choice about the way in which he or she was rooted in the maternal womb shortly after conception. But there is a choice (theoretically, at least) in the way the person becomes basically orientated (rooted) as a sociosexual creature in the womb of eternity. He or she enters the next world with a particular sociosexual identity. Every person dies and enters eternity specifically in one or other of these three vocations.

Integrated Sexuality: Here and Hereafter (Part V)

The final part of the book begins with a discussion of what it means to be a loving sexual person in relation to people of the other sex (Chapter 18). The whole book is oriented toward helping the reader develop his or her potential for loving (meaningful) relationships (marital and non-marital) as a man or woman.

Chapter 19 (*this* one) suggests the unifying, symbolic theme of the book. Inner parenthood is the essence of being sexual in this world. As sexual persons we are all called to share the gift of self (the Child Within) with ourselves and with one another. Human sexuality is not so much a problem as a mystery--the mystery of sharing (with outselves and others, including God) the *mystery who we are*.

The next chapter concludes by reflecting on some of the future prospects for approaching human sexuality in an ecological manner.

The Child Within: Here

Early in this study of human sexual ecology (Chapter 2) the point was made that the way we come to know things (except, perhaps, in mathematics and logic) is just the reverse of the way in which they actually exist. The superficial things are known first. Then we gradually learn about things that are more important in themselves. These important things about any subject matter are the source of mystery and have so much to be known about them that we cannot comprehend them as we can comprehend certain aspects that are of lesser importance.

I noted how it is easy to regard the things that one first comes to *know* as the things that have first priority in the *existence* of the subject in question. I suggested that this confusion of priorities was especially evident in the common evaluation of the features of human sexuality. The perennial identification of genital and coital activity as the center of human sexuality was indicated as a case in point.

Parenthood is another area for re-evaluation of priorities. When most people think of parenthood, they think of the most obvious and dramatic kind: the physical generation of another human being on the planet earth in space and time. But this kind of parenthood is not the kind that can or should be exercised by every single human being. The population problems and crises within families, as well as in whole communities, are ample evidence. In an ecological age, parenthood as simply an option in the fulfillment of personal (not communal) sexuality will become better understood.

Parenthood, however, has an inner, essential meaning
for everyone. Inner parenthood is really more intelligible in itself--though less intelligible immediately
to us--than "outer parenthood." We as intelligent, self-
determining beings are the father and mother of our mysterious inner self. We are called to reverence, nurture,
and unconditionally affirm the goodness and potential
of our whole self. This inward vocation of motherhood
is crucial in our being able to share the gift of self
with self and others (our being sexual). We are likewise
called to respect, protect, and challenge our inner potential. This inward vocation of fatherhood is also
needed for healthy sexual development.

What I am calling *inward parenthood* is *not* being
so called because it is *like* the physical and moral activity of conceiving and raising children who are other
persons. Rather, it is being called that because the
begetting and educating of offspring is like *it*. What
we normally term parenthood is an undertaking which symbolizes (signifies externally and participates in) the
inner care and protection of every human being's Child
of Self-identity.

Human sexual ecology, first and foremost, is the
sexual care of one's sexual self. It is the activity
of being a parent to the celibate within. Each person
is a whole being who is physically, psychically, and
spiritually either a male or a female celibate within.
This single, whole sexual character of oneself is the
inner Child of Self-identity that *is* one sex or the other
as an emphasis in be-ing.

But a human person *as a person* is necessarily responsible for the *growth* of self-identity. One has intellect and will, two complementary powers for guiding and
determining the destiny of one's self-identity. By these
specifically spiritual powers the person is, as it were,
beyond self within self. The person mothers and fathers
the whole of self in the ways that ultimately determine
happiness or unhappiness (fulfillment or unfulfillment
as a person).

As suggested earlier (Chapter 18), the human intellect functions in an emphatically female sort of way
(relative to will) while the human will functions in an
emphatically male sort of way (relative to intellect).
Intellect is the power to be spiritually present to,
and in union with, all beings. By our intellects we receive the being in knowing the being. Will, on the other
hand, is the power to direct the intellect to whatever

is to be known and to hold it there while the conception
of the thing naturally occurs in the intellect as the
result of impregnation by that which is known. By our
wills we give to ourselves what we are knowing when we
are knowing it. The intellect is the spiritual womb in
which our *ideas* of things can gestate and grow. The will
makes this possible by its activity of initiating, guiding, and determining *which* things we know.

In *self*-knowledge and *self*-direction, then, the intellect and will intimately interact in a reciprocal way.

The intellect's activity is an emphasis on receiving
in a giving kind of way. Self is known and affirmed unconditionally. Self is utterly received, even as it is
embraced by means of the necessary, but ever-limited,
fruit of this reception--the self-concept.

The will's activity is an emphasis on giving in a
receiving kind of way. Self is given attention and a
challenge (qualified affirmation). Self is rested in
(received) only to the extent that it is developing in
accord with proportionate standards for selfhood determined through the action of the (motherly) intellect.
Through our wills we specifically protect our fragile
self-identities from unwarranted meddling and imposition
on the part of other people's desires for us or on the
part of our own instinctive impulses to develop passively
in accord with the "first standards to come along." It
is not surprising that we have the expression "will power." Will is the power to be decisive in the determination of how well or poorly we shall develop as human
beings.

Intellect is a *seeing* (receiving) power, emphatically
though not exclusively.[4] Will is an *executing* (giving)
power emphatically though not exclusively. One cannot
do without the other. If one were to use intellect without will, it would be like a person who can see but is
entirely paralyzed, unable to move. If one were to use
will without intellect, it would be like a person who is
totally blind and does not know where to direct his or
her movements.

The intimate interactions of intellect and will represent the most crucial (spiritual) expression of the
inner Adam and Eve, Animus and Anima, in the human person.
Upon the success or failure of this inner marriage depends
the effectiveness of the inner parenthood and ultimately
the destiny of the whole person. The inner celibate receives nurturance and protection for growth only to the

362

extent that he or she is mothered and fathered by these
ultimate, spiritual powers of self-knowledge and self-
direction (intellect and will). But this inner parenthood
is only as wholesome as the interactivity of these two
intimates of spiritual life. How well an individual person grows depends upon how well he or she freely fulfills
the natural, God-given marriage of intellect and will.

The Child Within: Hereafter

Becoming sensitive to the Child Within that we mother
and father here and now in this world inclines one to
believe in some kind of personal immortality. One is
disposed to contemplate the birth of this indwelling child
at the moment of death. (A Christian might think in terms
of the end of marriage as known in this life, union of
the good in the marriage of the Lamb, and the postmortal
existence of the celibate Child Within, that Jesus likely
meant when he said, "Of such is the kingdom of heaven.")
The immortal dimensions of sexuality begin to stand out
in relief.

The Child Within that we mother and father is destined (after death) to be one with the Child Within that
we are. The latter Child Within includes our mothering
and fathering powers and activities. When we have ultimately succeeded or failed in the activity of parenting
ourselves, then there is no need for this personal function of participating in our redemption. It will cease
because we will be perfectly healed in the happiness of
eternal life, or else we will be thoroughly frustrated
in the hellish divorce of self-knowledge from self-
direction (of intellect from will).

Sexuality is part of our eternal destiny. The ultimate condition of happiness would seem to be a supremely
ecstatic sharing of the gift of self with self and others.
(For the Christian this sharing of self in beatitude involves sharing in the very life of God. The person who
has attained the freedom and friendship of self-perfection
known as heaven ecstatically participates in God's life
of sharing Self with Self in the Triune glory, within
which this person was originally created.)

The Creator Self (in whose likeness all other beings
have come to be) can be regarded as the ultimate mother
and father of the Child Within--of the Child Within that
we ourselves mother and father in this world *and* of the
Child Within that we are. People who parent other persons
in this world are dramatically symbolizing, by the exercise of their coital-genital powers, the creation of every

being within the heart of the Triune God. Coitality and
genitality are the major physical symbols of the fundamental structure and dynamics of all genuine love: the
receiving kind of giving and the giving kind of receiving
that constitute our sharing of the gift of self in the
likeness of a Triune God. Not everyone is called to this
beautiful and dramatic participation in the gift of self-
giving that the exercise of life-giving is designed to
effect. But, in this life at least, everyone is called
to be a good parent to the Child of Self-identity, created
in the image and likeness of God who makes this Child to
be forever.

NOTES

1. *Life*, April 30, 1965. Nilsson's photography of prenatal life
is featured along with text by embryologist Claes Wirsén and obste-
trician Axel Ingelman-Sundberg in *A Child Is Born: The Drama of
Life Before Birth* (New York: Dell, 1966)--originally published in
Sweden in 1965.

2. Albert W. Liley, "The Foetus in Control of His Environment,"
in *Abortion and Social Justice*, eds. Thomas W. Hilgers and Dennis
J. Horan (New York: Sheed and Ward, 1972), p. 27.

3. Ibid., p. 35. See also A. W. Liley, "The Foetus as a Personality," *The Australia-New Zealand Journal of Psychiatry*, 6 (1972):
99-105.

4. The intellect is a receiving power *relative to will*. In Chapter 20, I will discuss one way in which it may be regarded as a
giving power, as well as a receiving power.

THE FUTURE OF SEXUAL ECOLOGY

Ecology is the science of environmental carrying-power. Environmental biology and human sexual ecology participate in a common spirit and perspective. The genius of the ecological approach to reality is the perception that any given element is dependent on its womb, which is constituted by *all other* elements in the system. Each component is viewed as implanted in the totality of everything else.

Environmental biology is a study of living organisms as they interrelate not only with one another but with the total physical environment. Each element in an ecosystem is regarded as intimately dependent upon many other elements--all thoroughly interconnected.

Human sexual ecology is the study, of the human being as a self-determining individual, who in his or her power of moral choice, is interrelated with all other human beings (withinness, super-relatedness--the female emphasis) and yet utterly alone (uniqueness, otherness--the male emphasis). Human sexual ecology also includes interrelationships with all beings other than fellow human beings. The human person is rooted in nothing less than universal being, and ultimately in the eternal being of God. He or she is the participant in a threefold ecosystem within each person and between individual persons-- the physical, psychic, and spiritual energy systems which thoroughly interpenetrate one another and provide the dynamics of every personal (moral) act.

Sexual ecology is, then, a philosophy of the ultimate
environmental conditions for human action as a sexual
being. These conditions are examined, explored, and
made meaningful in relation to the sexual dimensions of
any given human act. Sexual ecology, however, cannot
be concerned only with the conditions of human action
itself. It must include consideration of what lies beyond, and yet directly influences, the human environment.
Thus, I have made explicit reference (however brief) to
the ultimate maleness and femaleness of the Creator, within whom and toward whom every creature with immortal destiny comes to be.

The development of human sexual ecology is as crucial
to the survival and welfare of humankind as the development of environmental (physical) ecology. In terms of
both ecologies, the people of so-called developed nations
have been moving the planet to the brink of disaster.
The "dominion by exploitation" mentality toward land,
water, and air has resulted in physical pollution caused
by careless industrial, military, and urban expansion.
The pollution of minds and hearts by anti-fertility and
anti-life solutions to sexual problems has resulted in
physical pollution wrought by drugs and devices that can
be lethal to women, as well as by abortifacient chemicals
and surgeries that are inevitably lethal to millions
of children.

If, as I have claimed, human sexuality is the personal capacity to share the gift of self (social, as well
as individual, self), then human sexuality goes right
to the heart of both ecological crises. Pollution is
essentially a social phenomenon, with physical results.
A morality of self-restraint in being man and woman will
quite naturally affect the quality of all social relationships, not just coital and genital ones. The relationship
of man and woman is the center of both ecologies.

Before closing this introductory study of sexual
ecology some comments on the prospects for further development will be offered.

First of all, the present study has opened up some
relatively new perspectives in the field of sexual ethics.
These perspectives and many others deserve special cul-
tivation. The crucial role of attitudes (especially Be-
Attitudes), the three interpenetrating areas of vocational identity (celibacy, marriage, and parenthood),
and the suggested task of reconceiving and interrelating
the moral virtues within an ecological framework--all
require further attention. Of course, one cannot overlook

the obvious need to develop the concepts of the fundamental human Goods and the modes of responsible action, and to refine the meanings of sexuality, genitality, and coitality.

Apart from the particular approach and scope of this book, there are various sources of insight and inspiration in contemporary psychology, theology, and philosophy. I have already cited my special indebtedness to Anna Terruwe and Conrad Baars in the field of psychology, and to Mary Rosera Joyce and Germain Grisez in the area of philosophy. In this final chapter, I wish to discuss two sample approaches--one in psychology and one in theology--that have creative and decisive implications for the philosophy of human sexual ecology. I will then suggest three special needs from a religious and philosophical point of view, and will conclude with a comment on the most practical sign of a breakthrough in sexual ecology: the movement toward natural family planning.

Identity and Intimacy

The future of sexual ecology will depend on how cogently many thinkers can defend and elucidate the constancy of human self-identity. It will also depend on how well they explore the ever-growing potential of the human being for meaningful, if fluid and changing, relationships. The gift of self that we share in being sexually effective persons is both male and female. There is constant need to keep a balance between self-identity and self-development--between one's uniqueness and one's super-relatedness as a self.

On the one hand, the introspective turn in modern and contemporary philosophy, especially significant in the religious existentialists such as Kierkegaard, Marcel, and Buber, has underscored the radical otherness of the individual self, independent of the community and the masses. On the other hand, recent trends in clinical and social psychology, led by such popular mentors as Carl Rogers, Abraham Maslow, and Frederick Perls, have produced almost a religious fervor on behalf of the fluid self, ever changing in relation to new partners, new ideas, and newly discovered features of the human potential. Both orientations--emphasizing uniqueness and super-relatedness, respectively--are readily exaggerated.

A bright light on the subject of self-identity has been provided by psychologist William Kilpatrick in his book, *Identity and Intimacy*.[1] The book is basically a telling critique of the excesses in the human potential

movement and in its ally, the idea that we are fast becoming a global village through a change in emphasis from
print media to electric media. His analysis is conducted
at a broadly psychological level and is buttressed by the
insights of certain existential psychologists--notably
Erik Erickson, Rollo May, and Victor Frankl.

Kilpatrick warns that a self-in-process is really
no self at all, unless it is also a stable resource on
the basis of which one can make decisions about one's
destiny and can make commitments to other people. If
the self is entirely fluid, as the human potential movement often seems to suggest, one has no grounds for fidelity while participating in basic goods of life, such
as friendship and marriage.

Kilpatrick also criticizes the New Tribalism advocated by Marshal McLuhan and others, who assert that we
are entering a new age of global consciousness and community. Kilpatrick claims that electronic media, such
as television and stereophonic headsets, foster just the
opposite of human community. They tend to develop the
isolated egoism of the users who are only passive con-
sumers of the information and of the here-and-now feelings
that these media convey. Tribal people, he points out,
actually interact with one another; they become intimately
involved in one another's destiny. The neotribalism of
the electronic age does not really produce a village at
all, but only the illusion of involvement and an ever-
greater preoccupation with a narrow self-actualization.
Kilpatrick is convinced that self-actualization and self-
realization strongly tend to make self-definition (hence,
commitment and fidelity) practically impossible.

There can be little doubt that, as Kilpatrick indicates, many people are regularly weakening their capacity
for commitment and true intimacy by being satisfied only
with warmth and closeness. The essential self of the person can readily be sold for a mess of potential. No one
can realistically begin to activate (let alone actuate)
in this short span of spatio-temporal life most of his
or her human potential. Those who would make their practically unlimited potential as an individual take ascendancy over commitment to fundamental human purposes that
transcend the individual self are destined to bring chaos
to the exercise of their capacities.

When one's potential is more important to oneself
than the self itself, one cannot begin to share oneself
as a gift. True love becomes impossible. Feelings swamp

meanings in the frenzy for meaningful *experiences*. As
Kilpatrick says,

> 'Feelings accompany the metaphysical and meta-
> psychical fact of love, but they do not constitute
> it.' In the writings of Buber, Kierkegaard and
> Erickson we find this persistent theme: love is
> a matter not of feeling, but of choosing. And
> choosing is a matter of identity. By our choices
> we create ourselves, and that is why we ought to
> try to be faithful to them.[2]

This conclusion is thoroughly in harmony with the ethics
of sexual ecology.

We choose who we shall be. We do not choose *whether*
we shall be. Nor do we choose the fundamental kind of
being that we are. We choose to actuate and celebrate
the unique being that we are among the beings of our fundamental kind. And we have a profound sexual identity
of which we must take particular account if we would
choose well and grow in genuine feeedom and love.

A sound philosophy of man and woman does not place
commitments and feelings in opposition. In the present
volume, I have implied that growing commitment actually
evokes deeper and more lasting emotional identity with
others to whom the commitment has been made. Yet, at
the same time, we need to recognize that true love--the
heart of any authentic commitment--is centered in will,
rather than in feelings.

Kilpatrick recognizes, too, that the unfortunate
feature of the human potential ideology is not its emphasis on fluidity, but its removal of fluidity from
the context of commitment. He proposes "fluidity-within-
commitment" as the only sane approach to attaining true
identity and intimacy.[3] His recommendations for resolving
or alleviating the contemporary identity crisis are definitely ecological.

Human sexual ecology of the future needs to assimilate competent critiques of fashionable drifts. William
Kilpatrick has provided a valuable critique. But the
development of sexual ecology also requires in-depth
elucidation of the many valuable insights afforded the
careful student of the psychology of human potential.
Rogers, Perls, Berne, and particularly Maslow, have opened
up many individuals to new richness, much-needed self-
esteem, and a unique joy in living out their practically
unlimited personal potential. When one has developed a

relatively mature and quite stable sense of self-identity,
then the intelligent exploration of personal potential
can fulfill the basic ecological principle of dynamic
equilibrium.

The more diversity among species in a given environment, the greater the stability of the ecosystem. The
greater the number of interrelated species, the more adap-
table to changing conditions the whole system tends to
be. The human person, even in his or her psychic being,
seems to partake in this paradoxical condition of stability through diversity. A variety of experiences,
circumstances, and friends will enhance one's ability
to be at home with self and the world, but only if the
person has first attained a relatively strong sense of
uniqueness and differentiation within the human community.
The psychology of self-actualization is an important component of human sexual ecology.

The Crisis in Eden

Another significant area for development, having
implications for human sexual ecology, is the impact
of the physical environmental crisis upon theology and
religious education. *Crisis in Eden*, a provocative study
by Presbyterian minister Frederick Elder, reveals the
need for theologians and pastors to rethink the emphasis
given to the two creation accounts in the Book of Genesis.[4]
Elder points out that the first creation narrative (Genesis 1-2:3), God creating the world in six days, is known
as the priestly account. God is the center of focus in
that rendering. The second creation narrative (Genesis
2:4-3:24), man naming and having dominion over all other
creatures, is called the Yahwistic account. Man is the
primary figure.

Elder claims that the age-old propensity in Judeo-
Christian thought has been to emphasize the message of
the second account--man's domination over the rest of
material creation--to the detriment of humankind itself.
He sees the contemporary environmental crisis as, in no
small way, the result of an exploitative attitude arising
out of an exaggerated sense of man's importance in the
whole of material creation.

According to Elder there are at least two contrast-
ing ways in which nature can be understood. The term
nature can refer to all physical systems which form an
environment for human beings and their civilization. In
this view, nature is everything that would remain if

mankind were suddenly and completely removed from the
earth. Man is understood as standing over against nature.

But nature can also be understood in another way.
Nature is viewed as all of material creation, including
mankind. This definition is more comprehensive and includes human beings and all processes of civilization.
Mankind is regarded as an inextricable part of nature.

According to Elder, the first view may be called
"exclusionist." It has a long history in Western civilization. This highly anthropocentric orientation to the
world has many proponents in our time. Elder portrays
and critiques three thinkers whom he regards as major
contemporary exponents of this view: Teilhard de Chardin,
the paleontologist-philosopher who envisions mankind
moving toward a point of complete humanization in fusion
with "God-Omega"; Harvey Cox, the theologian who has described the "secular city" that will be the completely
dominant reality of the future and that represents the
separation of human being from nature; and Herbert Rich-
ardson, whose book, *Toward an American Theology*, is an
argument for a "wholly artificial environment" under the
leadership of American technology, which Elder interprets
as involving the utter submergence of the non-human order
of nature.

One can readily question Elder's interpretation of
the significance of these three "exclusionist" viewpoints.
[Teilhard, for instance, is treated only from the perspective of his major work, *The Phenomenon of Man*, and
exceptional stress is placed on his methodological focus
(man) without exploring the significance of his working
assumption that the noosphere (mind-sphere) is a part
of the biosphere.] But one can hardly deny that all of
us have suffered from the exclusionist tendency to separate mind and matter, soul and body, man and "nature."

Elder calls the second perspective an "inclusionist"
view. He says that the heterogeneous group of those who
include mankind in the definition of nature is largely
composed of life-scientists--biologists, botanists,
anthropologists, ecologists--as well as certain urban
planners and landscape architects. This group is intellectually distinguished by what Elder calls its "holistic
approach"--by its awareness and elucidation of "the interrelated web of life." This orientation is common to
the naturalist Rachel Carson, the botanist Edward Sinnott,
the landscape architect Ian McHarg, and the conservation-
ist Aldo Leopold. But the star of Elder's constellation
of life-scientists and environmentalists with a common

371

vision of the essential interdependence of man and the rest of nature is the evolutionist Loren Eiseley. He regards Loren Eiseley as the leading light among the inclusionists because of his gifted awareness of the numinous in everyday natural events.

Viewing nature, he sees not only empirical inter-relatedness and he senses not only aesthetic enjoyment, but he also perceives in it and through it the holy, the miraculous--that awesomeness which has marked religious consciousness from the beginning. In his awareness there is a preternatural perception that gives a sanctity to all life, a depth of feeling and insight that is worthy of formal religious attention, especially in a day when so much formal religion has removed itself from such consciousness.[5]

In a chapter on Biblical and theological determinations Elder argues persuasively for the prospect of shifting the emphasis from the man-centered account of creation to the God-centered account. He cites further Biblical passages in support of this shift. God is seen as the unity of *all* natural systems. He takes his cue from the inclusionists who emphasize that as emergent man tries to extricate himself from the web of life he will be subject to dire repercussions.

Interpreting this theologically we can say that where man, either because of arrogation or ignorance, lives too far out of balance with the natural order, he meets God, the author of that order as well as the Immanent One within it who binds it together, as the God of wrath and judgment.[6]

Elder is aware that his position may be repugnant to many people in an age that has been largely devoted to the glorification of man. But he insists that it is an implication drawn from a truly comprehensive "systems" theology, in which God stands as the unity of all natural systems.

What Elder calls "environmental theology" is characterized not only by the immanence of God in every part of nature--nature's unity in God--but also by the uniqueness of every individual element of nature. Each person and each grain of sand are recognized and celebrated as unique, even while they are perceived as inextricably and universally related to all else.[7] In this way, his theological perspective is quite harmonious with the founda-

372

tions of human sexual ecology. Uniqueness and super-relatedness, otherness and withinness, are the reciprocal attributes of all being that have grounded this study of the nature of human sexuality.

Crisis in Eden is remarkable for its timing. Written in the late sixties, before environmental ecology was popularized, it listed and discussed many ecological and demographic features of the crisis. Elder is sanguine about the prospect for appealing to people's aesthetical consciousness. Utilitarian concerns, economic interests, and the drive for "progress," tend to be overwhelming. As he indicates, not many people will be motivated to clean up smog because it is unsightly. They require proof that it can be deadly. While it is true that many people are still capable of wonder and awe at the more dramatic beauties of nature, others seem to be more like the individual (whom Elder once observed) standing at the rim of the Grand Canyon, seeing it for the first time, and blurting out, "Man, what an ashtray!"[8]

As a result, the empirical evidence for the need to change our attitudes is given particular consideration. Elder discusses eleven areas for serious attention: overpopulation, urban sprawl, air pollution, water pollution, radioactive contaminants, solid waste disposal, noise pollution, the "weak-link" aspect of narrow approaches to solving problems (such as the non-selective character of pesticides), deforestation and soil erosion, the extirpation of animal species, and the stress induced by living in crowded conditions. Because of the interplay of so many unfortunate trends, Elder believes that unless major changes in approach and procedure are seriously adopted civilization as we know it will not endure. He thinks we could "go down in history as an elegant technological society struck down by biological disintegration for lack of ecological understanding."[9]

The present study of human sexual ecology has included a similar underlying thesis: we are an egregiously utilitarian (second-level freedom only) society that is already in a condition of considerable moral disintegration because of a lack of attention to *sexual* ecology.

Elder proposes for the future a desperately needed "modern asceticism." His proposal would not mean a withdrawal from the world, but a new way of thinking and acting toward and *with* the world. His three fundamental requirements are: (1) restraint, (2) an emphasis on quality existence, and (3) reverence for life. These elements of the new asceticism are in accord with the

373

practical attitudes needed for the furtherance of human sexual ecology.

Restraint means (in sex as well as any other human endeavor) that just because we *can* do something, it *does not* mean that we *will* do it.[10] Quality existence means that more and bigger is not better (in orgasms as in other things).[11] Reverence for life means that a person has a strong biological balance and proportion, develops a symbiotic conscience, and demands that every form of life be accorded consideration beyond the measure of its utility.

In other words, Elder holds that all life has third-level meaning and value, beyond the second-level freedom of means-and-ends. He believes that abortion on demand, for instance, represents the same narrow-answer approach that has brought humanity to the threshold of catastrophe. With reverence for life as a basic value, he asks whether solving the population problem by abortion is on any higher ethical plane than solving it by means of forced starvation and nuclear weapons.[12]

Natural family planning would seem to fit best in Elder's general criteria for ecologically responsible control of population. Yet the author of *Crisis in Eden* makes no mention of any particular form of birth control (other than his rejection of abortion). His optimism about inclusionistic environmentalists repudiating abortion as a method of population control may be regarded as stretching the boundaries of realism. Scientific and medical ignorance of the effectiveness and viability of NFP among people who have acquired a new asceticism, proportionate to our environmental crisis, is a massive obstacle. The irresponsible rhetoric and myopic moral perspective of many ecologists, such as Paul Ehrlich and Garrett Hardin, constitute a major factor in clouding the issue of genuinely human means of sex-control through self-control.[13] And the almost universal allegiance to a "Ptolemaic" view of the center of human sexuality--even among many of those who choose to develop natural family planning as a morally responsible way of life--may itself be attributable, in part, to what I suspect is a serious flaw in the inclusionist philosophy itself.

Elder's own inclusionist perspective on nature needs to be greatly expanded. In their view of nature, the inclusionists do not include enough. Nature, for them, involves the totality of the material world, including human beings, who are regarded as thoroughly, if not exclusively, biological.[14] Without denying the (limited) efficacy of such a meaning for nature, the term needs to undergo a meaning-expansion in which it becomes commensurate with all beings.

God and exclusively spiritual beings are natural, too. They are part of the total order of nature. Divine nature is supernatural with respect to *our* particular (human) nature. But God's infinite being is *natural* to God. Environmental theology (which Elder very perceptively advocates), as well as human sexual ecology, needs a concept of total Nature--the Nature of all being. God can be numinously present to insightful inclusionists precisely because God's nature--so immanently present to the simplest particle of matter--is *infinitely* other than both the perceiver and the perceived. God is the eternal womb in whom we all live and move and have our being-- inclusionists and exclusionists alike.

Crisis in Eden concludes with an assertion that environmental theology and its concomitant, environmental ethics, must emerge. The new asceticism must be proclaimed so that "man at last becomes biologically sophisticated and materially reverent."[15] Analogously, my contention is that, in the ethics of man-woman relations, a holistic philosophy of all being and its concomitant, human sexual ecology, must emerge. I have tried to develop the outline of a major revolution in man-woman relations so that people, at last, may become sexually sophisticated and *beingfully* reverent.

New Religious Synthesis Needed

Environmental theology, such as Elder and others would advocate, needs to become, or to be encompassed by, a theology of our total environment. A theology which sees God within every part of the physical universe needs to be complemented by a theology that sees every bit of creation as within God. God is the ultimate womb. Every being is within all other beings, and most intimately within the being of the Mother Person of God.[16]

Sexual ecology of the future will attempt to incorporate present attempts at a theology of the physical environment. The task will be extremely difficult in practice because we are all suffering, as Elder specifies it, under the dominance of the man-centered story of creation.

The anthropocentric fixation seems to have taken hold decisively in our culture at the time of the introspective revolution in philosophy inaugurated by the seventeenth-century French philosopher René Descartes. This mathematical genius searched for philosophical clarity and certainty akin to that attainable in mathematics. He developed a method of doubting the authority of other people and of all previous learning, and he also began to distrust the testimony of his senses. He is famous for his manifesto of philosophical certitude, "I think, therefore I am."

Along with this radical turn toward personal consciousness (human subjectivity), Descartes developed a criterion of truth divorced from sense experience and from direct contact with the physical world.[17] He began to regard clarity and distinctness of one's ideas as the only serious standard for judging truth or falsity. If one could have a clear and distinct idea of the matter, it was judged to be true; if not, false.

Most Western philosophers and theologians have been profoundly influenced by the great wedge that Descartes drove between the thinking self and the bodily world. Descartes' distrust of sense knowledge led him to regard his personal self as quite independent of the physical world, which he could know only indirectly. The Cartesian cataclysm, in which human nature was effectively deprived of its material existence, is perhaps far more responsible for the ecological crises of our times than the much longer historical emphasis on mankind's dominion over the birds of the air and the fish of the sea.

One of the unfortunate results of this turning point in the history of Western thought was that philosophers and theologians began to abuse the careful distinctions made earlier concerning the meaning of nature and grace, of reason and faith.[18] Nature and grace came to be regarded as quite separable, so that philosophy was supposed to confine itself to nature, and theology was to use some of the basic principles developed in philosophy while devoting itself to grace. Nature was regarded as the structure of things that could be known by human reason without any aid from the supernatural, which is known only through the power of faith.

Even before the time of Descartes the originally careful *distinction* between natural and supernatural (created and uncreated nature) was beginning to turn into a *separation* at the hands of some scholastic philosophers. Yet, after Descartes, the separation hardened. The excitement over new scientific discoveries in method and in content, wrought during the age of the enlightenment, led many thinkers to exploit the difference between matters of nature and supernature, reason and faith. The intellectual convenience of not having to stop and to integrate their discoveries about the strictly physical world with the testimony of revealed religion seems to have served as strong motivation for the neglect of theological and philosophical ecology. Today we are paying an inflationary price for the mutual neglect of theologians by scientists and of scientists by theologians.

Later, it became fashionable for philosophers to play games with the distinction between reason and faith. They spoke as though the light of faith could be turned off, while the thinker attempted to use only the light of reason to see what he could see about the world.

The condition might be likened to a situation where someone advises us to turn off the light in a room so that we can see what we can see, using only the light of the setting sun through the window. When the dim but natural light of the sun is our only source of illumination we can still see many things in the room that we saw before the "supernatural" (over-and-beyond the natural) light was turned off. Perhaps people and chairs are still visible, as well as pictures on the wall. We can still get around the room. But we have lost a great deal of illumination and have little chance of seeing much detail, such as facial features, printed words on publications that may be available in the room, finer elements of pictures on the wall, and so forth.

Of course, for those who do not admit that there is any light other than the natural light of reason, a person who claims to be aided by an additional light is being deceived. For strict naturalists, there is no distinction to make into a separation and to play around with. Such people are philosophizing with everything they have (at least at a conscious level).

But to those who claim to be graced with a light of truth additional to the natural light of reason the question should be asked: Why play games in the discovery of truth? If they really do have access to such light, they ought to philosophize with everything they have, making allowances, of course, when in dialogue with others who do not admit a light of faith.

The seeds of separation can be found in the original distinctions between nature and grace, reason and faith. Those who carefully and ingeniously wrought the original distinction seem to have relied heavily on images of *seeing* and *targeting*. Seeing something and "zeroing in on it" appears to have been a constant analogue from the world of sensation on behalf of the world of intellection. Thomas Aquinas held that sight was the most "spiritual" of the senses because of the distance from the objects of sensation which it presupposed.[19]

I suggest that this observation is astute, but excessively male in its bias. The emphatically male image of seeing and "zeroing in on" an object needs to be complemented by an emphatically female image.

Perhaps another analogue could be drawn from the world of sensation that would equally support the life of intellection and help to correct the traditional overemphasis on the otherness side of the remarkable distinction of faith and reason, grace and nature.[20] We need an analogue that will aid us in appreciating intellectively the unity and togetherness of the components in the distinction. My suggestion is that a phenomenology (careful philosophical description) of the activities of listening and feeling would help us understand the meaning of the difference between God's nature (grace) (the principal object of faith) and the nature of all other beings ("nature") (the principal object of reason).

Listening is a human activity in which the object sensed (sound) is globally experienced. Seeing is a human activity in which the object sensed (color) is linearly experienced. Sound surrounds the listener; color is apprehended at a distance and in a particular location. The listener is, as it were, invaded from all sides when sensing music that fills the room. The see-er is, as it were, an invader of the colorful objects of attention when seeing them.

In order for sound to be heard properly, there must be a linear sequence in time as it reaches the listener, but there is no such spatial sequence necessary for the message or meaning to be conveyed. The perception of colors, however, must be stretched out in linear sequence, both spatially and temporally. While a person cannot listen well to all sounds at one and the same time, he or she can listen to them coming from many different directions at once. The seeing of things requires both one thing at a time and one thing in one place.

In summary, when listening, one senses from *within* in a relatively emphatic way. The listener's action is a response to stimulation which comes as a global, all-directional bombardment. When seeing, however, one senses from *without* in a relatively emphatic way. The see-er's action is a receptive invasion of selected parts of the visible environment. (Even the placement of the initially decisive physical structures of listening and seeing like-wise reveals a mutual emphasis. The ear drum is quite internal, relative to the lens of the eye.) From a sexual perspective, listening can be said to be a giving kind of receiving (more female than male); seeing, a receiving kind of giving (more male than female).[21]

In terms of the person's response to these two primary forms of sensing, it might be suggested that listening more readily evokes feelings, while seeing more readily evokes doings. Both listening and seeing elicit feelings and doings, but there would seem to be an ecological balance of emphasis that can be called sexual.[22]

For instance, it was noted earlier how women tend to be initially more interested in *feeling* loved than in *having* sex. Men seem to be oppositely inclined. At least in our culture, men tend to be emphatically bent on an ocular approach to sex stimulation and a concomitant drive to "do it." They are seeing (and targeting) in their primitive sex tendencies. Women, on the other hand, tend to be more inclined toward a listening approach to sex stimulation (How readily does a woman tire of being told she is loved?) and to a concomitant longing for emotional satisfaction. The way to sex for a man is emphatically through his eyes. The way to sex for a woman is emphatically through her ears.

The much-needed synthesis of faith and reason, grace and nature, will require greater sensitivity to the interior kinds of intellection that are correlative to an expanded exercise of the thinker's own Anima. The religious thinkers of the future would be wise to support their attempts to understand and articulate the new synthesis with analogues from human sensation that reveal the ecological wholeness of human thought and its philosophical content.

In order to appreciate how far away we are from accomplishing this epistemological task, one only has to reflect on the four terms: faith, reason, grace, and nature. In the history of Western thought, with hardly an exception, three of them have been used in a thoroughly sexless way. Only "nature" in the narrow sense that signifies material creation apart from human spiritual powers is regarded as including sexual elements. Not only are nature and grace cut off from each other within our minds, but the material world and the spiritual world are secret-ly--and sometimes blatantly--separated. The "Copernican

379

Revolution" in human sexuality, advanced in this book must be accompanied by a similar revolution in other areas.

I have already noted the importance of a paradoxical logic (Chapter 13). We need to be able to say that sexuality is not *either* material *or* spiritual but that it is *both*. But, more generally, this paradoxical logic needs to be brought into play within an epistemological revolution such that we can make distinctions without separations. We need to be able to affirm unities in the same breath as we acknowledge differences.

The future of human sexual ecology will bring special integrative insights to bear on people's philosophy of life. Believers will be able to say meaningfully that everything temporal is eternal (that you are reading these words at this moment in time is an eternal and absolute truth) though not everything eternal is temporal (the love of the Persons in the Triune Godhead is not temporal). Similarly, we will be able to see clearly and know certainly that everything which is material is immaterial (a tree has a kind of immateriality about it, otherwise it would be relatable neither to God's mind nor to ours), but not everything which is immaterial is material (an act of human or Divine intellection is not itself material).23

In the spirit of this kind of synthesis, which unites even as it distinguishes--distinguishing features of even the fullest of unities--we can likewise understand that sexuality is relevant to the order of grace as well as nature, and to faith as well as reason. One can say that everything that is of faith and grace is sexual, though not everything sexual is of faith and grace. Sexuality can be understood as being a part of every being that is spiritual because it is the crucial sharing-dimension. Brute animals and plants have sex but not sexuality because they are material beings that are not also spiritual in their own right.

Most thinkers still do not really distinguish sexuality from genitality and coitality. Thus, when they hear that sexuality is distinguishable as an attribute of beings who are spiritual in their own right, they are still identifying sexuality with genitality. Hence they are inclined to deny the distinction.

Genitality and coitality--not sexuality--ought to be regarded as specific to human beings inasmuch as they are bodily. Genitality is a sharing power; but it is a

special kind of sharing power--one that necessarily involves body. Our genital power (which is quite other than
our sexual power, though intimately related to it) is
our capacity for generating another human being in space
and time. In other words, it is a bodily capacity that
everyone naturally possesses and that is highly influential in everything we do, even when it is never actualized
in its specific form. I have indicated this particular
significance of genitality in discussing the pervasive
influence of fertility patterns in the life of men and
women (Chapter 13).

A given person's influence on self and others by
virtue of his or her being sexed is not the same as the
influence by virtue of being genital. The specifically
sexual dimension of every cell in the human body--those
that are somatic and not gametic, as well as those that
are gametic--underscores the difference between our *being*
man or woman and our being potential father or potential
mother. *Being* man and woman necessarily means one is
potentially a father or a mother, but it is not the *same*
as the capacity for parenting.[24]

Parentive capability necessarily (naturally) flows
from sexuation in the world of matter and motion. It
is a definitive expression of our being-in-the-world.
Human beings are beings-in-the-world in their essentially
bodily being. Their being *persons*, however, capable of
sharing in all of their own acts, springs not from their
being-in-the-world or from their materiality of essence,
but from their being simultaneously (or correlatively)
self-reflective and beyond-the-world--from their spirituality of essence. Human nature is *both* fully material
and fully spiritual.

Our either-or logic tends to be overapplied and our
power to employ a both-and logic readily goes unexercised
when we contemplate the paradoxical reality of human nature. Our *eco*logical power is cramped and we do not
realize the total womb of our nature. Thus, when we
regard sexuality we tend to identify it with only *one*
side of our nature. The easiest thing to do is to identify it with genitality and the necessarily material side
of human nature. But with an expanded consciousness of
the human potential we can come to recognize that what
we are doing is logically fallacious. We are attributing
to the whole (sexuality) the attributes of a part (genitality).

Human genitality, however, is not just the capacity
for "reproduction." It is a certain kind (logically a

part) of sharing power: the power to share the gift of human life in space and time. Perhaps because it is so dramatic, this particular sharing power is still regarded, almost universally, as the center--if not the whole--of human sexuality.[25] The future of human sexual ecology is dependent on whether (and how) religious thinkers can come to see the centrality of sexuality in the *spiritual* life and to recognize it as the essential dimension of that life which we call sharing.

In order for the needed breakthrough of insight to happen or for the complementary synthesis (of faith and reason, grace and nature) to be effected, religious think-ers will have to examine, more seriously than hitherto attempted, the meaning of the mind-body rupture wrought by Descartes and many subsequent thinkers, as well as the seeds of its occurrence in the earlier age of the Great Distinctions.[26] They will also have to take serious account of biological, psychological, and anthropological data on man and woman--both in the way they go about thinking (methodological) and in the conclusions they draw (contentual). A new religious synthesis, incorporat-ing considerations of sexuality into the concepts of faith, reason, and grace, as well as nature, would be in some respects a significant help to, and in other re-spects the happy result of, development in human sexual ecology. Such a religious or theological re-synthesis can hardly proceed effectively, however, without a con-comitant development in the philosophy of being (metaphys-ics).

The Meaning of Being

The question of being--what does it mean to *be*--is not the first question that arises in the mind of either child or scholar. The human mind seems to be awakened, and often remains satisfied, by questions of nature--what does it mean to be this or that? But the most mean-ingful kind of question is the kind in which we wonder what it means for anything to *be at all*, to be something rather than nothing--not just to be this, rather than to be that.

Questions of nature are obviously important. They make it possible for us to grow into a differentiated consciousness of the world. But questions of being are necessary if we are going to retain our sense of unity in the midst of all the diversity of natures that we ex-perience and come to know. Questions of nature spring from our intellective Animus--our penchant for manyness of meanings. Questions of being arise from our intellective Anima--our inward yearning for the oneness of meaning.

Human sexual ecology is the study of sexuality with a special purpose. The student of sexual ecology makes a determined effort to keep the meaning of sexuality integral. Both the oneness and manyness of meanings for sexuality are appreciated. In this study I have made many distinctions. But I have tried constantly to show how all of the many parts of the sexual universe are integrally "alive" in the "womb" of *being*. This philosophy of man and woman has been partly an endeavor in ecological ontology.[27]

An eco-ontology requires more than the pursuit of *what*ness--what is a man, what is a woman, what is a celibate, what is a spouse, and so on. It serves a fuller purpose than the important but easily overregarded excursions into *how*ness--how to magnify sex pleasure, how to have a happy marriage, how to be your own best friend, how to parent effectively, and the like. Human sexual ecology develops primarily in the light of these questions: why *is* there sexuality at all, and what does it mean to *be* a man or to *be* a woman? The meaning of *being* and the meaning of *being* one's sexuality personally-- not just "doing" it--are the ecological conditions for the panoramic perspective and for the systematic examination undertaken in this philosophy of man and woman.

The development of sexual ecology will depend on the future course of ontology. Insight into the meaning of *being* is the radiant center that' illuminates and integrates all the arts and the sciences, including theology. Without abandoning the rich and vigorous growth in contemporary psychology, the fullness of meaning for human sexuality can only come through a resurgence of the metapsychological encounter with the structure of our *being*.

In order to ensure genuine growth in human sexual ecology, our greatest need is for an inclusive, integrative science of being. We do not need more metaphysics in the narrow ("faithless") sense. Nothing will suffice short of an holistic approach to the meaning of being, God, mankind, and the world.

This eco-ontology of the future will elucidate the meaning of being through careful articulation and explication of universal principles such as:

"Everything that is, is related to everything else."

"Every being is utterly unique and in *no* way the *same* as anything other than itself."

"Every being is related *uniquely* to every other."

"Every being, in each of its acts, affects (not necessarily changes) *every* other being."

"To be dependent is necessarily to be related, but to be related is not necessarily to be dependent."

"Every being, as such, is *within* (immanent to) every other being."

"Every being, as such, is wholly other than (transcendent to) every other being."

"An absolutely infinite being (God, by nature) can only be known by absolutely finite beings (us, by nature) through the perspective of being (the common ground)."

"Through the perspective of being, God is known as the *infinitely* unique Being who is *both* absolutely other *and* absolutely within us."

"God creates beings who (or which) create themselves."

These and countless other propositions need clarification and defense if philosophy itself is going to meet the challenge of future expansion in depth-psychology, social anthropology, theology, and the many parts of its own discipline--not to mention all other areas of the natural and social sciences. Ethics (moral philosophy) in general and sexual ethics in particular need desparately the backdrop of principles such as the foregoing. Everyone today needs a philosophy of the environment. But, even more importantly, we stand in need of an environment of philosophy--a philosophy directly explicative of the environment of *being* in which we ever wonder, think, and lead our lives.

In the context of eco-ontology, then, sexuality as sharing the gift of *being* who we are can be enormously expanding and freeing.

The Human Person Is His or Her Acts

In the ethical area of sexual ecology perhaps the greatest need for future development is a sound understanding of the nature of human acts. Much contemporary

384

criticism of past ethical theory centers around what is regarded as an unduly narrow focus upon the individual act and insufficient attention to the basic moral orientation of the person as manifest in a series of actions. The idea that in matters of sexual morality there is no such thing as an act that is intrinsically wrong has achieved widespread currency. The question of whether some acts (such as rape, incest, and directly procured abortion) are always objectively wrong, independent of the disposition of the agent, must come to some kind of reasonable resolution before one can proceed on a course of evaluating sexual activity from an ecological standpoint.

In Chapter 9, this question was discussed briefly. My contention was that human (moral) acts are personal acts--having the whole person present in each of them to some degree--such that it is possible for someone to affect his or her *ultimate* moral destiny in any *one* of his or her acts. The person determines self in a given moral act because he or she *is* the act, and does not simply *use* it. The person is *more* than his or her acts. But moral acts are not just something done by the person. They are part of the person's very self. I also suggested that any moral act has many consequences that a person might not foresee.

Human moral life is fed by the influences that every moral action necessarily affords its agent. As in physical consumption of food there can be nutritious influence and anti-nutritious influence independent of the intentions of the one who eats, so in the development of the person as a person through moral actions there can be good and bad effects independent of the intentions of the one who chooses a particular course of action. Ingestion of poisonous food--however unwittingly done--is an objectively wrong action. The choice of certain kinds of moral action--however well-intentioned--are likewise objectively wrong.

If one argues that no action is *necessarily* wrong from a moral standpoint (because of the greater good which might accrue under certain, admittedly-unusual circumstances), one is tacitly lowering all moral action to the level of a means-to-an-end (second-level freedom only) and is regarding the moral person--every person--as a puppet of ultimate circumstances. Such an ethical position effectively kills the ethical enterprise itself by treating the person as a *means* to the execution of goals (second-level "purposes") which necessarily lie outside the meaning of his or her every action.

385

Some personal (moral) actions must be regarded as wrong in themselves. Otherwise, ethics is no more. In fact, actions can be said to be ethically relevant *only* to the extent that they involve some degree of value in their own right--on their own, independent of the goals or purposes *toward* which they may be directed.

But this moral autonomy of an action cannot be reasonably regarded as coming from the will of the agent, since the agent does not will his or her own nature as an ethical being. The moral agent participates directly--in ways that are healthy or unhealthy--in his or her nature.

The moral autonomy of the agent is an autonomy different from the moral autonomy of the action. The moral autonomy of the agent springs from his or her own natural capacity to choose responses to the being that he or she has been given and that he or she is increasingly called to receive from within. The agent does not produce his or her moral autonomy, but exercises it well or poorly with every moral action. The moral autonomy of the agent is a *response* to the moral autonomy of the *nature* of his or her acts. The agent does not create his or her acts, but creates a unique personal destiny in, through, and with those acts, which he or she *is*.28

An ecologically sound ethics, then, will be steeped in the paradox of human freedom and action. It will be attuned especially to the paradox of *each* and *all* of a person's acts. Each act is inextricably connected to all others and to all parts of the moral ecosystem (intentions, motives, attitudes, values, and the rest). Consequently, any individual moral act *can* be *the* one to break the person's whole world of moral soundness. Any moral action (such as murder, rape, torture) that directly affronts a fundamental human Value seriously ruptures the agent's interrelationship with the whole ecosystem of freedom and values, and needs only the agent's deliberate intention as such--even if made only on this one occasion--to effect a complete break with God, self, and the world. Moral abortion of the Child Within may be more or less common than physical abortion of children, but it surely must occur if there is any serious meaning to the idea of human freedom and any real significance to the ethical enterprise itself.

Those who deny any objective wrong in certain actions that are manifestly direct attacks on the nature of being human--despite the presumed "good will" of the agent-- are really saying that we create our own human nature and its values in and through the choices we make. But since, under this assumption, we could not possibly have shared in those values before we created them through the moral choices we made, these values amount to goals (second-level ends) which we project onto ourselves (and others, consciously or unconsciously). The great interior human enterprise of engaging our power to be free is thereby vitiated at its source. Our choices are no longer acts of sharing--giving and receiving--but sheerly exercises in projecting ("giving") and making for ourselves an "essence" that covers over the radical structure of our being, massively inhibiting our power to receive (right within our actions) the being who we *are*.[29]

An ethics without an objective nature in accord with which one must creatively act is the ultimate form of pollution and the polar opposite of ethical ecology. Human sexual ecology is, among other things, an attempt to heal the rupture of self-consciousness right at the core of the human potential to share the gift of being with self and with others.

A genuine ethics of man and woman flows from an ethics of the person and his or her acts. This ethics provides a rational basis on which nature can be respected and creatively cared for in every moral action because the person is present there precisely *as a person*. There is no such thing as a moral act without a person. There is likewise no such thing as a moral person without an act. Any *one* act, in which a certain kind of stance toward basic human Value (third level) is being taken implicitly or explicitly, can revoke a phenomenal trail of previously good or bad acts and be determinative for the ultimate destiny of the person--so free is that person in *each* act, and so important in itself is each act of that person.

The freedom of a person in each one of his or her acts is a major premise of authentic sexual ecology. Another crucial provision is the recognition of the deeply human and moral significance of genital and coital activity. Together these two standpoints underscore the importance of what might be regarded as the pivotal issue in human sexual ecology today: whether contraceptive intercourse is ever a morally sound action. Apart from considerations of "practicality"--which are not adequate for decisive ethical evaluation--is contraceptive intercourse an objectively wrong action, despite the obvious good will of so many of its practitioners? In this study, the answer was that contraceptive intercourse is objectively wrong, but that morally sound and practical alternatives do exist. Natural family planning was

387

delineated as ecologically sound on both moral and physical grounds.

Total Sexual Ecology and Natural Family Planning

Total sexual ecology means, above all, that coital-
genital sex and all other forms of sexual expression are
not simply means to an end, but actually ends in themselves, when they are undertaken under the proper conditions. Coital orgasmic intercourse, for instance, on
the part of loving married people choosing a parentive
vocation is a natural invitation to the physical, psychic,
and spiritual good of giving life while giving love. The
proper intercourse with human genitals, like the proper
intercourse with the human tongue (conversation), regards
carefully and responds generously to the total ecology
of a personal (moral) act.

As soon as sexual expression--with genitals, tongues
(voices), arms, or whatever--becomes *primarily* a *means*
to something else, such as pleasure or power over one's
partner or ego-fulfillment, it insinuates a radical break
in the personal and communal sexual ecology. The participants may or may not realize it. Yet the great good of
human sexuality is thereby degraded to the level of a
goal. Despite the rhetoric often used to exalt such activity as a good, it is not being considered a good in
itself, but a good in its *use*. It is being regarded primarily as a means. The person who participates in any
action that is *primarily* a means is making into a means
or instrument a great part of himself or herself. Sexuality is a great part of one's personhood. But instru-
ments--whether they are pencils, typewriters, teacups,
clothing, or whatever--are always *other than and separable
from* the person who uses them.

When, for instance, a person deliberately misrepre-
sents the true state of conditions upon which he is re-
porting to someone who has a right to the information,
then the action is one of lying. This action, in effect,
treats one's tongue and its activity principally as an
instrument. Whether the person realizes it or not, a
considerable part of himself or herself--including the
moral powers of mind and will--is regarded as a sheer
means to the goal of diverting the listener from the
truth. The act of lying violates one's naturally harmonious relationship with the truth of things. Since
every being is intimately related to everything else--
even though we may be totally unaware of what that particular relationship is--the deliberate rupture of one's
relationship to one set of conditions (the lie) pollutes

388

the entire ecosystem of the moral world and has consequences for self and all others in the physical, psychic, and spiritual energy systems.

Even when a person tells the truth, moral pollution can occur. If he or she conveys the message *primarily* as a means rather than as an end, the action is--attitudinally at least--subpersonal. The moral health of any person is dependent upon the degree to which his or her individual acts are done as goods in themselves. That they are also means to an end (a goal) is important, but nonetheless secondary, in the development of moral ecology.

In the most dramatically obvious form of sexual activity--coital-genital union--any attempt to separate, by way of intention or by way of action, the life-giving power (procreative) from the love-giving power (sexuative) treats genitality (the personal and social power to share the gift of life) as primarily a means to coitality (the personal power to share the power to give life). Unlike the approach advocated in the authentic natural family planning movement, wherein both the life-giving potential and the love-giving potential of the action are regarded as ends in themselves, contraceptive (or deliberately sterilized) intercourse disintegrates the one power (procreative) for the sake of the other (love-giving). As a result, even the love-giving power turns into a means of satisfying a goal-seeking tendency (such as mutual ego-satisfaction), and becomes the instrument actually used in contrast to the instrument not used (procreative power).

Love can really be given neither by nor through an instrument. Love is always activity as a primary good in itself. So, the contraceptive expresses the participant's *un*willingness to regard the action as an act of *love*, in which there would necessarily be an attitude of detachment from any one form of expression. Contraceptive intercourse necessarily treats the great personal powers of genitality and coitality as means to a goal, and thereby instrumentalizes and dehumanizes the very persons of whom these powers and their activities are profoundly intimate dimensions.

True sexual love is integrative. The primary purposes (goods in themselves) of human sexuality, namely, intimacy and creativity (resulting from the giving kind of receiving and receiving kind of giving respectively, that constitute the inscape of all genuine sharing), are integrally realized in any authentically personal action.

Truly loving genital union (for instance, of mother and the child with whom she shares life) is always integrated with sexuality as the sharing power of the person. Truly loving coital union--the union of genitals--is never separated from (and is always integrated with) genital union and is thus an authentic sexual (sharing) union of self with an other-than-self. This integration of one's life-giving power with one's love-giving power naturally requires the restraint of sometimes very obstreperous coital-genital tendencies--for a short or long time with one's marital partner, and for all time with anyone else. Integrated love is the key to total sexual ecology.

When people are really loving, every single act of restraint or of indulgence presents within itself the whole person *as a person*, not as a thing. In every authentically personal interaction the union of persons is totally ecological--where all parts of the persons involved are regarded as *personal*, including their fertility. In every action each person presents self as ready to share the gift of self as a whole (as a person) rather than as a part (as a thing). The rhetoric of "love talk" aside, the human person presents self to the world, in the simplest or the most complex activity, as a lover or as an unlover. Human sexual ecology is rooted in the totality of the human person.

In the present study I have particularly cited natural family planning as the authentic light of mankind's coital-genital future. NFP involves scientifically validated methods of conception-regulation in the context of self-regulation. Through the reflective practice and communication of the methods of NFP many outstanding couples around the world are raising people's consciousness concerning NFP as a way of life. Couples who seriously practice the method, in attitude as well as by intention, begin to realize that it is not really so much a method (a means) as it is a philosophy of married life (an end).

The sources of technical and philosophical significance, through which the efficacy of NFP can be carefully evaluated, are growing. In terms of the philosophy of man and woman presented in this book, NFP might be regarded as a living philosophy of parentive sexuality, that extends itself to the whole of parenthood by teaching sex to children right within the ecological heart of society--the interpersonal relationship between mother and father. Here there are no limits to growth in joy through responsible indulgence and restraint.

390

If a person sees the value of NFP as a good in itself for those who have chosen the parentive vocation, then the philosophy of a natural (inclusionist sense) sexual life delineated in this book will serve as a support and perhaps a motivation. Natural family planning is total sexual ecology in action--especially within the most obvious area of sexual life, the coital-genital. In this movement one can find *tangible* hope for renewing the sexual face of the earth.

The Philosophy of Man and Woman

The destiny of man and woman on this planet will be determined largely by the quality of the philosophy of sexuality which prevails. As I noted in the introductory chapter, the philosophy of man and woman throughout history has been fragmentary at best. This whole book has been an argument for raising the quality of the perspective and the analysis. Quality of life is thoroughly dependent on quality of thought. The perennial inclination to take sexuality much less seriously than issues such as the best form of government, the value of private property, the relation between science and religion, and even the value of human life itself, has kept the quality of discourse on the meaning of man and woman exceptionally low.

But, as someone put it, philosophy buries its undertakers. Those thinkers and non-thinkers of the past and present who would inhibit critical reflection on the nature and value of sexuality seem to be already on the verge of obsolescence. The rise of the women's movement in the past one hundred years or so in the United States, the recent budding of male awareness, as well as the sprouting of sex-oriented philosophical literature within the past decade, appear to threaten this time-honored status quo.

Many philosophers--professional and non-professional--must work to develop the philosophy of man and woman. Metaphysical principles are crucial, but not enough. This philosophy must be spelled out in a value system and in an ethics that offers much more than the ideology of "anything goes as long as one is loving." Reflective people from a wide range of disciplines need to come together to contribute to the thought-and-action task ahead.

The development of the sense of human sexual ecology that has been delineated in this book could one day become a cultural norm. Whether it ever does or however long it might take, there is satisfaction in knowing that intimacy with inner space in human sexuality has always been attained by individuals and couples who have dared to break through the sociocultural limitations of a "Ptolemaic" sexual existence. The reader and the author can be encouraged by the presence of those, here and there throughout the ages, who have lived in special, man-woman friendships. We can likewise be confident in the practical potential of increasing multitudes, here and now in various parts of the world, who are responding in their own way--with or without articulate philosophical attention--to a "Copernican Revolution" in man-woman relations by practicing a thoroughly ecological form of birth control.

In some ways, the future of human sexual ecology is the future of human beings on the planet earth.

NOTES

1. William Kilpatrick, *Identity and Intimacy* (New York: Dell, 1975).
On this theme, cf. Paul Vitz, *Psychology as Religion*. He concentrates on four of the most influential self-theorists: Eric Fromm, Carl Rogers, Abraham Maslow, and Rollo May.
2. *Identity and Intimacy*, p. 225. Here Kilpatrick quotes from *I and Thou*, the contemporary masterpiece of the Jewish philosopher, Martin Buber.
3. *Identity and Intimacy*, pp. 239-240.
4. Frederick Elder, *Crisis in Eden* (Nashville: Abingdon, 1970).
5. *Crisis in Eden*, p. 15.
6. Ibid., p. 102.
7. Ibid., pp. 40-42.
8. Ibid., p. 106.
9. Ibid., p. 128. Elder is quoting, in agreement, David M. Gates, director of the Missouri Botannical Gardens, testifying before a House subcommittee on science and technology.
10. My own idea in parenthesis.
11. My own idea in parenthesis.
12. *Crisis in Eden*, p. 155.
13. One of many absurd and grossly irresponsible perspectives is phrased by Ehrlich this way: "As Professor Garret Hardin of the University of California pointed out, [equating a zygote or fetus with a human being] is like confusing a set of blueprints with a building. People are people because of the interaction of genetic information (stored in a chemical language) with an environment." Paul R. Ehrlich, *The Population Bomb* (New York: Ballantine, 1968), pp. 147-48. This incredible piece of biological reductionism exemplifies the prevalent contemporary rationalizations used to cover

392

up insensitivity to the weakest and most innocent members of the human family. Apparently, Hardin does not realize that this "biological blueprint" grows and eventually speaks, reads, and writes, if given an environment sufficiently benign. A building blueprint, however, never becomes part of the house, unless it is used to paper the wall. For a direct philosophical treatment of the common arguments in favor of abortion, see R. E. Joyce and Mary R. Joyce, *Let Us Be Born: The Inhumanity of Abortion* (Chicago: Franciscan Herald Press, 1970). Also, Germain Grisez, *Abortion: The Myths, the Realities, the Arguments* (New York: Corpus Books, 1970); and Donald DeMarco, *Abortion in Perspective* (Cincinnati: Hiltz and Hayes,1974).

14. *Crisis in Eden*, pp. 49-50.

15. Ibid., p. 162.

Another Christian ecologist, Paul Folsom, has written a short, beautiful book on the need for a morality and theology of environmental care. He writes explicitly of a Christian ecology, gives a wide range of testimony through Biblical passages, points to the incarnation of Christ as the central ecological mystery, notes how the whole earth is sacramental, and celebrates St. Francis of Assisi as the universal patron of ecology. See *And Thou Shalt Die in a Polluted Land: An Approach to Christian Ecology* (Ligouri, Mo.: Ligourian, 1971). The title is taken from Amos 7:17.

16. A particular theological speculation suggested earlier. See Chapter 14, note 5.

17. This introspective turn in the history of philosophy has also brought distinctive benefits. Without it, psychology itself probably could not have developed to such an extent that in our day we take for granted the importance of the human psyche as well as the body and soul. Analytic psychologists are particularly insightful on the newness and importance of attending to the personal life of the psyche as a whole. On the importance of the radically subjective to psychology, James Hillman is enlightening. See, e.g., his essay, "Abandoning the Child," in his book *Loose Ends: Primary Papers in Archetypal Psychology* (Zurich: Spring Publications, 1975), especially pp. 5-8. Also see his *Re-visioning Psychology* (Zurich: Spring Publications, 1975).

18. A helpful treatment of the interrelationships between faith and reason is provided by Germain Grisez, *Beyond the New Theism* (Notre Dame, Ind., University of Notre Dame Press, 1975), pp. 6-12.

19. For example, see his differentiation of the psychic powers of human beings, including the five "external senses," in *Disputed Question on the Soul*, 13, c. Thomas Aquinas, *The Soul*, trans. J. P. Rowan (St. Louis: Herder and Herder, 1949), pp. 165-70.

20. Oriental philosophy provides rich sources of idea and imagery in a global, rather than a narrowly-focused, way. The Upanishads are replete with the wisdom of Atman as a maternal cause--a fullness that reveals itself--ever subtly, in myriad forms. In studying Hindu thought one is readily impressed with the idea of the Absolute as a nurturant source. Also, the term *shastrayonitvat* (third sutra of Badarayana) means that Scripture is the womb of knowledge concerning Brahman, the supreme reality. In several ways, Indian

philosophies are more intelligently represented by the image of the
Child Within than is the perennial philosophy of the West. For a
basic comparison of the Indian and Aristotelian-Thomistic philosophies see John B. Chethimattam, *Consciousness and Reality* (Maryknoll,
N.Y.: Orbis Books, 1971). An increasingly popular source of Chinese
wisdom is the classic *Tao Te Ching*, in which one finds several sa-
lient female images for the Absolute (*Tao*)--an absolute like
Heidegger's *Being* rather than like the Hindu *Brahman* or the traditional *God* of the West. Authoritative commentary on each chapter
of the *Tao Te Ching* is given by Wing-Tsit Chan, the translator of
the Bobbs-Merrill edition: *The Way of Lao Tzu* (Indianapolis: Bobbs-
Merrill, 1963).

21. I do not wish to claim that women are more competently auditory and men are more competently visual. But I suggest that there
is a possible favoring of the one over the other in most men and
women. My observation is rather akin to the conclusions of the
major research survey by Eleanor Emmons Maccoby and Carol Nagy
Jacklin, *The Psychology of Sex Differences* (Stanford: Stanford
University Press, 1974) (See pp. 351-52.) that girls have greater
verbal ability and that boys (adolescents and adults) excel in
visual-spatial ability. But my basic idea centers on the similar
proportion in the positioning of the "working organs" of eye and
ear as compared to the outer-inner emphasis of the "working organs"
of genital sexuality.

22. Listening, of course, does evoke action (e.g., "faith comes
through hearing") and seeing often stifles it (e.g., social passivity
as a function of mesmerization by excessive television viewing).
My point is that both listening and seeing evoke both feeling and
doing, but that there is a natural emphasis in each form of sensing.
The doing that listening tends to evoke is inclined to be more in-
ternal--commensurate with the natural structure of the listening
activity. Emotions are the powerhouse of external action. Feelings
are internal doings that may eventually flow into significant external action. Seeing, in contrast to listening, tends to produce
images that are direct or indirect models for externalizing and
directing one's plans and actions. Seeing is an emphatically
"possessive" kind of sensation. Listening is a sensation in which
one is emphatically "possessed."

23. The term *immaterial* signifies that by which a thing can be
said to be free of dependence on matter. Matter can be understood
as that by which something can be said to have parts (or be extended
"in space"). Thus, a tree is relatively freer of matter than a
stone, and a squirrel is relatively freer than a tree, because the
principle of life (soul) in each of them lets them be freer to
move (i.e., to go beyond being sheer parts and "taking up space").
But both squirrel and tree are (even with respect to their souls)
intrinsically dependent on matter. They are only relatively free
of matter. Human beings, however, (with respect to their souls and
the powers specific to them--intellect and will) are absolutely free
of matter because they can act (and therefore *be*, to that degree or
in that way) in a manner that is intrinsically independent of matter,

394

even while being extrinsically dependent on it. See Chapter 3, note 1.

24. Parenting here signifies initiation of life through gametic sharing of the gift. If cloning of humans is ever successful, such that a new individual is developed by way of the genetic material of a donor's somatic cell, the process would be akin to twinning, not parenting. The natural process of twinning or of the natural unfolding of any number of human embryos developed from a single conceptus (monozygotic) can perhaps best be understood as nature's own way of "cloning."

25. Coitality--an even narrower focus--is the practical center for sexuality in the minds of most people today, who regard "sexuality" and "reproduction" as quite separable.

26. The great distinctions in the age of scholastic theology and philosophy, from Anselm (A.D. 1109) to Duns Scotus (1308).

27. In my opinion, anti-ecological ontology in the Western world got its start with the decadent scholastic philosophy that, for the most part, came after the thirteenth century. The scholastic philosophers who hardened and passively transmitted the concepts and distinctions of some of their great predecessors paved the way for the anti-ecological crisis in philosophy which Descartes turned into a catastrophe. Contemporary existentialists and phenomenologists (Heidegger, Buber, Marcel, Husserl, Merleau-Ponty, Ricouer, et al.) have made valiant attempts to return to the roots and wellsprings. Their work is, in my opinion, but a promise of the radical ontology needed for creative continuance of the perennial philosophy of the West, as it becomes increasingly nourished by the perennial philosophies of the East.

28. The idea is that human nature is not a static given, but a dynamic, stable given that can radically change through the agency of the person himself or herself. In fact, one of the basic principles of human sexual ecology might be stated this way: The unique, God-given nature that is yours is so dynamic that it continually changes--not by "becoming" a different nature (which is absurd), but by becoming better or worse--with or without your deliberative agency. We can change for the worse, just by *neglecting* to exercise our powers for responsible action. Human ecosystems are at the mercy of our personal freedom.

29. The contemporary existentialist Jean-Paul Sartre has written about "bad faith" involved in acknowledging a transcendent source or one's sheerly spontaneous self. But the accusation could be leveled at him for his implicit confusion of goals with goods. Implicitly Sartre has regarded the idea of a dynamic, stable structure (nature) of the self prior to freedom of choice as setting up a goal for man to aim toward and be directed by. And all too often traditional philosophers have characterized it as such. But nature is not a goal that we "measure up to" in bad faith, but a good that we participate in because it is what we *are*--and a great *part* of what we are is what Sartre has emphasized to the point of gross exaggeration: radical freedom to choose our destiny. We are free to determine the outcome of our nature. We are called from within

("by our nature") to act *in accord with* our nature (to *cooperate* with nature), not to be imposed upon by it. In so doing, we act in "good faith."

Index

397

About the Author

Robert E. Joyce, Ph.D., is Associate Professor of Philosophy at St. John's University, Collegeville, Minnesota. He did his graduate studies in philosophy at De Paul University, the University of Notre Dame, and International College. Over the past twelve years he has taught courses, given lectures, and conducted workshops on the philosophy of human sexuality and the value of human life. With his wife, Mary, Professor Joyce is the co-author of *New Dynamics in Sexual Love* and *Let Us Be Born*. His articles have appeared in a variety of scholarly and popular periodicals, including *Cross Currents, Improving College and University Teaching, The New Scholasticism, The International Review of Natural Family Planning,* and *Marriage*.